PRINCE2™

FOR

DUMMIES®

2ND EDITION

PRINCE2™
FOR
DUMMIES®
2ND EDITION

by Nick Graham

 **WILEY**

A John Wiley and Sons, Ltd, Publication

PRINCE2™ For Dummies®

Published by
John Wiley & Sons, Ltd
The Atrium
Southern Gate
Chichester
West Sussex
PO19 8SQ
England

E-mail (for orders and customer service enquires): cs-books@wiley.co.uk

Visit our Home Page on www.wiley.com

For general information on our other products and services, please contact our Customer Care Department within the U.S. at 800-762-2974, outside the U.S. at 317-572-3993, or fax 317-572-4002.

For technical support, please visit www.wiley.com/techsupport.

Wiley also publishes its books in a variety of electronic formats. Some content that appears in print may not be available in electronic books.

British Library Cataloguing in Publication Data: A catalogue record for this book is available from the British Library

ISBN: 978-0-470-71025-8

Printed and bound in Great Britain by Bell and Bain Ltd, Glasgow.

10 9 8 7 6 5 4 3 2 1

WILEY

About the Author

Nick Graham is the founder and Managing Director of Inspirandum Ltd, a small and specialised company focused on achieving excellence in project management. In his company he has set very clear objectives to teach all project approaches and methods in a practical way so that they can be applied intelligently and productively.

With a career that has covered both the public sector and the private sector, Nick is able to communicate readily with managers in both communities and he's been involved in project consultancy and training for more than 15 years. Nick's experience with structured methods in projects goes back much further, and in the PRINCE method it goes back to before it was even called PRINCE.

Nick is an experienced project practitioner and trainer and he's also a qualified teacher. His work has taken him world wide and those attending his courses have described his style as energetic, lively, fun, very practical, and very informative. Nick's consultancy work has ranged from helping to plan individual projects to advising senior managers on how to implement PRINCE2 throughout their organisation. He teaches regular open PRINCE2 courses in London UK and in Hong Kong as well as running courses 'in-company' for clients in the UK and world wide.

When not away on consultancy or training assignments, Nick lives in Weymouth in Dorset. His company's offices are on the tip of the Isle of Portland overlooking the sea and the famous Portland Bill lighthouse. His wife Kath also works for Inspirandum.

Nick is a member of the Association for Project Management (APM) and the Institute of Directors (IoD).

www.inspirandum.com

Dedication

This book is dedicated to Li Yat Chuen – 'YC' – and Christina Lai in Hong Kong who, by their dedicated professionalism and enormous kindness, have demonstrated so consistently that you can indeed combine business and pleasure.

Author's Acknowledgements

Writing a book takes enormous patience – from other people. I really want to thank Rachael Chilvers at Wiley who was such an encouragement for the first edition of the guide, and then Simon Bell for the second edition. In both cases, I valued their advice and positive support so very much.

At home and in the office I have to thank my wife Kath, who also works for Inspirandum, for her patience as I spent hours in my study pounding a keyboard and for sheltering me from so much of the day-to-day pressure of running a business.

It's so good when some of those people who come on an Inspirandum training course stay in touch, and better still when some go on to become friends. It's great fun to have Philipp Straehl as a friend, but I'm also grateful for him so freely sharing his thoughts and ideas based on very substantial project management experience. It's not that often that you go out to dinner with a friend and grab a bit of paper halfway through the main course to write down something he just said to quote it in a book. Watch out for the quotation as you read *PRINCE2 For Dummies*.

Publisher's Acknowledgments

We're proud of this book; please send us your comments through our Dummies online registration form located at www.dummies.com/register/.

Some of the people who helped bring this book to market include the following:

Commissioning, Editorial, and Media Development

Project Editor: Simon Bell
(*Previous Edition: Rachael Chilvers*)

Content Editor: Jo Theedom

Commissioning Editor: Nicole Hermitage
(*Previous Edition: Samantha Spickernell*)

Copy Editor: Anne O'Rorke

Technical Editor: The Office of Government Commerce

Publisher: David Palmer

Production Manager: Daniel Mersey

Cover Photos: Getty Images/Gallo

Cartoons: Rich Tennant
(www.the5thwave.com)

Composition Services

Project Coordinator: Lynsey Stanford

Layout and Graphics: Samantha K. Cherolis, Nikki Gately, Joyce Haughey

Indexer: Claudia Bourbeau

Contents at a Glance

Introduction *1*

Part I: How PRINCE2 Can Help You *5*

Chapter 1: So What's a Project Method and Why Do I Need to Use One?................7
Chapter 2: Outlining the Structure of PRINCE2.....................................15
Chapter 3: Getting Real Power from PRINCE2.......................................27

Part II: Working Through Your Project *39*

Chapter 4: Checking the Idea Before You Start 41
Chapter 5: Planning the Whole Project: Initiation 67
Chapter 6: Preparing for a Stage in the Project 93
Chapter 7: Controlling a Stage...109
Chapter 8: Building the Deliverables..121
Chapter 9: Finishing the Project 131
Chapter 10: Running Effective Project Boards.....................................145

Part III: Help with PRINCE2 Project Management *167*

Chapter 11: Producing and Updating the Business Case.............................169
Chapter 12: Deciding Roles and Responsibilities 187
Chapter 13: Managing Project Quality 209
Chapter 14: Planning the Project, Stages and Work Packages.......................223
Chapter 15: Managing Project Risk..253
Chapter 16: Controlling Change and Versions 275
Chapter 17: Monitoring Progress and Setting Up Effective Controls....................295

Part IV: The Part of Tens *311*

Chapter 18: Ten Ways to Make PRINCE2 Work Well 313
Chapter 19: Ten Tips for a Good Business Case 319
Chapter 20: Ten Things for Successful Project Assurance............................325

Part V: Appendices *331*

Appendix A: Looking into PRINCE2 Qualifications 333
Appendix B: Glossary of the Main PRINCE2 Terms.................................337

Index *351*

Table of Contents

Introduction *1*

About This Book 1
Foolish Assumptions 2
How This Book is Organised 2
    Part I: How PRINCE2 Can Help You 3
    Part II: Working Through Your Project 3
    Part III: Help with PRINCE2 Project Management 3
    Part IV: The Part of Tens 3
    Part V: Appendices 3
Icons Used in This Book 4
Where to Go from Here 4

Part I: How PRINCE2 Can Help You *5*

Chapter 1: So What's a Project Method and Why Do I Need to Use One? 7

Getting the Low-Down on PRINCE2 8
Giving You Some Facts about Projects 8
    Fact 1: A lot of projects go wrong 9
    Fact 2: We know why projects go wrong 10
    Fact 3: We know good ways of preventing a lot of those things 11
    Fact 4: PRINCE2 is free to use 12
Making Your Life Easier with PRINCE2 12
Clearing Up Some Misunderstandings about PRINCE2 13
Working Through Your Project 14

Chapter 2: Outlining the Structure of PRINCE2 15

Getting to Know the Process Model 16
    Getting things going 17
    Repeating as necessary 18
    Shutting down: Closing a Project 19
Introducing the Themes 20
    Understanding the themes 20
Working in Line With the Principles 23
Appreciating the Six Control Variables 24
Fitting in Project Techniques 25
Putting it all Together 25
    The environment of a PRINCE2 project 26

Chapter 3: Getting Real Power from PRINCE2 27

Understanding the Problems 27
Remembering that PRINCE2 Is a Tool 28
Getting the Power: Adjustment...30
    Leaving out activities 30
    Adjusting the degree to which you do activities 31
    Altering the sequence of activities within a PRINCE2 process 31
    Shifting activities between processes 32
    Using PRINCE2 in a hurry – parallel initiation.........................33
    Running the project without a project plan, just stage plans........33
Fitting PRINCE2 to the Project 34
Taking It Seriously: Being Professional..38

Part II: Working Through Your Project **39**

Chapter 4: Checking the Idea Before You Start 41

Understanding 'Starting Up a Project' 41
Seeing Why You Really Need Start Up 42
Getting Start Up Done Fast 43
Starting Up Start-Up – a Mandate 44
Filling Project Roles...45
    Appointing the first two key people 45
    Appointing more Project Board roles 46
    Deciding on the remaining roles...48
Creating the Daily Log...50
Learning Lessons from the Past 51
Checking the Project's Viability...52
    Writing the Outline Business Case 53
Checking the Approach and Writing the Project Brief 55
    Thinking through the Project Approach......................................56
    Writing the Project Brief 57
    Getting it together with the brief 59
Planning the Planning: Initiation..63
Deciding to Plan in Detail – or Not 65

Chapter 5: Planning the Whole Project: Initiation 67

Getting to Grips with Initiating a Project..68
Understanding Why You Need Plans 69
Looking at What's in a PID..70
Getting Strategic 71
    Thinking about risk management 71
    Thinking about quality management...73
    Thinking about Configuration Management...............................76
    Thinking about communications 79

Deciding on Controls..82
  Breaking the project into blocks.......................................82
  Setting up the other controls 83
Planning Your Project..85
Working on the Business Case...86
  Building the full Business Case 86
  Planning the measurement of benefits...............................87
Preparing for the First Delivery Stage......................................87
Fitting PRINCE2 to the Project 88
Writing the Extra Bits of the PID..88
Putting the PID Together 89
Looking at How You Use the PID...90
  Asking the Project Board to commit to the whole project.............90

Chapter 6: Preparing for a Stage in the Project 93
Understanding the Process of 'Managing a Stage Boundary' 94
Providing Key Information at End Stage....................................95
Triggering an End Stage...96
  Stage planning in Start Up and Initiation 97
  More about exceptions and stages....................................97
Planning the Next Stage 98
  Using product planning in more detail 98
  Preparing the Product Checklist..98
  Getting detailed with quality 99
  Updating the Project Management Team 100
Building an Exception Plan..100
Updating Project Documents and Plans 101
  Updating the Project Plan..101
  Updating the Project Approach 102
  Reviewing Risk 102
Checking the Business Case...104
Preparing an End Stage Report..105
  Reporting any lessons..107
Asking for Sign-Off and Authority to Proceed with the Next Stage.......107

Chapter 7: Controlling a Stage 109
Understanding the Process Controlling a Stage.......................109
Controlling the Flow of Work to Teams....................................111
Dealing with Risks and Issues 113
Monitoring and Progress Reporting..115
Correcting a Stage or Reporting an Exception.........................118
  Correcting the stage 119
  Reporting an Exception...119

Chapter 8: Building the Deliverables **121**

Understanding the Process Managing Product Delivery......................121
Unpacking the Work Package...123
Building the Work Package Products..127
    Receiving the Work Package 127
    Building the products...127
    Returning completed products 129

Chapter 9: Finishing the Project **131**

Closing a Project...132
Planning the Planned Closure..133
    Making sure that you've done everything 133
    Checking for sign-offs and acceptances..133
Planning a Premature Closure 134
Handing Over the Final Product(s) 135
    Checking the working environment 135
    Looking at business benefits 136
Reviewing How the Project Went 137
    Recording the follow-on actions 140
    Writing the End Project Report...140
    Writing the Lessons Report 140
Recommending Closure...142
    Closing down the logs and registers 142
    Storing the project records 142

Chapter 10: Running Effective Project Boards **145**

Introducing the Process Directing a Project..145
Understanding Five Key Responsibilities for the Project Board 146
    Taking ownership of the project..147
    Managing, not working...147
    Getting sufficient authority...147
    Checking availability 148
    Appointing small boards..149
Taking Individual Responsibility 149
    Business viewpoint – the Executive 149
    User viewpoint – the Senior User(s)...150
    Supplier viewpoint – the Senior Supplier(s) 150
Taking Joint Responsibility...150
    Making decisions without stepping over the line..........................151
    Listening to the Project Manager...152
Deciding the Level of Control 152
    Setting Project Manager authority levels 152
    Deciding on the management stages...153
    Fixing the level of risk acceptance...155

Determining highlight reporting 155
Sorting out project and quality assurance 156
Giving Advice When Asked.. 158
Getting Involved at Specific Points.. 158
Starting up 159
Initiating the project.. 159
Getting involved during a delivery stage........................... 161
Ending a stage 162
Ending the project 162

Part III: Help with PRINCE2 Project Management 167

Chapter 11: Producing and Updating the Business Case 169

Understanding Two Key Documents 170
Knowing Who's Responsible for the Business Case 170
Justifying the Project 170
Compliance projects.. 171
Benefits-driven projects... 171
Hybrid justifications 173
Keeping It Current: A 'Living Document' 173
Getting Help When It Gets Complicated 174
Dealing with Organisational Finance 176
Writing a Business Case.. 177
Setting down best case and worst case 180
Being sensitive 181
Checking If a Benefit Really Is a Benefit 181
Being Sure That You Can Deliver 182
Not claiming benefits that don't exist 182
Being prudent.. 183
Avoiding benefits contamination.. 183
Actually Measuring Benefits Delivery 184
Measuring during the project, at the end of
the project and after the project.................................. 184
Understanding the responsibilities 185

Chapter 12: Deciding Roles and Responsibilities 187

Getting the Right People Involved.. 187
Understanding PRINCE2 Management 188
Having roles, not jobs... 188
Sticking to small Project Boards.. 189
Seeing the project from three viewpoints 190
Viewing the Project Board as central................................... 191
Keeping the Project Organisation stable.............................. 192

Structuring the Organisation of PRINCE2.................................192
The PRINCE2 Project Management Team...............................193
Examining the Project Board 194
    Understanding the three Project Board roles...............194
Looking at Project Assurance 199
    Knowing that Project Assurance isn't optional 199
    Deciding how to do Project Assurance.........................200
    Working with, and not against, the Project Manager....200
    Blowing the whistle 202
Understanding Organisational Assurance.............................202
Changing Things – Board Authority.......................................203
Getting to Know the Project Manager....................................203
Considering Team Manager(s) 205
Knowing How Project Support Helps.....................................206
    Setting up a Project Office 206

Chapter 13: Managing Project Quality.........................209

Product Planning with Quality Built In 210
Taking Quality Seriously, Very Seriously 210
    Delivering appropriate quality.....................................211
    Sticking to quality 212
Specifying Criteria for Project Acceptance 212
    Customer quality expectations.....................................212
    Acceptance criteria 213
Writing a Quality Management Strategy................................213
Planning Stage- (and Team-) Level Quality 216
Controlling and Auditing Quality..216
    Controlling quality...217
    Auditing and the Quality Register................................217
    Making sure of assurance 219
Checking Products with Quality Review 219
    Roles in the quality review 220
    Finding, not correcting, errors.....................................220
    Staying 'ego-less'...220
    Signing off – the three options 221
Recording Quality...221
    PRINCE2 quality records..222
    Generic quality records 222

Chapter 14: Planning the Project, Stages and Work Packages.....223

Thinking about the Planning..224
    Considering organisational requirements.....................224
    Thinking about money 224

Planning with Products...226
    Looking at the planning problem..226
    Focusing first on what you must produce........................226
    Identifying products in the project....................................227
    Using the Product Flow Diagram.......................................228
    Writing Product Descriptions...232
    Defining the project...236
    Giving the product list some structure..............................237
Moving On to Activity Planning..239
Estimating – the Easy Bit..240
Scheduling and Resourcing...241
    Activity networking and precedence networks 242
    Activities with Gantt charts..246
    Activities and resource levelling..246
Checking Risk..247
Explaining the Plan...248
    Adding explanations for those who read the plan 248
    Financial planning...249
Planning at Three Levels 250
    The Project Plan..250
    The Stage Plan..251
    Team Plans 251

Chapter 15: Managing Project Risk **253**
Starting with the Basics: What Is Risk?....................................254
    Deciding your strategy for handling risk..........................254
    Understanding the sections of the strategy 255
Managing the Risk Budget 258
Using a Risk Cycle..259
Managing Risk with the Risk Procedure 260
Identifying Risk 261
    Assessing risk..264
    Making the 'before or after' decision 268
    Planning how to deal with a risk..269
Implementing the Risk Responses...271
    Actually taking the planned action....................................272
Communicating Information About Risk 272
Registering a Risk . . . or Not 273
    Making a Risk Register entry 274
Safely Leaving Out Risk Management 274

Chapter 16: Controlling Change and Versions **275**

Allowing Change, but Not Scope Creep 276
  Taking control 276
  Avoiding a change freeze 276
Defining a Project Issue 277
Categorising Issues 277
  General Issue or 'Problem/concern' 277
  Request for Change (RFC) 278
  Off-Specification (Off-Spec) 278
  Conceding a concession 279
Handling an Issue 280
  Step 1 – capturing the Issue 280
  Step 2 – examining the Issue 282
  Step 3 – proposing action 283
  Step 4 – deciding action 283
  Step 5 – implementing any work 284
Understanding Authority Levels 285
  Setting up a change budget 285
  Setting up a Change Authority 286
Controlling Versions – Configuration Management 287
Deciding How Much CM to Do 287
Writing the Configuration Management Strategy 288
Keeping CM Information on Products 290
Additional CI Information 292
Seeing that CM Is a Different Control 293

**Chapter 17: Monitoring Progress and Setting Up
Effective Controls** **295**

Controlling at Different Levels 295
Reporting: Time-Driven Controls 296
  Highlight reporting 296
  Checkpoint reporting 296
Using the Event-Driven Controls 297
  Controlling the project with stages 297
  Making decisions at four key points 299
Ordering Project Closure at Any Time...299
Managing 'By Exception' 300
Specifying the Limits: Tolerances 300
  Setting unequal tolerances 301
  Guarding against wishful thinking – tolerance lines 302
  Outlining the six types of tolerance 304
Reporting Projections Outside of Tolerance: Exception 305
  Giving an Exception Report 305
  Deciding what to do...306
  Revising the plans 306
Using Tolerance at Different Levels 307

Monitoring Progress and Controlling Projects...308
        Controlling teams with Work Packages 308
        Measuring progress with the Product Checklist 308
        Avoiding 'percentage complete' 309
        Controlling quality..309
    Looking for Financial Controls...309

Part IV: The Part of Tens................................... 311

Chapter 18: Ten Ways to Make PRINCE2 Work Well 313
    Staying Flexible – Using PRINCE2 Differently............................313
    Keeping the Documentation Down...314
    Making PRINCE2 a Standard..315
    Insisting on PRINCE2...315
    Training People in PRINCE2 316
    Implementing Project Assurance 316
    Actually Doing the Benefit Reviews 317
    Maintaining Product Planning...317
    Using the Product Checklist..318
    Keeping the Plans Up To Date 318

Chapter 19: Ten Tips for a Good Business Case..................319
    Measuring Benefits – Wherever You Can 319
    Understanding that Some Projects Don't Have Benefits 320
    Reviewing the Business Case Regularly 321
    Being Prudent (1) 322
    Being Prudent (2) 322
    Owning the Business Case...322
    Aligning the Business Case with Corporate Requirements....322
    Standing Firm on the Figures 323
    Updating the Business Case During Stages..............................323
    Thinking 'Business Case' in Issue Handling 324

Chapter 20: Ten Things for Successful Project Assurance 325
    Making Sure You Do It...325
    Being Flexible about Assurance..326
    Selecting Experienced People...327
    Avoiding List Tickers 327
    Steering Clear of Nit-Pickers...328
    Working Co-operatively 328
    Separating Assurance and Support...328
    Being Careful When Using Other Project Managers 328
    Getting Project Board Ownership 329
    Being Clear on What You're Assuring..329

Part V: Appendices *331*

Appendix A: Looking into PRINCE2 Qualifications .... .333
Choosing PRINCE2 Training 333
Looking at Sample Papers 334
The Foundation Exam 334
The Practitioner Exam 334
Staying Up To Date..336
Getting Qualified and Locating Exams 336
Getting Help With the Exams 336
Answers to the Sample Questions..336

Appendix B: Glossary of the Main PRINCE2 Terms .... .337

Index *351*

Introduction

．．．

*F*or a very long time, people have been doing projects, and for a very long time some people have been messing up their projects. Good approaches and techniques are 'out there' but some people just don't know they're there.

PRINCE2 is a structured method that gives a clear but very flexible approach to running projects and builds in the things that work well. PRINCE2 helps you do the job of running a project, and also helps you avoid messing up. Whether you're very experienced in running projects, or absolutely new to it, you'll find PRINCE2 very powerful and may go on to become a PRINCE2 fanatic like me. Well, hopefully not as fanatical, but certainly enthusiastic! Enthusiastic because this stuff really works.

You may have heard some bad things about PRINCE2; that PRINCE2 makes a mountain of paper, that it's only for very big projects, that it only fits very formal projects. None of that is right and when you read this book, you'll soon see why.

If you see poor PRINCE2 projects, don't make the mistake that so many people do and confuse the result with the tool. If you don't use a tool properly, you can't blame the results on the tool! Used well, PRINCE2 – with its 30 years of project experience – is amazing, and it really earns its keep.

About This Book

This book is based very much on practicality. You'll find a fair bit of technical content here, but that takes a back seat to understanding the logic and thrust of PRINCE2. Once you have the logic clear, the technical bits become straightforward. For the fine detail of all of the PRINCE2 documents, consult the PRINCE2 manual – *Managing Successful Projects with PRINCE2* by the Office of Government Commerce (published by The Stationery Office). *PRINCE2 For Dummies* isn't intended as a complete replacement for the manual but rather as a practical commentary. I hope that the explanations in this book give you the thrust of the method with practical information on how to apply it well and productively, whereas like most manuals, the PRINCE2 manual can seem a bit fragmented and dry, and even rather theoretical.

PRINCE2 is a process-driven method and the processes cover from just before the start of the project until project closure. The Part II chapters that cover these processes each have a diagram – a process model. Just to warn you up front, these diagrams can look complicated but the trick is not to get too focused on them at first. Just have a quick glance to get the overall idea, then read the chapter. At the end of the chapter, have another look at the process model and you'll see it as a simple roadmap for that part of the project. Everything falls into place!

PRINCE2 expects you to be using a particularly effective way of doing planning in the project, called *Product-led* or *Product-based* planning. If you haven't had much project experience, be happy, because you'll probably take to this way of working like a duck to water. But if you've done a lot of project planning using the more traditional start point of activity planning, you might find the product approach a bit more difficult. Don't give up, though, because it'll suddenly click into place. It took me a while to get my head round this way of planning when I first came across it – but it's really easy now. So stick with it. Product planning is very, very powerful and it's worth a bit of perseverance to understand it.

Foolish Assumptions

I assume that you:

- ✔ Don't know anything about PRINCE2 at all yet. If you do know a bit, that's a bonus.

- ✔ Want a project method to help you in your drive towards a successful project outcome – not to bury you under a pile of paper.

- ✔ Are practical and pragmatic, and prepared to be flexible to get the job done.

- ✔ Really want to use the method intelligently to get the maximum possible power from it.

How This Book Is Organised

This book broadly follows the structure of the PRINCE2 method with processes and themes. It looks first at the processes (*when* you do things), followed by the themes (*what* you do).

This section gives you an idea of what lies ahead.

Part I: How PRINCE2 Can Help You

In case you're not too sure about methods, this section sets the scene and shows you that you already use methods, and even that you quite like them. Part 1 also covers how to get the power out of PRINCE2, so it's a good dipping section.

Part II: Working Through Your Project

Part II is all about the processes, and it works through the project from start up right through to project closure. The processes in this part are the suggested *when* you do stuff. It also has a chapter on running Project Boards well.

Part III: Help with PRINCE2 Project Management

Part III covers what are known as the PRINCE2 *components themes*. These are about *what* you do – such as risk management. This Part also covers planning including the powerful product-based approach.

Part IV: The Part of Tens

Here you find some handy lists giving condensed advice on making PRINCE2 work well, writing sensible Business Cases, and doing Project Assurance (project auditing) really well. You can find even more advice free on the Dummies website, so point your browser at www.dummies.com.

Part V: Appendices

Here you find a bit about the PRINCE2 qualifications and also a useful glossary of the main PRINCE2 terms to give you a handy look-up when someone uses a term that you can't quite remember the meaning of. Of course, you can learn the terms by heart and impress people at dinner parties with your grasp of technical language.

Icons Used in This Book

To help you navigate through the book, these icons highlight some of the key points:

The information next to this icon helps you understand a point, often using a real project.

The method has seven principles such as the 'continued business justification' of the project, and this icon shows significant points where the principle is worked into the method.

The key points are things that are really core to your understanding of the method, so make sure that these snippets really stick in your mind.

These are clear explanations of PRINCE2 terms (you can also find help in the glossary at the back of the book).

This icon draws your attention to an important pointer to bear in mind.

These snippets are all about stuff to steer clear of. They tell you how things can get really messed up, sometimes with details of how other people have done exactly that. Laugh at them, but don't fall into the same trap!

Important things to keep in mind as you apply the techniques and approaches discussed.

Where to Go from Here

The great thing about *For Dummies* books is that you don't have to read them all the way through. You can simply turn to the bit you want. The Table of Contents and the Index help you out. Of course, as a structured method, PRINCE2 has a structure, but even that won't stop you moving in and out of chapters. When you're starting up the project you may want to read Chapter 4 on checking out the project idea which covers that start up work. But then you may go off to look at the theme chapters for the Business Case (Chapter 11) and risk management (Chapter 15) to help you do that work.

Part I
How PRINCE2 Can Help You

The 5th Wave — By Rich Tennant

'The new methodology has really helped me become organized. I keep my project reports under the PC, budgets under my laptop, and memos under my mobile.'

In this part . . .

Why use a method? Some people really hate the idea and the very word is enough to send them speeding away like Road Runner until they're a dot on the horizon. But methods are really helpful and in fact you already use them.

In this part I set out the idea of a method and how the PRINCE2 method can really help you plan and control your projects. Method isn't an extra overhead, it's a powerhouse. I also show how the different bits of the method fit together – the structure – and how to apply it so that it works for you every time, no matter what type or size of project you happen to be working on this time around.

Chapter 1

So What's a Project Method and Why Do I Need to Use One?

. . . .

In This Chapter

▶ Exploring what a project method is and how it works

▶ Establishing how PRINCE2 can help you run a project successfully

▶ Knowing what a method's about – and that using one isn't difficult

▶ Explaining how PRINCE2 gets a bad name when used wrongly

. . . .

*Y*ou must have seen newspaper reports of projects that have gone wrong, resulting in a waste of money, lost opportunities and disappointed people. The big question is: 'Do projects have to be like this?' The short answer is a resounding, 'NO!' That's a pretty bold statement given the scale and complexity of some projects. But the fact remains that the underlying causes of project failure are generally very well known – and, interestingly, so are strategies to prevent those problems and to help plan and control projects more effectively.

Now if only somebody would get all that information together from the huge pool of experience of planning and controlling projects. If only they'd package it up in a form that's really usable and walk you through a project in a way that avoids the known pitfalls and builds in things that are really useful to help you, based on those years of experience of what works and what doesn't work. If only. Well, read on – because between the covers of this book is some extremely good news for you.

Chapter 2 explains the overall structure of PRINCE2 but this chapter gives some context and looks at why a method such as PRINCE2 can be a very real help to you on your projects. To start with, we pick up the point mentioned at the beginning of the chapter and think about some project problems and what you can do to avoid them.

Getting the Low-Down on PRINCE2

PRINCE2 actually stands for *PRojects IN a Controlled Environment*, but don't worry too much about that; they had to call it something. PRINCE2 is currently on Version 2, hence PRINCE2. Small changes and developments are made from time to time and are released in new editions of the PRINCE2 manual.

PRINCE2 is a project method and it happens to be rather a good one, as PRINCE2 is the result of many years of hard work by many people feeding in practical ideas. You can use PRINCE2 on just about any type of project and of any size, from the very big down to the really small.

If the word 'method' spooks you, that's understandable. The very mention of a method makes some people break out in a cold sweat, reminding them of their worst nightmares, fighting through a mesh of never-ending administrative procedures and struggling up a mountain of paper. One senior manager in a large organisation asked us about PRINCE2 because she'd heard the name and wondered what it was. But as soon as she heard PRINCE2 is a method she flatly refused to hear anything more about it.

But methods don't have to be bureaucratic nightmares. Used properly, methods are sensible, helpful, productive and simple. In fact, you already use them – and you like them.

No doubt you've done a jigsaw puzzle. How do you like to set about a jigsaw? Do you start with the edges or do you go for the corners first? Perhaps you begin by putting together those bits of the puzzle where you can see that the pattern is the same. Or maybe you prefer to start with the sky. Either way, you have . . . well, a method. A method is an approach that helps give a bit of structure to what you're doing and then helps you do the job.

The difference with project methods is that they aren't just one person's approach: Lots of people have an input into setting down a good way of doing things. If a lot of experienced people think a particular approach is a good way of doing something – which is the case with PRINCE2 – then you can expect it to help you too.

Giving You Some Facts about Projects

The reason that PRINCE2 works well with all types of projects is that some parts of planning and control are common to every project. Many, or even most, project problems are common too and the rest of this section looks at those problems and how you can use PRINCE2 to overcome them.

Fact 1: A lot of projects go wrong

Project failures are common. A failure can be the loss of the entire project or something can go wrong in one or more aspects. The things that bother most people are time and money, though they need to bother about rather more than this – notably quality. But sticking to the most common concerns, projects are often late and almost always overspent. Sad though this is, many organisations expect nothing else.

One PRINCE2 project manager caused a big problem when he delivered his project on the day he had specified. The part of the business responsible for taking over the project deliverables for operational use was not ready. The project manager questioned this because he had confirmed the project's scheduled end, and the senior manager responsible for the operational area replied that they had not believed the date because projects were always late.

Now there's a lot of debate about 'failure'. If a project is just five per cent over budget but does everything that's required, is the project really a failure? Even more attention is given to deciding whose fault the failure is. When a periodical for the IT market published an article suggesting that IT staff who failed to deliver the goods should be fired, IT professionals reacted strongly, saying that project failure wasn't just down to them. They were right, because an IT project relies on much more than merely the competence of IT staff. If business areas don't supply knowledgeable staff to tell the IT people what they want in a new computer system, they shouldn't fall over in shock when the delivered system doesn't work as required.

This book is concerned with what can help avoid a failure, whether in IT projects where failure does tend to be measured to some degree, or in business projects where the failure goes largely unreported. But along with the method, the book goes further than just avoiding failure and gives you powerful tools that make your life easier in planning and control and help you speed the project forward.

After a large survey that revealed substantial failure in IT projects, Bryan Cruickshank, UK head of information risk management at KPMG, was reported as saying: 'Blind application of methodologies doesn't tend to work very well and it's certainly not something you can do straight out of university.'

I very much agree. Such 'blind application' is frighteningly common and often results from people just following the manual page by page as if every project were the same, or attending poor-quality training courses that only teach the 'what' of PRINCE2 and how to pass the PRINCE2 exams.

In *PRINCE2 For Dummies* the focus is on explaining the method in a practical way, with the 'how' and 'why' as well as the 'what'. It helps you apply the method well, with understanding, and therefore successfully. For the precise and full detail of the 'what', you can invest in a PRINCE2 manual. For explanations of how to make PRINCE2 work really well and productively on your projects, keep reading.

Fact 2: We know why projects go wrong

Here are some of the main causes of project failure. As you can see, the list is fairly predictable. Please note the kindness of using the word 'they' and not 'you' – because you don't face any of these problems in your organisation, do you?

- **No clear objectives:** They weren't really sure what the project was about.

- **Unrealistic finance:** They were never going to be able to do a project of that size on such a low budget.

- **Unrealistic staffing:** They were never going to be able to do a project of that size with so few staff. Or perhaps they have enough staff, but what they didn't take on board was that all the people had other responsibilities and were only available to the project for 10 per cent of their time; the project team was only one-tenth of the size they thought it was.

- **Poor communications:** Nobody knew what they were supposed to be doing or what anybody else was supposed to be doing, and people were unsure who they should report to and who could make decisions.

- **Poor planning:** Actually that's a kind way to put it. No planning at all is actually the problem in many projects. Then they hit problems in the project that they could have found and solved, during planning.

- **No effective progress monitoring:** The project was going off track but nobody even noticed, much less did anything about it.

- **Unclear scope:** Nobody was really sure what was in and what was out of the project. When they discovered essential things that nobody had talked about before, they had to include them. As they weren't in the original plan, the project went over time and over budget.

- **No change control:** They added in all sorts of things with no attempt to check if they were sensible or affordable, or worth the effort or cost. This is known as 'scope creep'. Sometimes the cumulative impact of a lot of uncontrolled small changes overwhelms and kills the project.

- **No risk management:** The project got killed by something that they clearly could have foreseen, controlled, or even prevented.

- **The project was not actually sensible:** A manager said that he wanted it, but nobody realised that it would cost considerably more than it would save.

Fact 3: We know good ways of preventing a lot of those things

The sad thing – or the good thing if you take a PRINCE2 perspective – is that most of the ways of preventing problems are straightforward. That suggests in turn that PRINCE2 is pretty straightforward, and actually it is. It contains a lot of detail in places because the method can tackle some pretty big stuff, but nothing is difficult. You may say, 'If everything is so easy, how come nobody did it before?' Good question. But happily someone has done it now.

You can accuse me of being simplistic here, but if that's the worst insult I ever have to face I'll have an easy life indeed. Most of the problems have obvious solutions.

✔ **Lack of planning:** Do some planning. PRINCE2 has a rather different but really powerful approach to this. You can look forward to some real help when you look at the planning chapter, Chapter 14.

✔ **Lack of clear objectives:** Set down clear objectives. And following on from this point, don't allow the project to start until the objectives are both clear and agreed.

✔ **Lack of risk management:** Do some risk management. Again, the method incorporates some really helpful and simple stuff. You may need rather more risk management than the method provides, but that doesn't take away from the fact that it gives a great foundation.

✔ **Lack of a business case or project justification:** Don't start the project until the business case demonstrates clearly that it's worth doing. Oh yes, and do actually produce a business case.

✔ **Lack of change control:** Do some change control . . . Okay, you get the picture.

The problem is that although most people can come up with most of the answers for themselves, they seem to think they don't need to apply these sorts of project disciplines on 'this project'. On 'this project' we can get away with it. Wrong, because obviously all failed projects were 'this project' to somebody. To have the best chance of project success, taking these actions has to become automatic, the way the organisation does projects.

By adopting PRINCE2 as a method and using it sensibly, it becomes standard practice – and with that comes the inherent protection of an approach that avoids known project problems. One objection may be that the method takes up too much time and time is at a premium in 'this project'. Don't let that put you off. You can use PRINCE2 in a very rapid way indeed once you see how the method works and how to apply it flexibly.

Fact 4: PRINCE2 is free to use

An amazing number of organisations say that they have their own standard for planning and controlling projects. But why reinvent the wheel? Why make up a project standard if a well-proven one already exists? The really good news is that PRINCE2 is basically free. You may want to buy a manual and go on a (good) training course, but you don't have to pay to use the method. You don't need to ask anybody's permission or pay any fees to use PRINCE2, you just use it. There are restrictions on using the name and logo though, or taking core bits of the method and including them in other things – the legal minefield of intellectual property and copyright – so be careful out there.

Making Your Life Easier with PRINCE2

I teach PRINCE2 to a lot of people on training courses. One of the things I often say at the beginning of a course is: 'If PRINCE2 doesn't help you plan and control projects better, faster and more easily, then why bother? Just do whatever else you'd do if you weren't using PRINCE2.'

And that's the point. Any method has to earn its keep – used with understanding and intelligence, this one does. PRINCE2 can make your life easier for lots of reasons, many of which this book unpacks later on. But here are some to start with.

PRINCE2 can be a real help in project planning and control because it . . .

- ✔ Provides a 'checklist' approach to help make sure that you've thought about everything you need to think about at this point in the project

- ✔ Takes a powerful and logical approach to planning that helps make sure that you don't miss anything out – that the plan is complete

- ✔ Sets down really clear roles and responsibilities, which goes a long way in helping prevent misunderstanding and communication problems

- ✔ Brings in managers at key points to make clear decisions about the project, such as if it should continue

- ✔ Builds in conscious decisions to carry on with the project at control points, so you don't just carry on by default even if things are going wrong

- ✔ Provides one of the most effective progress-monitoring controls seen in projects and one based on fact, not on estimates of percentage completion of activities

- ✔ Integrates risk management into the routine of project management so that you don't forget it

✔ Makes sure that an approved business case with measurable benefits drives the project

✔ Includes regular reviews of the business case, so if circumstances change, you re-evaluate and perhaps even stop the project

✔ Makes sure that all parties with an interest in the project are involved with the management of it, so it includes the users but also the suppliers – those doing the project work

✔ Makes sure that one person is ultimately in charge of the project so that things happen and decisions are not fudged

✔ Builds in auditing of the project to make quite sure that everything is running well and that management information about the project is accurate

✔ Links quality management to deliverables to keep it specific and measurable

✔ Is hugely flexible and adaptable to fit different sizes of project, different types of project and different project environments – it's not a 'standard approach' because projects themselves are not standard

The list can go on and on. But, in short, PRINCE2 can really help you on your project, whether big, small or something in between. PRINCE2 is really powerful and really helps you do the job when you use it properly. And using it needn't cost you much more than the price of this book, so that saves you the work of writing your own method!

In fact, in all the years of teaching PRINCE2, including to many project staff with a lot of experience as well as people with none, I've only ever found one person who claimed not to find it helpful. Well, you can't win them all, and we work hard to focus our courses on real, practical, productive PRINCE2 use.

Clearing Up Some Misunderstandings about PRINCE2

When organisations do still make up their own project method, this can be because of misunderstandings about PRINCE2. Here are a few of them.

✔ **PRINCE2 is for big projects only:** No, actually it zips down to a very small size and you can use it on very small projects. For example, its design allows for very informal use, so while it has a number of reports, these reports can be verbal.

✔ **PRINCE2 is a method designed by government for government projects:** That in itself doesn't mean that you can't use the method for non-government projects, but actually the statement is untrue. PRINCE2 started out as a method designed by a private company and then the UK government purchased it for use on its projects. And most of the development of PRINCE2 was by private companies, although the government made sure that it stayed suitable for their projects as well as private-sector ones.

✔ **PRINCE2 has huge overheads and is very bureaucratic:** No it doesn't and no it isn't. Unless, that is, you use it wrongly. In fact, one of the first signs of the method being used badly is that people on the project describe it as 'bureaucratic'. If you're on a project and you hear the words 'PRINCE2' and 'bureaucracy' in the same sentence, then worry.

✔ **We don't have time for PRINCE2:** Yes, you do. You can always find time to project manage, unless you want to fail. People who say this just don't know how to use the method rapidly.

Working Through Your Project

Just like having a method for doing a jigsaw helps you to get started and work through the problem of completing the puzzle, so having a method for doing a project 'walks' you through the project and helps by pointing out what to think about at each point. PRINCE2 does this, from a point even before the project begins right through to the end. PRINCE2 uses seven processes, which form helpful checklists of what to do (these are covered in Part II, with the Planning theme covered in Chapter 14). This is really helpful, provided that you bear in mind something that this book reinforces again and again in different areas: A checklist doesn't mean that you have to do everything. Mostly you will, but if you don't need something on a particular project, then for goodness sake keep your brain in gear and don't do it.

Chapter 2

Outlining the Structure of PRINCE2

In This Chapter

▶ Introducing the main structure – the processes

▶ Outlining the themes

▶ Setting down the principles

▶ Explaining where project techniques fit in

*T*he PRINCE2 method can seem a bit fragmented at first, especially in the 2009 edition of the PRINCE2 manual which doesn't help too much. But when you see how all the parts fit together as you read this edition of *PRINCE2 For Dummies* then it'll make sense. Parts II and III of this book look at the various elements of the method, but this chapter ranges across the whole of PRINCE2 at a higher level so that you can see how it all slots together.

You may need a little while to get to grips with all the detail, but the framework in this chapter is to help speed up that process by giving you a sort of map. PRINCE2 is very logical, so if you have any experience in projects at all, even limited experience, you'll find you can predict to some degree what will be in the different parts of the method.

When you have the structure of PRINCE2 clear and then hang on the detail, it just becomes the way you run projects. You find that your concentration turns away from what the method is and on to how you're going to use it on your next project (or if you react like some of the delegates on my courses, how you wish you'd run your last one!). And even if you have a lot of project management experience, you may still find the framework in this chapter helpful before you get into the detail.

A brief history of PRINCE2

PRINCE2 isn't new and in fact its track record is quite impressive. It started out more than 30 years ago as a method called PROMPT II (PRoject Organisation, Management and Planning Technique) and was developed by a private company. The UK government bought the rights to it for computer projects. A new government version took on board suggestions for improvements and was renamed PRINCE2 (PRojects IN Controlled Environments) to make it distinct, but it was just PROMPT II with some changes and was still very much geared to computer projects.

The UK government decided to make PRINCE2 publicly available without charging for its use, and it spread out through different types of organisation and through different countries. But something interesting happened. Although

PRINCE2, like PROMPT II, was aimed solely at computer projects – and the manual was written that way – people took the principles of PRINCE2 and applied it to business projects that had absolutely nothing to do with computers. And it worked. Looking back, that's not particularly surprising because the principles of planning and control are much the same across most projects. This wider use was recognised and in Version 2 the method was given a new structure that made it very much easier to use but, importantly, the IT terminology was taken out. When PRINCE2 was launched in 1996 it was as a business project management method, suitable for all projects and not only IT ones. The result was an astounding success and PRINCE2 continues to grow in use worldwide.

Getting to Know the Process Model

The main part of PRINCE2's structure is the process model, shown in Figure 2-1.

This model takes you through your project from the part before the project, known as Start Up or, to use the full PRINCE2 name, Starting Up a Project, through to closure. Seven processes walk you through the project and set down what you need to think about and do at each key point. The processes represent the chronology or time span of the project. You can think of the processes as the suggested 'when' of PRINCE2.

Processes, activities and actions. The seven main blocks are the processes that take you through the project and some run in parallel. Each of these has activities that give more detail on what's going on. This is where some people start to draw back and think: 'Oh no. My worst fears confirmed. You have to go through loads of steps.' But when you use it intelligently, PRINCE2 just isn't like that at all. Then at a third and final level below are the recommended actions for each of the activities.

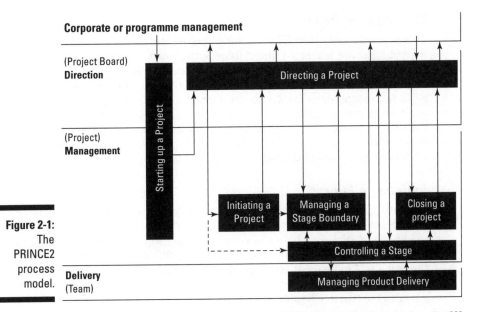

Figure 2-1:
The
PRINCE2
process
model.

Corporate or programme management

(Project Board)
Direction

Directing a Project

Starting up a Project

(Project)
Management

Initiating a Project

Managing a Stage Boundary

Closing a project

Controlling a Stage

Delivery
(Team)

Managing Product Delivery

Based on OGC PRINCE2 material. Reproduced under licence from OGC.

Beware of people who say you have to do absolutely everything on every project because PRINCE2 is a standard approach to projects. You don't and it isn't. Just pretend that you didn't hear them and read on.

You can think of the activities within each process as a helpful checklist. When you do, suddenly the whole method comes alive. Just because something is on a checklist doesn't mean that you have to do it. In fact, a checklist can be really helpful to show you what you *don't* need to do as well as what you *do* need to do. You may be starting to see how PRINCE2 really can help you on your projects. The activities help you think through very rapidly indeed what you need to do, and so speed you up and bring clarity.

The processes set down the main progression through PRINCE2. But they aren't linear, because you'll use some in parallel and one set repeats. The repeating block is to do with the control of delivery stages and these cycle round for as many stages as you have in your project. Later chapters in the book go into detail on each of these processes.

Getting things going

The first two processes, and part of a third, are to do with getting the project under way, taking decisions about it (the work of the Project Board) and planning at three different levels of detail.

Starting up a Project

This is the part of PRINCE2 that comes before the project. It covers sketching out what the project is about in order to make a decision on whether going forward into full planning would be worthwhile. Sometimes a quick look at an idea reveals that it's not so good after all and that the right thing to do is to stop immediately. Start Up also looks at roles and responsibilities, and normally you put the Project Organisation in place now. This includes the Project Board: the group of managers with oversight of the project, who decide if they should start the project and take it on into full planning. Start Up has six activities and Chapter 4 explains how they work.

Initiating a Project

This process drives the first stage of the project, the Initiation Stage, which is for project planning. The work covers the production of the project plans – in the broadest sense – which together form the Project Initiation Document (PID). This is not simply an activity plan. The PID includes elements such as the Quality Management Strategy, the Risk Register with the risk actions, and the whole package of things that define what the project is and how you're going to control it. Chapter 5 explains all about it.

Directing a Project

Figure 2-1, the process model, shows that the process Directing a Project runs right through PRINCE2, from initiation to project closure. It covers the work of the Project Board, which in turn breaks down into two broad areas. The first covers the key decision points. I mentioned the first in the section 'Starting up a Project. The board decides if the Project Brief looks promising and whether to start the project and do the detailed project planning – the Initiation Stage. But another activity runs right through the delivery stages and that's giving 'ad-hoc direction', or advising the Project Manager whenever necessary. Chapter 10 tells you what you need to know about ad hoc direction, but briefly it's where the Project Board functions as the Project Manager's boss. Just like you may need to go and talk to your boss about something, so the board must be available to the Project Manager to give direction when needed.

Repeating as necessary

The next three processes repeat for as many delivery stages as you have in your project. The only exception is in the last stage of the project, where you trigger project closure (see the later section 'Closing a Project') instead of the Stage Boundary process to prepare for the next stage.

Managing a Stage Boundary

In PRINCE2 the stages are an extremely important control feature and the stage boundaries mark important decision points. At the end of each stage the Project Board has to decide whether to authorise the next stage and allow the project to continue, or shut the project down. The activities in the Stage Boundary process cover the work of the Project Manager in getting information ready for the Project Board so that it can make that decision. For example, the processes cover things such as getting the plan ready for the next stage and updating the Business Case to reflect the very latest information and projections of benefits.

You use the Stage Boundary process at the end of every stage in the project, including the Initiation Stage – the one where you plan the project in detail. The only exception is with the last stage because at the end of that you close the project down instead. For more information on the Stage Boundary work, dash ahead to Chapter 6.

Controlling a Stage

Although Controlling a Stage is the busiest process in terms of activities – it contains eight – it isn't difficult to understand. The process represents the Project Manager's day-to-day work during a stage (except for the final work of the stage to prepare the next one, because the process Managing a Stage Boundary covers that bit). The eight activities involve actions such as giving out work to Team Managers, checking progress and reporting to the Project Board at set intervals. Chapter 7 has more detail.

Managing Product Delivery

Managing Product Delivery is a small PRINCE2 process with just three activities, but a huge process in terms of project work. This is where all the specialist work to build the deliverables – or products – is done and also the testing. The process represents the work of the Team Manager in receiving instructions on a work assignment or Work Package, building the relevant products and handing the products back again. Each Team Manager works through a series of Work Packages within each stage, so the process cycles round a lot of times. Full information on the activities is in Chapter 8.

Shutting down: Closing a Project

The last of the seven processes covers closing down the project. This can be the planned close or an early or premature close. You may shut down early if, for example, business circumstances change and you no longer require the project.

The Closing a Project process includes reporting back to the Project Board for the board to confirm the closure. The activities cover things like checking that everything is done, making sure that products can move smoothly through into their working life and producing an End Project Report.

If the project is shutting down early, then you don't need to make sure that everything is complete, because it won't be. Instead, you check to make sure that you identify any usable stuff from the project to minimise waste. Chapter 9 covers closing a project.

Introducing the Themes

The second model shows the seven themes, which you can see in Figure 2-2. The themes are the suggested 'what' of PRINCE2 and are effectively project disciplines, or subject areas. You use them right through the project.

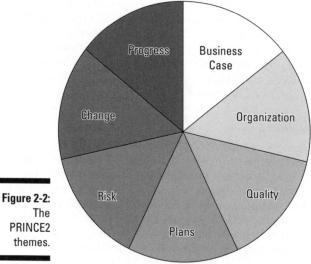

Figure 2-2: The PRINCE2 themes.

Based on OGC PRINCE2 material. Reproduced under licence from OGC

Understanding the themes

You will find a lot more about the themes later in the book – in fact there is a whole chapter on each one – so this is a quick overview to give you the general idea. As with the processes, you will see that they are not difficult and you can probably guess a lot of the content just from the title of each one.

Business Case

The Business Case is the main driver of PRINCE2. The project is not about having fun or occupying your time, but rather about delivering business benefit; well, usually. This theme sets down the suggested content of the Business Case, which you sketch out before the project begins, work into full detail in the Initiation (or project planning) Stage, and then keep up to date throughout the project. Chapter 11 has much more information on the Business Case.

Organization

PRINCE2 has very clear roles and responsibilities. Lack of clarity in this area is a common cause of project problems, so the fact that PRINCE2 is so clear is necessary as well as being really helpful. The word 'role' is extremely important in PRINCE2 because it opens the way to great flexibility in fitting the method around the needs of each individual project. On a small project, one person may have more than one role; so you may need fewer people involved in the management of the project than you may think. In fact, the minimum number of people needed on a full PRINCE2 project, including all the team work, is two people working part time. So PRINCE2 is suitable for very small projects right up to very large ones. Chapter 12 explains organization in more detail and explores why the minimum number of people is two.

Just in passing, and in case it looks odd to you, the 2009 edition of the PRINCE2 manual has standardised to use 'z' instead of 's' in words such as *organization*. If you're a reader from the USA, you can be pleased that in the UK we are flexible and our government's project method has followed your use of the English language in this instance. But please be advised that we continue to fiercely resist driving on the wrong side of the road.

Quality

Quality is the vital third dimension of project management. You may focus on time and cost, but delivering sub-standard, non-functioning deliverables on time and within budget doesn't get you anywhere. Your results need to meet the right quality level – so that they actually work!

I ordered a cooling unit with fans to put under my laptop computer. It was advertised as being very effective, with two super-quiet fans, and it was reasonably priced. The unit arrived surprisingly quickly and well before the promised date. However, one of the two fans vibrated and was far from super-quiet, and the other fan was indeed super-quiet as advertised – it didn't work at all. If I'd only been concerned about time and cost, I'd have been happy with it.

Quality management is very realistic in the PRINCE2 method because it doesn't insist that you go for the very highest quality in every project. This is sensible because not every project is a life or death situation. You may have a genuinely 'quick-and-dirty' project. PRINCE2 focuses on what quality is appropriate for this particular project and then helps you to deliver at that level.

Plans

A 'product-based' – or product-led – approach to planning is used in a number of different project approaches and is expected in PRINCE2. The product-based approach is where you first look at what the project is to produce; in other words the deliverables. Then you move on to the more familiar activity planning with techniques such as activity networks and Gantt Charts. Product-led planning is amazingly good and used to be explained in the PRINCE2 manual – albeit with some mistakes. Sadly, in the 2009 edition, it has been 'dumbed down' and the examples relegated to an appendix. Rumour has it that this is because some trainers had difficulty in teaching the technique and some didn't see the point.

In training courses delivered by my company, we have always gone into full detail on product planning because it is extraordinarily powerful in planning but also for project control. Now some of the people I have taught are even more fanatical about the product techniques than me – hard to imagine I know! Product-based planning is arguably one of the biggest advances in business project management in recent years and even in courses on the 2009 edition of PRINCE2 we continue to teach the full detail. The good news for you even if, mysteriously, you don't book one of my courses is that this *For Dummies* book will help you. It's hard to overstate just how good the product-based approach is and Chapter 14 describes the techniques in some detail.

The method works at three levels of detail in planning. A project plan covers the whole project from the end of the Initiation Stage, where you do the project planning, until the end of the project. More detailed stage planning comes where you plan a stage just before the end of the previous one, using the very latest information available. And finally team plans for individual work assignments or Work Packages, where the Stage Plan does not provide enough detail. This may be where a Work Package is particularly complex.

Risk

It won't come as a shock to you that PRINCE2 includes risk management as a theme. This is an essential part of project management and many projects have come to grief because they didn't take risk management action to identify and then control things that could cause damage. The amount of risk management you do will vary according to the risk exposure of the project and how important that project is. PRINCE2 allows for good risks as well as bad and includes mechanisms for exploiting this 'upside' risk as well as controlling the 'downside risk'. Chapter 15 covers the risk theme.

Change

A very common project problem is scope creep; uncontrolled change. You won't have been too surprised then to see change control included as one of the seven themes. It covers change mechanisms and authorities but also touches on something called 'Configuration Management'. That's rather a mouthful and a slightly strange expression for most business users of PRINCE2. In simple terms Configuration Management is version control or *versioning*. Clearly, if a document or other project deliverable goes through changes, you want to know which edition is the latest. Depending on the product, if the latest one is badly wrong, you may also want to roll back to the previous version and have another go.

Progress

PRINCE2 has excellent 'event-driven' controls that kick in at certain points, but also a couple of 'time-driven' ones that take the form of reports. Progress control is particularly effective if it is based on delivery, strongly locking into the product-based planning approach as covered in this book. A common problem with progress control is that managers tend to do too much (control freak) or too little (you never see them). The method has an excellent mechanism in the stages that keep the Project Board in control, while at the same time giving the Project Manager some space to get on and do her job.

Working in Line with the Principles

PRINCE2 has seven principles, and allegedly you're not running a proper PRINCE2 project unless you comply with all seven. Don't worry too much about them if you're reading this chapter before looking at the process and theme chapters. That's because where each one comes into the method then *PRINCE2 for Dummies*, helpful to the end, clearly points it out. Just to make life easier if you're using this list for reference, you can see that each entry has a cross reference to the chapter that's the most relevant. For example:

1. Continued business justification (Chapter 11, Producing the Business Case).

2. Learn from experience (Chapter 4, Checking the Idea).

3. Defined roles and responsibilities (Chapter 12, Roles and Responsibilities).

    4 Manage by stages (Chapter 17, Monitoring Progress).

    5 Manage by exception (Chapter 17, Monitoring Progress).

    6 Focus on products (Chapter 14, Planning).

    7 Tailor to suit the project environment (Chapter 3, Getting real power from PRINCE2).

Appreciating the Six Control Variables

In the section earlier in this chapter, which was about the Quality theme, I made the point that project management isn't just about time and cost. Quality is important too. But PRINCE2 goes on to show a total of six variables that need to be controlled and balanced. See Figure 2-3 below.

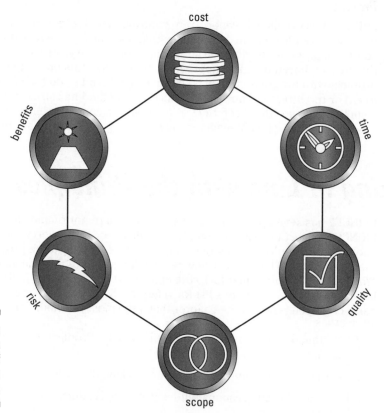

Figure 2-3:
The six areas of control in PRINCE2.

The areas interact so, for example, if there is pressure on time then you may need to re-balance cost or quality or both. The six control areas are referred to quite often in different parts of the method so you will be encountering this list again in later chapters of the book.

Fitting in Project Techniques

Finally, a bit about PRINCE2 techniques. There aren't any. Instead the method says, like some others, that suitable techniques are well documented elsewhere. The PRINCE2 manual does include some panels listing suitable techniques but leaves you in the dark as to where to find them. Some techniques will be covered in later chapters of this book, but even we don't have space to list the dozens of techniques that you can use. Try a search on the Internet for books and folders which provide a project techniques toolbox. Having said that, PRINCE2 does give a bit of information on two techniques in particular:

- **Product-based planning:** Chapter 14 gives you an insight into the power of product-based or 'product-led' planning and explains four techniques to help you do it.

- **Quality Review:** This technique uses a meeting to look for errors in a written product such as a report. It's not solely a PRINCE2 technique – the older ones among us can remember quality walkthroughs long before PRINCE2 or even PROMPT II on which PRINCE2 was based. Chapter 13 offers more information on quality including Quality Review.

It also outlines a few more such as a risk technique that's covered in this book in the risk chapter, Chapter 15.

Putting It All Together

You can think of the processes 'calling in' the themes when they're needed, and they do this extensively. Then the process and themes are supported by the principles. Figure 2-4 gives a graphical view of the integration of these three areas.

Risk management illustrates the point of using a theme while you're working through processes. You need the risk theme during Start Up to assess the overall amount of risk. If the benefits of the project idea are fairly small but the risk of the project is huge, then the project may not be worth doing. Then Initiation 'calls in' the risk theme. Initiation is more detailed project planning and risk analysis, and deciding on risk-management actions is very important at this point. During the project, you're going to discover new risks and you certainly need to monitor the existing ones. So you use the risk theme over and over as you work through the processes. At the end of the project you may pass on some risk management actions back into the organisation if they're needed in the working life of products, so it figures in your work in Closing a Project.

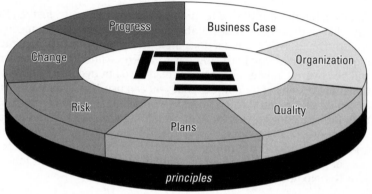

Figure 2-4:
The integra-
tion of the
parts of
PRINCE2

Based on OGC PRINCE2 material. Reproduced under licence from OGC.

The environment of a PRINCE2 project

Finally, you have the context of a 'customer / supplier environment'. PRINCE2 expects there to be a customer side and a supplier side in a project, and it manages the potential conflict of interest between the two. For more on this aspect go to Chapter 12, Roles and Responsibilities.

Chapter 3

Getting Real Power from PRINCE2

In This Chapter

▶ Knowing that PRINCE2 isn't a standard approach to projects

▶ Understanding why some people hit problems with PRINCE2

▶ Adjusting the method to fit exact project needs

*P*RINCE2 is a really logical and helpful way of planning and controlling projects. This chapter shows you how to get the true power out of the method, adjust it to fit real-life project situations, and avoid the problems that come from poor understanding and inflexible application of PRINCE2.

This chapter is ideal for you to dip in and out of. You may want to have a look at the chapter early to get some idea about the flexibility of the method, and perhaps discover the cause of any problems you've heard about when other people have been using PRINCE2. Indeed, you may have flicked to this chapter first and even now be standing in a bookshop wondering if *PRINCE2 For Dummies* can give you answers to problems like that. It can. After you've read other parts of the book and seen how everything fits together, you can come back to this chapter and think these things over in a bit more detail.

Understanding the method well and then using it intelligently is very important. In that sense, PRINCE2 is like most tools: If you don't know how to use the tool, you may well end up causing some damage to yourself and other people too.

Understanding the Problems

Two misunderstandings are at the root of most poor uses of the method: That PRINCE2 is a standard approach to projects and that PRINCE2 is merely a method for documenting projects:

- ✔ **PRINCE2 can't be a standard approach:** PRINCE2 can't be a standard approach to planning and controlling projects for one simple but overriding reason: projects themselves are not standard. They vary enormously from very small, low-risk, very simple projects to huge, business-critical, high-risk, very complex projects. Thinking that you need to plan and control all projects in the same way is highly illogical, as well as dangerously simplistic.

Projects vary enormously and so your personal applications of PRINCE2 may be very different depending on the projects you're working on. The really good news is that you can adjust your use of PRINCE2, and quite dramatically so. The method has been built for flexibility and you can adjust almost everything in it to fit the needs of individual projects. Indeed, that's one of its great strengths.

The PRINCE2 manual mentions a few limits on its adaptability, though not many. But in this book – particularly in this chapter – I show how you can exceed some of these limits to make PRINCE2 more widely applicable than the manual suggests.

✔ **PRINCE2 is not a documentation method:** Not much more to say here – other than that people thinking PRINCE2 is just about filling forms in is extremely sad because they are missing out; big time. In fact PRINCE2 is an active and powerful method that really helps you get the job done.

As I write this update to *PRINCE2 For Dummies* to reflect the changes in the 2009 edition of PRINCE2, a project management organisation is planning a debate. The debate is to be held at a major UK university and is to discuss the problem that PRINCE2 has so much documentation. This demonstrates the degree (no pun intended) to which PRINCE2 is being misunderstood and mis-applied. It's being taught as a documentation method and then applied as a documentation method. Follow this book to see how you can apply the method intelligently without excessive paperwork. And while we're on the subject, do beware of any not-so-good Project Offices that idolise their filing formats and documents and push you down the path of excessive documentation in the name of 'standardisation'.

When thinking about how to 'tailor' PRINCE2 to fit the project, a lot of people look at the whole of the method in all its detail and try to work out which bits they can chip off. But usually it's better and easier if you begin at the other end. Start with a simple implementation of PRINCE2 and justify any complexity. Remember that every bit of project overhead costs money and it also costs time, so be sure you need it. On the one hand don't skimp on necessary and sensible planning and control, but on the other hand don't do things on your project just because they're in the PRINCE2 manual. In short, keep your brain in gear.

Remembering that PRINCE2 Is a Tool

Some of the strange and even funny things people say about PRINCE2 illustrate the wrong concepts they hold. I mention some of them here because it helps you see what the method isn't, and understand more how it can help you.

✔ **I have enough to do on the project already without having to do all this PRINCE2 stuff as well.**

This shows a misunderstanding of the 'tool' nature of PRINCE2. The method becomes the way in which you plan and control projects, not some additional bolt-on work. You'd be surprised to hear a carpenter say, 'Oh, no. As well as building a table, now I have to use a mallet and chisel as well.' Using the mallet and chisel makes it easier to build the table; like PRINCE2, they are tools that help get the job done well and more easily.

✔ **PRINCE2 doesn't really fit my project.**

This takes us back to the wrong idea of a 'standard approach' where an organisation tries to have a fixed use of PRINCE2 across all its projects. Managers fail to understand PRINCE2's enormous flexibility to adjust to the needs of different projects in different project environments. Almost certainly, managers pay for this misunderstanding with excessive project overheads and probably with project delays.

✔ **Isn't PRINCE2 bureaucratic? It makes you do all this stuff you don't need.**

Once again, the organisation doesn't appreciate the flexibility of the method. If you don't need something on a project, don't do it. Things really are as easy as that. However, this doesn't mean that Project Managers can start leaving out bits of PRINCE2 because they can't be bothered to do them. The adjustment of the method comes under the full protection of the project auditing function known as Project Assurance, which you can find out about in Chapter 12.

✔ **I know this is stupid, but PRINCE2 made me do . . . and . . .**

This stems from a failure to appreciate the need to fit the method to the project and also is a symptom of the 'standard approach' mentality. The short answer is: 'If you know that something's stupid, why are you doing it?' PRINCE2 doesn't 'make' anyone do anything – it's a book and a book can't jump off the desk, twist someone's arm and force him to do something! People saying this reveal that they didn't think through what they did – and didn't – need and so are now using the method inappropriately.

✔ **We don't have time to do PRINCE2 on this project.**

Oh yes you do. You always have time to project manage, and actually the less time you have before delivery, the better the planning and control needs to be. If the delivery date of the project doesn't much matter, then the plans and controls don't need to be as tight. What this organisation is really saying is that its staff don't know how to apply the method rapidly.

Principle 7 – Tailor to suit the project environment.

Focusing on flexibility

If you want one key to success with PRINCE2, flexibility has to be it. You fit the method around your project. You don't fit the project around some standardised and inflexible implementation of PRINCE2 and force the project to do things that are unnecessary, illogical and wasteful.

Getting the Power: Adjustment

I hope that you get the picture that PRINCE2 isn't some strict, step-by-step approach to projects, but rather a powerful and dynamic method that really helps you plan and control projects better, faster and more easily. Here are some of the ways in which you can adjust the method to fit your project.

Leaving out activities

In Chapter 2, which discusses the structure of the method, I said that you can think of the activities within each PRINCE2 process as being like a checklist. This reminds you to *think about* everything, but it doesn't mean that you have to *do* everything.

Here's a simple analogy. Perhaps you have a standard shopping list that you use for a weekly shopping trip. The list includes a bag of flour, because usually you use one bag each week. However, last week you ate out a few times and other dishes didn't use much flour, so you hardly used any of last week's bag. Do you leave the flour on the list and go and buy another bag? No, of course not: You cross it off because you don't need to buy flour this week.

The shopping example may be a simple one, and as an experienced project professional you may think that weekly grocery shopping is definitely something to delegate to someone else. But it shows exactly how you handle the activities in PRINCE2. If you don't need an activity on this particular project, then don't do it – or you may start to complain about the method not fitting the project or about excessive overheads.

A group of people I call the 'List Tickers' make this worse. The List Tickers go round projects insisting that absolutely everything is done so that they can tick the boxes on their standardised control sheets. I refer to List Tickers again later and I don't like them any better in those places either. The point is that you have to *think*, not follow the manual blindly.

Beware of List Tickers – they can seriously damage both your patience and your project budget. But don't confuse List Tickers with Project Assurance and Quality Assurance, both of which are genuinely helpful when performed properly.

Adjusting the degree to which you do activities

Although you don't need to do every activity you'll end up doing nearly all of them. So then you need to decide the degree to which you do an activity. For example, one of the activities that you use in the main part of the project is about checking progress. You obviously need to check progress, so you can't leave it out altogether. But how much or how often do you check progress? That depends on the characteristics of the project. You may do a very detailed and exhaustive check with careful forward predictions twice a week. Or you may be happy with a fairly high-level check once a fortnight and that may be enough for a small and straightforward project.

Altering the sequence of activities within a PRINCE2 process

The process diagrams in PRINCE2 (shown in the chapters in Part II of the book) have arrows that show the order in which to do the activities. But this is a suggested sequence, not an imposed sequence. You may deliberately go against the direction of the arrows, and that's absolutely fine.

The arrows between activities are a suggested sequence, not an imposed sequence.

For example, suppose that when you work on the Business Case in Start Up, it indicates that the project is certainly worth at least planning out in more detail. So the Initiation Stage is started to do exactly that. But you know that the benefits were difficult to assess accurately in Start Up and you think that when the more detailed work is done, the Business Case may fall apart. Well, in that case, you might well want to do that Business Case work first of all in the Initiation Stage, so if it's going to collapse, it does so early on before you've wasted time on other planning work.

Taking that example and translating it into PRINCE2 activities, you'd actually be altering the PRINCE2 sequence as set down in the manual. The activities and the arrows between them show that you write strategies such as the

Risk Management Strategy and plan the project, and only after that do you work up the Business Case into more detail. Going back to your preferred approach for this project though, you're doing quite a bit of Business Case work before you do the strategies and the plan. If the Business Case still looks good when you've done the more detailed work, you then catch up with the strategies and other planning and make any final tweaks to the Business Case after that. You're going against the flow of the arrows in the process diagram but that's completely justifiable and sensible in this case.

The acid test for any adjustment of PRINCE2 to the project is always to ask: 'Is this sensible change for this project?' If the adjustment is better for the project than the default in the PRINCE2 manual, then it's a good one.

Shifting activities between processes

Many PRINCE2 practitioners must have 'done time' in prison I think (perhaps some dodgy projects) because they seem to think of the processes as prison cells from which activities mustn't be allowed to escape. However, in some circumstances you may want to move activities (or bits of them) from one process to another. This may send the List Tickers into apoplexy, but if it's sensible, do it.

An example is with making appointments to project roles in Start Up. The normal PRINCE2 way is to appoint the main project board role, the Executive, and then the Project Manager. When they're in place, the rest of the Project Management Team is designed and the people are appointed. This means explaining their roles to them and making adjustments if they aren't happy.

Suppose, though, that you need to go really fast in Start Up. In fact, the Executive and Project Manager need to do Start Up in just two hours. At the end of this time, the Executive will decide whether or not to take things forward, start the project and authorise the full project planning with an Initiation Stage. In that two hours, the Executive and Project Manager must scope the project, look at likely risks, build a Business Case and see if the project looks as if it'll be justified. In those two hours they won't also have time to decide on other appointments, call those people in, brief them and make any adjustments to the roles if people aren't happy. In 'real life' the other appointments would be left until later and done while the planning is going on in the Initiation Stage.

Translating that into activities, the start up work of designing and appointing the Project Management Team is taken out of the primary process 'Starting Up a Project' and moved into the process 'Initiating a Project'.

You may also want to delay appointments for other reasons, such as you're not sure who the right people are until the Project Brief is agreed. Delaying these appointments is not uncommon and can be very sensible.

Using PRINCE2 in a hurry – parallel initiation

Some people argue that they need to move fast to meet a short end date and so don't have time to do Project Initiation. This is a poor argument, because proceeding without the sensible plans and controls that Initiation puts in place is dangerous. But if you really are under pressure, you can often speed up the front end of the project without losing the power of PRINCE2. The early work of the project can be very predictable and often you can run it with a very simple plan. If that's the case, you can simply overlap the Initiation Stage with the front part of the first specialist stage of the project.

This doesn't mean that you leave the Initiation Stage out, just that its work proceeds in parallel with the front part of the first delivery stage. Using parallel initiation is the only time in PRINCE2 that you consider overlapping management stages. When you produce the Project Initiation Document (PID) at the end of Initiation, if the Project Board decides that the project is not worth doing after all, then you've wasted the specialist work that was done in parallel. Is that acceptable? Well yes, probably, because in such extreme circumstances if you don't overlap the two, then you won't ever manage to do the project at all.

But this overlap is still bad news, so try hard not to do it. You're much, much better off running the Initiation Stage rapidly, making a decision using the PID on whether to commit, and then moving promptly on to the specialist stages. Overlapping really is a last resort for when you need to move very quickly indeed, so don't make it routine.

Running the project without a project plan, just stage plans

PRINCE2 does have some boundaries, but you can break these and the method is actually rather better than the official manual indicates. The manual says that of the three levels of planning detail – project, stage and team – only the Team Plan level is optional. The idea sitting behind this is that in many projects the Stage Plan carries enough detail for Team Managers to control their work assignments or *Work Packages*.

Logically though, the Stage Plan cannot be mandatory. If you have a very small project with only one delivery stage, then the Stage Plan and the Project Plan are the same thing and you only need the Project Plan.

But going further than this, the method indicates that you must always have a Project Plan that runs from the end of the Initiation Stage until the end of the project. But what if you don't know what the end of the project is? To take an extreme example, what if you can only see as far ahead as the first delivery stage? The answer is not to regard each stage as a separate project – that's a sure way to massively drive up overheads. The answer is to challenge the PRINCE2 assumption about having to have a Project Plan.

An example here is with research projects. Say you're doing research on a major disease. Can you tell me when you're going to find a cure because I want to write the date in my diary? Clearly, life just isn't like that. You often can't see too far and you certainly aren't able to see up until the end of the project. But most research projects have stages. So you can plan and resource the first block of research, and at the end of that stage things are clearer and you can plan and resource the next stage. So the staged approach of PRINCE2 fits most research projects very well but you don't have a Project Plan. You have a succession of stage plans, and you check the ongoing viability of the research before committing to each new stage.

Fitting PRINCE2 to the Project

The following panels go through a few of the environments you may encounter, together with some tailoring tips. This covers the major environments mentioned in the PRINCE2 manual. But in looking at the specific environments mentioned in the method, don't forget the factors covered earlier in this chapter. Bearing those in mind, you can fit PRINCE2 to just about anything, not just the specific areas that follow.

Programmes

A programme is a group of projects that are being run together and which need to be co-ordinated. If your project is part of a programme, think about:

✔ Having 'programme' liaison on your Project Board; it may be sensible to combine a board role with a programme role.

✔ The communications implications. For example, it's common to copy project progress reports (Highlight Reports) to programme level.

✔ Checking that your project plan fits in with the programme plan.

✔ Budgeting and change. For example, will change funds be held at programme level with a mechanism so projects can bid for additional funding for worthwhile changes?

✔ Resource conflicts between projects, not just inside your own, if you're sharing resources across the programme.

✔ Inter-project dependencies in planning, such as another project can't do part of its work until you've copied across some specifications being written in your project.

Chapter 14 gives more information on modelling and controlling inter-dependencies.

✔ If any management actions might be done more economically or simply better at programme level. For example, the monitoring of some risks.

✔ If project support can be combined across the projects in a Programme and Project Office?

✔ If the project Business Case may be influenced by the programme Business Case and so need to make reference to it. For example, your project may be an 'enabling project' which allows other projects to run (Chapter 11 has more detail on project justifications).

Simple projects

The PRINCE2 manual refers to a common question: 'which elements of PRINCE2 can be relaxed on simple projects?' and the reply is given that there's no easy answer. Well, there is an easy answer: 'none'. Not where people are looking for an excuse to leave things out anyway and the very fact that they're asking the question indicates that they don't fully understand how to apply the method in different circumstances. What you do in simple projects is what you do in any project, and that is to adjust the degree to which you apply the processes and activities and the way that management is to be carried out. This isn't relaxing any of the planning and control, but rather it's scaling it and applying it appropriately, intelligently, but

no less professionally. In simple projects think about:

✔ Having verbal instead of written reporting, or skeletal written reports that record only the key facts, the rest of the information being given verbally.

✔ Reducing the size and complexity of reports by combining sections.

✔ Deciding what planning techniques you need to use – you may not need all of them, but I strongly suggest that you don't leave out product planning (please see Chapter 14).

✔ Having a small number of delivery stages – perhaps only one.

Commercial supplier environment

All projects have a customer/supplier environment but they have a different characteristic if the supplier isn't internal (such as 'our Works Department') but is a commercial company; or perhaps more than one. If your project has commercial companies providing project team resource, think about :

✔ How to identify suppliers that can help you achieve your Business Case and at the same time still achieve theirs (normally to make a profit on the work, but it can be to gain experience of the work area). Strangely, many organisations phrase ITTs – invitations to tender – to exclude small companies and only consider the big experienced ones. But it's often the big experienced companies that care most about their monthly profit targets and 'selling in' more days, and least about your needs. To a smaller company you're usually much more than just an 'account' and it will be more focused on meeting your requirements.

✔ Using the Work Breakdown Structure in planning to divide the project deliverables into contract groups (please see Chapter 14 for more on how to apply this technique).

✔ Planning in more detail up front to work out what contracts you need and what you need in those contracts. The tendering and contract process, of course, takes time.

✔ Considering your contract requirements. Talk to your legal or contracts people early so that they get the right things drafted; they may be specialists but they're not mind readers. In particular make sure that you have a clause that allows you to close the project early if you need to.

✔ How you will explain the working environment to suppliers. They needn't necessarily know that you're using PRINCE2 if you specify the interface clearly.

✔ How you'll integrate suppliers' working practices with your own. This requires you to go into the strategies, such as the version-control arrangements being set down in the Configuration Management Strategy. If you don't yet know who your suppliers are going to be at the time of drafting the strategies when first planning don't worry, you can add this detail later.

✔ The visibility of key documents such as the Risk Register. Normally you want everyone to be able to see these (though not to make entries in them) so everyone is knowledgeable and vigilant about the project. Getting suppliers to sign non-disclosure agreements is preferable to hiding things, so only keep separate what you really have to.

✔ How you'll arrange board-level meetings. One or more Senior Suppliers will be from the commercial companies involved in the project and there may be things that need to be discussed without the suppliers present. Keep the Project Board meetings as set down in PRINCE2 with the suppliers present, but you may then arrange some additional customer side meetings where just the Executive and Senior User roles meet up. Don't feel bad about that because the suppliers' interests will be discussed in private meetings in their companies when they look at how the contract is going and what the profit projections are.

Multi-organisation environment

Where organisations are collaborating on a project, life can get difficult. This is both in terms of delay to the project where a hundred and one agreements have to be obtained to get anything to move and where even one organisation can veto something and so bring the project to a halt or make it disappointing because it always delivers to the lowest common denominator! If your project involves more than one sponsoring organisation, think about:

✔ Whether the participating organisations have sufficiently common objectives and cultures to work together. Conflicting cultures can bring projects to grief and waste large sums of money and if it's obvious that clashes are there, you're better not to start. But if you have to, such as in some government work, then address the culture problems as part of setting up the project and lay down rules for how problems are to be addressed and then resolved.

✔ If one organisation holds the 'purse strings' and so can sway the project their way too easily to the detriment of others. That may need some tough up-front talking to come up with a fair way of dealing with disagreements between the sponsoring organisations.

✔ If there's a lead organisation for the others to support. In that event, they agree up front that in the case of dispute, they'll accept that lead organisation's decision. In that case, that lead organisation should supply the Executive for the Project Board.

✔ How you'll handle communications and decision-making involving all of the sponsoring organisations. Remember that a Project Board should have a maximum of around six members, which may give a problem if you have 12 collaborating organisations all of whom want to be heard! See Chapter 10 for ways of keeping a Project Board to a manageable size, and not becoming overwhelmed by too many 'user' members.

The PRINCE2 manual suggests that the roles of Programme Manager could be integrated with Executive of projects. This isn't usually a good idea. In a programme of any size, the Programme Manager is almost certainly a 'project professional' not a business manager, and focuses on the day-to-day co-ordination and management of the projects. The Executive role needs to see things from the point of view of the business and in the context of the business. However, you can consider integrating the roles of Programme Director (or Senior Responsible Owner) who isn't so involved in the day-to-day detail with that of one or more Executive positions on the member projects. Those roles are more compatible as, like an Executive, the Programme Director focuses on the business.

The PRINCE2 manual suggests combining the processes 'Starting Up a Project' and 'Initiating a Project' in simple projects. This isn't usually a sensible thing to do at all. Starting Up a Project can be done very rapidly and as argued in Chapter 4, Start Up is not only logically necessary but very advantageous, simple project or not. The circumstances where the processes may, unusually, be combined don't relate to the simplicity or otherwise of the project but rather to things like the availability of information.

The PRINCE2 manual warns of the need for things like having two separate progress reports from each commercial supplier team. One to the project and one to their own company managers, which include things such as new business opportunities. However, don't even start to get bogged down in all this. You needn't concern yourself with the supplier's internal communications and you certainly can't start specifying them. Anyway, no commercial supplier is going to start telling you all their internal communication arrangements just so you can complete some strange and excessive project documentation!

Taking It Seriously: Being Professional

The last part of getting the power out of PRINCE2 concerns the people, which is what all projects come down to in the end. The organisation has to be as professional about managing its projects as it is about any other management activity.

Everyone involved needs to be professional in their outlook and not play 'project games'. As part of this, the Project Board, the senior managers overseeing the project, must take their responsibilities seriously, just as a head of department takes managing the department seriously. They must also treat the audit function of the project, Project Assurance, as seriously as accounting functions take internal audits.

Organisations are often very professional in their mainstream work, but then act strangely when it comes to projects, as if somehow projects don't represent a significant use of resources. Project management doesn't have to be given a higher profile than any other branch of corporate management, but it does need to be taken as seriously and carried out conscientiously. Where projects fail, the impacts are business impacts. That alone signals that good project management is an important business matter, no matter if your business is private sector, public sector or third – charity.

Part II
Working Through Your Project

The 5th Wave   By Rich Tennant

In this part . . .

This part covers the time-driven part of the PRINCE2 method – the processes. Each of the eight top-level or primary processes covers a bit of the project from start up through to closure. One process – planning – is covered with other planning information in Chapter 12 in Part III.

Each primary process has a process model that shows the sub-processes inside that top-level process. Don't worry about these models – some look a bit complicated at first sight. They form a sort of checklist and road map of what the process is about. When you read chapters in this section, have a quick look at the process model to get a general idea, then read the chapter and come back to the process model again. On your second visit to the model you'll find it really simple.

Chapter 4

Checking the Idea Before You Start

In This Chapter

▶ Checking that your project is really a project

▶ Finding the right people and appointing them

▶ Taking on board lessons from earlier projects

▶ Writing a rough (Outline) Business Case

▶ Identifying important planning information

▶ Sketching out the project idea – the Project Brief

▶ Planning the first stage of the project up front

▶ Starting up – the processes and products you use

*P*RINCE2 gets going before the project gets going, and this chapter looks at the part of PRINCE2 that you do before the project: You take a quick look at the project idea to provide information for an important management decision – whether to start the project and get stuck in to planning it in detail, or abandon the whole idea because it doesn't look worth it after all.

The PRINCE2 name for this pre-project work is, predictably, 'Starting Up a Project'. This chapter describes exactly what that work is and the key points to help you run this first part of PRINCE2 effectively and successfully.

Understanding 'Starting Up a Project'

PRINCE2 has seven processes that walk you through your project and 'Starting Up a Project' is the first of these. Like the others, Starting Up a Project – or 'Start Up' for short, then has activities inside it. (Have a look at Chapter 2 for more on how to use the processes.) Remember that you don't follow the activities as a slavish list. They're more like a checklist and can sometimes really help you because you can see what you can safely leave out of your project, as well as what you do need to cover.

As with all of the process models in this section of the book, have a quick look at the diagram in Figure 4-1 to get the general idea, and then come back again at the end of the chapter when you've read all about it. The models can look a bit intimidating at first, but after reading all about them they're simple enough.

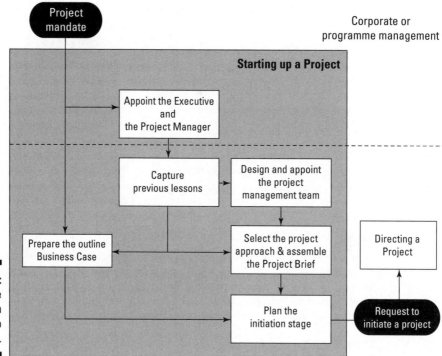

Figure 4-1:
The
Activities in
Starting Up
a Project.

Based on OGC PRINCE2 material. Reproduced under licence from OGC.

Seeing Why You Really Need Start Up

Imagine that I ask you to plan my project, 'The Office Move Project'. With just this information, can you get on and produce a set of plans? Actually, no. After pausing for a moment to think about it you fire off a whole series of questions:

- What exactly is this project – who's moving?
- Are there any constraints on the move – for example, do you need to stay in the city or move outside it?
- How much money is available?
- Do you face financial restrictions, such as when you can spend money?
- Do you have a time limit by which you must complete the move?
- Does this project include selling the old building, or is it literally just the move and another project perhaps deals with the sale?

Before you get into the detail of planning any project, you have to sort out some basic things and collect some basic information. Welcome to Start Up. This is important stuff and you can't go on to planning until you know this information. So you can now see that starting PRINCE2 before the project itself is rather logical.

But Start Up also answers an important question – 'Is this really a project at all?' Perhaps the task is just a simple unit of work that doesn't justify the overheads of project control. Or perhaps the really great idea for a project isn't so great at all, except in the mind of the person who suggested it!

Next, Start Up helps you, well, get started. You appoint some people to manage the work. You set down what the project actually is. You look at likely costs and benefits. You check on any constraints such as on technology or delivery date. Then you put all this information together in order to make a decision on whether to proceed to full planning or stop right here.

Some people argue that you can leave out the start-up work or simply include it in the main planning when the project is under way. The best advice I can give you for when you meet that argument is . . . don't! This part of PRINCE2 is really useful and more than earns its keep. It can save you hours of wasted time spent planning a project that you then find isn't worth running after all. And you can normally do the start-up work very rapidly anyway. Like the rest of PRINCE2, Start Up is pretty simple, so don't be daunted that you're at the beginning of some huge, overwhelming process. In fact, Start Up is quite the opposite and is really logical and straightforward. Even if you're already very experienced in projects, Start Up is a sensible, helpful and fast approach.

Getting Start Up Done Fast

You can usually do Start Up very quickly. It may take two weeks, but more likely two days and it can even take just a couple of hours.

Try running a Start Up or Project Brief workshop to collate information quickly. Get together a group of people who can give advice on what work the project involves (specialists) and requires (users). Ideally, aim for a group of between 4 and 12 people. (You can include more, but the problem with larger groups is that some people may avoid speaking up – but to minimise this, you can use break-out groups for some parts of the workshop.) Work through together what the potential project is about, what sort of work it involves, how much the work is likely to cost and who needs to be involved.

On one £1.25 million project, a workshop group did most of the Start Up work in just one morning. The group discussed points and wrote information on a flip chart, then later someone produced a short document based on the flip chart and finalised the project team appointments that the participants didn't complete during the workshop.

Starting Up Start Up – a Mandate

PRINCE2 starts with an instruction, usually a document but it can sometimes be a verbal instruction from the organisation, a *Project Mandate*. A Project Mandate is effectively an authority to do the Start Up work with a view to running the project. The Mandate can set out a fair amount of detail of what the intended project is about and, if it does, it can save a lot of work that you otherwise need to do in Start Up. However, usually the Project Mandate contains very little information. I know of one project where the mandate was simply the name of the project. But at the very least the Mandate should outline the project idea and name a manager who'll be the Executive and take responsibility for Start Up and then the project overall. PRINCE2 doesn't cover what should be in a Mandate, so to be helpful – as always – this book gives you a steer on the sort of information you should normally be looking for in a good Mandate.

Getting key information – a Mandate

The format and content of a project mandate may be defined already in your organisation, but if not, here are the key bits of information you should be looking for:

✔ **Scope:** An outline of what the project is about and what it will deliver.

✔ **Responsibilities:** Who is to be in overall charge of the project (the Executive), and

also who the Project Manager is to be, if this has already been decided.

✔ **Objectives:** What the project is expected to achieve (savings, faster customer service and so on).

✔ **Key constraints:** Things that will limit the project, such as an absolute delivery date, maximum budget, integration with related business procedures.

With the mandate to hand, you can start the work of Start Up, and the first thing to do is get some people in place.

Filling Project Roles

Clarity in 'roles and responsibilities' is very important in projects. Vagueness causes a lot of project communication problems, because people don't know what they need to do or what other people are doing. Indeed, project roles are so important that two other chapters of this book are devoted to them. This chapter summarises the main roles, but you can find the full detail in Chapter 12, which deals with the Organization theme. Chapter 10 is also relevant as it covers how to set up a successful Project Board (the senior management group with oversight of the project).

Principle 3 – Defined roles and responsibilities.

Appointing the first two key people

The first two appointments are an Executive, who has overall control of the project, and a Project Manager. The organisation's management appoints the Executive. The Executive must be able to take a business perspective. If a Project Manager hasn't already been identified by someone in the organisation, then the Executive must find and appoint a suitable person. Although you can divide most PRINCE2 roles between more than one person where necessary, these first two roles are the exceptions. You can only have one Executive and one Project Manager in a PRINCE2 project.

Selecting the Executive

The Executive is a vital role in PRINCE2. The manager taking the role of Executive must

- ✔ Have a strong business viewpoint
- ✔ Have an aptitude for seeing things clearly and in the full context of the project and the business
- ✔ Have sufficient authority to make project decisions

As well as decision-making authority the Executive needs to have the courage to take action, perhaps very bold and decisive action, where justified.

A project in a large, European-based company had already spent around £250,000 when the managers in the business area involved said that, due to work pressure, they could only supply a small part of the user staff resource they had promised to help deliver the project. The project teams would just have to manage the best they could. The Executive immediately stopped the project. When the user managers protested, the Executive's response was that if they couldn't supply the staff, then there was insufficient staff resource to run the project. The user managers were a bit shocked by this and said that the Executive couldn't just stop the project – a quarter of a million pounds had already been spent. The Executive's reply was not only that he could, but that he just had!

Project Board. In PRINCE2 a group of managers takes responsibility for the project. This group is known as the *Project Board*. The Executive, who is the first person to be appointed and who, as the manager with overall responsibility, is the most important participant, heads up the Project Board.

Only one person can be the Executive; two people cannot share the role. And the Executive must be a person so, for example, you can't have the senior management board as the Executive.

Deciding on the Project Manager

The role of Project Manager is a key one. The *Project Manager* is someone with project skills and, particularly at this early point, project planning skills. The Project Manager has day-to-day responsibility for the project and works for the Project Board.

As well as having strong management and project skills, the Project Manager must also have a practical understanding of how to apply the PRINCE2 method to make it work well and productively. Like the Executive, she must have sufficient time available to devote to the project.

Appointing someone to project manage a business-critical project who's already struggling to keep many other vital organisational balls in the air is asking for trouble. Many organisations try to do too much at the same time and end up delivering very little or, in some cases, nothing at all. You're often better off running projects sequentially and rapidly, rather than trying to do everything at once and delivering very slowly and with lots of things going wrong thanks to over-extended managers.

Appointing more Project Board roles

If you look back at the process diagram at the start of this chapter, you can see that the remaining appointments are made after looking at lessons from previous projects. But here, we'll carry on and deal with all the roles now so as not to chop and change the subject.

In PRINCE2 the Project Manager's boss is the Project Board. The members of the Project Board, not the Project Manager, 'own' the project.

The board members are active and extremely important to the project. The Project Board has three roles and these represent the three key interests of

- ✔ Business
- ✔ User
- ✔ Supplier

The Executive represents the business interest. Within the Project Board, the Executive is in ultimate charge and always chairs the meetings. For more on the role of Executive, flip back to the section 'Appointing the first two key people', earlier in this chapter.

Although the Project Board incorporates three roles, it doesn't necessarily have to contain that many people, though it often does. Because of role sharing the board may involve more than three people, but a top limit is around six people. The minimum number is just one person, who takes on all three roles. Personally I always think that a better minimum number is two because then you have someone to talk things through with other than the Project Manager.

Big Project Boards are bad news and can cause significant problems. One of the difficulties can be that the full board never actually meets because there are always some people missing. For more on setting up successful Project Boards and avoiding common problems, please see Chapter 10.

Choosing the Senior User(s)

The _Senior User_ represents the viewpoint of users and is responsible for specifying, then delivering, the business benefits of the project. A suitable person for this role is someone from the management of the business area that the project affects: the people who actually use what the project delivers. If the project affects more than one business area, the Executive may appoint more than one person to the Senior User role on the Project Board, and they then share the role.

As well as checking that the project delivers things that are 'fit for purpose' for the business area, the Senior User(s) must also provide user staff for the project. The project may need this resource, for example, to help specify what the users require and to test project deliverables to make sure that they work in the way the users want. The Senior User(s) must obviously have authority to commit that resource.

Selecting the Senior Supplier(s)

The Senior Supplier is a manager who can commit team resource to the project and who represents the viewpoint of suppliers. Again, if more than one area is involved, you may want to appoint more than one Senior Supplier. You can find out more about the Senior Supplier in Chapter 12.

Dealing with Change

The Project Board members normally make decisions on project changes that are beyond the authority they're willing to delegate to the Project Manager. However the Board has an option to set up a Change Authority and delegating some of its authority to make changes to this intermediate level – it comes between the Board and the Project Manager. If you cringe at the thought of it, you're right that it can be problematical as well as helpful, and Chapter 16 on Change includes an examination of the pros and cons.

Ensuring Project Assurance

Project Assurance is basically auditing – checking that the project runs correctly and that complete and accurate information gets to the Project Board. In a small project the individual board members themselves often do this assurance work. In a larger project the board may appoint people to do the checking on their behalf and report back, though they can still do the work themselves if they want to.

Project Assurance is important and you need to set it up properly. A bad, but very common, practice is to ignore Project Assurance and think of it as optional. It's not optional. Organisations waste many billions of dollars each year because they run projects badly and the projects then fail as a consequence. In the same way that financial audit is necessary for a business's accounts, Project Assurance is necessary for a project.

Deciding on the remaining roles

Other roles involved in administration and managing project teams are not part of the Project Board but are included in the management of the project and form the rest of the PRINCE2 Project Management Team.

The Project Management Team. The PRINCE2 roles together are known as the Project Management Team. That's more than just jargon: The concept of the Project Management Team emphasises that everyone is on the same side, on the same team. They work together for the success of the project. For example, the Project Board can't delegate the project to the Project Manager and disappear until the end of the project then claim the credit if the project succeeds, or fire the Project Manager if it fails.

Providing Project Support

Project Support at its simplest is administrative support. Providing a good administrator rather than having the Project Manager spend a lot of time on routine administration makes sense and is more effective, including cost-effective. The administrative support also means the Project Manager can concentrate on running the project rather than be distracted with routine admin.

Some organisations have a central Project Office that supports all their projects. Projects finish and new ones start, but the Project Office is permanent, helping all the current projects. A particularly large project may justify having its own Project Office.

Allocating Team Manager (s)

The PRINCE2 method may only involve one Project Manager, but you can have many Team Managers. A number of teams may work on the project at any one point. Some of these may be from inside the customer organisation and some may be from external supplier companies. Each team has a Team Manager who reports to the Project Manager.

Defining the Project Management Team

Don't forget that you don't necessarily need as many people as in this list – one person can have several roles and two or more people can share some roles.

The Project Board roles are:

✔ **Executive:** A role for one person only who is ultimately in charge.

✔ **Senior User:** This person represents those who use what the project delivers. You may have more than one Senior User.

✔ **Senior Supplier:** This person represents the teams doing the actual work of the project, except user activity. You may have more than one Senior Supplier.

✔ **Change Authority:** The Project Board members can choose to appoint a group or a person with an intermediate level of authority between the board and Project Manager. The board then delegates some

or all of its authority for making changes to the project to that Change Authority.

✔ **Project Assurance:** Board members may do this 'audit' function themselves or appoint others to check on their behalf and report back.

Other roles are:

✔ **Project Manager:** A role for one person only, who has day-to-day responsibility for the project and is accountable to the Project Board.

✔ **Team Manager(s):** It may be too early to say exactly what teams are needed, but where you do know, you can name the Team Managers. You have one Team Manager for each team.

✔ **Project Support:** This role concerns project administration. The Project Support can be one or more people – the same person who is the Project Manager or separate support staff.

During Start Up, before the project has got as far as detailed planning, it is often too early to decide on the Team Managers. However, sometimes you're already clear that you need particular teams, such as an installation team. Where this is the case, you can include these managers and their teams in the list of roles and responsibilities: The project management team structure. In a small project where the Project Manager runs the team, you can leave out the role of Team Manager.

You may not be able to make all the appointments at this time, perhaps because you haven't yet agreed the scope of the project or you're running Start Up very rapidly. You can delay appointment of some roles until the Initiation Stage, the first stage after the project starts. The minimum that must be in place is the Executive (for decision making) and the Project Manager (for project skills and especially planning skills).

Creating the Daily Log

One of the first acts of the Project Manager is to set up the Daily Log. This has a couple of functions. The first is like a diary in which the Project Manager can note reminders, actions and other day-to-day information. The log is very useful and can save a lot of paperwork when used intelligently. For example, the Project Manager may record a decision and thereby save the need to write and send letters or memos. The second function is as a 'catch all' to record any project information that none of the other PRINCE2 management products cover. Having said that, PRINCE2 is quite comprehensive, so this second use is rare.

In Start Up, the Project Manager starts to use the Daily Log straight away. For example, to record information such as risks that will later be transferred to the more formal *Risk Register* if the project goes ahead to full planning – Initiation.

You can have a completely unstructured format to the Daily Log, just a date and some text. PRINCE2 does suggest some headings though.

The Daily Log

Date of entry	Target date
Problem, action, event or comment	Results
Person responsible	

You may want to think about making the headings more comprehensive and store the log in the form of a spreadsheet. That way you can sort it in different ways just by clicking on column headings. It depends a bit on how much information you expect to hold as spreadsheet columns aren't suitable for storing large amounts of text.

Learning Lessons from the Past

It's been said that history repeats itself because nobody listens the first time. It's sad when a good project fails, but tragic if it's for the same reasons that a previous project failed (yes, it still happens) because nobody 'learned the lessons'. But sometimes you can miss out on good things too. Perhaps something different was tried out on a previous project and it worked really well and you can repeat the trick in this project.

PRINCE2 looks at lessons in two time frames. One is a look into the future. The method uses the Lessons Log to record things found out in this project – good stuff as well as bad stuff – to pass on to future projects. But the second is here, at the start of a project, to look back at previous experience – the lessons learned from the past.

You create a Lessons Log for the project now, at this point in Start Up, and then write into it the things you need to bear in mind in this project. The PRINCE2 manual gives three ideas of where to get information, but with a bit of thought you can do better than that.

- ✔ Lessons Reports from previous projects (where they reported information based on their Lessons Logs) and any other reports from those projects

- ✔ Corporate guidance, if you are in a large organization.

- ✔ People who worked on a similar project run previously in your organisation: Project Managers, Team Managers and team specialists.

- ✔ People in similar, non-competitive, organisations. This can be especially useful in the public and charity sectors. If you find an organisation that has already run a project similar to yours, you can often find someone willing to spare you some time if you visit, or even in a phone call, to share experience and some tips.

- ✔ Your own personal notes of what has worked for you on previous projects and what didn't.

- ✔ Project articles in the specialist press.

- ✔ Reviews and reports on the Internet – some surprisingly candid information is around.

The Lessons Log

Lesson type: To be applied to the project, in the organization or both.

Lesson detail: Why it is a lesson and details such as the cause of the problem.

Date logged:

Logged by: This is a misnomer and really means who identified the lesson as usually only the Project Manager (or Project Support on her behalf) actually makes log entries.

Priority:

You can use this lessons information in the other activities in Start Up, such as Design and Appoint the Project Management Team. 'Whatever you do, don't let X or Y even get near a project – they're the kiss of death.' Well, hopefully not quite that, but you get the idea.

Principle 2 – Learn from experience.

Checking the Project's Viability

You can easily get enthusiastic about some great project idea and rush into planning it (or not!) and 'getting on with it'. Often the urgency comes from a senior manager who has at last managed to find the resource to run her wonderful project. Now she wants to 'get on with it' and fast – or, more often, she wants *you* to get on with it and *really* fast.

But jumping straight into a project isn't a particularly good idea. You need to validate the idea to make sure that this really is a worthwhile project. The UK Treasury, the government department responsible for government finance, has a document called 'The Green Book'. The Treasury produced this for government employees who have to write business cases for their work, including projects. The document's freely available as PDF files and you can download it and print it off if you're interested – simply search for 'HM Treasury Green Book' on the Internet.

The Green Book describes the common problem of 'optimism bias'. It says that managers tend to be over-optimistic in two areas. First, they think that the project can run at lower cost and faster than is really the case. Second, they think that the project can deliver considerably more business benefit than is actually the case.

I was talking to a very experienced project consultant a while ago and we agreed that far too many projects start with high expectations but finish with disappointing results, to the point of being a failure. Or projects stop part way through when managers realise that the project can't deliver anything like the level of benefits anticipated.

You can often prevent such costly mistakes with a short upfront review of the project that estimates likely costs, timescale, benefits and possible risks. This upfront review is exactly what PRINCE2 does in Start Up.

The project is not the property of an individual manager or even a department. The organisation pays for the project and so needs to check that it's viable and sensible from the perspective of the whole business. The project must normally deliver some worthwhile benefit, and support the business. You don't want people doing their own thing – even if they have the budget – if doing so causes significant problems in other parts of the organisation.

A public-sector organisation let each of its sections improve efficiency by installing whatever new computer systems they wanted within their area and without reference to anyone else. The trouble was that the resulting systems were incompatible. So if a person sent in a change of address, for example, staff had to separately input it into each of the different systems because they wouldn't 'talk' to each other due to the different technical and data standards. This incompatibility wasted a lot of staff time, and caused some embarrassing problems when one system got left out of the update. What made sense in isolation within each section didn't make sense overall. The wider considerations should have been properly thought through and managed.

Writing the Outline Business Case

And please note the 'outline' bit. The Business Case at this point is rough and not the polished and full justification that comes when the project is planned in detail – if it gets that far. At this point, in Start Up, the Outline Business Case is to support the decision on whether it's worth going forward into full planning (Initiation) or not. It may be that very little information is needed to make that decision.

Producing the Project Product Description

Having said that this is about the Outline Business Case, the method actually requires something else before starting work on the business aspects. That is, to define what it is that the project is going to deliver. That definition is documented in the Project Product Description.

To make sense of this part, you need to take on board that PRINCE2 focuses on project deliverables, or 'products'. Chapter 14 is dedicated to this 'Product-Based Planning' approach. The chapter explains how to set about planning with products, including writing a Product Description for each deliverable that defines what the product is, what quality criteria it must reach and how it's to be tested to make sure that it does. The Project Product Description is basically the same, except that it's for the whole project and some of the content is slightly different.

Towards the end of a major construction project in the UK a national newspaper reported an argument between the construction company and the customer organisation. The construction company said that the customer must check the build before handover. The customer organisation said it must be handed over before they could check it. There was talk of taking the matter to court at some considerable cost to resolve it. Clearly, stating and agreeing the 'acceptance method' up front would have avoided the problem, as would the product-based planning approach.

The Project Product Description

Title: The name by which the project is known.

Purpose: The purpose the project fulfils and who'll use it.

Composition: The major deliverables of the project.

Derivation: Where any prior products come from, such as a feasibility study report.

Development skills required: Includes where the resources are to come from.

Customer's quality expectations: Overall quality level expected and reference to any known standards or processes needed.

Acceptance criteria: A list of criteria that the project's product must meet before the customer will accept it. This may be prioritised and some may not be essential.

Project level quality tolerances: Tolerances on the quality criteria – sometimes a band of acceptable values exists such as making deliveries to customers faster by between three and five days.

Acceptance method: How acceptance is to be confirmed. This can be merely notification or anything up to formal signed and legal handover, including a phased handover.

Acceptance responsibilities: Who is to be responsible for confirming project acceptance.

The information here is sensible, but as always in PRINCE2 you can adjust it in any direction. You can add extra sections in a more complicated project environment, or take some out if you don't need them. If you do need to add anything, do remember that you're in Start Up at the moment and try to keep things simple. You can always adjust it a bit in Initiation when you do the full planning.

A Business Case, put simply, is the justification for a project. Normally, a viable case shows that the benefits of running the project are significantly greater than the costs. But be careful to keep your brain in gear because benefits aren't the only justification. The project may be justified on different grounds, such as compliance. The project is being run, for example, because it's a head office instruction, and the fact that little or nothing exists in the way of benefit is immaterial.

For the full detail of the Business Case, please turn to Chapter 11. You can find all of the section headings for it there, it's just at this point in Start Up some sections are missed out and others only have skeletal information in them. For example, you're not usually going to do investment appraisal in the rough Business Case in Start Up, but you may do substantial appraisal work later on when you produce the full Business Case.

Getting Business Case approval

Although the Executive with the rest of the Project Board has authority to make decisions, they don't always have the authority to approve the Outline Business Case. In that case, as soon as it's prepared and has been agreed by the Project Board, the Outline Business Case passes to whoever in the organisation can give approval. No problem, but do take into account any time delay involved in going through an approval process. This is particularly so if, perish the thought, the Outline Business Case has to go to a committee.

Principle1 – Continued business justification.

If you're working on very large-scale projects, the term 'Outline Business Case' is likely to have a very different meaning. In the context of PRINCE2 'outline' means 'sketchy', consistent with its place in Start Up.

Checking the Approach and Writing the Project Brief

After looking at things like the roles and the Business Case you can now get down to thinking more about the project itself. Unless you have some devastatingly boring financial project to do, this thinking is good fun.

There are two parts to this activity. The first is to look at something PRINCE2 calls the Project Approach. This information on how you need to 'approach' the project may include constraints, such as on the type of equipment you have to use or the security requirements you need to observe. The second is to write the Project Brief, which is a sort of sketch plan of what the project is about. We'll take these one at a time because being a dummy I can't write in stereo – but don't be too critical because you probably can't read in it either.

Thinking through the Project Approach

Identifying key project information is an extremely useful, but often neglected, part of Start Up. You need to think about any constraints that may affect the planning and control of the project, as well as the outcome. You then record this information in the *Project Approach* which goes on to form part of the Project Brief.

The Project Approach can list constraints on the outcome of the project, or the 'solution' if it's that type of project, but it should also include any other information that affects how the project should be plan and run.

When considering how to approach your project, think about:

- **Resources:** You may face a constraint to use only internal or only external staff, for example.

- **Security:** The project may need to meet a particular security level, which in turn may affect resource planning of who can do what.

- **Legal/compliance:** Legal constraints may exist, such as health and safety regulations, and financial or industry codes of practice that the project must comply with.

- **Type of solution:** For instance, when you require a computer system and have to buy a packaged solution, the project is simply to find which is the best system.

- **Technology:** You may need to stick to a particular brand of machinery on the production line, for example, so that the company doesn't have to maintain lots of different brands with many different maintenance contracts.

These days my consultancy work is mostly with business projects, but I started out in computer projects, where I was a systems analyst involved in getting requirements together and then designing and installing computer systems. When I was about to start my very first development project, I was taken into the computer room and shown a super-mini computer in the corner. I was told that was the computer my system would run on. I therefore had no choice of technology and I had to design to fit that hardware, unless something overriding happened that justified my challenging the constraint. Nothing like that did happen, and so my first system did indeed run on that computer.

Another example illustrates a different aspect of the Project Approach, this time with staffing. A large and world-renowned photographic company was involved in a project to develop a new, highly innovative product. The project was very commercially sensitive. The company took extraordinary care to make sure that competitors did not get any idea of the development and forbade staff talking about any aspect of it outside the project. In that environment, the organisation only wanted to use its own permanent staff on the project. Part of the Project Approach was that under no circumstances should the project recruit any new or contract staff onto the teams. So how did I find out about this to use it as an example? Well, that's top secret – so I could tell you, but then I'd have to kill you.

In the Project Approach you can set out the options in different areas such as resources or technology, and then you can state the options selected together with their reasons. That selection may be done by people such as Project Board members or technical experts and not the Project Manager. However, you can also use the Project Approach more simply, just to list the things that affect planning.

If you have to achieve a high level of security on a project, it may involve very considerable security-related work, so be careful to find out about all the implications when preparing the Project Approach. You need to include all the security work in the project plan. That might include things like computer system security or physical security for part of a building with access control and CCTV. Don't skip over this only to get hit by a lot of extra security work after the project is running – with all the hassle and project delay that causes – all because you didn't check it out up front.

Writing the Project Brief

The Project Brief needs to be . . . well, brief. A common mistake is to do far too much work and go into completely unnecessary levels of detail. In turn, that extra work extends the Start Up period – instead of getting through the work quickly, it takes weeks or even months.

To illustrate this, assume that you're a very senior, intelligent and highly paid member of staff – which is almost certainly true if you've had the foresight to buy this book to see how to use PRINCE2 well. You decide that to use up some of the huge amount of money your organisation pays you each month, you want someone to build a house for you. You go to an architect and say that you want a house, please. What does the architect reply? 'Yes, that's fine. I'll get busy on some scale drawings and come back to you in eight weeks'? No. Instead the architect gets some scrap paper and asks you to sit down and describe the sort of house you have in mind. She draws a sketch as you talk. 'Okay, 50 bedrooms, 51 bathrooms (always good to have a spare), a huge living area overlooking the lake and mountains . . .' When you say, 'Yes, that's pretty much what I have in mind,' the architect then goes off to produce scale drawings that comply with planning and building regulations. The process starts with a sketch, not full architectural drawings.

The Project Brief is that sketch on some scrap paper, not the architectural drawings for the project. If you decide to go ahead with the project, more detailed planning produces the project equivalent of scaled drawings.

The Project Brief is a simple, and usually short, document that provides enough information for you to make the decision whether to start the project and take things forward into full planning, or to stop here because after this quick look the project doesn't look viable after all. Don't confuse the Project Brief with the more substantial Project Initiation Document (PID) that comes later (see Chapter 5).

The Project Brief

Project definition, explaining what the project needs to achieve. It should include:

Background

Project objectives (covering time, cost, quality, scope, risk and benefit performance goals)

Project scope and exclusions

Constraints and assumptions

Project tolerances

The user(s) and any other known interested parties

Interfaces

Outline Business Case

Project Product Description

Project Approach

Project Management Team structure

Role descriptions

References

Although the PRINCE2 activity refers to assembling the Project Brief, actually that's only part of the job. You do quite a lot of thinking, discussing and writing before actually getting to the point of assembling the whole brief.

You may not need all the sections in the brief, but like so much in PRINCE2, the headings in the box 'The Project Brief' act as a useful checklist so you can think it through, even if you find that you don't need some parts.

Don't ever fill in all the sections of a PRINCE2 document (or create documents in the first place) just because those sections or documents are in the method. Always think through carefully what you need for this particular project. Remember, first you put everything down, then you check it, and then someone else reads the documents. That all takes time and costs money, so always keep things as simple as possible. If you produce something in PRINCE2, be quite sure that you know why.

Getting it together with the brief

Keep the Brief as simple as possible: The headings of the document make a useful framework to explain the information and where it may come from. Some of the information may come from the mandate – possibly a substantial part, depending on how good the mandate is. (For the lowdown on the mandate, see the section 'Starting Up Start Up – a Mandate', earlier in this chapter.)

Getting the Brief together does need some effort, but you'll recognise a lot of the content from the earlier Start Up activities – so expect quite a few references back to things covered earlier on in the chapter.

Project Definition

As the name suggests, the Project Definition sets down exactly what the project idea is. If the idea isn't clear – which isn't at all uncommon – you may need a lot of discussion first. Some subsections of the Project Definition can help you with this.

Background

The Background describes how the project idea came into being. It sets the rest of the definition into context.

Your Background section may read 'This project was listed in last year's annual report as part of our drive to reduce delivery times to customers by at least 60 per cent,' or 'This is Project 3 in a programme of five projects to bring the company into line with the corporate governance requirements of Sarbanes Oxley in all our divisions.'

Project objectives

For the same project, different people can have different objectives. The project objectives set down the agreed objectives that everyone can then sign up to. PRINCE2 locks these objectives into the context of achieving goals for each of the six control factors: Time, cost, quality, scope, risk and benefit performance. You may find that a bit limiting. If so you can always add on objectives that don't fit easily into these categories.

Project scope and exclusions

Project scope and exclusions constitute a valuable section, not only because it sets down what is part of the project, but also because it specifies what is not. Knowing the project's scope is important in managing expectations. A list of what's in the project isn't necessarily enough, and at the end business users can be disappointed because you haven't included something and the business area didn't notice it was missing from the scope. These exclusions aren't the whole of the planet outside the project, but rather those areas where misunderstanding may occur.

Saying what the project excludes has two valuable benefits. First, doing so manages expectations so that the business area can see what it will get and what it won't get. Second, specifying the scope and exclusions can lead to a challenge. The business area may argue that the scope shouldn't exclude the element concerned but rather make it part of the project. They may prefer to have that in place of another part if the organisation doesn't have the time and resource to do both. Adjusting the project boundaries may be very beneficial in getting a better project.

Your Project scope and exclusions section may include something like this: 'This project will review all the company's financial procedures, but with the exception of the customer invoicing procedures in the Parts Department. The department reviewed these procedures recently and installed a new computer system that meets the exact current requirements. That system is logically separate and does not cause conflict with any other financial procedure or data set.'

You can specify the scope according to function, as in the example just given, or by departmental area, or sometimes even by time. In a project to prepare a major mountaineering expedition, the scope may be time based, to include everything up to arrival at base camp with the right people and the right equipment.

Constraints and assumptions

Although you may identify constraints on the scope, don't confuse them with things like planning constraints (see Chapter 14 for an idea of what these include). Constraints in this section of the Project Brief typically refer to the minimum scope that the project will cover.

Project tolerances

You may know some project tolerances at the outset and if so you can set them down in the Project Brief. A tolerance is an acceptable range that always has a plus and a minus. You may state this as a number or percentage, but usually working with a numeric range is easier. So, a project to investigate a business process and suggest improvements should take 12 weeks, plus or minus five days. It may sound a bit odd to say minus five days but it represents completing the project ahead of schedule. A minimum time may be sensible if the organisation wants the investigation to be thorough.

The two tolerance limits don't have to be the same. You can specify, for example, that the project tolerance is plus five days and minus ten days or plus $10,000 and minus $5,000. Tolerances can apply to different elements such as the project's scope, but the most common areas are time and cost.

Try to resist any pressure from your organisation to impose specific tolerances at this point. Remember that Start Up only deals with a rough outline of the project idea and you haven't done the detailed planning yet. Being very specific about tolerances doesn't often make sense until everyone has a much better idea of what's involved and you won't have that until Initiation – the project planning.

The user(s) and any other known interested parties

This section refers to stakeholders, which includes those who'll use what the project finally delivers, but goes beyond to others who may be affected. Again, you may not know all of them at this point, but you can list the ones you do. This will be helpful in working out who to involve and consult when doing the detailed planning in Initiation and as a start to stakeholder management.

Interfaces

This section shows how the project may interface with other areas. Interfaces can include:

- ✔ Other business areas that have links with the area that the project covers.

- ✔ Other organisations that the project outcomes may affect and that you need to consult. This element can be especially important if you're in a public-sector organisation.

- ✔ Interfacing business procedures that use outputs from an area covered by the project, or provide inputs to it, or both.

- ✔ Related projects that can have an impact on this project, and vice versa.

Outline Business Case

The Business Case is the justification for the project idea. This section of the Project Brief sets down the business benefits, the estimated cost of the project and the project's likely timescale. See the section 'Writing the Outline Business Case' earlier in this chapter, and for the full detail see Chapter 11.

The whole Project Brief is a sketch plan, and at this point in its life the Business Case that you include in the Brief isn't detailed. Instead, it's 'quick and dirty' at this point, an Outline Business Case. You aren't costing the project down to the last pop rivet. Rather, the aim is to show that the idea looks worthwhile and so to justify the more detailed planning in the Initiation Stage.

A common problem in organisations is that finance departments require very detailed cost cases up front as soon as you even mention the possibility of a project. Where possible, talk your finance people out of this. At the time you're writing the Brief, you may not be at all convinced yet that the project is even worth planning, let alone worth running. When you show that the project is at least worth planning, then you can do more detailed work, including a fully detailed Business Case, with investment appraisal if necessary, that fully meets the requirements of the finance department. Doing detailed finance work at Start Up goes against the whole concept of a quick sketch and often makes Start Up painfully, and unnecessarily, long.

In the Outline Business Case you also need content to show that the project lines up with organisational strategy and policy, not working against the rest of the company or going off at a tangent.

Project Product Description

Have a look at the section earlier in this chapter 'Producing the Project Product Description'. You make this definition while working on the Outline Business Case and it includes the quality level required in the project required by the customer: The Customer Quality Expectations. What you need here for quality is an idea of the overall level for this particular project idea. On the one hand, the project may be safety-critical where people's lives depend on the quality of the deliverables, and the quality-related work, including quality planning, is considerable and rigorous. At the other extreme, the project may be 'quick and dirty' and justifiably exempted from the normal minimum quality requirements in the organisation's projects.

Putting the Project Product Description in the Brief can be helpful in two ways. First, some people find it hard to grasp what some projects are about, but if you say clearly what the project will deliver, they immediately understand. Second, two people can talk about the same project idea but have very different ideas about what the final deliverable may be. In either or both cases, this section makes the outcome clear.

In a major healthcare project, a document described some problems that a project needed to address. However, the project scope was ambiguous. In one place the document suggested that the project would investigate the problems and come up with a recommended solution. In another place the document included implementation of that solution. So, then: what was the final deliverable, a recommendation or an implemented solution? Senior managers agreed and signed off the document, but in signing, what had they actually authorised?

Project Approach

This is described in the section earlier in this chapter 'Thinking Through the Project Approach'. This information is extremely useful when doing the full planning in the Initiation Stage, and even before that towards the end of Start Up when you're planning the Initiation Stage.

Project Management Team Structure

The good news is that this is really simple. You'll have decided, normally, on roles and responsibilities earlier in Start Up. See the section earlier in this chapter 'Filling Project Roles'. Now you get to play with a diagram editor to draw up an organisation chart for the project. You can spend happy hours adjusting the layout and colours – or perhaps you're much more disciplined than me.

Role Descriptions

Don't get carried away here. The PRINCE2 manual, contrary to the impression it gives, can save you some serious time and often you just don't need to do role descriptions. If your use of roles is standard, you don't need to start writing detailed descriptions because they're all printed out in Appendix C of the manual. Concentrate instead on spelling out anything that is non-standard – if you have any roles that are non-standard.

You can find much more on roles in Chapter 12 on the Organization theme.

References

This is where you record any references to other documents. You might refer to an organisational strategy, for example, or a policy paper that has a bearing on the project.

Planning the Planning: Initiation

The final part of Start Up is to prepare for the Initiation Stage. If the Project Board decides to start the project and run the Initiation Stage then you need to have a plan in place so that you can start the work without delay.

The Initiation Stage: PRINCE2 calls the first phase or stage of the project which is devoted completely to planning, the *Initiation Stage* (Chapter 5 has more details). You create two important PRINCE2 products in the Initiation Stage. The first is the fully developed project plans, packaged together to form the Project Initiation Document or PID. Then you prepare the plan for the stage after that, the first delivery stage where the main work of the project starts. In PRINCE2, you always produce a stage plan just before that stage begins, so you can base the plan on the very latest information available. Following that pattern, you produce the plan for the Initiation Stage towards the end of Start Up, and the plan for the first working stage towards the end of the Initiation Stage.

Project Initiation Documentation: The Project Brief is the sketch plan of the project. If the project goes ahead then you need to develop the Brief into a more detailed set of project plans. This package of project-level plans makes up the *Project Initiation Documentation* or PID. To find out much more about the PID and what's involved in producing one, please see Chapter 5.

When you plan Initiation, don't forget any work to create baseline measures. If the Business Case claims that the project is going to make a 15 per cent saving in costs over the present business procedures, do you know what the business procedures cost at the moment? Similarly with claims for time savings – do you know how long current procedures take? In order to measure the savings of the 'after', you need to have accurate figures for the 'before'. You need to include work to take those measurements in the Initiation Stage plan.

Unless your project is very large, you can usually keep the Initiation Stage plan fairly simple. Remember that you're planning the planning, so don't get carried away with unnecessary detail.

Thinking through the Initiation Stage plan

The Initiation Stage is when you plan the project, so you need to think carefully how much planning you need to do. Consider what's involved, referring to the Project Approach but not limiting yourself just to that.

✔ **Risk:** How much effort do you need to devote to doing a risk analysis as part of the Initiation Stage? Perhaps you need just 30 minutes in front of a flip chart, or maybe you require an analysis lasting several days and involving expert risk consultants from outside your organisation, or something in between.

✔ **Quality:** How much effort do you need to plan the management of quality in the project? If the project is fairly 'quick and dirty', you may not need to invest much effort. But if, for example, you're working with a safety-critical project, you may require a huge amount of quality-related planning in Initiation.

✔ **Version control:** You may already know that significant version control will be needed in the project if you're going to be dealing with a large number of project products that go through a significant number of changes. In turn, this affects the level of work that you need in the Initiation Stage to plan and set up those controls.

✔ **Project filing:** How much project documentation do you anticipate? If the amount is substantial, such as in major construction projects, then part of the planning and Initiation Stage involves setting up file libraries and even computer systems to control the documentation. Alternatively, your filing requirements may be very simple indeed. Whatever the extent of that work is, you need to include the time and resource for it in the Initiation Stage plan.

Deciding to Plan in Detail – or Not

At the end of Start Up, a package of information goes to the Project Board, who then decides whether to go ahead with the project and authorise work to start on the Initiation Stage and do the full planning, or whether to stop things at this point because the project doesn't look viable.

If the board does decide to go ahead, its members are only committing to the Initiation Stage at this point. Only at the end of the Initiation Stage, if things still look good, does the board commit to the whole project.

Checking out the Products of Starting Up a Project

In Start Up you create and adjust several management products, but be careful not to do too much. The time to work the management products into detail is in the Initiation Stage, not here in Start Up. The Project Brief is the major output of Start Up. Here's an overview of the products for at-a-glance information:

✔ **Daily Log.** This log is set up by the Project Manager and functions mostly as a sort of diary.

✔ **Lessons Log.** This log is set up by the Project Manager and is used in Start Up to record lessons from previous projects that need to be applied in this one. Later it's used to record lessons learned in this project that will be useful on future projects.

✔ **Outline Business Case.** A 'quick and dirty' Business Case that's not fully detailed but has sufficient information on which to make a decision on whether to start the project and do the full planning, or stop now. The Outline Business Case forms part of the Project Brief.

✔ **Project Approach.** Very useful in full planning – Initiation – this is a statement of things that will constrain any project 'solution' (such as technology) and the way that the project is run (such as a secure environment). The approach goes in the Project Brief.

✔ **Project Brief.** An outline of the project idea and the justification for running the project. This contains other things that are products in their own right, such as the Business Case, and other information that aren't full products, such as the Project Management Team structure. See the panel 'The Project Brief' earlier in the chapter for full details.

✔ **Project Product Description.** A definition of what the project is about. This is included in the Project Brief.

✔ **Stage Plan for the Initiation Stage.** The Initiation Stage is the first stage in the project and so needs a Stage Plan. Following the PRINCE2 pattern that a stage plan is always produced just before that stage starts, the Initiation Stage plan is produced towards the end of Start Up.

Chapter 5

Planning the Whole Project: Initiation

In This Chapter

▶ Thinking through risk, quality, change and communications and how best to manage them

▶ Deciding on the degree of control you need and what mechanisms to use

▶ Planning the work of the project

▶ Working the Business Case into full detail

▶ Creating the Project Initiation Documentation (PID)

Chapter 4 is about the PRINCE2 process of Starting Up a Project and how the Project Manager and the Executive produce a Project Brief. The Project Board uses this 'sketch plan' of the potential project to decide whether the project looks worth planning in more detail. And that's where this chapter comes in. Initiation is that planning in more detail.

The first project stage, which is driven by the process 'Initiating a Project', is devoted entirely to project planning and doesn't involve any other work. A very common cause of project failure is poor planning – or even a total lack of planning – and this stage in a PRINCE2 project helps to make sure that doesn't happen.

The completed set of project plans form the *Project Initiation Documentation* or PID, a precise definition of exactly what this project is. But then you also need to plan in more detail for the first delivery stage of the project (the one after the Initiation Stage), so that if the board decides to go ahead with the full project the first of the delivery Stage Plans is in place and ready to roll.

If you're involved in doing a feasibility study as part of your project, be careful not to confuse that feasibility work with project Initiation, or indeed with Start Up. The work involved in the feasibility study and writing the feasibility report is the work that you need to project manage. What you do in the Initiation Stage is plan that feasibility work and decide how best to project manage it.

Project Initiation Documentation (PID): This is the documentation set that contains all of the project-level plans – not only activity plans but things like the management strategies for controlling risk and quality. Even if you're new to PRINCE2 you may be familiar with this type of document and know it as a Project Definition Report (PDR), a Project Definition Document or a Project Charter.

Getting to Grips with Initiating a Project

As with all of the PRINCE2 processes, a lower-level model of Initiating a Project shows you the activities that are inside. It gives you a road map of what Initiation is all about. Have a quick look at Figure 5-1 now. It may look a bit complicated but after you've read this chapter, the detail falls into place and you see it's actually quite simple.

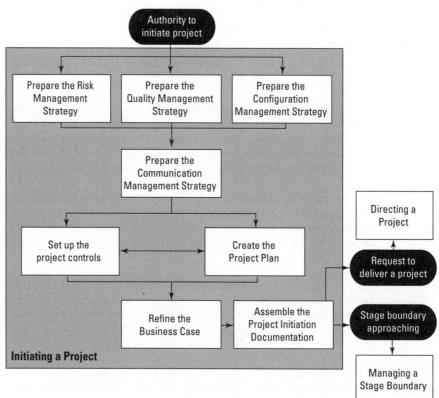

Figure 5-1:
The activities in Initiating a Project.

Based on OGC PRINCE2 material. Reproduced under licence from OGC.

Initiation involves some big subjects like risk, quality and planning so expect lots of references to other chapters where these themes are covered in more depth. As you'll see, this chapter gives you the main things to bear in mind, but the main subject chapters give more detailed coverage.

Understanding Why You Need Plans

So, the first stage in every PRINCE2 project is the Initiation Stage. This stage is mandatory in the method and the word 'initiation' here basically means 'project planning', but in the widest sense of those words. The activities in the process give you a helpful checklist of what you need to think about and work through.

The argument for planning is really a no-brainer. When you go on holiday, you have to think through what you need and plan your trip. With a project that may be business-critical to your organisation, planning is even more important.

The old saying goes: Fail to plan, then plan to fail. If you don't plan, you can be fairly confident of failure. In contrast, in PRINCE2 you plan thoroughly – although only in proportion to the needs of your particular project.

When working through any project, problems always crop up – some predictable and obvious and others that come out later during the project work. So when do you want to find out about the more obvious problems and deal with them? While planning, so you can sort out those problems on the plan, or would you prefer to hit them during the project itself? Clearly, if you find the problems during planning, you can deal with them at that point and the project will then run more smoothly. Some unforeseen difficulties are still bound to occur, but why struggle with other things that you could have noticed and sorted out earlier? The time and energy you waste in 'fire fighting' all the problems is much greater than the time taken to plan things properly in the first place.

A common project problem is resource overload. You want to use particular people at a particular time, but then find at the last minute that they're not available – perhaps they're working on another project. If sorting out the resource availability is part of the planning – which of course it should be – then you can identify that conflict and plan the project around it. And that planning avoids people running around in a panic during the project, shouting, 'Where are Mary and Cheng? Why aren't they *here*, and why aren't they here *now*?' Sound familiar? No, of course not!

A further argument for effective planning is project control. In order to monitor progress, you need to have something to measure against – a plan. If you don't know where you expect to be at any given point, how can you know whether you're on track?

The answer to the problem of under-planning isn't over-planning – don't react by going to the opposite extreme. Think carefully about just what degree of planning and control is sensible for your particular project. For more on this see 'Planning Your Project', later in this chapter.

Looking at What's in the PID

It's easier to understand the process Initiating a Project if you have a quick look at the contents of the PID first. Then as you work through this chapter you'll see that Initiation simply covers the thinking, consultation and writing needed to produce the various sections.

The Project Initiation Documentation (PID)

Project definition

Background

Project objectives and desired outcomes

Project scope and exclusions

Constraints and assumptions

The user(s) and any other known interested parties

Interfaces

Project approach

Business Case

Project Management Team structure

Role descriptions

Quality Management Strategy

Configuration Management Strategy

Risk Management Strategy

Communication Management Strategy

Project Plan

Project controls

Tailoring of PRINCE2

Because the PID defines what the project is and what the Project Board approves, you can see it in terms of a contract between the board and the Project Manager. This is the project that the Project Board is asking the Project Manager to run on a day-to-day basis on their behalf, and the PID gives the Project Manager the authority to do that.

Getting Strategic

The first four activities in the process are about thinking through how you'll manage four key aspects of this particular project: Risk, quality, version control and communications. For each of these four you develop a strategy, which is usually a written document.

As with all documents in PRINCE2, keep things as simple as you can. Don't get carried away with documentation and build a paper mountain that wastes your time in writing masses of stuff that isn't really needed and other people's time in reading it all. If each strategy can be a few notes, or a reference to an existing organisational project standard, that's great.

The 2009 edition of the PRINCE2 manual is more than a bit strange when dealing with Initiation, so do be careful out there. It looks as if the Project Manager locks himself away in his office to write the bits of the Project Initiation Documentation, including the strategies, and the Project Board just approves them all. Clearly that isn't the case and considerable interaction with the Project Board is needed during Initiation, not least in the formulation of the strategies. Board members must make themselves available during the Initiation work to give input and generally talk things through with the Project Manager.

Thinking about risk management

The first strategy is the *Risk Management Strategy*. This is an overall strategy so don't confuse it with how you plan to deal with individual risks. Information on the management of each individual risk is contained in the *Risk Register* that you also create during this activity. More on the Risk Register in a moment.

The Risk Management Strategy is how you'll manage risk overall on this project. For example, who is able to take decisions about risk? Do any procedures need to be put in place and if so what should they be? Should there be a separate budget for risk management within the project? How should risk status be reported? For full details on the Risk Management Strategy go to Chapter 15, which focuses on the risk theme.

Opening the Risk Register

Information on risks that are to be formally managed should be put into the Risk Register but as you haven't got one yet, now is the time to create it. The full information on this, including the register headings, is in the risk chapter, Chapter 15. The register can be set up by Project Support – the administrator function in the project – but normally the Project Manager can set it up faster than reaching for the phone to ask Project Support to do it. In my training company, Inspirandum, we provide a full set of templates free to everyone who books us for a course and they can really speed things up when creating the basic control documents in a project.

PRINCE2 allows for risks to be managed in two ways. Formally, by entering a risk into the Risk Register, or informally by the Project Manager by just keeping track of that particular risk in his Daily Log. Up to this point the Project Manager has only had the Daily Log and any risks identified during Start Up were noted in that. So now, those risks that should be formally managed are transferred to the Risk Register.

Logs and registers. PRINCE2 has two logs and three registers. A register is for things that are to be formally managed in the project, such as with the Risk Register. The two logs are for informal use by the Project Manager to keep track of things that he can deal with on his own and which don't need formal tracking.

Analysing risk during Initiation

You may well decide to do some risk analysis at this point too and work the Risk Register up into full detail, though the official PRINCE2 manual is strangely silent on the point. In Start Up you only list the main risks and even then only in basic detail. In any risk analysis you record the full details on each risk in the Risk Register, including exactly how you're going to handle them in the project. That's not the end of the story though because you'll undoubtedly find more risks as you go through Initiation – not least while you are developing the project plans – and so you can expect to add more risks and do more analysis before you're done with this 'Initiating a Project' process.

Watch out, because risk analysis can take quite a lot of time and it involves the Project Board as well as the Project Manager. But as always, balance this. If the project is very low risk you may not need too much time and effort on it, no matter how large the project. But equally, don't cut back too much. Better to spend a bit more time now and manage the risk really well, than find you need time-consuming and costly effort later in the project because you didn't see problems coming that you could have spotted easily if you'd done a bit more work in Initiation. Who knows, a bit of thought may mean that by taking some very simple actions, you can prevent some of the risks ever happening at all.

Thinking about quality management

In this book I make the point several times that project management isn't just about time and cost – the two things that many organisational managers are exclusively concerned with. What's the point of delivering a load of unusable garbage 'on time and within budget'? Clearly, producing the products – the project deliverables – to the required level of quality is of prime importance.

PRINCE2 has a very strong focus on quality, deeply embedded in the method. You think about quality even before the project – in Start Up. But the real quality work begins now, in Initiation, when you think through a strategy for quality across the whole project and record it in – you've guessed it – the *Quality Management Strategy*.

You may think it odd to tackle quality early in Initiation, and before you've done the project plan. But as you get to grips with the Initiation work you can see the logic. When you get to the project planning you then benefit from knowing the overall level of quality you're aiming for and the sort of things involved with that, such as the amount of testing, what skills and resources you're likely to need, and the timing of some quality activities.

Most of the time you decide on individual tests and their timing when you do the really detailed quality planning as part of stage planning just before each stage begins. However, some things go across stages. For example, you may need to book a fire officer in Stage 3 for a fire inspection that you need in Stage 6. If you think through what standards you need to comply with as part of your quality strategy here, early on in Initiation, you note that element and keep it in mind for when you come to the project planning.

The Quality Management Strategy is, not surprisingly, strategic while the quality work in stage planning is more tactical. You leave the tactics of exactly what tests you need and when and who is to do them, for that stage planning, when you have a clear picture of the precise requirements for things you'll be producing in that part of the project.

Quality in Initiation is all about strategy. Don't confuse this with the more detailed and tactical quality planning that comes later as part of stage planning. At this point at the beginning of the Initiation Stage, it's far too early for the detailed quality planning, because you haven't even planned the project itself yet, let alone worked out the detailed deliverables of the stages.

Get real – not every project is safety critical

Some people think – wrongly – that good projects should always achieve the very highest levels of quality possible. That idea's a long way from the truth. The PRINCE2 method is more realistic than that, and you need to be realistic as well.

The correct level of quality for your project may genuinely be a low level. Running a 'quick and dirty' project to do something rapidly without rigorous quality isn't at all wrong. Not every project is safety-critical with thousands of lives hanging in the balance. That doesn't give you an excuse to abandon quality where you do need it, but it does emphasise the need to balance the level of quality against the needs, the cost, and the time you require to achieve it.

Quality management in projects and in PRINCE2 is about delivering the appropriate level of quality, not the maximum level possible.

Writing the Quality Management Strategy

Chapter 13 covers the full detail on quality management in PRINCE2, including the strategy. But here are a few things to bear in mind now.

First, establish just what level of quality you're going for – for that you may need to talk to other people:

- **Project Board members:** Ask what they need from a customer viewpoint and what they want to pay for.

- **Known suppliers:** Discuss quality in the specialist parts of the project. Technical or industry standards may be involved.

- **Specialists:** Find out about any specialist quality requirements they have, perhaps including legal constraints.

- **The Quality Department (if you have one):** Establish organisational quality requirements such as quality procedures, standard checks and quality responsibilities.

But the Project Board itself does the main quality decision-making. The board includes the Senior User, who says what the user community requires; the Senior Supplier, who's aware of specialist quality requirements (such as industry codes of practice); and the Executive, who represents the organisation and who is usually paying for the project.

Don't aim too high. A common problem is setting quality at an unrealistically high level, then realising how much work achieving that involves and, faced with time pressures on the project, abandoning the lot and delivering zero quality. The Project Board as well as the Project Manager need to be realistic from the start and ask what quality level is justified in the context of what the organisation can afford. And what the organisation can afford doesn't just mean money, but time as well.

Very high quality is extremely expensive in terms of time as well as money. In your very highest-quality projects, how much project effort do you estimate is wholly devoted to quality? What percentage of project activity is taken up with designing tests, performing tests, making corrections and retesting? If your answer is 20 per cent of the total project effort, that's high – the equivalent of one day a week. If these activities take up 50 per cent of the project effort, that's extremely high, because you spend as much time testing as building the project deliverables in the first place! But even that level is low compared with some safety-critical projects, such as developing flight controls for large passenger aircraft, where the quality work can be up to 85 per cent of the project effort.

In the Quality Management Strategy you need to set down what level of quality is appropriate for this project, how to achieve it, and who's responsible for achieving it. The strategy has to be practical and achievable.

So, for the strategy you need to think through and record:

- ✔ **Who:** Who's responsible for delivering and checking quality? This can include people from outside your project (perhaps from head office) or even from outside your organisation (perhaps building inspectors).

- ✔ **What:** What level of quality do you *want* to achieve and what level do you *need* to achieve? For example, you may face legal requirements such as safety standards, as well as what the business users want to have.

- ✔ **How:** What controls and procedures do you plan to put in place to make sure that you actually deliver the required quality and don't just talk about it?

Don't look on the Internet for examples of quality strategies or plans to copy for your project. People rarely do a great job on them. While writing this section, I found one PID in which the writers completely left out the quality thinking and didn't mention quality in the PID at all. Another I looked at had four short paragraphs under the quality heading, which were so generalised that they were effectively meaningless. The last paragraph covered project progress monitoring, which has nothing to do with quality anyway. And just in case you think that such problems only affect small projects with inexperienced staff, this second PID was for a UK government project, and one of the members of the Project Board was from 10 Downing Street and an adviser to the Prime Minister on government projects.

Thinking about outside suppliers

For the Quality Management Strategy you need to think carefully about any project teams from outside your own organisation – perhaps from supplier companies. Their approach to quality may be entirely different to yours. These project teams may have different patterns of quality responsibility, different procedures and different ways of approving products. Your strategy may need to include mapping these teams' quality procedures to show how they'll align to, and interface with, your own project procedures.

Updating the Quality Management Strategy throughout the project

You may be wondering what you do if you don't yet know who your external suppliers are, because your organisation isn't going to award the contracts until part way through the project. Don't worry, this is quite common and PRINCE2 covers that – of course! Although the Quality Management Strategy forms part of the PID and the Project Board use it to give the go-ahead at the end of the Initiation Stage, it is then kept up to date throughout the project. The Project Manager can update the strategy at the end of each stage, so any new information, such as the details you need to deal with different suppliers' procedures, can be put in then.

Preparing the Quality Register

The Quality Register is effective and simple, an excellent combination. It acts as an audit trail to help with project assurance and to make sure that planned tests and checks actually get done.

The Project Manager, or Project Support on his behalf, makes entries in the Quality Register before the start of each stage, listing all the planned quality activities, such as tests and checks, each with a reference number and the target date on which it is due to take place. When a test or check is done, the testers sign it off in the Quality Register and the Error Sheet or other test notification is often filed in the register too. Signing the register shows that the test was done and the Error Sheet demonstrates that the team cleared any errors. It's a good idea to file each Error Sheet as extra evidence of a test, even where there is a 'nil return' because no errors were found in the product.

Team Managers, the Project Manager and Project Assurance staff will repeatedly check the Quality Register, and each of those checks takes mere moments. These repeated checks mean that forgetting a test is just about unimaginable.

For more information on the whole topic of quality, see Chapter 13. You will find full details there on the exact contents of the Quality Management Strategy and the Quality Register.

Thinking about Configuration Management

Thinking about . . . what? If you're not from an IT or engineering environment you may wonder what on earth Configuration Management (CM) is. Don't get too worried, it's basically about controlling versions. 'So why don't they just call it Version Control?' you ask. Why indeed. But Configuration Management it remains, despite my repeated protests, so you and I have both got to live with it. But look on the bright side, at least we can sound knowledgeable and important. 'Ah yes Mr Smith. I think we definitely need a bit of configuration management with that one!'

The document you're working on here is the *Configuration Management Strategy*. It sets down how you do the version control, and how you protect project products from unauthorised change. The full detail is in Chapter 16, which is about managing change. But as with quality in the previous section, here are a few guidelines for writing the strategy.

Writing the Configuration Management (CM) Strategy

As with the other strategies, remember this is about how you're planning to control the versions. It's not about actually controlling them; that happens mostly in the delivery stages. Here you need to think through what protection and procedures you're going to need. For example, should anyone on the project be able to get at things without restriction or anyone stopping them? Perhaps so, in which case you won't need any protection. But perhaps you don't want to allow free rein, so you need to think who can get at what, and what security you need to stop other people getting at information they shouldn't have easy access to. That may involve physical security such as fences and locks, or perhaps computer security with usernames and passwords.

If project staff can't just get at something without authority, you need to decide what procedures to put in place to issue documents and make sure that they come back. You may need 'booking in' and 'booking out' procedures to keep track of who had what, and when. The design of those procedures is part of the Configuration Management Strategy.

Watching out for suppliers

Mapping suppliers' procedures to your project procedures is very important in this context of CM. What if your external suppliers have different version control procedures and identification systems to yours? Or worse still, if you work in information technology, what if the suppliers have the same procedures and identification systems as yours? If the supplier writes some program code and gives it the same identifier as a different program being written by someone from your own IT department, in the worst case, someone's code may get overwritten by mistake.

Keeping the CM Strategy up to date

Like the other strategies, you will be keeping the Configuration Management Strategy up to date throughout the project. So if, for example, at the start of Stage 5 you let a contract and the winning supplier has a different CM procedure to yours, you may then need to update the strategy to show the mapping of the two procedures and how the interface will work.

Keeping track of things to be configuration managed

If you're going to version control something you obviously need to record information about it. In PRINCE2 that is called a *Configuration Item Record*. It's far too early to do this for most things because you haven't even done the planning yet. However, you need to version control some of the project management things as well, such as the Business Case. Because you know about them now, and indeed are working on them during Initiation, you can set up the Configuration Item Records for them here and now.

For the full detail on the information on a Configuration Item Record, have a look at Chapter 16. But don't be put off by the bureaucratic image that the term 'Configuration Item Record' conjures up. The information this record contains is actually very sensible and enormously useful in preventing a range of project problems.

Setting up the Issue Register

Before explaining the *Issue Register*, it's probably helpful to say what an Issue is in a PRINCE2 project. An Issue is a communication from anyone with an interest in the project straight to the Project Manager at any time and about anything. Now is that flexible or is that flexible? The Issue may be to ask for something to be changed, it may be to report a problem, it may be to put forward a good idea, it may be, well . . anything. When the Project Manager gets the Issue, he must make a decision about whether to deal with it formally or informally. If his decision is to deal with it informally, he simply records in the Daily Log. Chapter 4 on Start Up explains more about the Daily Log, but in short it's like a project diary. If the Issue needs to be managed formally, the Project Manager records the details on an Issue Report and then keeps track of its progress with an entry in the Issue Register.

So, having come to the register by following the track of an Issue, you can pretty much guess what it contains. Again you can see that PRINCE2 is pretty logical overall, and therefore predictable. You need to record who sent in the Issue; when; briefly what it's about; the current status (such as 'under investigation') and finally when it was closed so you can tell which Issues have been resolved and which ones are still being worked on. You set up the Issue Register here, in Initiation, ready for use in the delivery stages.

You may like to go against the normal sequence of the process model and set up both the Quality Register and Issue Register as soon as you start the Initiation Stage. This way, you can use them during the Initiation Stage as well, not just in the delivery stages.

For more on Issues, Issue Reports and the exact content PRINCE2 suggests for the Issue Register, please see Chapter 16 on the Change theme.

Thinking about communications

Hang on in there, this is the last of the four strategies. But actually it's a particularly powerful and useful one . . . the *Communication Management Strategy*.

The concept of the Communication Management Strategy is simple enough. What communications do you expect to take place inside the project, from inside the project to interests outside it, and from outside the project into it? This covers things like progress reports and information about risks.

The Communication Management Strategy is helpful because it lists the communication needs so that they won't be forgotten. But it also includes things like who should receive information and who'll create it, and when and how the information is to be communicated. You may think that it sounds a bit over the top, but actually it isn't because it can save a lot of effort. That's because it can help cut out unnecessary communications and help you make the remaining ones as efficient and appropriate as possible.

Think about communications very carefully. Many projects produce far too much paper, or electronic documents with huge distribution lists. In the 'old days' the problem was insufficient communication and people didn't know what was going on, or found out far too late. Today, the problem is very much in the other direction. People are drowning in vast quantities of information with over-communication. How many people add you to an email distribution list 'in case you want to know', but actually you don't and would much rather have fewer emails to wade through each day?

One Project Manager told me that she gets about 150 emails a day and it takes her around three hours to go through them. About 85 to 90 per cent of her emails are from people who send them in case she wants to know, but she doesn't. The other 10 to 15 per cent are genuine communications or sent in case she wants to know and she finds that she does. Only when she opens an email and scans the first couple of paragraphs does she know which category it falls into. This Project Manager never takes more than five days' holiday at a time because she refuses to spend three hours a day looking at emails while she's on holiday, and she can't bear the thought of more than 15 hours' backlog when she gets back to the office.

Writing the Communication Management Strategy

When writing the Communication Management Strategy, you think through each of the anticipated communications and how best to do it. You can record a lot of this information as a simple table, it doesn't have to be flowing text. Your list should include:

✔ What information is going to be communicated (information moving around inside the project as well as information going outside it and coming in from the outside – such as progress information)?

✔ Who is to produce the communication?

✔ Who needs to receive it (perhaps one person or a distribution list of many)?

✔ The frequency of the communication (this can be regular, such as a monthly statement, or event-driven, so only triggered when something happens).

✔ The format of the communication (this can be anything from a phone call to a formal presentation).

Thinking wide – not just 'document'

PRINCE2 is often accused of being paper heavy, but this is based on a mis-understanding. Yes, some documents are needed but some things can be communicated in other ways. The Communication Management Strategy lists how particular communications should be made and the options can include things like presentations, podcasts, websites and even carrier pigeons if you want. Think about the best way of communicating each item and don't just think 'document' no matter what your trainer may say if you're reading this on a not-so-good-but-cheaper PRINCE2 training course! That last comment isn't made idly because a lot of over-documentation on PRINCE2 projects results from trainers having taught people that PRINCE2 is about filling forms in.

Remembering that it's good to talk

British Telecom's catchphrase 'It's good to talk' is worth remembering here. You don't have to write reports; they can be verbal. This comes as a big surprise to many organisations using PRINCE2, who wrongly assume that they must write down everything – and then blame the method for creating a paper mountain! But verbal reporting can be fine. For example, if something goes wrong that causes a stage to go beyond limits that the Project Board specified (such as time), the Project Manager must inform the board with an Exception Report to explain the problem and give a recommendation for action. In a small project with few people involved the Communication Management Strategy may record that the Project Manager can give the infor-mation to the Project Board using . . . a phone call.

Although I've emphasised that over-communication is a problem, you must be balanced here. Problems still do occur because insufficient communica-tion takes place and this can sometimes be expensive.

Considering communication needs

Think systematically about who must communicate throughout the project, including:

External needs

✔ Programme roles, such as the Programme Director

✔ Management Boards and/or individual senior organisational managers

✔ Agencies that have responsibilities (such as building inspectors)

✔ Other people that the project may affect; stakeholders such as major customers

✔ Finance managers and/or the finance director

✔ Organisational safety and quality managers

✔ Legal specialists

✔ Other projects (where interdependencies exist) Internal needs

✔ Project Board members (for progress, new copies of plans)

✔ All project staff, including team members

✔ Project Assurance staff and Quality Assurance staff

You keep the Communication Management Strategy up to date throughout the project and check it, especially at each stage end, so that you can include additional communication needs as you find them.

A multinational company was running a project that involved work in London and in New York. Because the project was so important, those involved decided to hold a face-to-face meeting each month instead of having a phone or video conference. To be fair on everyone, the location of these monthly meetings alternated between the London and New York offices. Before a scheduled meeting in New York, the London staff were advised that some of the Americans may be missing from that meeting because it was a public holiday in the States. When the London staff arrived at the New York office, they suddenly realised that no American staff were present at all; everyone in the room had travelled from London. The meeting cost thousands of pounds in air fares and hotel expenses.

The Communication Management Strategy doesn't fit into any of the main theme areas of PRINCE2, so here's the detail of the headings now. As you can see it isn't difficult, but you may still want to simplify it for your project.

The Communication Management Strategy

Introduction: The purpose, objectives and scope.

Communication procedure: How communications will be made and, possibly, recorded.

Tools and techniques: Any comms tools, such as video conferencing.

Records: What records need to be kept and how they'll be stored. Remember that some comms can be verbal, but if they're written, how are they to be retrieved? In a lot of projects this is simple and documents are held in preconfigured directories of the project area on a file server.

Reporting: What reports will be produced, by whom, when and who should receive them.

Timing of communication activities: You could specify this separately using this section, but for a lot of timings you simply record it along with the type of communication. So for each report listed under the previous heading you say how often it is to be produced.

Roles and responsibilities: Again, although there may be some general responsibilities here, it usually makes sense to record responsibilities for individual communications, such as reports, against the information, with the information on that communication.

Stakeholder analysis: Who has an interest in the project and how such stakeholders should be managed. Clearly, this has an impact on communication and information flows.

Information needed for each interested party: This covers inbound and outbound information over the project boundary together with the format of the communication, frequency and content. It includes communications involving stakeholders: listed under the last heading. This part of the comms plan lends itself rather well to being summarised in a table. If you use a table though, you need to change the order of this section to list the communications, then against each one who needs it, rather than listing the interested parties, then what communications they need to be involved with.

Deciding on Controls

In PRINCE2 you can't really say the word 'control' without immediately thinking 'stages'. The project stages are *the* big control, though you need to think about other controls as well as you work through this part of Initiation.

Breaking the project into blocks

The stages of the project represent the main blocks of work. In PRINCE2 these are *management* stages that represent the Project Board and Project Manager's view of the world, not technical stages that are the teams' view of the world and relate to the characteristics of the activities they're working on, such as 'design' and 'build'. You may choose to map management stages onto the technical stages, but you probably won't.

Put simply, a management stage represents a unit of work that the Project Board is happy to authorise in one go. That may be three or four months of work or even more. Clearly, this is a Project Board decision, although the Project Manager may advise and make suggestions on suitable boundary points. A management stage may include more than one technical stage, and the management stages may even cut across technical stages. This may sound a bit messy, but actually it saves considerable time in unnecessary meetings.

The fact that one technical stage finishes and another one starts may hold little interest for a Project Board, except as an indication of progress that you can communicate some other way. To illustrate this point, imagine yourself at a Project Board meeting as a Project Board member. You're very busy, but you've cut an hour out of your busy schedule, plus travelling time to and from headquarters. The meeting starts and the Project Manager tells you that Team C have now finished their work and left the project, and that Team D have arrived and are about to start their work. What's your reaction? More than an hour of your valuable time was used up – for *that*! You may gently remind the Project Manager of the existence of the phone and email. The board has nothing to decide and didn't need to meet. Progress information like that can be communicated more effectively in a simple report; it doesn't require a meeting.

At what points in the project *does* the board need to meet? Those mark the management stages. These stages are extremely important in PRINCE2, not least because they provide Project Board control points that are relatively infrequent in the project. The Project Manager will talk about this with the Project Board before putting the stage boundaries onto the Project Plan. You can find much more information on management stages and the factors involved in deciding on them in Chapter 17, which is on the Progress theme.

Setting up the other controls

Other controls include things like progress reporting and problem handling. On progress reporting, at what frequency should progress reports be made and should they be copied to organisational managers, not just to Project Board members?

All projects involve making important decisions and as part of setting up the controls you need to be clear who can decide what. When does the Project Manager have the power to decide and at what point must he refer something to the Project Board for a decision? The Executive has to be involved in deciding authority for the project, because the Project Manager can't choose his own authority level.

Controls decided in Initiation

Progress reporting: What reporting is needed between the Project Manager and the Project Board? How often should this be, what information is to be included and what form should it take?

Risk reporting: You may have already set this down in the Risk Management Strategy, but if not, it needs thinking about now.

Authority limits: These are the 'tolerances', which are the plus and minus limits of the Project Manager's authority. An example is with normal spending limits. None of the project stages are going to go exactly to plan so at what point does the board want to be told about a spending deviation? If the projection is one penny more or less than the expected budget for the stage, more than £1 million more than projected?

Issue handling: No, not just problems though it includes that, but good stuff too. Normally this is done by people sending an Issue to the Project Manager, but if for some reason this is impractical then you may need a different procedure and you decide that here.

Change authorisation: What authority should the Project Manager have to make changes to deliverables and at what point should he go to the Project Board or Change Authority to get permission?

Financial monitoring and reporting: The PRINCE2 manual doesn't mention this, but that doesn't mean you don't have to think about it. It's an essential part of control and may involve much more than just a tolerance. For example, are there reporting requirements to advise organisational finance staff on what money has been committed and in which financial year, irrespective of whether that spending is in tolerance or not? Financial reporting may be done via the Project Board or it may be direct, but you need to decide that here too.

If a Project Manager has a change budget of £100,000 and someone asks him to authorise a change costing just £5 and taking three minutes, should he do it? Well, perhaps not if that change commits a multinational company to an action that affects all its offices worldwide. Authorities may need to be very specific so, in this case, the Project Board may authorise the Project Manager to approve changes up to a value of £20,000 each, within a total of £100,000, before he needs to go back to the board. However, they may go on to say that this applies only to changes that affect the business area in which the project runs. The Project Manager must refer anything that has an impact outside of that business area to the board, no matter how little it costs.

For this activity to set up controls, the PRINCE2 manual talks about looking at the frequency and format of communication between the management levels. But this isn't true for the communication between the Team Manager level and the Project Manager level. A lot of that communication is actually decided later on and is done Work Package by Work Package – as the manual makes clear elsewhere. And that's for an extremely good reason, which I explain in Chapter 7 on Controlling a Stage – just to keep you in a bit of suspense here.

As you can see, project controls in PRINCE2 are generally straightforward, and to make things even clearer it can be helpful to spend a moment comparing it with work in a department in an organisation – a parallel that's helpful with roles and responsibilities too. In any department, there must be clear authorities so people know when they can make a decision and take action and when they need to refer something to their boss. There must also be clear reporting of progress and problems. Well, so too with the project. The Project Manager must know what authority he has, and everyone needs to know the mechanisms for things such as progress reporting.

Updating the Communication Management Strategy

You may have noticed several references to reporting in this section on controls and if you're especially wide awake, it may have crossed your mind that this overlaps a bit with the Communication Management Strategy covered earlier in the chapter. If so, you were right. The controls and communications are closely linked and a control decision, such as on reporting, may lead to you adjusting the Communication Management Strategy. No problem, just do it and keep the other strategies in line too as things get clearer as you work through Initiation.

Planning Your Project

The general planning covered so far in this chapter is good, but planning the project work itself is where the excitement really starts! The good news is that PRINCE2 expects you to be using the particularly powerful 'product-based' approach to planning, which starts with identifying and understanding what the project must *produce* – the *products*.

Sad to say, those in the PRINCE2 community generally don't really understand this approach and the associated techniques and the PRINCE2 manual doesn't now do all that much to help. As a result, people undervalue 'Product-Led Planning' to the point of frequently leaving it out. That's more than tragic, because Product-Based or Product-Led Planning is a very real help. It helps in planning but then also opens the door to effective progress control and quality management, as well as helping significantly with risk management. The full detail on planning is in Chapter 14, including lots to help with using the product techniques.

PRINCE2 expects this same basic product-led approach no matter what level of detail you happen to be planning at the time. You work at three levels of detail through the project: Project, stage and team level.

In the Initiation Stage, you work at the first two of these levels. You produce a Project Plan for the whole project and then a more detailed Stage Plan for the first delivery stage; the one that immediately follows the Initiation Stage.

When you're doing the project planning, guard against getting sucked down into a mass of detail and effectively start working at a stage planning level of detail. Don't work too hard here! It's a big temptation and a common mistake to get very detailed when you should be focusing on the higher-level view of project planning. The danger is that you miss some big, important and even 'obvious' things at high level because you're down on the floor with a microscope. Besides there is usually little point in planning the later bits of the project in a lot of detail because things will almost certainly have changed by the time you get there. You'll be pleased to know that a neat way exists of enabling you to stick to the right level of detail for each level of plan – yes, it's another advertisement for Chapter 14 and the full works on planning!

You do plan a delivery stage towards the end of Initiation, but only the one that comes after Initiation. You don't need to plan the whole project in fine detail at the beginning. Indeed, one of the strengths of PRINCE2 is that you only plan each stage as the preceding stage is coming to a conclusion. In that way, the Stage Plan reflects the very latest information available and any changes to the project and the business environment. As the project moves along, you keep the higher-level Project Plan up to date from those Stage Plans.

Working on the Business Case

In Start Up, an outline (quick and dirty) Business Case is prepared which helps the Project Board decide whether the project is worth planning in detail. In Initiation, where you're doing that planning, now is the time to add the detail to the Business Case.

Principle 1 – Continued business justification.

Building the full Business Case

The business justification for the project may need considerable work, or it may be very simple (such as with a compliance project, when you do the project because someone told you to), or anything in between. The Executive is the owner of the Business Case and is primarily responsible for making sure that the right level of detail goes in, although frequently the Project Manager is heavily involved with the research work and the Senior User(s) takes responsibility for identifying the benefits.

As with all the management products in a project, PRINCE2 does not give a format but rather just a list of suggested contents. For the Business Case in particular, you need to check what your own organisation requires. Your corporate management may need you to include particular information in the Business Case, and may even want it to be in a particular format to fit in with organisational approval procedures. Adjust the contents of the PRINCE2 Business Case to meet your organisation's requirements and preferred layout. You may already have that information to hand if you've done a project before, or if you recognised the importance of that Business Case format and procedures when you thought through the Project Approach in Start Up.

You may have a great deal of work on your hands with the detail of the Business Case – allow for this in the Stage Plan for the Initiation Stage.

A UK police force was considering a project to build a new headquarters using private investment that would be paid back over a long period. A considerable amount of work effort and time was required to meet government requirements to apply for such funding, so researching and writing the Business Case was made a project in its own right.

Planning the measurement of benefits

Many business benefits won't be clear until after the end of the project, whereas some others may be clear at the end of it. But particularly in business projects where things may be being taken into operational use at several points during the project, not one 'big bang' at the end, benefits may come on stream much earlier than project close down.

To set down exactly when benefits will be visible, when they should be measured, by whom and how, PRINCE2 has a *Benefits Review Plan.* You prepare this now, as you work on the fully detailed Business Case, but you need to keep it up to date during the project if things change, such as you find some additional benefits that weren't spotted at the outset.

You can find the full detail of the Benefits Review Plan, along with the Business Case, in Chapter 11.

Preparing for the First Delivery Stage

In line with the PRINCE2 approach of planning a project stage in detail towards the end of the previous stage, you now need to plan in detail for the first delivery stage – the one that comes after Initiation. This is no different from project planning in that it uses the same techniques, but of course you're working at a lower level of detail.

The end of the Initiation Stage is just like the end of any other project stage, so in PRINCE2 the 'Managing a Stage Boundary' process handles this, including the stage planning for that first delivery stage. Have a look at Chapter 6 for the full detail on the Managing a Stage Boundary process and at Chapter 14 for planning, including stage level planning.

Fitting PRINCE2 to the Project

Part of the final work of Initiation – though you may choose to do it a bit earlier in the stage – is to decide how the PRINCE2 method is to be used on this particular project. You need to think this through carefully and you may want to consider some of the advice in Chapter 3, 'Getting Real Power from PRINCE2'. Put simply, you need to balance your use of PRINCE2 against the characteristics and control needs of the project.

An explanation of how you're fitting PRINCE2 to the project goes into the Project Initiation Documentation and forms the last section of it. Chapter 2 gives you more on adjusting PRINCE2 to fit the project.

Writing the Extra Bits of the PID

Most of the content of the PID is made up of major products like the Communication Management Strategy, but you need to add in a few additional sections before the PID is complete.

Project definition

The definition section does slightly more than define the project, as the subheadings indicate. The section also explains the nature of the project.

Background. Information on why the project idea came into being, such as being part of the five-year organisational development strategy.

Project objectives and desired outcomes. Objectives should be agreed, and a good way to get them agreed is to put them into the PID so that they're clearly stated and then signed off. That's true of desired outcomes too, but that's also helped by the Project Product Description (see Chapter 4 for more on that one), which is included in the Project Plan.

Project scope and exclusions. This says clearly what is in, and out, of the project. You can think of exclusions as 'negative scope' and specifically stating what the project doesn't cover can really help with scope clarity. The exclusions help avoid misunderstanding with later disappointment when people don't get something they had thought was included in the project.

Constraints and assumptions. This sets down any limitations on the project, such as that it must deliver by the end of the financial year. Stating assumptions is also good because if things change, everyone recognises that an adjustment to the project is justified. An example is an assumption that another project on which this one depends will finish on time or no more than four weeks late. If that other project ends up six weeks late, everyone understands that a time impact is now on this project and the plans need to be amended accordingly.

The user and any other known interested parties. This is to show who will be impacted by the project and who may therefore need to be consulted. The main user interests will be represented by a role on the Project Board.

Project Approach

The Project Approach sets down things that affect how the project is run and the nature of the final deliverable. Please see Chapter 4 for more detail as this information is identified during Start Up.

Project team management structure and roles

You can find out more about this in Chapter 12 on roles and responsibilities. But basically this section of the PID is an organisation chart for the project that you've put together, or at least begun, in Start Up.

Interfaces

This final part lists interfaces such as with other projects, other organisations or things such as operational or business procedures.

Putting the PID Together

When you put the extra parts listed in the last section together with the main products covered earlier in the chapter you have yourself a PID.

Beware of big PIDs. In some organisations people work hard to make the pile of paper as high as possible, as if they'll win a prize for the biggest PID. Personally, I'm far more impressed with concise PIDs and perhaps someone really should give prizes for those. You need to work hard to keep the PID as simple and as small as possible while providing all the information that you need for the project.

To get a clear picture of a PID, think of it as being rather like a folder that contains a number of documents, many of which are other PRINCE2 management products – things like the Risk Management Strategy, the Business Case and the Project Plans.

When you take a closer look at the content of the PID, you may think that some of it looks rather like the Project Brief. If so, you're right. You can see considerable overlap, but remember that these same things are now in much greater detail. For example, the Business Case was an important element of the Project Brief. But in Start Up that Business Case is sketchy and incomplete – an *Outline* Business Case. By the time you get to the PID, you've done a full Business Case possibly including investment appraisal. So yes, the Business Case appears again in the PID, but now complete and in much greater detail.

Looking at How You Use the PID

You can use the PID in three ways in PRINCE2. The first is to define the project in Initiation and to support the decision of the Project Board at the end of the Initiation stage regarding whether to authorise the whole project or to stop after the planning because it doesn't look worth doing after all. A bit more on this first use of the PID in a moment.

A second way you can use the PID is as an ongoing reference for staff joining the project. This can help particularly in larger projects when lots of staff are coming and going as different parts of the work are done. Giving the PID to new staff to read can save a lot of explanation of individual areas of project control. Potentially, you can give the PID to any of the project staff, but Team Managers find it particularly helpful.

Finally, a very important third use of the PID is to check on the achievement of objectives. The Project Manager uses this information when creating the End Project Report, which in turn informs the Project Board (and possibly a programme or management board) if the project has been successful. For more on this use of the PID during project closure, turn to Chapter 9.

Asking the Project Board to commit to the whole project

The focus of a normal stage boundary is to check whether everything is okay and decide whether or not to continue to the next stage. But the decision at the end of Initiation is rather more important. Here, the board members are being asked if they want to commit to the whole project and then specifically to authorise the start of work on the first delivery stage. Up to now, the

Project Board has only committed to planning in more detail – the decision they make at the end of Start Up. The end of the Initiation stage and the production of the PID mark the point where they make the major go/no-go decision for the project. The board might stop the project prematurely if something goes badly wrong or if new conditions mean that it's no longer needed, but their intention now is to run it through to the end.

Checking out the Products of Initiating a Project

You may find this list helpful to make sure that you have everything you need when initiating your project. For the PID see the panel earlier in this chapter for the exact headings. Don't forget that you can add to the contents, or simplify the products, to fit the particular needs of your project.

✔ **The Project Initiation Documentation (PID).** A document set, and although it is often presented as a single document for approval, it contains a number of different project level control documents, including the Project Plan.

✔ **Benefits Review Plan.** Details of when benefits will be seen – this may be at one or more points during the project as well as after it – and how they're to be measured.

✔ **Business Case.** The justification for the project and information on the overall cost, timescale and the business benefits that will be gained.

✔ **Communication Management Strategy.** What communications are expected in the project, who is involved and the way the communication will be made, for example, phone call.

✔ **Configuration Item Records.** Records containing version control information for management products such as the Business Case.

✔ **Configuration Management Plan.** How version control will be done in the project, what procedures will be operated and how things will be protected from unauthorised access.

✔ **Issue Register.** Ready for use to record the existence, progress and outcome of Issues that are being handled formally in the project.

✔ **Project Plan.** A plan of the whole project covering the delivery stages. It includes product plans as well as activity, resource and finance plans. In turn the product section of this plan includes the Project Product Description.

✔ **Quality Management Strategy.** How quality will be done and controlled on this project.

✔ **Quality Register.** Set up ready to list quality activities and sign off when they're done.

✔ **Risk Management Strategy.** How risks will be controlled in the project and any procedures for doing that.

✔ **Risk Register.** Ready to record the existence of each risk, who is responsible for taking action on it and what action is to be taken.

✔ **(Stage Plan).** Although not produced by the Initiating a Project process, don't forget this must be presented to the Project Board at the same time as the PID.

Pens are powerful things and most managers in most organisations world-wide really don't like using them when giving authority – so it's not just a problem in your organisation! Important documents like the PID and Stage Plans need to be physically signed. Such sign-off encourages clear commitment from the board, reinforces the importance of their responsibility and gives the Project Manager clear authority.

If getting people to sign things in your organisation is difficult, you can build up the expectation beforehand. Inform the Project Board up front that you'll be asking them to sign particular documents to approve them. Then, when a draft goes out, have a signature panel on the very first page saying 'Executive, signature, date; Senior User, signature, date' and so on. The board members then see that soon you'll ask them to sign. When you hand round the final version, pass each member a pen! This applies to the Project Brief, the Project Initiation Documentation and each Stage Plan.

Although the plan for the first delivery stage is produced by the process 'Managing a Stage Boundary', you do this towards the end of the Initiation Stage in parallel with the final work covered by the Initiating a Project process. It's normally presented to the Project Board at the same time as the PID.

Chapter 6

Preparing for a Stage in the Project

In This Chapter

▶ Looking at stages – the big control in PRINCE2

▶ Knowing how and when you trigger an End Stage

▶ Forcing an extra stage boundary if you need a major re-plan

▶ Checking the ongoing viability of the project

▶ Providing vital information for the Project Board

*Y*ou can't say the word 'control' in PRINCE2 without immediately thinking 'stages'. Stages are the highest level of control and are powerful because at the end of each one, the Project Board must take stock before deciding whether or not to specifically authorise the next part of the project – the next management stage. This chapter covers the work of the Project Manager towards the end of a stage, getting ready for that Project Board decision by providing up-to-date information as decision support and also by creating the plan for the next stage.

As with other key decision documents in PRINCE2, the information that the Project Manager provides at the end of a stage shouldn't come as a huge shock to board members, because they'll have been consulted informally while the information was prepared. If you're using the PRINCE2 manual alongside this book then look out because the manual gives the strong impression overall that the Project Manager goes away and does this work without any reference to the board. The diagram, Figure 6-1, shows you what I mean because there's no reference to Project Board 'ad hoc direction'. But that's wrong and board members must make time available to talk to the Project Manager to help get things ready for the next stage. You can see just how much that's needed as you follow the activities within the 'Managing a Stage Boundary' process covered in this chapter.

This work of the Project Manager towards the end of a stage is logical and so very predictable. As with just about all the rest of PRINCE2, this work is also very straightforward. Some projects may need quite a bit of work, but the overall concept isn't difficult.

Understanding the Process of 'Managing a Stage Boundary'

Five activities cover the stage boundary work in PRINCE2. These activities are the responsibility of the Project Manager who in turn consults with other people, including Team Managers and Project Board members, for the stage ahead.

Don't get too bothered about the activities at first. Have a quick look at the diagram to get an overall idea and then read the chapter. Then, when you come back and look at the diagram again, it will all fall into place easily.

The stage boundary work has two alternative start points. The first is the normal planned close of a stage, and the other is corrective action if something's gone significantly off track and calls for a major re-plan. To be clear on exactly what 'significantly' means, please see 'Triggering an End Stage' later in this chapter and Chapter 17 on progress and controls.

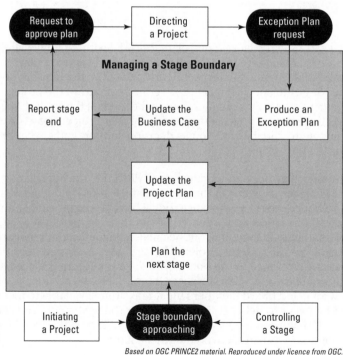

Figure 6-1:
The activities of Managing a Stage Boundary.

Based on OGC PRINCE2 material. Reproduced under licence from OGC.

Providing Key Information at End Stage

To show that this End Stage work is very logical, imagine you're a Project Board member attending a meeting at the end of a stage and the Project Manager asks you to authorise the next stage. What do you want to know before picking up your pen to sign and give your authority? You almost certainly want to know:

✔ **How did the last stage go?**

- Did it run smoothly to plan or keep going off track – ahead, behind, ahead again?

- What happened with changes to the management of the stage? Were the adjustments due to genuinely unpredictable things and changes in the business area, or were they mostly corrective, for things missed off the plan or wrongly estimated?

- How did the stage finish in relation to tolerances (a range with a target value and then a plus or a minus maximum) on time and cost, but also against any other elements such as the scope?

- Were any significant problems encountered in the last stage that will affect the rest of the project?

- Is the project in control or can you see signs of delivery starting to slip and the spend edging upwards? If the stage did end within tolerance, was it by the skin of its teeth?

- Were there any problems with quality or was everything delivered to the right standard?

✔ **Is the Business Case still okay?**

- Is the project still needed? Sometimes business circumstances change quite dramatically and you might need to stop the project rather than authorise the next stage.

- Is the project still on track to deliver the expected benefits, or does new information from the last stage indicate that the benefits may be lower, or higher, than anticipated?

- What are the latest estimates of cost and time and how do those now relate to the expected level of benefits?

✔ **What about risk?**

- Have any significant new risks come to light that affect the balance of the project justification?

- Has the status changed on existing risks? Sometimes, of course, a project can go to a higher plane of risk not because of one big new risk, but a small increase across many risks – a cumulative effect.

- Is the risk under control, or are things starting to get out of control?

✔ **What about the plan for the next stage?**

- Is the next Stage Plan realistic and achievable? Don't even take the top off your pen with a thought of authorising the next stage unless you're convinced that the plan is workable. If you sign off a plan that won't work, then the failure that follows is your fault.

- Are the resources in place to do the work at the times set down on the plan, including any user resource from the business area?

In a nutshell this is a look-back – how did the last stage go?; a look at where the project is now – are the Business Case and risks okay?; and a look forward – is the next Stage Plan achievable?

If you're a board member you can get help with checking that the Stage Plan and Project Plan are achievable and workable. You can appoint Project Assurance (the audit function of the project) to help check out exactly this sort of thing. Have a look at Chapter 12 for more on Project Assurance.

What about when the board can't meet – say they're in different parts of the world? You can use another mechanism, such as a video link, telephone conference, or even e-mail. These ways are decreasingly effective, though – e-mail is less effective than a phone conference, which in turn is less effective than a video link. Nothing is quite as good as a face-to-face meeting, so do hold one unless this is impossible.

Triggering an End Stage

During the project two things trigger the End Stage work:

✔ **The planned end of a stage (including the Initiation Stage but excluding the final stage):** The Project Manager checks the stage status and sees that the end of the stage is approaching. Therefore, now's the time to start planning the next stage and preparing for the End Stage Assessment – the meeting of the Project Board.

✔ **Exception:** If the projections for the stage show that it may exceed the tolerances (such as time and cost) for the stage, the Project Manager refers this to the Project Board. If the Project Board decides to run the stage differently to get it back on track – perhaps using different products, different activities and different resources – then you can't use the existing Stage Plan to control the stage. Instead, you need to do a major re-think and produce a replacement plan. This *Exception Plan* is a replacement Stage Plan that covers the period from the point of the problem until the end of the stage. This forces a new stage boundary and so the work now comes under that category.

End Stage Assessment (ESA). The Project Board meets at the end of a stage to conduct an ESA, in which they check the project, especially the stage just finishing, and either authorise the next stage or stop the project. Instead of ESA, people commonly use the phrase 'stage gate', which is much more descriptive and a whole lot better.

 Exception Plan. You replace part of an existing plan with an Exception Plan because something changes that makes the existing plan unusable. This swap usually takes place at stage level, but it can have a knock-on effect on other plan levels as well; often the Project Plan.

Stage planning in Start Up and Initiation

In PRINCE2 you plan each stage just before that stage is due to start so, with one exception, that's towards the end of the previous project stage. The exception is with the plan for the first stage of the project, the Initiation Stage, where no stage comes before it. But the pattern of 'just before' is still the same because you prepare the Initiation Stage Plan towards the end of Start Up. However that planning work is covered in the 'Starting Up a Project' process as it isn't an End Stage and you don't need the other End Stage stuff (such as an End Stage Report) covered in this chapter.

The plan for the first delivery stage – the one that comes after the Initiation Stage – is done towards the end of the Initiation Stage. So, while the Initiation Stage is primarily to plan the whole project at a project level of detail, it also includes the lower-level Stage Plan for the stage that comes straight after it.

More about exceptions and stages

Having a stage boundary when the stage isn't complete may seem odd, but this is part of exception handling and is logical when you think it through. For example, say a stage is one-third through and a significant problem arises that changes things substantially so that the rest of the stage now needs to be run differently. The Exception Plan covers the point between now, one-third through, and the end of the stage. But what about the one-third that's already completed? Obviously, you don't need to plan what's already done, so instead that third is closed down as if it were a stage end. The remaining work is re-planned with an Exception Plan and the previous work in the stage is reported on as if it were an End Stage, even with an End Stage Report.

The End Stage behaves exactly as normal and the board authorises work to continue the stage as if it were a brand new stage.

Exception Assessment. In an Exception Assessment the Project Board meets to approve an Exception Plan and authorises work to commence on the basis of the plan (unless they close the project instead). This assessment is like an End Stage Assessment; the difference is that you didn't plan the stage boundary originally; it's reactive because of the exception situation.

Principle 4 – Manage by stages.

Planning the Next Stage

You may have a lot of work to do to create a Stage Plan for the next stage, but as is usually the case in PRINCE2, the concept is straightforward enough. It's a plan for just one management stage that's very like the Project Plan in terms of content and techniques. It's just that it covers a single management stage rather than the whole project and is in much more detail than the Project Plan.

Using product planning in more detail

When preparing a Stage Plan, PRINCE2 expects you to use the *product-based* approach to planning. Products are effectively what the teams deliver, or produce, in each stage – the *deliverables*. Products are things like brick walls, computer programs and new logo designs. At project planning time you identify 15 to 30 products for the whole project. In each Stage Plan you go into more detail on the products that'll be built in that particular stage – maybe 3 out of the 30 – and break them down to a lower level until you have 15 to 30 again. So at project level you may have identified the product 'new business procedures' but now, for the stage in which those procedures will be designed, you show the six individual new procedures that make that up. For lots more help on the product planning and the activity and resource planning that are also included in the Stage Plan, please see Chapter 14 that also explains the powerful product planning techniques in detail.

You also create documents needed for version control of the new lower level products – *Configuration Item Records* – but please see Chapter 16 for full detail on version control.

Preparing the Product Checklist

You develop one additional product planning element when you're stage planning – the Product Checklist. When you've identified the 15 to 30 lower-level products that will be developed in the stage, write them out as a list.

After you do the activity planning and risk analysis you can then determine the delivery date for each product and add that to the Product Checklist.

This checklist now forms an extremely simple but powerful progress monitoring tool for running the stage. As each product is completed (which means it's been quality checked and signed off), the delivery date is noted on the Product Checklist and the milestone is completed. Doing this shows exactly where the stage is with no debate or human judgement: Is the product delivered – yes or no? There are 15 to 30 products in the stage, and so 15 to 30 milestones where you can determine progress very exactly – and all for free with product-led planning. Although the PRINCE2 manual says you shouldn't use every product as a milestone, you lose the huge power of the Product Checklist if you follow that advice. Please see Chapter 17 on progress and controls for more on progress monitoring.

You can extend the Product Checklist to include other dates, such as the date you plan to send the product for testing and the date it actually goes. That can be really useful to get early warning of likely delay in product delivery, but the ultimate power lies with delivery dates themselves.

Getting detailed with quality

You prepare the Quality Management Strategy in the Initiation Stage as part of the Project Initiation Document (PID), but the strategy is exactly that, a strategy. As you come to stage planning you need hard detail and in PRINCE2 that's locked in with the product planning. That lock-in makes quality very clear and specific as Chapter 13 on Quality explains.

The quality criteria for individual stage-level products are decided and recorded on the Product Descriptions that define those products. Together with the criteria, the way that each product will be tested is set down (Quality Method) and then also the responsibility – who does those tests (Quality Check Skills and then the Quality Responsibilities). If any new quality requirements are thrown up during this work you may need to update the Quality Management Strategy. No problem, and in fact you keep all four of the strategies up to date throughout the project.

You then take this testing information forward into the activity planning. Enter the quality related activities onto your Precedence Network and Gantt chart, and for the Gantt you enter the resource information of who does the test. So you deal with specific quality at stage level by actually building it into the product and activity plans.

A vital action now is for you to update the Quality Register with a list of all the tests that must be performed during the stage, together with a planned test date. To do this you extract two bits of information from the Stage Plans.

You can take the details of the tests themselves from the 'Quality Method' sections of all the Product Descriptions or from the activity plans, and the planned test dates and responsibilities from the schedule – usually a Gantt chart.

The Quality Register is set up in Initiation and is simply a list of quality activities, including tests, that you carry out in a stage. As the stage progresses and each test is done, it gets signed off in the Quality Register. This forms a very simple but highly effective audit trail. You can see at a glance whether a test has been done or not, and because several people check the register, you won't forget a test. Chapter 13 explains more.

Updating the Project Management Team

As part of stage planning the PRINCE2 manual says that you should check for changes to the Project Management Team Structure. You may prefer to do this when you make checks across all project-level documentation to keep it up to date (see 'Updating Project Documents and Plans', later in this chapter) – that's fine, as long as you do check at some point.

Movement often occurs in and out of teams around a stage boundary, although it can happen during the stages too. Look out for changes with the other roles as well. For example, perhaps a change of Senior Supplier is not only necessary but was planned for this point. Perhaps one external supplier company put in teams for the first six months of a year-long project to do structural work, and a second external supplier company is now taking over to do the final six months' work in fitting out. This is the one valid exception to the general line that the Project Board needs to be stable.

Building an Exception Plan

You may be doing stage boundary work not because it's a planned stage end, but in reaction to an exception – where the stage goes significantly off track (see 'More about exceptions and stages', earlier in this chapter). It may have been decided to re-plan the rest of the stage and do it differently to recover from the problem.

One other reason to have an Exception Plan is to build in a major change that's a really good idea and worth all the re-planning effort. Chapter 16 explains this as part of change control.

The Exception Plan is, effectively, a Stage Plan, but for just the remainder of the stage. It has a few characteristics that are worth bearing in mind:

✔ The Exception Plan only covers from the point of the problem until the end of the stage, so don't waste time re-planning what's already done.

✔ An End Stage Report covers the work done up to now in the stage, just as with a planned End Stage.

✔ The text of the Exception Plan is usually a bit more problem-focused than a Stage Plan, because the Exception Plan needs to explain how the plan addresses the exception.

✔ Although the Exception Plan does change the stage, a lot of the work is likely to be the same, so you can bring forward the relevant information from the Stage Plan that you replace – you don't start from scratch.

Updating Project Documents and Plans

You keep at least some parts of the PID up to date throughout the project. With the information from the Stage Plan you just finished, and armed with the new information from the Stage Plan you just produced for the stage ahead, now you make sure that the project information set is up to date and consistent.

Updating the Project Plan

Updating the Project Plan may sound an odd thing to do if you use a computer scheduling tool, because as you update the stage level of detail on a Gantt chart, for example, you keep the project level in line with that automatically; they form a single computer file. But don't forget that you may need to adjust other parts of the plan besides activity networks and Gantt charts. For example, you may need to adjust the project-level product plans.

Sometimes updates to the Project Plan are considerable because you reach a point in the project where for the first time you can see to the end clearly. The PID may describe this entirely predictable update.

In a project to perform ten-year maintenance on an industrial installation, the first part of the project was to close down the plant and do a thorough survey to see what machinery needed to be replaced – including components not normally visible because of heat shielding – what could be maintained, and what didn't need any work. It wasn't until that survey had been done that the exact nature of the rest of the project could be determined with complete accuracy. The organisation knew the normal amount of work for a ten-year service on this type of installation from previous experience, and the initial Project Plan, produced at the start of the project, was based on that. But significant change to the plan in either direction was possible when the results of the survey were available.

Updating the Project Approach

In the light of new information coming from the last stage and the production of the new Stage Plan, you may need to adjust the Project Approach. For example, you may need more information to develop the new business procedure than you first realised, and some of that additional information may be commercially sensitive. You may therefore need to comply with additional security requirements, not only for the operation of the new business procedure itself, but also for the project because project teams will now be working with that sensitive information.

Other changes can affect things such as technology, where newly available equipment from a new manufacturer is so advantageous that it removes a previous constraint to only use equipment from the normal manufacturer in order to minimise maintenance costs.

Reviewing Risk

Part of the work in the 'Update a Project Plan' activity is a systematic review of every risk in the Risk Register, together with thinking about whether any new risks are now apparent. The PRINCE2 manual always was a little light on this review but it's now positively featherweight with only a short bullet point reference. But be alert because you may face significant work here – especially, of course, if yours is a high-risk project. For example, if you decide that a risk has changed significantly and that you also need to change the risk management actions, this may involve changes to the Stage Plan just produced. It may also need quite a lot of discussion with a range of people in the project (depending on the nature of the risks) to perform the risk analysis and with the Project Board.

In fact one of your key consultations regarding risk is with the Project Board members and especially the Executive. The board members own the project and at Initiation they decided what level of risk they were willing to accept and what management actions were appropriate. They also decided how much they were willing to pay to control the risks. Therefore, any change to the level of risk, or any planned action to control new risks, needs similar consultation.

Things to review for risk

You need to think about a few things when reviewing the risks. Are there any new risks? If so, you need to analyse them, create a Risk Register entry if they're to be formally managed, and make any adjustments to the plan, such as increased contingency time or staff resource for risk management actions.

Then, for each risk already appearing in the Risk Register, answer these questions:

- ✔ Is the risk still current or can it be given the status 'dead'? Some risks are only a threat for a particular part of the project and may no longer exist, or new information may come to light to show that the particular risk can't affect the project after all.

- ✔ Did you find any new information during the stage or at End Stage that changes the status of the risk, perhaps to make it more probable? For example, a risk that the project may not be able to recruit enough specialist consultants at a later point in the project may increase if that specialism is now even more in demand and the specialists are more scarce than ever.

- ✔ Has the probability of the risk increased, decreased or stayed the same?

- ✔ Has the impact of the risk increased, decreased or stayed the same?

- ✔ Does any change in the business environment mean that although the impact of the risk is the same in terms of, say, money, its effect is actually more of a problem? Perhaps, for example, company profits at the end of the financial year were significantly lower than expected and this in turn has put pressure on project budgets. Although the impact of a risk of £50,000 may not have been that severe in the last financial year, the same amount may be very much more of a problem in the new financial year.

- ✔ Are the risk responses still appropriate?

The Executive is especially important, as the Executive is the final 'owner' of the project and, representing the business viewpoint, is primarily responsible for ensuring that the project is value for money. Planning actions that cost any significant amount without checking them with the Executive isn't acceptable. The Executive is also more aware of what's happening in other parts of the organisation and so is well placed to help evaluate how changes in the business impact risks. This involvement is part of the ad-hoc, informal direction from the board – even though the diagram from the manual in Figure 6-1 doesn't show this happening. You can read more about the need for board members to give a steer in this way in Chapter 12. It's a bit like your boss being available to you if you need to talk something through.

You also need to consult others in the project, not just the board members. Team specialists and suppliers may identify changes in the environment that can have an impact on risk. Although you may say that the specialists and suppliers should have reported these changes during a stage and not waited until End Stage (and you may be right), the fact remains that sometimes people don't realise something until you specifically ask them. How many times have you started a sentence, 'Well, now you come to mention it . . .'?

This review of risk is extremely important on the stage boundary, as it gives the members of the Project Board the exact and latest position on risk for their decision on whether or not to authorise the next stage. The review of risk interacts with the review of the Business Case. If the risk increases but the benefit projections fall significantly, the board may well decide to stop the project. This level of risk exposure may not be worth facing for this reduced business benefit. However, if the risk increases slightly but the benefit projections increase by a large amount, the board may decide that continuing, and even spending more on risk management action to help secure those benefits, is worthwhile.

If you detect a change in risk that affects the way that risk as a whole should be managed in the project, then you may need to update the Risk Management Strategy, but once again this needs some discussion with the Project Board and especially the Executive. Please see Chapter 15 for more information on the Risk Management Strategy, on risk analysis and management, and when you carry these out, including at End Stage.

Checking the Business Case

In a PRINCE2 project, the Business Case must be reviewed at least at the end of each stage. Project Board members then have the very latest information to hand on which they can base their decision on whether to carry on with the next stage or not. The Business Case may have been modified during the stage in the light of problems or new information, for example.

At the end of the stage you conduct a more thorough and systematic review of the Business Case, including checking the projection and timing of benefits, the cost of the project, the time you need for the project, and the risks. You take the cost and time from the Project Plan, which has now been updated using information from stage planning. If there's any change to how and when benefits will be reviewed you'll also need to update the Benefits Review Plan.

Principle 1. Continued business justification.

While on the subject of the Business Case and benefits, it's possible that benefits start to be seen during the project itself and not just at the end or after it. This is especially the case if project deliverables are being taken into operational use throughout the project and not just in one 'big bang' at the end of it. The Benefits Review Plan shows when benefits should be measured, and if one of those points is at the present End Stage then the measures should be taken and you must make sure that they're reported now. These measures, where done, will be included in the End Stage Report.

Things to review for the Business Case

Here are a few things you need to think about when updating the Business Case.

✔ Has the justification changed? If the justification for the project was compliance, for example, does the requirement still stand? Sometimes those who insisted that a project take place change their minds – not least government bodies when faced with the impracticalities of their instructions.

✔ Check the benefits projections. Does any information indicate that the level of benefit is likely to be different from what you stated in the last version of the Business Case? Also check the expected timing of the benefits coming on stream. The project may be on track to deliver savings of £500,000 a month, but whereas the plan was for this to commence three months after the end of the project, you now expect the savings to

start two months after the project's end, a gain of £500,000.

✔ Include the latest cost and time projections from the new Stage Plan and updated Project Plan.

✔ Update the risk section with any shift in status of existing risks or identification of new ones.

✔ Check the overall balance of the Business Case and if necessary update the Executive Summary. If anything else has changed that affects the balance, the Project Manager should bring it to the attention of the Project Board in the End Stage Report but she should discuss it immediately with the Executive, and the Senior User(s) if it affects benefits.

Preparing an End Stage Report

The End Stage Report is the Project Manager's report to the Project Board on the stage just finishing. You think through the form and content of the End Stage Report in the Initiation Stage and record the details of it in the Communication Management Strategy. Normally small is beautiful, and informal (such as verbal reporting to the Project Board) can be pretty attractive for some projects too.

The contents of the report are predictable: basically, how did the stage go, what did it cost, how long did it take in comparison to the plan, and were the quality requirements met? In full, the report is very extensive but as always, do cut it down wherever possible for your organisation and project.

One problem with the PRINCE2 End Stage Report is that it has a lot of headings and many Project Managers feel obliged to write a fair amount under each heading to show that they've completed the document thoroughly and so did their job well. This backfired quite nicely in one organisation where a Project Manager caused project delay because he couldn't think what to write, but then the project proceeded to the next stage without the End Stage Report being presented but promised later. In that way the PRINCE2 documentation was completely divorced from the project management and this stripped the method of its power – the project proceeded without the method and PRINCE2 was reduced to just some documentation system lagging some weeks behind where the project really was.

End Stage Report

Arguably, rather too many headings are here for a 'normal' End Stage Report. Be careful that you don't swamp your project with excessive documentation. Having said that, one problem lies with the choice of wording for the headings and the content is actually simpler than it looks at first sight. But some sections, not least the 'Review of Products', are overkill for a lot of projects and a Project Board won't thank you for a huge report re-stating stuff they already know.

Project Manager's report: How the stage went from the Project Manager's viewpoint.

Review of the Business Case: Particularly draws attention to any change, such as projection of total benefits. This section is also for reporting any benefits already seen and a comment on the total risk exposure. Please see Chapter 11 for full detail on the Business Case.

Review of project objectives: How the project currently stands including against the six control areas (cost, time, quality, scope, risk and benefits) and if strategies and controls are proving effective.

Review of stage objectives: How the stage just finishing met its objectives, again on things such as cost and time.

Review of team performance: Any performance metrics and a 'mention in despatches' for team members who've performed particularly well – but don't get patronising!

Review of products – comprising:

✔ **Quality records:** Which quality activities were planned and completed.

✔ **Approval records:** Which products were completed and approved.

✔ **Off-specifications:** Things that weren't done or not to standard.

✔ **Phased handover (if applicable):** Confirmation that operational areas are ready to receive products delivered before the end of the project

✔ **Summary of follow-on action recommendations (if applicable):** Any actions already noted that need to be done by the organisation after the project.

Lessons Report: Any lessons that need to be passed back into the organisation at this stage. Please see the section after this panel 'Reporting any lessons'.

Issues and risks: A summary of the position on risk and any current Issues.

Forecast: The Project Manager's forecast for the project and the next stage for the six control areas, although things like time and cost are largely self-evident from the plans submitted along with the End Stage Report. But there may be value in having it concisely in one place.

Reporting any lessons

You keep the Lessons Log up to date throughout the project, which means during the stages (for more on this log, please see Chapter 4). But having said that, the point at which you write the End Stage Report is a great time for reflection on the stage as a whole: Think about whether any more can be learned from the experience that would be of value to others in future projects – both good things that worked well, and bad things to try to avoid if similar circumstances arise.

A mechanism is available for reporting lessons back to the organisation at the end of the project, but if something comes up that the organisation would benefit from knowing now, it can be reported now. The Project Manager can prepare a Lessons Report, which is then included in the End Stage Report and which the Project Board can then pass back into the organisation. Chapter 9 has more on the Lessons Report, as it is produced anyway at project closure.

Asking for Sign-Off and Authority to Proceed with the Next Stage

The Stage or Exception Plan goes with the End Stage Report (if this is a written report), the updated Business Case, and the updated Risk Register to the Project Board, who then hold an End Stage Assessment (ESA) or, in the case of an Exception Plan, an Exception Assessment. The board members must approve the stage that just finished and then give their authority to proceed with the next stage – or else stop the project. That authority on a stage boundary helps avoid the problem of projects that just carry on blindly even if things are going badly wrong.

You can make it very simple for the board to give authority to proceed at stage boundaries. Just put a signature panel on the front of the Stage Plan. If the board members sign, they authorise work to start on the basis of that plan.

Checking out the major stage boundary products

Stage boundaries involve a lot of PRINCE2 management products. Here's a reference to help you make sure you have everything you need and to think through how much you need. Remember, as always, to keep things as simple as you can. Everything you produce in writing has to be checked and then read. That all takes time and drives up project costs, so don't do more than is justified for the project just because it's in the manual.

(continued)

(continued)

↙ **Benefits Review Plan:** Notes any changes to how and when benefits will be measured.

↙ **Business Case:** You undertake a thorough review and update the benefit projections.

↙ **Configuration Management Strategy:** You may need to update the Configuration Management Strategy if you find, for example, that newly appointed suppliers have different configuration management procedures that you need to map to the project's procedures.

↙ **Configuration item Record:** A document created for each product carrying version control information such as the latest version number.

↙ **End Stage Report:** This is the report of the stage you just finished, including 'actuals'.

↙ **Exception Plan:** Here, you plan for the remainder of this stage if you're using the stage boundary because you can't handle an exception within the limits of the existing Stage Plan.

↙ **Follow-on Action Recommendations:** Itemises things that you can already see will need to be done by the organisation after the end of the project. You normally save these recommendations until the end of the project, but some may need to be passed on earlier than that.

↙ **Issue Register:** Not mentioned specifically in the chapter, but this Register is maintained and consulted all the time and, of course, includes End Stage.

↙ **Lessons Log:** Although this Log is maintained throughout the last stage, producing the End Stage Report often reveals more things that need to go into the Lessons Learned Log.

↙ **Lessons Report:** A report of any lessons that should be passed back into the organisation now, rather than waiting until the end of the project. It's included in the End Stage Report.

↙ **Project Approach:** The more detailed stage planning for the next part of the work may lead to changes in the approach.

↙ **Project Management Team Structure:** You can update this if any roles are changed.

↙ **Project Plan:** You can update the Project Plan if any changes happened to products, for example, or for major activities.

↙ **Quality Management Strategy:** Includes the more detailed planning of the next part of the work – the next stage – that may affect the strategy for quality in the whole project.

↙ **Quality Register:** You add to the Register details of tests and checks to be carried out in the next stage so that they can be checked off when they're done.

↙ **Risk Register:** You update the Risk Register with a systematic review of every risk to bring it up to date with the latest information. You also include any new risks.

↙ **Stage Plan:** You develop this plan for the next stage at a planned stage end.

Chapter 7

Controlling a Stage

· ·

In This Chapter

▶ Understanding the day-to-day work of the Project Manager

▶ Giving out assignments to Team Managers and keeping an eye on the work

▶ Checking and reporting on progress

▶ Dealing with problems and referring some things to the Project Board

· ·

*T*his chapter deals with the day-to-day work of the Project Manager during a delivery stage. That includes picking up on any problems and reporting progress. The chapter doesn't cover the activity of the Project Manager towards the end of the stage in getting ready for the Project Board meeting to approve the next one. Chapter 6 describes all that work, which is mostly done as the stage boundary approaches.

Understanding the Process Controlling a Stage

Like the other six processes in PRINCE2, Controlling a Stage has a lower-level diagram that shows the activities taking place inside it and the order in which they're normally done. It's the busiest of the processes – if you take the number of activities as a sign of busyness. But happily the process is not only straightforward but actually one of the easiest to follow. If you just think about what a Project Manager is doing in the main part of a delivery stage, you could build the model yourself:

✔ Giving out work assignments to Team Managers, checking the progress of that work and then getting delivery of products when they are finished – built and tested

✔ Dealing with any inbound risks and issues (– including problems – and taking any necessary action to deal with them

✔ Keeping track of the progress of the whole stage, and reporting that progress to the Project Board at the frequency they asked

✔ Taking any action needed to keep the stage on track, or passing the matter up the line to the Project Board if things have gone beyond the limits the board set down at the start of the stage

Having set down those four main areas of work, have a look at Figure 7-1 that contains a diagram of controlling activities.

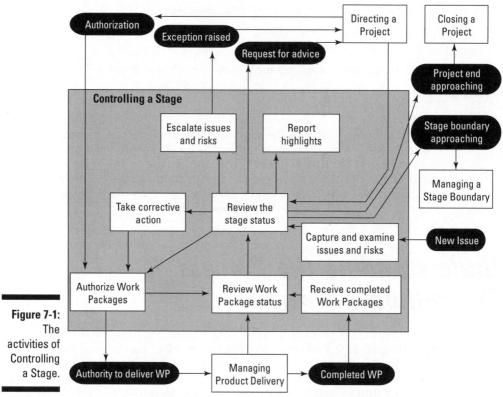

Figure 7-1: The activities of Controlling a Stage.

Based on OGC PRINCE2 material. Reproduced under licence from OGC.

The eight activities in the diagram map relate to the four work areas. The bottom three activities are to do with controlling work assignments, or *Work Packages*. The upper one on the right-hand side is to do with handling Issues, which are things like reported problems, and any newly identified risks. The two on the far left deal with correcting problems in the running of the stage. This is done by the Project Manager taking 'corrective action' within his own authority or by 'escalating' the matter to the Project Board if it's beyond his authority. The two activities in the middle deal with progress checking and reporting.

The rest of this chapter looks in detail at the activities in the four main groups just described.

Controlling the Flow of Work to Teams

The Project Manager, as the role title suggests, manages. This means that Team Managers and their teams don't just start doing stuff when they feel like it. Instead, the Project Manager authorises work a bit at a time using *Work Packages*.

Work Package. An instruction pack given to a Team Manager by the Project Manager that asks him to build one or more products that it makes sense to build together. Each Team Manager normally works through a series of Work Packages in each stage in which his team is involved, but of course he may only be involved in a single one.

Figure 7-2 shows you how Work Packages fit in with the stage. As to the exact content of a Work Package, you can find all the detail in Chapter 8, which covers the work of the Team Manager in receiving the Work Package and then building the products it describes.

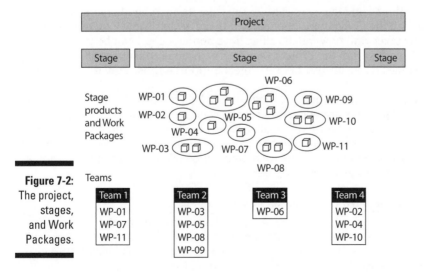

Figure 7-2: The project, stages, and Work Packages.

Giving out the Work Packages

If you're the Project Manager and you give a Work Package to a Team Manager, the two of you won't end up having big disagreements. You'll have already talked things through with all of the Team Managers when you drew up the Stage Plan and resolved any problems then. Discussion at this point is fine-tuning to make sure that the Team Manager involved is clear on what's required, including controls and reporting while the work's being done.

If the Team Manager decides that he needs a more detailed plan than the Stage Plan to control the Work Package, then this *Team Plan* will be agreed with the Project Manager before work starts.

When giving out the Work Package, the Project Manager – or Project Support – may need to create Configuration Item Records for the version control of products involved, depending on the approach being taken. You can read more about this version control, including CI Records, in Chapter 16.

Checking progress on Work Packages

While the teams are working to build the products, Team Managers will be reporting progress to the Project Manager using Checkpoint Reports. You can find more on this reporting in the next chapter, Chapter 8, which covers the Team Manager's responsibilities in PRINCE2.

Checkpoint Report. A progress report that a Team Manager gives to the Project Manager. The required content and format of the report is specified by the Project Manager in the associated Work Package.

Usually the Team Managers send in time sheets and spending information along with the Checkpoint Reports and these *actuals* (how long things have actually taken and how much things have actually cost) can be fed into the Stage Plan. If you're the Project Manager you can do this yourself, but if you have some administrative help – Project Support – those staff do it for you.

To keep an eye on the quality, the Project Manager also checks to make sure that the right tests are being done at the right time by the right people while the products are built by the teams. This is really simple and fast in PRINCE2 because the information is all in the Quality Register (see Chapter 13), which is basically a list of all the quality actions to be taken, such as testing, and a record that they were properly carried out.

Receiving completed Work Packages back

When all of the products in the Work Package are completed, the Team Manager delivers them to the Project Manager or notifies him that they're complete if that's more appropriate – the sections of a suspension bridge are often too big to fit into an envelope without tearing the sides.

Importantly, because the completed products are excellent progress milestones the delivery date is put against those products on the Product Checklist. Chapter 14 on planning explains how to create and use the Product Checklist because it forms part of the plans.

Dealing with Risks and Issues

If you're the Project Manager you can expect to receive project Issues – and in some projects, you can expect to receive a lot of them. Strangely, in the PRINCE2 themes, Issues are covered under the heading of Change Control (for the detail please see Chapter 16). That's odd because the Issue needn't be to do with a change at all – perhaps the Team Member is passing on a good idea, for example.

Issue. A communication sent directly to the Project Manager from anyone in the project or, if you're brave and agree with the PRINCE2 manual, anyone with an interest in the project. An Issue can be sent in at any time, and can be about anything to do with the project.

Deciding how to handle an Issue or risk

If you are the Project Manager, then when you receive a Project Issue, your first decision is on whether or not you need to handle it formally or informally. If the answer is that it's best handled informally, you can simply note it in the Daily Log. If it needs formal tracking, then a register is used; use the Risk Register, fairly obviously, for a risk and if it's an Issue then use the Issue Register. In the case of an Issue, you first transfer the details of the Issue into an Issue Report.

Issue Report. The formal record of an Issue that's normally created by the Project Manager on receipt of an Issue, but if it comes from someone knowledgeable in the project, such as a Team Manager, he may already have written an Issue Report and submitted the Issue in that form.

Examining the issue or risk

After you record the issue or risk you look to see what action, if any, you need to take. This work is sometimes called *impact analysis*.

You're probably not a subject expert in all areas of your project. But you have other people available who are. Often when you receive an Issue, your reaction is, 'I don't have the faintest idea what this is about or what to do.' That's fine, really. Just go and talk to the people who do know.

As part of this analysis, you need to look at a number of dimensions. Ask yourself the following questions to see which dimensions are relevant:

- ✔ Is the issue really an issue or the risk really a risk? Sometimes a team member has misunderstood something and you can reply and close the matter within a minute or two.

- ✔ Does it affect cost?

- ✔ Does it affect timescales?

- ✔ Does it affect the Business Case or the timing or level of benefits?

- ✔ Does an issue affect the nature of a product or products?

- ✔ Is the impact of any issue or risk contained within the present stage, or does it knock on into future stages or even the whole project?

- ✔ Is it likely to affect any other projects and so does it need communicating to other Project Managers or, if you're in a programme, to programme level?

- ✔ What action can you take to address the issue or risk, and is that action within your own authority limit or do you have to go to the Project Board?

To help answer these questions, you may need to talk to a number of different people, such as:

- ✔ Team Managers.

- ✔ Team specialists (for example, for technical implications).

- ✔ Supplier companies.

- ✔ Project Board members (for example, on resource matters).

- ✔ Project Assurance (for example, Business Assurance to look at impacts on the Business Case).

- ✔ Project Managers of other projects, or the Programme Manager if your project is part of a programme (if you need to assess the impact on other projects or on the whole programme).

Having looked at the possible courses of action and the impacts, as Project Manager you then need to work out whether you can deal with the issue or risk within your own authority or whether you need to go to the Project Board. Part of that decision depends on where you are at the moment. If the action requires £12,000 and you have £15,000 to spare for adjustments like this, then you can get on with it. If, however, you have only £15 to spare, you need to take the matter to the board. Those options are covered by the two actions in the Controlling a Stage process of 'Take corrective action' and 'Escalate issues and risks'. In the latter case, the Project Manager then awaits the Project Board's guidance on what to do.

Checking how the possible actions sit with where you are at the moment carries on neatly on to the next heading of 'Monitoring and Progress Reporting'.

Even if the Project Manager is working within his delegated authority (tolerances) he can still go and talk something through with a Project Board member informally. This is a bit like any staff member going to discuss something with his boss to get the boss's view on it, even though the staff member is fully within his authority to take the decision. Chapter 10, on the Project Board, has more explanation on this 'ad hoc' or informal contact.

Monitoring and Progress Reporting

You must check regularly during the stage to see where you are against the plan. But you also need to check where you are if you're dealing with an Issue in order to see if you have capacity to absorb the impact of any action, or if you must refer the matter to the Project Board.

This activity is all about making a thorough check on the progress of the whole stage, including forward projections, to see whether you're still likely to finish the stage within the limits – or tolerances – that the Project Board set down at the beginning of the stage. This progress check is much more thorough than the 'Review Work Package Status' activity, which is a much higher-level check and limited to the progress of a particular Work Package.

Checking risk and the Business Case

As a minimum, you review and update the Business Case and Risk Register at the end of each management stage, but you certainly want to check them and maybe update them more often than that. In a high-risk project, for example, you're likely to do a systematic review and update of all risks at regular intervals during each stage and the required degree of control will have been defined in the Risk Management Strategy.

Strangely the method only refers to checking if any benefits should be measured as part of this activity, not checks of the Business Case itself. But in many projects you need to check the Business Case regularly too in order to be satisfied that the project is still on track to deliver the expected benefits – as previous manual editions made clear. Although you may well do this checking as part of the analysis of inbound information coming in on Issues, a regular review is often more than advantageous and not least if a benefits tolerance has been set by the Project Board.

Firing off other parts of PRINCE2

This status check of the stage can trigger other work, depending on what you find. You may find that the project is:

- ✔ **Going off the plan but still within delegated limits:** Can you deal with it within your own delegated authority? If so, fine, get on and do it. (See the later section 'Correcting a Stage or Reporting an Exception').

- ✔ **Going off the plan and finishing outside delegated limits:** You need to report any Exception (a projection that you will go outside the tolerance limits for the stage) to the Project Board. Again, you can read more later in the chapter in the section 'Correcting a Stage or Reporting an Exception'.

In Exception. A stage is said to be 'in Exception' when it's projected to go outside one or more of the tolerance limits set down by the Project Board, and the Project Manager can't correct this by taking action within his own authority. But exception also refers to the position of the whole project. It could be that some new information comes in and although that doesn't have an impact on the current stage, it does affect a future one and will cause a breach of the project tolerance limits. In that case, the Project Manager must report it immediately, just like a stage exception.

You don't need to report an Exception if you can adjust the running of the stage to bring things back within the specified limits. Exception is where you can't 'project manage' your way out of the problem and you'll breach the limits no matter what you do.

- ✔ **Getting near the end of a stage:** Okay, time to start the End Stage stuff and then to get ready for the Project Board meeting. Turn to Chapter 6 for all the detail on the End Stage work.

- ✔ **Getting near the end of the project:** When you approach the end of the last stage, start project closure. The detail of the closure work is in Chapter 9.

Reporting progress to the Project Board

The Communication Management Strategy included in the Project Initiation Document (PID) sets down how you'll report stage progress to the Project Board, including the information you give and how frequently. In PRINCE2, this progress report is called a *Highlight Report*. As with all PRINCE2 reports, the report can be verbal, but again the Comms Strategy determines that (for more on the Communication Management Strategy, please see Chapter 5).

The PRINCE2 Highlight Report isn't supposed to be a huge, unwieldy thing. Rather, you should spend less than an hour producing it and usually fit it on just one or two sides of A4. Some people use a dashboard-type layout with things like budget status shown as a petrol gauge. Being visual can be effective as well as concise.

Highlight Report

Date.

Period.

Status summary.

This reporting period:

✔ Work Packages, pending authorisation, in execution and completed in the period.

✔ Products completed in the period.

✔ Products planned but not started or completed in the period.

✔ Corrective actions taken in the period.

Next reporting period:

✔ Work packages to be authorised, in execution and to be completed

✔ Products to be completed in the next period.

✔ Corrective actions to be completed during the next period.

Project and stage tolerance status.

Requests for change.

Key issues and risks.

Lessons Report.

The Highlight Report needs little explanation because, once again, the contents are straightforward. If you think it's rather detailed and your Project Board is unlikely to be interested in that level of detail, don't forget you can adjust it. The Communication Management Plan is where you define and agree the content and format of Highlight Reports for this particular project.

Warning the board of issues and risks

As you can see from the report headings, the Project Manager has the opportunity to tell the board members about any significant issues and risks, but contrary to an impression given by PRINCE2, he doesn't need to tell the board absolutely everything. The idea of the board as the Project Manager's boss is helpful here. If a subordinate tells his boss absolutely everything, the boss may wonder why he hired that person. Managers expect their staff to inform them of significant things only, not a mass of routine detail.

Reporting on progress with the Product Checklist

PRINCE2 has a very useful control document that doesn't figure in the Highlight Report, but you may want to take advantage of it. It's the *Product Checklist* mentioned earlier in the chapter in the context of noting the delivery of products completed by teams. The Product Checklist is useful in the context of the Highlight Report to show which products have been delivered that are due to be completed in the next reporting period. The Product Checklist is a particularly powerful progress monitoring and reporting tool and readily understandable for a Project Board.

Chapter 14, on planning, has more information on the Product Checklist and how, very simply, you can make it even more useful to the Project Board than covered in PRINCE2 by combining it with another technique. But it's worth emphasising here that the checklist is extraordinarily powerful as a progress measure and the PRINCE2 manual has always understated its value and continues to do so.

Logging and reporting lessons that have been learned

The Lessons Log is for the Project Manager to record which lessons from previous projects can be applied to this one, and which lessons are being learned in this project that may be of value to future projects. Although such lessons can be noted at any time, obviously one or more may come to mind as the Project Manager reviews the stage. In that context, one final thing to single out from the Highlight Report headings is the *Lessons Report*. If something significant has been learned and logged, it may well be worth passing it back into the organisation now so that other projects can make immediate use of the information, and the Lessons Report serves that purpose. Read more about the Lessons Report in Chapter 6 that covers the stage boundary work, because that's the more usual place for lessons reporting.

Correcting a Stage or Reporting an Exception

Projects go off track, which is why they need Project Managers. If the stage does go off track, clearly you need to react and do something about that. What you do depends on the nature of the problem and if you can bring it under control or not. You'll have discovered the *deviation from the plan* (to use the PRINCE2 term) when checking the status of the stage – covered in the 'Monitoring and Progress Reporting' section a bit earlier in this chapter.

Exception Report

Exception title: An overview of the exception. (You might use 'Stage Budget Exception').

Cause of the exception: A description of the cause of the deviation from the current plan.

Consequences of the deviation: The implications if the issue isn't addressed.

Options: Different things that could be done to address the deviation and the effect of each.

Recommendation: Of the available options, which one the Project Manager is recommending to the Project Board and why.

Lessons: What can be learned from the exception.

Correcting the stage

If you're the Project Manager and can make some adjustments to the running of the stage that would mean that the stage would finish within the tolerances, then you get on and do that. That may mean making some changes to the plans and the work given to the teams. But the important point is that you're working within your delegated authority and so can do this without reference to the board. This is just the same as ordinary business management where you'd expect one of your staff to get on and solve problems if he can, and not bring them all to you.

Reporting an Exception

If the Project Manager finds that no matter what action he takes within his own authority, he cannot adjust the running of the stage to finish within the limits of the tolerance, he must report this to the Project Board immediately. The stage is now 'in Exception'. He must not take any action at all other than quickly to investigate the size of the problem and produce an Exception Report in the format set down in the Communications Management Strategy (which is in the Project Initiation Document). The Exception Report isn't necessarily a document, but may be a meeting or a phone call.

Escalating apparently minor matters

Although the Project Manager can take action to get the stage projections back down inside the tolerance limits, he may not be able to if something else limits his authority to take action. For example, if an adjustment would cost only one penny and take one minute to do but would have huge business implications, the Project Manager almost certainly won't have the authority to take that action. He has to go to the Project Board and in turn the board probably has to take it to more senior managers in the organisation.

With an exception, the Project Manager *recommends* how it should be dealt with, but the Project Board *decides* how it will be dealt with.

Checking out the products of Controlling a Stage

Here's a summary of the main products in use when controlling a stage:

- ✔ **Benefits Review Plan:** Checked by the Project Manager to determine what reviews of benefits, if any, to do in the stage to quantify benefits that have already come on stream.

- ✔ **Business Case:** The Project Manager must check that the project is still on track to deliver benefits and he may also update the Business Case with new cost and time information. He will also check the Business Case when establishing the impact of any Issues and risks.

- ✔ **Checkpoint Report:** Received from Team Managers, these progress reports on individual Work Packages provide information to determine how the whole stage is going.

- ✔ **Configuration Item (CI) Record:** A record for version control of a product.

- ✔ **Exception Report:** The Project Manager uses this report to advise the Project Board if the whole stage will breach a stage tolerance.

- ✔ **Highlight Report:** The Project Manager gives this report, which highlights progress on the whole stage, to the Project Board. It may include a Lessons Report.

- ✔ **Issue Register:** The Project Manager (or Project Support, on the Project Manager's behalf) uses this register to record the existence and progress of Issues under formal control.

- ✔ **Issue Report:** The Project Manager formally records an issue on this report on receipt of an Issue.

- ✔ **Product Checklist:** The Project Manager uses this checklist to monitor delivery of products during the stage.

- ✔ **Quality Register:** The Quality Log records the planned quality actions, such as tests, and is normally completed by the people doing those tests. The Project Manager keeps an eye on the register to ensure that the quality actions are being taken.

- ✔ **Risk Register:** This register is used as a reference when managing risks during the stage, but also to enter any new risks or any changes in status of existing ones.

- ✔ **Stage Plan:** Using this plan helps the Project Manager to check progress and act as a reference for the controls that are in force in the stage.

- ✔ **Team Plan:** A Team Plan may be created by a Team Manager on receipt of a Work Package. If so, the plan will be agreed with the Project Manager.

- ✔ **Work Package:** This is a unit of work that the Project Manager gives to a Team Manager. The Work Package is in the form of an instruction pack and authority to the Team Manager to build one or more products. See Chapter 8 for a full description.

Chapter 8

Building the Deliverables

In This Chapter

▶ Getting a work assignment and checking it out

▶ Building project products and getting them tested and approved

▶ Checking and reporting on progress

▶ Checking the acceptances and handing over completed work

*T*his chapter is going to be short. Conceptually it is by far the easiest part of PRINCE2 and the process is the simplest of the seven, but strangely this is where the huge majority of the project's work is done. The process covers the work of Team Managers in building products during the delivery stages and getting them tested, approved and handed back.

Understanding the Process Managing Product Delivery

If you're reading the book in chapter order, you've just finished Chapter 7 covering the work of the Project Manager in controlling the stage and you've read about three activities to control the work assignments, or *Work Packages*, given to Team Managers. Those activities were to give out a Work Package, check progress as the products are built, and then receive the products back when they're finished. The process Managing Product Delivery is simply the mirror image of those three activities, reflecting the Team Manager's perspective. Only three activities are here and those are to receive the Work Package, build the products and then hand them back when the whole Work Package is completed. Mind-blowing in complexity, isn't it?

As with the other chapters about processes, the process diagram, shown in Figure 8-1, comes first and the chapter then walks you through the activities involved.

Before looking at the handling of a Work Package, it's helpful to look in a bit more detail of what one contains. It has a number of headings but the concept behind it is very straightforward: it's an instruction pack from the Project Manager to a Team Manager asking them to build a deliverable, which PRINCE2 calls a product, or perhaps more than one if it makes sense to develop them together. The Work Package defines what products are involved and sets down any constraints and requirements for the way the work is to be done. That includes the basic and obvious things like the requirements for progress reporting.

Work Package

Date.

Team or person authorised.

Work Package description.

Techniques, processes and procedures.

Development interfaces.

Operations and maintenance interfaces.

Configuration management requirements.

Joint agreements.

Tolerances.

Constraints.

Reporting arrangements.

Problem handling and escalation.

Extracts or references:

- Stage Plan extract.
- Product Description(s).

Approval method.

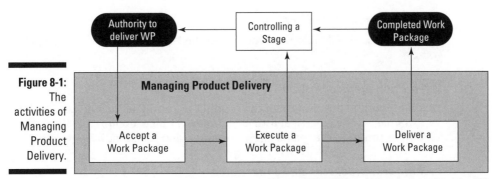

Based on OGC PRINCE2 material. Reproduced under licence from OGC.

Figure 8-1:
The activities of Managing Product Delivery.

Some people's first reaction on hearing about Work Packages is to think of them as yet more documentation and more bureaucracy. Well PRINCE2, used properly, isn't bureaucratic and although the Work Package is indeed a document it's a really valuable one. If something is to be built, someone has to define what that 'something' is and if things like progress reports are required, it obviously makes sense to set down the content needed and specify the frequency required. Work Packages contain sensible information, but as always, keep to the minimum in balance with exercising sufficient control.

In a very small project with only one team, the Project Manager may also manage the team and you don't need a Team Manager. That is quite okay. In effect then, if you're the Project Manager you give yourself a Work Package. The whole interface now becomes very informal to the point of ceasing to exist. Don't stand up in your office and start talking to yourself in order to agree the Work Package and then shake hands with yourself at the end. Your colleagues will think you're even weirder than they'd imagined.

Unpacking the Work Package

The Work Package content is logical and this section briefly explains each element of it.

Date

The PRINCE2 manual says that you put the date on which the Project Manager and Team Manager agreed the Work Package, but many people use this heading for the date on which the Project Manager actually issued the Work Package for work to begin, because these dates can sometimes be different.

Team or person authorised

This is simply who'll build the products in the Work Package; which team it's going to.

Work Package description

This is an outline description of the product or products included. It can be, for example, all the electrical fittings in the new office, comprising the lighting circuit product, the mains circuit product, and the standby generator.

Techniques, processes and procedures

This section simply shows how you build the product. In some types of project, particular approaches or standards may be important.

Development interfaces

The interfaces in this section tend to be communications interfaces, where the team must keep in touch with another team. You can see that this can be important, particularly in the area of change. If a team building one product in one Work Package ends up changing the product slightly, then they may need to warn other teams working on products that must fit in with it.

In computer rapid application development (RAD) projects, teams are empowered to de-scope products to fit a development 'time box'. If a team de-scopes a product, telling other teams who are building related products is usually extremely important.

Operations and maintenance interfaces

This sets out what the product(s) must eventually fit with. That may mean that you need to specify procedural interfaces, data interfaces, electrical interfaces, or even physical interfaces where something must physically fit something else.

Russian spacecraft and the American shuttle are both able to dock with the international space station. The space vehicle designs had to comply with this physical interface.

Configuration management requirements

Explaining the configuration management, or version control, requirements is especially important when the project involves teams from different organisations. These teams are likely to have different configuration management (CM) procedures and product identification systems. How the version control will operate in the project is set down in the Configuration Management Strategy which is explained in detail in Chapter 16.

Joint agreements

The agreements set down the resource and timescales for delivery of the products in the Work Package. The Team Manager must then manage the work to deliver in line with these limits.

Tolerances

Clearly, few Work Packages go exactly to plan, just as few projects go exactly to plan. Putting a plus and minus (a *tolerance*) on some of these delivery requirements, notably time and cost, often makes sense. The Project Manager doesn't want to know whether the Work Package will finish £1 over budget on a £100,000 Work Package. However, the Project Manager will be concerned if the Work Package goes £150,000 over budget and costs £250,000 against its budgeted £100,000. The tolerances specify the bands – Chapter 17 offers a full explanation of this control mechanism, which can be applied at project and stage levels as well as here, at Work Package level.

Tolerance. This is a plus and minus variation on a target, because almost nothing ever goes exactly to plan. For the Work Package, the tolerances set down the Team Manager's delegated authority and define the point at which something must be notified to the Project Manager. For example if the Work Package is now forecast to be more than four days late.

Constraints

The constraints section sets down anything that affects how the Team Manager and the team does the Work Package. In some environments you may have security considerations that affect, for example, who can enter certain restricted areas and when. Or if building works are taking place, limits may be placed on when builders can carry out noisy work, so that the work doesn't disrupt the functioning of the business.

Reporting arrangements

Under the heading 'Reporting arrangements' the PRINCE2 manual refers to the frequency and content of Checkpoint Reports, which is right, but it's not the whole story. Taking Checkpoint Reports first, you specify the frequency and content of these progress reports in the Work Package and not in the Communication Plan.

Checkpoint Report. A progress report that a Team Manager gives to the Project Manager at the intervals and with the content specified on the Work Package.

Being able to adjust the content and frequency of a Checkpoint Report between one Work Package and another is actually very powerful. In a very high-risk Work Package, for example, the Project Manager may require a

Checkpoint Report every two days. At the same time a different team working on a less critical Work Package may be asked to submit a report every two weeks. See 'Reporting progress on the Work Package', later in this chapter, for more details on the Checkpoint Report.

But this section of the Work Package is headed 'Reporting arrangements' and not 'Checkpoint Reporting arrangements'. An important reason for this has been rather lost sight of in the more recent editions of the PRINCE2 manual. That reason is that other reporting may be needed over and above the progress reports. Other requirements may cover things such as financial reporting to know when orders are being placed and what money is being committed in which financial year. Health and safety procedures can even necessitate daily reports to confirm things such as that fire exits have been checked each day.

Problem handling and escalation

If a Work Package tolerance is going to be exceeded, this is normally reported, or 'escalated' using an Issue. However, if the Project Manager wants the Team Manager to use a different procedure, this is where she would say so.

Extracts or references

This section is to pass on references to relevant other documents. For example, it may reference organisational security requirements or safety requirements for this sort of work. But it also includes project-related information and specifically two things

Stage Plan extract

Usually it's simpler for the Project Manager to give the Team Manager a copy of the whole Stage Plan rather than just an extract – the Stage Plan isn't usually that big – or it's a computer file. But if she doesn't want to do that – perhaps parts of it are confidential – she can instead pass on just that part of the plan needed for control of this particular Work Package.

Product Description (s)

PRINCE2 takes a product-led or product-based approach to planning (I explain this fully in Chapter 14). Part of this planning is to write a Product Description to define every deliverable or product to be created in this stage. The Product Description describes the product together with any quality criteria it must satisfy and details of how to quality-check it. As the Work Package may be to build more than one product, more than one Product Description may be included in this section.

Approval method

This section sets down who can approve the products in the Work Package after they've been built and tested. Sign-off is normally very simple, but can involve things like formal acceptances and even legal acceptances. If so, the details are set down here. This section also covers how the completed products in the Work Package are to be delivered. In some cases the Team Manager can hand them back physically or electronically to the Project Manager. But you can return the product(s) in a different way, such as into an automated CM (version control) system or by delivering direct to a final location. In this case the Project Manager needs to be notified that the product or products included in the Work Package are now complete and delivered.

Project communications don't have to be difficult. The Team Managers can notify Work Package completion by email or even phone calls. You often don't need to be formal, even in large projects, because the delivery of the product(s) can be verified in other ways.

Building the Work Package Products

For the Team Manager, things are actually very simple in terms of the method and as mentioned at the start of this chapter, there are just three activities.

Receiving the Work Package

The Team Manager discusses the Work Package with the Project Manager and makes sure that she's clear on requirements and can agree to it. The Team Manager must now decide if the amount of detail in the Stage Plan is sufficient to control the development of the Work Package. If it is, which is often the case, all well and good. If not, the Team Manager can draw up a more detailed Team Plan just for the work involved in this particular Work Package. This uses exactly the same approach as for all other levels of planning in PRINCE2, an approach that Chapter 14 covers in detail.

Building the products

Using the detail of the Stage Plan or Team Plan, the Team Manager gets her team working to build and test the products. The Work Package gives information on any constraints and also sets down the reporting requirements.

Reporting progress on the Work Package

The Team Manager sets up progress measuring points called Checkpoints to establish progress and ensure that she can deliver the Work Package in the agreed time.

Keeping the version control up-to-date

As products go through the different stages of their development, testing and approval, the configuration management information must be kept up to date. Each product being configuration managed has a Configuration Item (CI) Record. Depending on the instructions in the Work Package, the Team Manager may notify changes of state to Project Support who maintains the CI Record, or the Team Manager may update the record.

Checkpoint or Checkpoint Meeting. The Checkpoint to establish progress is often a meeting. Typically, the meeting is at the end of the week and the team gathers round a flip chart and reports progress made during that week. People hand in their time sheets and talk through the outlook for the next week, together with any problems. If the Project Manager is available, she may also attend the meeting, but the Checkpoint is primarily for the Team Manager to check progress with team members.

If you're the Project Manager, getting along to at least some of the Checkpoint meetings really helps. This has two very positive benefits. The first is that on large projects you're less distant and the team members feel that you're more a part of the project. The second is that you can find out a lot about what's going on in your project. This doesn't just concern listening to what team members say when discussing the work, but how they say it. Are they upbeat or downbeat? Do they sound enthusiastic and engaged, or de-motivated and worried? PRINCE2 focuses on planning and control and doesn't cover human factors, but the human factors – the people management – are vitally important in working towards a successful project.

The Team Manager reports the progress achieved and the outlook for the rest of the Work Package to the Project Manager, using a Checkpoint Report. As always in PRINCE2, this report can be verbal and the Work Package sets down the frequency and content.

The Checkpoint Report is all predictable stuff, but a bit over the top in a lot of projects, so you can often simplify its contents. If you use a Product Checklist at the level of a Team Plan, which products were completed and which are due for completion in the next period become self-evident.

Checkpoint Report

Date: The date of Checkpoint.

Period: The period covered by the report. This is often a week.

Follow-ups: The outcome of things mentioned on previous reports.

This reporting period: Activities during the period, with information on products built, quality activities carried out and any lessons learned that need to be passed on.

Next reporting period: Information on products to be worked on in the next reporting period, which products are due to be completed and what quality activities are scheduled.

Work Package tolerance status: The current position of the Work Package in relation to any tolerances set by the Project Manager.

Issues and risks: An update on any risks and current issues relating to the Work Package.

In large projects where the Project Manager may have regular meetings with the Team Managers, she can use Checkpoints to push information out into the project as well as gathering it in. The Project Manager can use a cascade mechanism to give information to her Team Managers and ask them to tell all their team members at the next Checkpoint.

Keeping an eye on quality

As well as monitoring progress during the work, the Team Manager also checks that the right tests and checks are being performed. This is done simply by checking the entries in the Quality Register, which lists all the required tests together with space for signing them off when they're done.

Returning completed products

When the product or products in the Work Package are all complete, the Team Manager checks them over one last time before delivering the product(s) or notifying their completion, as the Work Package instructs. The Team Manager's final checks include looking again at the Quality Register to make sure that all the tests required for these products have been completed and signed off. The Team Manager also confirms that all approvals and any other necessary acceptances have been obtained. For example, there may be legal or technical acceptances as well as user ones.

In a multi-agency project environment, there can sometimes be a large number of people involved in approving some products. Be careful to allow sufficient and realistic time for this in Stage and Team Plans.

Checking out the products of Managing Product Delivery

Here's a summary of the main products in use in the development of a Work Package.

✔ **Checkpoint Report:** In this report the Team Manager reports progress on the development of a Work Package to the Project Manager.

✔ **Configuration Item (CI) Records:** These records are to keep track of the state of products that teams develop and deliver. Chapter 16 outlines how to set up and use these records. Who actually does it depends on the instructions in the Work Package, which in turn are based on the Configuration Management Strategy in the PID.

✔ **Quality Register:** The Quality Log records the outcome of tests and is normally completed by the people doing those tests.

✔ **Team Plan:** The Team Manager produces this detailed plan that helps her to run the Work Package if the Stage Plan doesn't give sufficient detail. The Team Plan is optional, because the Stage Plan may be enough.

✔ **Work Package:** This is a unit of work that the Project Manager gives to a Team Manager. The Work Package is in the form of an instruction pack to build one or more products.

Chapter 9

Finishing the Project

· ·

In This Chapter

▶ Making sure that you're finished

▶ Closing the project early, if you need to

▶ Measuring any benefits and checking plans for further benefits reviews

▶ Recommending any actions needed after the project

▶ Preparing the report on how the project went

· ·

A lot of projects sort of fizzle out. People go off to do other things and organisational managers ask, 'Is that project finished or is someone still doing something on it?' Not so in PRINCE2. Closure starts with the work of the Project Manager, who checks that everything is really done, sees what needs to be passed back into the organisation and then reports how the project went. Closure ends when the Project Board agrees that everything is okay and that the project can be shut down.

This chapter looks at the first part of the closure: it covers what the Project Manager does to get ready for the Project Board's confirmation of closure. As always with PRINCE2, the work isn't difficult, but it's important, so don't be tempted to leave it out.

So where does this closure work fit into the project? 'Er, silly question,' you say, 'at the end, of course.' Yes, that's true, but I mean in terms of the project stages. In PRINCE2, the project closure work is something that you do towards the end of the last stage. Unlike some other approaches to project management, project closure isn't a stage in its own right. Having a closure stage does actually have some value, but that's not relevant in this introduction to the chapter because PRINCE2 just doesn't do things that way.

Closure can come at a time other than the planned end though and that's when you do an 'emergency stop' – which may be at any point. It may be, for example, that some new and unforeseen business development shows that you just don't need the project after all. Either way, project closure in PRINCE2 handles it.

Closing a Project

Closing a Project has five activities, which include two alternative entry points: you do the planned close for the project or you deal with an early or 'premature' close. Take a quick look at the model shown in Figure 9-1 to get the general idea and then come back when you've finished the chapter when you know exactly how it all fits together.

A repeated message in *PRINCE2 For Dummies* through both editions has been that you should always fit the method to the needs of the project. That's worth emphasising here because, as you'll see, in its full extent the work and documentation in closure can be extensive. But even in a very large project you may not need anything like this maximum so do think very carefully. Don't put your hand up for unnecessary work that not only takes time and money, but possibly annoys others with over-large documents. A common result of a document that's too big is that people, especially busy senior people, don't read any of it. A smaller one often has a much better chance of being properly considered.

I was told in one multi-national organisation that for their documents, the title is the Executive Summary. That's because when given a document their senior managers rarely manage to read more than the title!

Principle 7 – Tailor to suit the project environment.

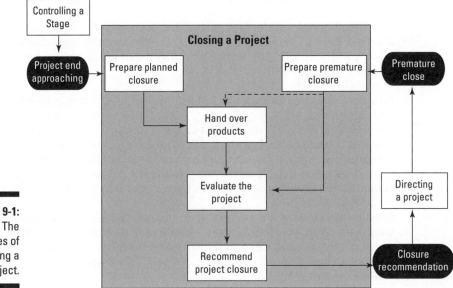

Figure 9-1:
The activities of Closing a Project.

Planning the Planned Closure

The name of the first 'entry point' activity is not very well worded because it involves rather more than just planning the closure, important though that planning is.

Making sure that you've done everything

When you say you're finishing a project, you need to check whether everything is done or nearly done. In a small project you may know this anyway if you're closely involved with the team, but even then sometimes a quick check does no harm to make sure that you don't overlook anything.

You also need to check that the project meets the Acceptance Criteria on the *Project Product Description*. Some of these criteria may relate to the project itself, and others may relate to specific final deliverables of the project, particularly if the project is the sort that makes one big delivery at the end. Please see Chapter 8 for more on the Project Product Description.

Three things help you check whether you've finished a project:

1. If you used the powerful progress measuring tool in PRINCE2, the Product Checklist, you can see if the sign-offs are done for most of the project deliverables or products. You can read more about the Product Checklist in Chapter 14 because you produce it when doing the planning.

2. The Checkpoint Reports (progress reports) from Team Managers on the remaining products to see how they're progressing.

3. The status information for products, which is part of the Configuration Management or version control information, to confirm that the status of all but the final few products is set to 'complete' – or 'approved' if you have the type of project where further approval is needed on some or all products. The Project Manager can ask Project Support to produce a *Product Status Account*. Chapter 16 has more on this.

Checking for sign-offs and acceptances

The completion check isn't complete unless you're sure that any necessary acceptances and handovers have been done properly. You don't usually get those acceptances now, but check that none have been left out when things may have been signed off – and even taken into operational use – throughout the project. Not all projects are 'big bang' with everything delivered in one hit at the end.

Acceptances and handovers

When checking through acceptances and handovers, you may need to include the following areas:

✔ **Legal sign-offs:** For example, you may need these when the company lawyers approve key documents.

✔ **External sign-offs:** These may include other organisations signing to say that they agree to the new business interfaces. Some may have legal implications as well, such as sign-offs from building inspectors that certify the structure is safe after the building works.

✔ **Supplier sign-offs:** You may need handovers from suppliers. This may be the formal handing over of a building from the development company to the customer organisation, for example. Or perhaps a sign-off of satisfactorily completed work which shows that payment to the supplier is now due.

✔ **Organisational handovers:** Examples of this include a development team handing a computer system over to the computer operations department or passing responsibility for a retail store back to the store manager after the project team has finished the brand change, refitting, and re-stocking work.

The need for formal acceptances will have been noted on the Product Descriptions and Work Packages that set down the exact requirements for deliverables. In turn they will have been influenced by the Project Approach in which you identified legal requirements and mandatory handovers. As with so much of this closure work though, this is a final check. Usually the other controls (such as the return of a Work Package) will have worked very well to make sure that nothing was missed.

Product Descriptions and Work Packages. A Work Package is a work assignment given to a Team Manager to build one or more products – or deliverables. Each of those products is defined on a Product Description. The Work Package is like an instruction pack, and part of it is to say how products are to be returned on completion, including sign-off requirements. (For much more on products see Chapter 14 and for more on Work Packages, please see Chapter 8.)

Planning a Premature Closure

Although this is a separate activity box in the process diagram at Figure 9-1, it isn't hugely different from planning the planned close. The key differences are the following:

✔ **You usually go faster than usual.** The objective is to close the project quickly so as not to use any more resource than is absolutely necessary.

✔ **You don't check that everything is complete.** Instead, you look to see if any of the work that the project did carry out is worth saving, to get at least some benefit from the project. As with the planned close, you may use a Product Status Account but this time to establish what has been finished and how far through their development any unfinished products are. For example, if some are almost finished and would still be valuable to the business area, is it worth completing them?

✔ **You may need to tell people.** As staff resources are released early, there may be some people you need to warn. Equally on finance, you'll be releasing money that now won't be spent so your Finance Director may be more than a little interested. You may have some important work to do here, including work on the legal side if contracts are being ended prematurely. Let's hope you remembered to put a clause in the contracts to cover early close without incurring full costs!

✔ **Benefits reviews.** There may be benefits from products that have already been delivered, but it won't be the full range of benefits that would've been there if the project had been completed. You therefore need to adjust the *Benefits Review Plan* or, if there won't now be any worthwhile benefits, scrap it.

✔ **Your review of lessons learned looks at whether anyone could have seen this problem coming.** If someone had spotted the problem earlier, perhaps you could have closed down earlier and so saved more time and expense. Knowing that may help a future project in the same circumstances. If the project was shut down because it ran out of control, you need to examine the reasons for that. In turn, that may lead to *Follow-on Action Recommendations* (see later in this chapter) to change project procedures.

Handing Over the Final Product (s)

You will be passing one or more products back to the users of the project at the end, and it may be everything; the 'big bang' project. But in some cases it'll be the final deliverables or products because things will have been taken into operational use throughout the project; perhaps just drip-fed or in phases of release.

Checking the working environment

PRINCE2 is impressively responsible. The end project work includes a check to make sure that project products can move smoothly through into their working life. The planned work, especially during the last project stage, should already have done this but in the close-down process this final check makes quite sure of a smooth transition. That's very responsible, and very different from teams throwing products at users and running out quickly before people discover that nothing works!

The check should also make sure that enough resource is available in the early life of deliverables where users need more 'hand-holding' and where technical problems are more likely as things settle down or the need for small adjustments becomes apparent. Just in passing, these are actually some of the arguments in non-PRINCE2 methods for having a full stage dedicated to closure. Even in very high-quality environments, not everything will have been tested so you can expect some degree of trouble.

Looking at business benefits

Checking the business benefits falls into two areas. The first is those benefits that are visible immediately at the end of the project and that you can measure and report straight away. The second group is often bigger – those benefits that won't be clear for a while, and which you can't report accurately straight away. You need to measure and report this second group some time after the end of the project, and so after PRINCE2.

Measuring benefits that you can see now

No Project Board member wants to wait three months for the first report of benefits if some useful indicator already exists showing that the project seems to have been successful. So if you can measure and report any benefit now, even a single benefit, you do.

The Stage Plan for the final project stage includes any work to measure benefits during project closure, and the Business Case and Benefits Review Plan include information on what benefits need to be measured and how to measure them. The Project Manager includes this benefits information in the End Project Report – see 'Reviewing How the Project Went', later in this chapter.

Planning for benefits review after the project – did it deliver?

In many projects you can't measure most benefits accurately at the end. Things are still settling down and the exact level of benefits isn't yet clear. For a new business procedure, for example, in the first few weeks the staff are still getting used to it. Only after four or five weeks can you establish clearly how fast the staff can now operate the new procedure and the number of staff hours it saves. Measuring immediately while staff are going slowly because of unfamiliarity, for example, just isn't accurate.

PRINCE2 shuts down when the project shuts down. Therefore, neither PRINCE2 nor the project is still running when you do the benefits reviews after closure. The Benefits Review Plan covers reviews after the project as well as any within it and is checked as part of project closure before being passed on to someone in the organisation to do as a Follow-on Action from the project. That person will usually be the manager who was the Senior User on the Project Board but it could involve others, such as financial specialists.

Answering the question 'How long after the project should you measure benefits?'

A simple answer to this commonly asked question is when you can measure the benefits and report them accurately. Many people say that the length of time is always six months, but that's not correct; it's when the benefits can be measured. But anyway, you may need more than one review. For example, if you can see different benefits clearly at different times, you may have one review after three months, say, and another after six months. Or things may gradually become clear and you want a provisional review to give a ball-park idea of the benefits one month out, and then a precise one when things really settle down after four months. If your project is part of a programme of projects, you may need to have a review when the whole programme is finished and the full benefits are measurable. All of this should already be in the Benefits Review Plan, but you do a final check here before closing down and passing responsibility for reviews back into the organisation.

Reviewing How the Project Went

Now comes an important review of how the project went and, with that, the production of the End Project Report. This is where you look at the project in the context of the original Project Initiation Documentation (PID) – the detailed plan at project level – please see Chapter 5 for more detail. The PID includes things like timing, cost, and key objectives.

Follow-on action areas

When thinking about possible follow-on actions, have a think about these areas:

✔ **Ongoing product risks:** These are risks from the Risk Register that continue into the working life of project products. For example, if the project installed high-power machinery that has ongoing operational safety risks.

✔ **Ongoing business risks:** Many organisations now have corporate risk management alongside project risk management, and you need to be sure that you register ongoing risks into that corporate risk management system so that someone is now responsible for future monitoring and action.

(continued)

(continued)

✔ **Good ideas:** People in the project may have put forward good ideas, but the project had a fixed end date and wasn't able to include them. A recommendation may be to implement the ideas some other way.

✔ **Changes in standards:** Perhaps something from the Lessons Log has an impact on project management standards. So if the project discovered a better way of doing something, you may suggest that all projects incorporate that better way.

✔ **Temporary concessions:** As Chapter 16 describes, a *concession* means accepting something that's off specification. Perhaps you accept the product because, although not ideal, it's okay and you don't have enough time to rework it and still meet the fixed end date for the project. But although the PRINCE2 manual doesn't mention the possibility, that concession may be temporary. You may require that a supplier comes back after the project with a replacement that's up to specification. Therefore, a follow-on action is that some manager in the organisation makes quite sure that the supplier does just that.

End Project Report

As with the End Stage Report, you may find that some of this is excessive, particularly the 'Review of Products'. As with all reports, stick to what's necessary and not necessarily the exhaustive content as set down in the PRINCE2 manual.

Project Manager's report: A summary of performance but you can extend this to include a brief commentary on how the project went. However, it shouldn't be a reprint of the Project Manager's innermost thoughts from his personal blog or a repeat of the Lessons Log.

Review of the Business Case: A review that particularly picks up on:

✔ **Benefits achieved to date:** See 'Looking at business benefits' earlier in this chapter.

✔ **Residual benefits expected:** Those that will come after the project has finished.

✔ **Expected net benefits:** The total benefits after costs have been taken into account. This may be a dangerous thing to state in isolation though as it can give a distorted view by focusing just on finance whereas benefits may be far wider ranging. Please see Chapter 11 for a full explanation of the Business Case, including benefits and benefits measures.

✔ **Deviations from the approved Business Case:** This is a rather dangerous heading and wide open to problems. On one hand no project should deviate from an approved Business Case. If change is needed then that should be done through change control not by 'deviating' from what has been approved for the most important document in a PRINCE2 project. Don't confuse this with benefits tolerance because tolerance, by definition, is approved. If, on the other hand, this section is just used to report the final position of benefits projections within tolerance then fine, but it would be helpful for the PRINCE2 manual to have a clearer heading or at least to explain that.

Review of project objectives: How the project did against the six areas of time, cost, quality, scope, benefits and risk, but also a review of the effectiveness or otherwise of the strategies and controls set up in Initiation.

Review of team performance: The manual talks of a 'mention in despatches' for people who performed well (see also the End Stage Report in Chapter 6) but good though that may be, you should also be looking to put rather more information in this section such as performance metrics and a commentary on what helped performance and what hindered it. There may be some related lessons associated with this section.

Review of Products: You may want to cut down on this as it is more than unlikely for example that a Project Board, or anyone else, would want to read in an End Project Report all of the quality activities planned and completed right through the project. If someone actually wants that detail, they should go look at the Quality Register. It's putting in huge detail like this that gives PRINCE2 a bad name and a reputation for creating a paper mountain.

✔ **Quality records:** 'The list of quality activities planned and completed' – enough said in the previous paragraph.

✔ **Approval records:** Listing the products and their requisite approvals. Again, complete overkill in any project I can think of, even really big ones or perhaps especially big ones because of the large number of products involved. But you might want to list major products and confirm their approval, particularly in a multi-organisation project where approval was needed from several sources.

✔ **Off-specifications:** Things that did not meet their original specification. These should have been accepted as _concessions_. Chapter 16 on change control has more detail.

✔ **Project product handover:** The heading implies that this should confirm that the product has been handed over, which makes sense in the context of the process diagram at Figure 9-1 where this 'Evaluate the project' activity clearly follows the 'Hand over products' activity. However, the text of the PRINCE2 manual instructs that this section of the report should state that the appropriate areas of the organisation have confirmed that they are ready to receive the product. Well, the manual may be confusing on this point but you must make sure that you are not or you could get into the same sort of problems that a major construction project did in the UK. In that project there were opposing views on when handover should take place and talk of a very expensive legal action to resolve them.

✔ **Summary of follow-on action recommendations:** Follow-on actions are things that should be done after the end of the project, such as ongoing risk management actions for dangerous machinery, or a great idea that came up in the project but which you didn't have time or money to implement, or perhaps something like a recommended change to the version control procedures. The PRINCE2 manual says that this section is about the Project Manager asking the Project Board who each action should be referred to. But such consultation is likely to be long before this and probably verbal and you may want to think twice about using the End Project Report for discussion in this way; not least because it is often seen by people outside the project.

Lessons Report: This is a report based on entries that were made in the Lessons Log. It isn't negative – what went wrong and, importantly, whose fault was it? It is positive both in terms of preventing problems recurring in future projects and in recording useful things that were learned that will help future projects, such as a better and faster way of doing something. The full content of the Lessons Report is in the next panel in this chapter.

Recording the follow-on actions

You may have noted Follow-on Action Recommendations – things you recommend that the organisation does after the end of the project – right through the project but especially in the last activity in this process where you're thinking about products and handovers. The Follow-on Action Recommendations are summarised in the End Project Report. The Project Board should normally approve, and then make, the recommendations.

Writing the End Project Report

The Project Manager produces the End Project Report, which is his view of how things went, as well as a presentation of key facts and figures from the project.

The End Project Report goes with other closure products to the Project Board and then back into the organisation. But unless it is confidential, a copy of the report should then be stored where future projects can find it and refer to it, not in the bottom of a locked filing cabinet in the lower basement.

Writing the Lessons Report

In the review of the project and while thinking through what you will include in the End Project Report you may think of more lessons that are worth passing on. You can put these into the Lessons Log, but then you need to close that log and produce a Lessons Report.

Lessons Report

The Lessons Report is produced at the end of the project and included in the End Project Report. But if lessons need to be passed back into the organisation before project closure, then Lessons Reports can also be created at Stage Ends and included in End Stage Reports. Please see Chapter 6 for more on this end stage use. To give the usual warning, the content in this panel sets out the report in full but you may be able to simplify it considerably for your own projects.

Executive summary: An overview of what the report is covering such as lessons on risk budgets and project planning.

Scope of the report: This is simply to say if the report is a stage level one or the end project Lessons Report.

Review: What went right and what went wrong and, in the latter case, how it might have been prevented if that was possible. This review can include:

✔ **Project management method:** How PRINCE2 worked out on this project and if its use could be improved on future projects.

✔ **Any specialist methods used:** Comments on the use of other things used in the project, such as a risk management method that you integrated with PRINCE2.

✔ **Project strategies:** Any improvements that might be made in how strategies (quality, risk, configuration management, communication) may be improved in future projects.

✔ **Project controls:** The result of any adjustment made to PRINCE2 controls, or suggestions of how they may be adjusted in the future.

✔ **Abnormal events causing deviations:** A bit tricky this one, because if they're abnormal then it's likely that they're largely unpredictable and inconsistent and so hard to set down suggestions for the future. But if you can give help to future projects, this is where you do it.

A review of useful measurements, including:

✔ **Effort required to create the products:** A difficult entry for a Lessons Report because although this information is really useful for future estimating, it's going to be very lengthy if you list it all here.

✔ **Effectiveness of the Quality Management Strategy:** A slightly odd entry because it partly overlaps with the review of strategies earlier in the report, but it also goes into reporting quality statistics which can help establish the effectiveness of the quality strategy.

✔ **Statistics on Issues and risks:** The PRINCE2 manual gives no help on what this section includes, but keeping in mind the context of Lessons, it's worth pointing out trends such as that there were considerably fewer Issues submitted than were anticipated but that many more risks came to light during the project than were identified when it was planned. In turn that information may help with resourcing similar future projects (unnecessary to put quite so much time aside for Issue handling) and planning (devote more effort to risk identification during Initiation).

For significant lessons it is suggested that you also add for each one . . .

✔ **Event:** What led to the lesson involved, such as pressure on time led to a team member coming up with a faster way of doing something.

✔ **Effect:** Such as if it was a good or bad effect. So where a team found a faster and better way of doing something, this had a beneficial effect.

✔ **Causes/trigger:** What triggered the event that led to the lesson.

✔ **Whether there were early warning indicators:** This relates both to problems and to signs of a good outcome. So, the fact that one part of the project was done faster than expected was an indicator that a later and related part would also complete in a shorter time frame.

✔ **Recommendations:** If any action should be taken, what is recommended. This might include an adjustment to the organisation's risk management procedures for example.

✔ **Whether the triggered event was previously identified as a risk (threat or opportunity):** You may have noticed that the last few entries overlap with the area covered by risk management, but of course there can be lessons out of that too.

If you have a permanent Project Office, that's often a great place to keep Lessons Reports so that Project Office staff can tell Project Managers about relevant reports from previous projects. Or you may put the Lessons Report on a network directory. You may find it worthwhile to index these reports, or split up the recommendations so that you can search for individual items (such as all comments about Issue handling across all projects) as well as retrieve a whole Lessons Learned Report for a particular project. Again, Project Office staff can help you.

Recommending Closure

The last activity is very simple and that is to gather up the end project documentation and put it to the Project Board with the recommendation that the project be shut down. You will find the other end of this activity in the Chapter on the Project Board, Chapter 10, with the corresponding activity of 'Confirming project closure'.

You may need to warn people that the project is closing though, and then there is also a bit of tidying up to do.

Closing down the logs and registers

As part of the end project work, you close down the logs and registers. If any further action is needed on any items in the logs, you will have created Follow-on Action Recommendations.

Storing the project records

Clearly, where you have physical documents, you don't normally want to store stuff that was just working documentation and that you don't need in the operational life of products. But be careful not to overdo the weeding. You need to think carefully whether documents may be helpful for maintenance. You also need to consider whether you may need certain documents if anyone has to check back on the project as a final audit to make sure things were done properly. But even with physical documents, you can always scan them and store them electronically if you're in any doubt.

A problem with storing computer files over a long period of time is that, while the data records remain intact, sometimes the software and even computers and operating systems you need in order to read the files disappear. The BBC had a project many years ago to store information about what life was like in Britain at that time. All the computer data files are intact, but the BBC has had to ask whether anyone still has the type of old computers it used and the original software it needs to read that data. Those involved with archiving information have now realised that an excellent storage medium is . . . wait for it . . . paper. If something is on paper, you can scan it into new software and make a new electronic record.

So you need to think not only about *what* you need to store, but *how* you store it. How can you retrieve it? Storing something is pointless if you can't find the information you need because it's buried in a mass of redundant stuff. You can consider, for example, putting key information in one set of directories, and the larger mass of stuff that you probably won't need again in others.

 Some years after a motorway was built and opened, problems developed. Cracks appeared in some sections of the support structure, and although traffic volumes were greater than originally predicted, they were still well within the ultimate load capacity. The designs and records for the project were still stored in an old aircraft hangar and maintenance staff were able to consult the records to help establish the cause of the problem.

Checking out the CP products

You use a lot of products when closing a project, but some you only use for reference. As always, keep things as simple as you can. Don't start creating documents, or even filling in sections, where you just don't need to.

- ✔ **Benefits Review Plan:** To check what benefits need to be measured at the end of the project and to be sure actions are in place to measure benefits coming on stream later.

- ✔ **Daily Log:** Closed.

- ✔ **End Project Report:** This is the Project Manager's account of the project, including final costs and times, and achievement of project objectives as set down in the original Project Initiation Document (PID).

- ✔ **Configuration Item Records:** You check these version control records to make sure that all products have a status of 'complete' –

in other words, are you sure that the project is finished? The result of the review, often done by Project Support, goes on a Product Status Account – see below.

- ✔ **Follow-on Action Recommendations:** You recommend things for the organisation to do after the end of the project, such as the version control that needs to continue into the working life of products.

- ✔ **Issue Register:** This is closed, but you may carry some entries forward into Follow-on Action Recommendations (for example, a really good idea from a team member that the project didn't have the time or resource to implement).

- ✔ **Lessons Log:** You close this down after final entries and turn the content into a Lessons Report.

(continued)

(continued)

✔ **Lessons Report:** You develop this from the Lessons Learned Log and file it somewhere in the organisation so that future project staff can easily access it.

✔ **Product Status Account:** A report showing the status of all products in the last stage, or perhaps the whole project, to confirm that everything is done. In the case of a premature close of the project, it's used to establish just what has been completed and what hasn't.

✔ **Project Plan:** You complete this with 'actuals' of the final time and cost and delivery dates of the final products in the project going onto the Product Checklist. You'll also check on the acceptance criteria for the whole project using the Project Product Description which forms part of the Project Plan.

✔ **Project Initiation Documentation (PID):** You may check the original PID to help determine if the project has met its objectives. You need this for the End Project Report. You also use it to check the strategies and controls when commenting on how effective they've proved when you're producing the End Project Report.

✔ **Quality Register:** Closed.

✔ **Risk Register:** This is closed, but you notify any risks continuing into the working life of products as Follow-on Action Recommendations.

Chapter 10

Running Effective Project Boards

In This Chapter

▶ Understanding the vital responsibilities of the Project Board

▶ Knowing the key points of involvement and decision making for the board

▶ Avoiding common pitfalls

This chapter covers a vital subject, but one that organisations using PRINCE2 generally neglect: the effectiveness of the Project Board in controlling a PRINCE2 project. The *Project Board* is the group of managers who have overall responsibility for the project – a bit like the top management team of a department – and together they are the Project Manager's boss. (To see the overall management structure in which the Project Board roles fit, please see Chapter 12.)

This chapter shows how to avoid the pitfalls so common to Project Boards and, if you're a member of a board yourself, how you can be really effective in your role. Far too many Project Boards think that they can delegate responsibility for the project to the Project Manager and come back at the end to see whether everything is okay and, if so, take all the credit. If you're a Project Board member for a PRINCE2 project and your project fails through poor control and poor management, guess who gets the blame.

Being part of the Project Board isn't all doom and gloom, though. The chapter includes a step-by-step guide and real help on the key decision points and other times when the project actively involves the Project Board.

Introducing the Process Directing a Project

The work of the Project Board is covered by the process Directing a Project. If you're new to PRINCE2, have a quick look at the model in Figure 10-1 now, but come back to it again when you've read the chapter and it'll all make sense. Don't get hung up on the activities because this is all much simpler than it looks at first.

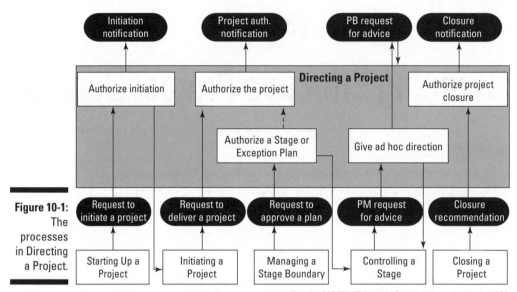

Figure 10-1:
The processes in Directing a Project.

One of the activities in the diagram is a bit different from the rest. That is the 'Give ad hoc direction' activity which, according to the PRINCE2 manual, goes on continually through the development stages of the project. This gives the Project Manager advice and input but in fact it also has to happen during the Initiation, or planning, Stage and also through the work of 'Managing a Stage Boundary' where the Project Manager is preparing for a further project stage.

Understanding Five Key Responsibilities for the Project Board

Many managers think that implementing PRINCE2 in an organisation is about training their Project Managers in the method. Unfortunately, implementation isn't that localised and involves others too, and the most significant of these are the Project Board members.

To have only the Project Manager functioning properly is an approach that I call 'PRINCE2 with a limp'. To have the method working well and stepping out strongly, the minimum is for the Project Manager and the Project Board to understand the method properly and then use it intelligently.

The principles for setting up and running an effective Project Board are not actually that difficult. They're very much the same as for organisational management. Remember that you can think of the project as a temporary department, and the Project Board as the group of senior managers in charge of that department.

The most important thing to remember is that as a Project Board member, you're responsible for the project and for ensuring that it runs correctly.

Taking ownership of the project

The project doesn't belong to the Project Manager, it belongs to the Project Board.

Taking the analogy of the department in an organisation again, the effective and correct functioning of that department is the responsibility of its senior managers and the head of department, not some operational manager further down the management chain. If the top management of the department decided to go on holiday for a year and just check back at the end to see how things went in that 12 months, they'd be sacked for failing to do their job.

Managing, not working

A board member's involvement in the project is to help manage it. Like any senior management function, board members must resist the very strong temptation to start getting involved in 'doing'. Things get a bit busy at certain points in the project with regard to advising and managing, but if you're a board member you're not involved with designing the system, or building the walls, or even specifying the requirements. Rather, your responsibility as part of the project management is to make sure that the project runs properly and delivers what's required of it.

If one or more board members need to get involved with the project activity as well, that's still not part of their Project Board work. They simply have two roles on the project – board member and also team member.

Getting sufficient authority

Project Board members need not be senior in the organisation, but they're senior relative to the project. If responsibility for the project has been delegated to you by someone more senior in the organisation, make sure that they've also delegated the necessary authority. Project Boards must have sufficient authority to make decisions about the project. You're ineffective if you have responsibility but no authority.

Ideas for keeping board membership down

You can agree that a board must be small, but things can be a bit different when you face people who really think they should be on the board and who may be quite senior and influential. Here are four ideas for keeping people off the board:

✔ **Focusing on roles:** If someone says that she needs to be on the Project Board, ask her which role she thinks she should fill. Often, she replies that she doesn't fit any of the roles, and that helps show that she doesn't need to be there.

✔ **Dealing with a lot of user interests:** Have a user committee or user forum, the chairperson of which sits on the Project Board to represent the user viewpoint.

✔ **Dealing with a large number of suppliers:** Appoint a lead supplier who sits on the Project Board to represent the supplier

viewpoint. This lead supplier can check things out with the others involved and get agreement on matters such as resource availability.

✔ **Identifying communications needs as opposed to control needs:** Often, Project Boards fill up because lots of people say that they need to be on the board so that they know what's going on. What they're expressing, when you think about it, is a communications need – 'I need to know what's going on' – rather than a management need. You can think about addressing that genuine need in other ways, such as a project news sheet, regular short lunchtime briefings, or a project website. You set down this communication requirement in the Communication Management Strategy, which is part of the PID (for more on these documents, please see Chapter 5).

Checking availability

The person with the ultimate authority in most organisations is the CEO (Chief Executive Officer) or general manager. But does that mean that she should be in charge of every Project Board for every project in the organisation? Clearly not. Actually, the CEO is unlikely to be suitable to serve on any board at all – not because of a lack of competence (well, not in all of them anyway) but more because of a lack of availability. If I need to see the CEO of a multinational for just two hours sometime today because something just happened on my project, what are my chances? Somewhere less than zero.

In the same way that managers in a department must make themselves available to their staff, so too must Project Board members be available to the Project Manager, and sometimes at short notice.

 A public body set up a 14-member board with very senior staff. When challenged over the number of people involved, the most senior person insisted that a board of that size was necessary. When asked about their personal availability to take part in a further discussion lasting two hours or so, the board members weren't able to make any more time available for about four weeks and even then not all the 14 could attend. In admitting this, they demonstrated that the composition of the board wasn't going to work in this project, which was high-profile and fairly fast moving.

Appointing small boards

In PRINCE2, small is beautiful when it comes to Project Boards. The ideal number is around three people, but you can have fewer. The minimum is actually one person who covers all three roles – Executive, Senior User, and Senior Supplier (see 'Taking Individual Responsibility', later in this chapter, for more on these roles). But a good maximum is about six, no matter how big the project is. Big Project Boards just don't work and actually rarely meet because somebody's almost always missing.

If you have a project where most of the work is being done by an outside supplier company, the minimum Project Board number is two because you need a manager from the customer side of the project and also one from the supplier who can authorise the team resource.

Taking Individual Responsibility

The Project Board consists of three roles, reflecting the three key viewpoints in PRINCE2 of business, user, and supplier. Chapter 12 explains the roles fully and they are covered here only briefly to put the specific duties in context.

Business viewpoint – the Executive

The role of Executive covers the business viewpoint. Although the project is the responsibility of the whole board, ultimately the responsibility lies with the Executive and this person is in charge. This role cannot be shared, so although the person who is the Executive can also have another Project Board role, two people can't be the Executive. The Executive must also be a person. I'm not discriminating against extra-terrestrial or robotic executives (though seeing some managers you may think . . . no, let's not go there), but rather saying that the Executive can't be a committee or an organisation.

The Executive either does the Business Assurance for the project or delegates the task to one or more people who then report back. Business Assurance is part of Project Assurance and, put simply, is project auditing to check that the project is running properly. Please see Chapter 12 for more detail.

Although the Executive can delegate the activity of this audit function, she can't delegate responsibility for the proper running of the project. This is like financial audit: If something is wrong, you don't blame the auditors.

User viewpoint – the Senior User (s)

The role of Senior User represents the user viewpoint. The Senior User is someone who represents those who'll use whatever the project delivers and who also specifies the business benefits that will result from doing the project. Unlike the Executive, this role can be shared and you can have more than one Senior User to cover different areas, such as departments.

The Senior User(s) either does the User Assurance for the project or delegates it. Again, User Assurance is part of Project Assurance, the project auditing.

Supplier viewpoint – the Senior Supplier (s)

The Senior Supplier represents the supplier viewpoint on the project. This is a manager who has control over supplier staff – the teams doing most of the actual project work. As with the Senior User, you can have more than one Senior Supplier. A common reason for multiple Senior Users is where you have organisational staff working on the project alongside project teams from an outside company. You may then have one Senior Supplier from your own organisation with authority over your staff, and another from the outside company who has authority to commit that company's staff to the project.

The Senior Supplier is responsible for Supplier Assurance for the project or can delegate the activity to others who report back. If you do have more than one Senior Supplier and one is from outside the customer organisation, you need to make sure that the assurance standards are consistent. Normally they follow the standards in the customer organisation.

Taking Joint Responsibility

Together the members of the Project Board are responsible for the project and take management oversight of it. They are part of the PRINCE2 Project Management Team. So, although 'senior', the board members are part of the team and must co-operate with and support the Project Manager and Team Managers.

The Project Board are on the same side as the Project Manager and the Team Managers. This is true even if the Team Managers are from an outside company. Remember, if the Project Manager and Team Managers do well, you, as a Project Board member, do well. If they do badly, you do badly as well because the project suffers.

Making decisions without stepping over the line

As a Project Board member you mustn't be afraid to make decisions. That's largely what you're on the board for. But in PRINCE2, as in general management, decision-making authority is set at different levels. The board must decide how much authority they give to the Project Manager. Although the Project Board do need to supervise the Project Manager, board members need to be careful not to interfere unless they have very good cause, such as following up a Project Assurance concern. To do otherwise undermines the Project Manager.

Jerry Madden at NASA produced '100 rules for NASA Project Managers'. Rule number 3 is: 'Management principles are still the same. It is just that the tools have changed. You still find the right people to do the work and get out of the way so they can do it.'

Responsibilities of the Project Board

These are the joint responsibilities of the Project Board members working together:

✔ Making key project decisions, such as whether or not to start the project.

✔ Deciding on key controls, such as the number of project stages.

✔ Approving plans at project and then at individual stage level.

✔ Deciding on the acceptable level of risk and on its management.

✔ Making sure that the resources are sufficient for the job.

✔ Giving authority to start successive stages.

✔ Assisting with problem solving when necessary.

✔ Checking that the project is running properly (Project Assurance).

✔ Monitoring progress and expenditure.

✔ Checking that the required quality level is delivered.

✔ Making decisions on matters that the Project Manager refers (for example, when the decision is beyond the Project Manager's delegated authority).

Listening to the Project Manager

The Project Manager attends the meetings of the Project Board, but isn't a member. The Project Manager can't have a role on the board, because if she does, she becomes accountable to herself, which rather defeats the object. Often, the Project Manager can advise and suggest action though, such as on a sensible number of stages when planning the project, or the action to take to overcome a particular problem. Board members need to listen carefully to the Project Manager's views, although they're not bound to follow them.

Deciding the Level of Control

The degree of control is a very personal decision. Just like in general management, as a board member you decide how much you want to supervise those working for you and what degree of autonomy you give them. Obviously, the more you supervise, the finer the degree of control you have, but also the greater the cost in everyone's time. Also, if you supervise experienced staff too closely and too frequently, you're likely to demotivate them – in the same way you get fed up if your boss checks up on you excessively and without reason. 'Control freak' managers don't usually have happy, productive staff.

Setting Project Manager authority levels

PRINCE2 uses three helpful mechanisms when setting Project Manager authority levels:

- ✔ **Exception Management:** Here the board can set upper and lower limits for the Project Manager's authority. If the Project Manager projects that a stage will exceed a 'tolerance', then she must report that to the board immediately. The two most common tolerances are on time and cost, but the board can also decide to set additional limits on any or all of risk, business benefits, scope, and quality. For full detail on Exception Management and tolerances see Chapter 17, which covers the Progress theme.

- ✔ **Change Budget:** The budget for each of the project stages is for what you plan to do. But what if someone wants a change? Unless the board want the Project Manager to come back to them at frequent intervals to get authority to do minor changes, allocating a Change Budget makes sense. The Change Budget can have two dimensions: a total Change Budget, but then with no one change being more than a set amount. A mid point is to set up a Change Authority between the Project Board and the Project Manager with an intermediate level of authority. Chapter 16 covers the Change theme including the handling of budget.

> ✓ **Risk Budget:** This is an authorised budget set against each risk where a valid action requires funding. If the risk occurs, the board has already authorised the Project Manager to spend the associated contingency money without the need for further approval. This risk management mechanism is set out in more detail in Chapter 14.

These three points don't cover everything and the board members need to talk through the specifics of project authority with the Project Manager.

PRINCE2 uses an Exception Management approach during each stage. This is a technique adapted from the world of finance. In financial control a budget profile is set at the beginning of a financial year. As the year progresses, as long as the spending or earning pretty much follows the profile, no one is particularly interested in it right up to the end of the financial year. However, if a budget bucks the trend in either direction, finance staff immediately start investigating to see why it isn't behaving as predicted. In the same way, if a stage is going to plan you have little to talk about. The Project Manager calls in the board only if she projects that the stage will go off the plan by more than the amount the board specified with the tolerances.

The traditional 'monthly progress meeting' doesn't exist in PRINCE2 and is unnecessary if the stage is going to plan. Instead, as a Project Board member, you'll receive regular Highlight Reports that advise on progress and things you should know about (see 'Determining highlight reporting', later in this chapter).

You may need to explore other authority limits in addition. For example, as a Project Board member you may be entirely happy for your Project Manager to go ahead with any change up to the Change Budget limit in each stage. But you may not want to give the Project Manager authority to commit your multinational company to a procedural change that affects operations world-wide, no matter how cheap it is.

Deciding on the management stages

In PRINCE2 the project stages are management stages and not technical stages. The board may be happy to authorise work on several technical stages that can be done in one block before another Project Board meeting takes place. You may have any number of management stages in a project, and the board members must consider a whole set of factors when deciding how much control to exercise and so how many stages they require.

Overall then, choosing how many management stages to have is a balance between control and cost. The more stages, the more control points but the higher the cost. Meetings can be expensive, but then producing Stage Plans involves a lot of work – so just how many stages do you want?

Factors for deciding stages

No calculation or algorithm can be formulated for determining how many stages you need for a particular type of project. Instead, the Project Board decides how many stages to have based on quite a large number of factors for each specific project:

✔ **Sensible units of work:** These are cohesive product sets. Sometimes where the stage boundaries go is just plain obvious in the context of the overall number of stages that the board think is appropriate.

✔ **Major deliverables:** If an important deliverable is required at a particular point in the project, that's often a good time to have a stage boundary so as to take stock and check that everything is okay.

✔ **Cost (1):** Although the board – usually the Executive – earmark all the money for the project, it specifically authorises the cash only one stage at a time. On a £25 million project, the board may decide not to authorise more than £4 million at a time. So if a stage costs £6 million, the board may require this work to be broken up into two management stages.

✔ **Cost (2):** A stage boundary should usually come just before, and not just after, a major spend such as on equipment. If the board meet at the end of a stage and decide not to go on with the project, the recent purchase of a large amount of equipment is probably a waste. Having a stage boundary just before that investment normally makes more sense. If the board decide that the project will continue, the next stage starts and the equipment can be bought.

✔ **Time:** Time is usually important. The stages are of different lengths depending on the work, but the board may specify a maximum on time so that its members never go more than, say, four months without a meeting.

✔ **Key decision points:** The time when an important decision needs to be made is often a good stage boundary, even though the Project Board may not be involved with that decision. Acceptance of a specification is an example. This often fits in with delivering cohesive sets of products. Although the focus here is on management stages and not technical stages, products can be of a different nature after a decision point. For example, in the case of the specification, you may start building major products after approval, whereas before you worked largely with documents.

✔ **Risk:** In a high-risk project the board generally want more stages than in a low-risk project.

✔ **Complexity:** This relates to risk. In a very complex project, the board usually want more stages and so a greater degree of control.

✔ **Business events:** Having a stage boundary to coincide with the end of a financial year, or just after a major strategy review, may be a good idea in case any implications require changes to the project.

✔ **The Project Manager:** Yes, the choice of Project Manager affects the number of stages and this relates to risk. If the Project Manager is very experienced, the board may be happy to authorise fairly large blocks of work and have few stages. On exactly the same project but with a different and inexperienced Project Manager, the board may want more stages, more control points, and to commit less money at a time.

One company issues all its senior managers with swipe cards, and outside every meeting room is a swipe card reader. When the managers go into a meeting room they swipe their cards through the reader. The reader is connected to a PC, which in turn interfaces with the payroll system to pick up each manager's hourly rate. At the front of every meeting room is an electronic display, and every 15 minutes it flashes up what that meeting has cost so far. Awesome. Whoever thought of that deserves fame and fortune.

Fixing the level of risk acceptance

In line with the Project Board owning the project, the board fix the level of acceptable risk. Again, there's no algorithm to help you with this and the level of acceptable risk depends on how 'gung-ho' the board are. If the board members all do parachuting and snowboarding in their spare time, they may be happy to accept a high threshold of risk with little control action. If they're very cautious members who think that going for a walk in the park is high adventure, then the threshold is low and they're willing to authorise, and pay for, a lot of action to control the risks. And 'pay for' is significant, because it indicates that the decision here is often a business one and so rests primarily with the Executive, though the whole Project Board have a say.

Determining highlight reporting

Under the Exception Management principle, the Project Board doesn't meet during a stage but only at the end of it. But PRINCE2 has a regular progress report, which the Project Manager produces, that keeps the board up to date during each stage – the Highlight Report. Chapter 7 covers this in more detail, but briefly it normally includes:

- ✔ **The position on delivery:** The report shows what products have been produced and what remains to be built in this stage. These are the powerful milestones in PRINCE2 that give superb progress visibility.

- ✔ **The position on schedule:** Often presented as a Gantt chart, this shows where the stage is in relation to time.

- ✔ **The position in relation to tolerance:** For example, the report may show that the stage is 1 per cent over cost but 7 per cent ahead on time, but within the plus or minus 10 per cent that the board set.

- ✔ **Any Project Issues:** These are things like problems, changes, and new risks, that the Project Manager wants the board to know about.

A Highlight Report is basically very simple, but highly effective. The Project Manager may be able to prepare one in an hour or so. Board members need to beware of requiring reports that are too complicated and therefore time-consuming and expensive: the board may never read the reports because of their complexity.

The Project Board must specify the content required in the Highlight Report, and also the reporting frequency through the project. This is recorded in the Communication Management Strategy, which forms part of the PID. (For more on these documents, see Chapter 5.)

Sorting out project and quality assurance

PRINCE2 identifies two levels of checking or auditing of the project to make sure that it runs well: Project Assurance and Quality Assurance.

Project Assurance

Project Assurance is the responsibility of Project Board members under their three key interest areas of business, user, and supplier (see 'Taking Individual Responsibility, earlier in this chapter) to make sure that the project is running properly. But board members can delegate the actual checking to other people if they want. This may be because board members are too busy to do the detailed work, or because they don't have those sorts of skills.

If the Project Board delegates Project Assurance activity, the board members must then make time available to work with assurance staff to explain what they must check, and then to receive and discuss the reports.

Project Assurance must be positive and as such welcomed by the Project Manager. In turn, board members must delegate to people who are positive and helpful rather than obstructive and fault-finding. But the other side to this is that if the Project Manager is hiding things from the board, then the board will get to know. Assurance is independent of the Project Manager and the people carrying out the assurance work aren't scared of reporting things as they find them.

Quality Assurance

Quality Assurance, as set down in the 2009 edition of the PRINCE2 manual, is the checking of the project from outside. Senior managers in the organisation may require that all projects are checked over, and that includes keeping an eye on the management activity of Project Board members. Although the idea of Quality Assurance is a check initiated from outside the project, Project Boards can find this really helpful as an independent view. The people involved in the check aren't involved with the management of the project and so are likely to see things more clearly. For that reason, Project Boards have an option to ask for Quality Assurance checks, not just wait for them to be imposed.

Sidestepping some other Project Board pitfalls

Some problems, such as big Project Boards, are covered earlier in this chapter. But here are a few more in this problem-rich environment:

✔ **Dominance of one interest:** Although on a Project Board the Executive can't be out-voted by other board members, sheer weight of numbers of a particular viewpoint on the board can give rise to an excessive influence. Be careful to restrict the total number on the board, but then also to balance the user and supplier interests within that.

✔ **'We have to have our monthly progress meeting':** Think hard about this because they can often be a waste of time. Trust the Exception Management process. In fact, doing so puts the board members in a fairly comfortable position. In PRINCE2 a good set of plans will have been drawn up and you have regular progress reporting with the Highlight Report (see 'Determining highlight reporting', earlier in this chapter). Then the amazingly powerful Product Checklist (see Chapter 14) shows delivery milestones and says exactly where the stage is. The board knows it'll be told immediately of an Exception and progress reporting has the safety net of Project Assurance, which checks to ensure that the information is accurate.

✔ **Accountability loops:** When someone with a role on the Project Board has a second role of team member, this creates a loop where the Project Manager is accountable to this person in his role as board member, but the person is accountable to the Project Manager in his role as team member. This may not be a problem if the person involved can wear just one hat at a time. But if this situation may cause problems, give the board role to someone different.

✔ **Neglecting a role:** If you're a board member and have two roles, such as Executive and Senior User, you're likely to neglect one role. In this example, the Executive role is often what suffers. You tend to say what you want (user) and forget to check whether the suggestion is worth the effort or not (business). Just being aware of this problem is most of the solution and you can be careful to think systematically from both viewpoints.

✔ **Doing the project in the Project Board meetings:** Boards don't exist to do the project; boards are a management function that makes sure that the project is done. The Executive needs to brief other board members carefully to make sure that they understand this at the outset. Doing project work, such as specifying user requirements, at Project Board meetings is inappropriate, expensive, and extremely inefficient.

Giving Advice When Asked

Using Exception Management significantly reduces the need for Project Board involvement in the main part of each stage. However, as a Project Board member, you must be available to discuss things informally with the Project Manager when she needs advice or a steer. This includes times when the Project Manager actually has the authority to make the decision but still wants to run it past the boss first. Two examples are:

  ✔ A control decision is needed to adjust the stage and although the Project Manager is still safely within the tolerance limits, she nevertheless wants to talk it through with the Executive before making a call.

  ✔ A change has been asked for by a member of the user staff. The Project Manager has the change budget to deal with it but would like to know the Senior User's view before making a decision on whether or not to go ahead.

Getting Involved at Specific Points

Being available to give advice is something that's ongoing throughout the project. But beyond that involvement, the Project Board has four very specific decision points, detailed in Figure 10-2. One, the decision about whether or not to authorise the next project stage, repeats for however many stages are involved in the project.

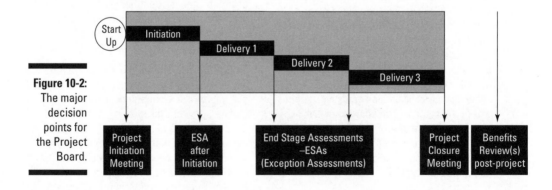

Figure 10-2:
The major decision points for the Project Board.

Starting up

The Executive is always appointed during Start Up, and the Project Board usually is too. The Executive has to establish the Business Case and develop the Project Brief – the outline of the project idea. The Project Manager and others may do much to help with both of these. The Senior User is particularly responsible for specifying business benefits that will result from running the project, and actually for delivering those benefits afterwards. But if it's not clear in Start Up who should be the Senior User, then benefits may be set down by the Executive and current Project Manager, and confirmed later by the Senior User when the appointment is made.

Then the board, and particularly the Senior Supplier, need to work with the Project Manager to identify anything that affects how the project is planned and run, and what the project delivers. This is known as the Project Approach. For example, there may be a constraint on the make of equipment used and on which staff are used and when. A constraint affecting the outcome or the solution (if yours is that sort of project) may be to limit the options for an office move. It may have to be a move out of a city location to where building costs are lower, for example.

> **Project Board decision point – at the end of Start Up:** At the end of Start Up, the board need to make the decision as to whether or not the idea looks good enough to take things forward, start the project, and run the planning or Initiation Stage. In making a decision to go forward and start the project, the board only commits to this first planning stage and not yet to the whole project.

Initiating the project

The Initiation Stage is the first stage of a PRINCE2 project and only covers project planning. No specialist work at all is done in this stage. Instead, the Project Manager works with the Project Board and others to develop the PID. For more on Project Initiation and the PID, please see Chapter 5 and please do look at that because as a board member you need to be very familiar with the PID; the whole of your project is based on it.

As a Project Board member, when you sign the PID you're responsible for it. Don't think it's the Project Manager's document, even though she may have done most of the work to write it. So be sure that you understand all of it and you agree all of it. No 'executive summaries' in the PID!

If, as a Project Board member, you say you haven't got time to go through all of the PID before you sign, you're really saying you shouldn't be on the board for this project. If you find that hard to accept, just go back to the analogy of the project being like a temporary department. Would it be acceptable for one of the top management team of the department not to have time to read the department's annual strategy and objectives document?

Although the process diagrams in the PRINCE2 manual can give the impression that the Project Manager goes away to write the PID and just brings it back to the board for approval, that's very far from the truth – as the text of the manual points out. Project Board members must be available to the Project Manager during Initiation, because they have a lot to discuss, a lot of decisions to make, and a lot of input to provide on the different management aspects of the project. Just some of the areas where board members must give input and make decisions are:

- How many stages do we need?
- How frequently do we want to see Highlight Reports, what information should be in them and how should they be presented?
- What staff resource is available and when?
- What should be the exact scope of the project be, and if there's pressure on time and/or resource and/or quality, what are the essentials and what can be left out?
- What is the trade-off between resource levels and delivery date?
- What degree of risk is acceptable, and what risk actions will we authorise?
- What level of quality do we require, and how much can we afford?
- What involvement does the user side require in testing project deliverables?
- Must the Project Manager always refer any changes to the board or a Change Authority, no matter how low the cost, or shall we authorise a change budget? Do we want to appoint a Change Authority?

The Project Manager will assemble all the Project Plans in the PID and as a board member you need to be sure that you're familiar with the whole document and agree with it. The PID is hugely important because it defines what the project is and exactly how it will be controlled. Nothing in the document must come as a surprise when you give it a final review before making a decision on whether or not to approve it and commit to the project. Accompanying the PID is also the plan for the first delivery stage (the stage after the Initiation Stage), so that if you decide to go ahead, the project can continue without delay.

Project Board decision point – at the end of Initiation: At the end of the Initiation stage, the board decide whether or not to commit to the whole project and specifically to authorise the first delivery stage.

The board may stop the project before the end if circumstances change, but the intention now is to run the project through to the end.

Getting involved during a delivery stage

As a Project Board member, you may get involved from time to time during the delivery stages. However, because of Exception Management this isn't usually a big time commitment – PRINCE2 actually saves managers a lot of time. During a stage, you may get involved to give what the method calls 'ad-hoc direction'; in other words, one-off advice to deal with something specific. Ad hoc direction includes:

✔ Receiving Highlight Reports and noting progress

✔ Having an informal discussion with the Project Manager if she asks for your view on something

✔ Doing Project Assurance work or receiving reports from whoever you delegated that work to

✔ Dealing with things referred to you by the Project Manager because they're beyond her delegated authority. This includes deciding how to deal with an exception if the Project Manager gives an Exception Report

Project Board decision point – when it receives an Exception Report: You may be able to resolve the exception easily and the Project Manager can then simply carry on. Perhaps the cost of a piece of equipment rose unexpectedly. The board may simply decide to authorise the extra funds and the Project Manager makes a note of that authority and carries on.

Sometimes, however, you need much more work to deal with the exception, to the point that the rest of the stage has to be completely re-planned. In that case things are more serious and an additional stage boundary is forced. Clearly, re-planning the work done to this point in the stage is pointless, so you shut that down as if it's the end of the stage. The remaining work is then re-planned by the Project Manager who brings this Exception Plan to a board meeting so that the board members can authorise it like any other stage-level plan.

 Exception Assessment. This is the meeting of the Project Board to consider an Exception Plan.

Project Board decision point – Exception Assessment: The board meet to approve the Exception Plan and, if it's okay, give authority to proceed with the rest of the stage on the basis of that plan. The board will usually agree to carry on because you can usually recover from a problem and you still need the project. If the situation was drastic enough to warrant stopping the project, then the board would probably have realised that when they received the Exception Report and called a halt then.

Ending a stage

At the end of a management stage, except for the last stage at the end of the project, the board meet to hear how the last stage went and to authorise the next one. The End Stage Assessment (ESA) is the name of the Project Board meeting on the stage boundary.

> ✔ **Project Board decision point – End Stage Assessment.**
>
> At the End Stage Assessment the board
>
> - Hears the Project Manager's account of the stage that just finished with the End Stage Report that covers the cost and time of that stage, how things went with risk management and quality, and any other factors, particularly if some may carry forward to the next stage.
>
> - Checks that the risk situation is still acceptable and that risk controls are appropriate for the present level of risk. The Project Manager has updated the Risk Log to show the very latest position.
>
> - Checks that the Business Case is still sound – that the project is still necessary and viable. The Project Manager will have updated the Business Case in consultation with the Executive.
>
> - Takes note of any early benefits reported from a benefits review, and checks to see that they're in line with what was anticipated. This is significant because if the predicted level of early benefits is not forthcoming, it may indicate that other benefits projections are over-optimistic and in turn that may call the project viability into question.
>
> - Ensures that the plan for the next stage is complete, workable, and achievable. Board members will normally have checked this out before the meeting or Project Assurance will have done this on their behalf.
>
> - Gives authority to proceed with the next stage or, if board members find that they can't sign up to the next stage despite having discussed it while the plan was being drawn up, they can order the project to be closed down instead.

Ending the project

Whether the project is closing down as planned or stopping early, the Project Manager goes through the closure activities (for more information on closure, please see Chapter 9). After that work has been done, the Project Manager comes to the Project Board for the board to authorise closure in a Project Closure Meeting or 'Close Out'.

The main things the Project Manager provides for the board are:

- ✔ An End Project Report.
- ✔ Details of acceptances and handovers.
- ✔ A Benefits Review plan for measuring benefits that will come on stream after the end of the project.
- ✔ Follow-on Action Recommendations – actions that the project is passing back into the organisation, such as ongoing risk management action.
- ✔ A Lessons Report (developed from the Lessons Log).

The End Project Report is the Project Manager's account of how things went on the project, including the final cost and time and delivery of quality. However, the Project Manager probably consulted Project Board members during this work, so as a board member you're probably already familiar with much of the content. You may need to pass the report on to others with an interest in the project, such as senior organisational managers.

Project Closure Notification. The method refers to a Project Closure Notification being prepared by the Project Manager, then sent by the board to others in the organisation to tell them the project is shutting down. But in practice relatively few business projects operate in such a formal environment, even very large organisations.

Measuring early benefits

If measuring any benefits is possible immediately at the end of the project, that will have been set down in the Benefits Review Plan produced for the PID. Any such measurements will have been made and the results set down in the End Project Report so that, as a Project Board member, you have an indication of whether the project was successful. You don't have to wait until Benefits Reviews that are after the project.

Post Project Benefits Review. A check at some point after the end of the project when benefits are clear and measurable. The review may be in the form of a meeting and there may be more than one if different benefits will come on stream at different times.

Checking acceptances and handovers

Acceptances, such as the legal acceptance of a new building from the company that built it, may have been obtained at different points in the project. At this stage you need a final check that the acceptances are all in place before the board authorise closure. This check is normally rapid, because the Project Manager has specifically checked these acceptances before getting as far as the Project Board and the closure meeting. Indeed, board members may already have checked acceptances themselves or asked any appointed Project Assurance staff to check on their behalf.

PRINCE2 doesn't cover benefits review after the project; it shuts down when the project shuts down. But the method includes planning for any such review(s), and the Project Board checks the Benefits Review Plan again before they finally close the project. This check is important because the board itself will be closing down and any further action on benefits measures will be passed to one or more staff in the organisation. Those organisational staff may well be same managers who were the Executive and Senior User in the project, but it could be others such as finance staff.

Follow-on Action Recommendations

Follow-on Action Recommendations are what the board recommend for the organisation to do after the project. The Project Manager assembles a list, but the board need to agree it. It can include things such as

- ✔ Good ideas put forward in the project as Project Issues, but which there was neither time nor budget to include in the project

- ✔ Ongoing controls, such as Configuration Management (version control) and Risk Management, which continue into the working life of products

- ✔ Recommendations for adjustments to organisational standards, such as project or risk management procedures, in the light of project experience

Checking out the products of Directing a Project

The PRINCE2 manual contains full details of the products that the Project Board use, but here's a quick reference of the main ones that you'll work with if you're a member of a Project Board.

At the end of Start Up

- ✔ **Project Brief:** This outlines the project idea, enough for you to decide whether planning it in more detail (the Initiation Stage) is worthwhile.

- ✔ **Initiation Stage Plan:** The plan for the Initiation or planning stage so that if you decide to go ahead with Initiation, the Project Manager can start the Initiation work without delay.

At the end of Initiation

- ✔ **Project Initiation Document (PID):** This comprehensive set of Project Plans (but perhaps short and simple nonetheless) defines the project and exactly how it will be controlled. The PID provides the information you use to decide whether or not to commit to running the whole project. The PID includes the Business Case, the Benefits Review Plan and four project strategies (risk, quality, communication and configuration management).

- ✔ **Stage 2 Plan:** This plan is for the first delivery stage, the one immediately following Initiation. If you decide to accept the PID and commit to the project, the Project Manager can start work on the first delivery stage immediately.

During a stage

✓ **Highlight Report:** The Project Manager sends this progress report to you on a regular basis and with the content and frequency that you asked for and which is recorded in the PID.

✓ **Exception Report:** In this report the Project Manager warns you that the stage is projected to exceed one of the *tolerances* (limits) that you specified. The report includes the Project Manager's recommendation on what to do. If the rest of the stage now needs re-planning, there'll now be a stage boundary with the remaining work in the stage being re-planned by the Project Manager using an Exception Plan and the work done so far in this stage shut down like a normal End Stage – you don't want the Project Manager to re-plan work that's already completed.

At End Stage

✓ **End Stage Report:** The Project Manager provides you with this report summing up the stage just finishing, including final costs, information about quality, and any ongoing problems.

✓ **Business Case (updated):** The Project Manager updates the Business Case as part of the End Stage work. You must check the Business Case to make sure that the project is still viable before authorising further work.

✓ **Risk Register (updated):** The Project Manager updates the Risk Log and you check that the level of risk is still acceptable and the risk management actions remain appropriate.

✓ **Next Stage Plan:** You review this plan for the next stage, and if you're happy with it you give authority to proceed with that next stage. If the stage boundary is part of the handling of an exception, you'll be looking at an Exception Plan instead (see next product).

✓ **Exception Plan:** You receive this instead of the Stage Plan if you're dealing with an Exception or large-scale change that means that the present Stage Plan can no longer be used and must be replaced. The Exception Plan covers the period from the point of the exception to the end of the stage.

At the end of the project

✓ **End Project Report:** The Project Manager reports to you on how the project went and provides information on things such as final cost and the level of any benefits that are already visible.

✓ **Benefits Review Plan:** This sets down who will measure benefits after the end of the project, how and when, and who reports back to corporate management. You make sure that you're happy with this before sending it on to the manager in the organisation who will take responsibility for it.

✓ **Lessons Report:** This report details what worked well on this project, what went wrong, and how future projects can benefit from the experience gained in this one. Again, you pass this back into the organisation, often to a Project Office, if you have one. If significant lessons have been learned during the project and it would be beneficial to report them immediately so other projects can make use of them, Lessons Reports can be submitted during the project as well.

Part III
Help with PRINCE2 Project Management

The 5th Wave   By Rich Tennant

'Before we start this project, I'd like to clarify what metaphors we'll be speaking in. Last time we used sports metaphors. How about using cooking metaphors? 'Half baked,' 'burnt,' 'simmering,' that sort of thing?'

In this part . . .

This part is about *what* you do in the project, which is different to the processes in Part II that are focused on *when* you do stuff. The things I cover in this section, such as risk management, are used throughout the project though some are used more heavily at some times than others.

PRINCE2 has some really helpful stuff here, but don't hesitate to add to it if you need a bit more to meet particular project needs. I also cover some techniques here, included in the relevant chapters. So, for example, you'll find the Quality Review Technique in Chapter 13 on quality management.

Chapter 11

Producing and Updating the Business Case

In This Chapter

▶ Justifying the project with the Business Case

▶ Driving PRINCE2 with the Business Case

▶ Identifying benefits and planning benefits reviews

▶ Making sure that the Business Case stays up to date

*P*rojects aren't about fun and the good of your health. They're usually about delivering business benefit. Projects *can* be fun and even healthy, but those aren't the drivers.

The Business Case is the main driver of PRINCE2 projects and just about everything else fits round it. The project has to be worth doing. The effort and cost you employ to do the project must result in something worthwhile. The media reports failed government projects (private companies often don't get found out) with headlines such as 'Government department spends £6 million in order to save £3 million'. In financial terms at least, clearly the project wasn't worth it; its Business Case wasn't valid.

The way that the PRINCE2 method builds in the creation and then update of the Business Case is neat and logical. If this isn't quite the same as the way your organisation deals with the Business Case then you have two options. Either change the way you use PRINCE2 so that the method does fit, or change the way your organisation works to reflect the underpinning logic of the PRINCE2 approach.

For most people, the Business Case that the method sets down is already a straightforward and sensible way to show that you can justify the project and, at the end, that the project did indeed deliver the goods. As with the rest of PRINCE2, the underlying ideas in this part of the method are simple enough.

Understanding Two Key Documents

Two key documents are concerned with the business perspective in PRINCE2. The first is the *Business Case* itself that records the justification for the project and which usually includes the benefits that result from the project. The second document is the *Benefits Review Plan*, which sets down when benefits will be measured, how and by whom. That measurement is often at the end of the project or after it, but in some cases benefits may come on stream earlier and start to be delivered during the project itself. This chapter deals with the Business Case first then, towards the end of the chapter, the Benefits Review Plan.

Knowing Who's Responsible for the Business Case

Most organisations are happy in the knowledge that the Business Case is the responsibility of the Project Manager. So here's the bad news (for those organisations, anyway): The Project Manager doesn't own the Business Case. She may do a lot of the work to construct the Business Case, but the responsibility lies with the Executive, the head of the Project Board who represents the business viewpoint on the project and, in the part concerning the identification and delivery of business benefits, the Senior User(s). These two board roles must make time available during Start Up, during Initiation and where necessary during stages and then at the end of stages, to get involved with the creation of the Business Case and the related plan for measuring benefits and then maintenance to keep them current.

Justifying the Project

The Business Case is pretty much about justifying the project. The focus in the PRINCE2 method is mostly on business benefits, but although that's sensible you need to take a wider view. In certain circumstances you can justify running a project that has no business benefits at all. The PRINCE2 manual, in its 2009 edition, has finally acknowledged clearly that a project need not be benefits driven. It lists five areas of business objectives and includes those where the justification may not be benefits focused in the sense of measurable financial benefits. The areas are compulsory projects, not-for-profit projects, evolving projects, customer/supplier projects and multi-organisation projects.

One justification that the manual still doesn't mention is 'enabling'. Sometimes the project won't deliver quantifiable business benefits itself, but it puts things in place that allow other projects to run and it's those other projects that will deliver benefits. An example is infrastructure projects.

People who like to argue that all projects must have business benefits may say that the infrastructure project is really just the front end of a much bigger project of which the later parts will deliver the benefits. But why have all the unnecessary complexity and risk involved in combining all of the projects into a single huge and unwieldy one just to avoid using a justification of 'enabling'? The infrastructure project may well be a self-contained, separately managed project, and all the better for that.

Compliance projects

Just to spell out the compliance justification a bit more, you may run a project because you've been told to. Things really can be that simple. As an example, think about legal requirements. Perhaps the government just announced that the tax rules are going to change . . . again. You need to run a project to amend your payment systems for your staff. This project doesn't save you money and you don't get better penetration into your market area; actually, you don't get any benefits at all. Well, don't run the project then. No, that's not an option because you have no choice; the tax change is a legal requirement and you must do it.

Again, some people who argue that every project must have business benefits would say that the business benefit here is that the Chief Executive Officer (CEO) or General Manager stays out of prison, but that's just silly, because this isn't a business benefit in the way we normally think about them. You're much better not to join in with such games and simply to state that the justification of the project is 'compliance'.

Benefits-driven projects

Most projects do indeed deliver business benefit. That's true even if the primary justification is something like 'compliance' – for more on this see the 'Hybrid justifications' section later in this chapter. Wherever possible you must be able to measure such benefits and the really bad news here is that you're probably going to have to think quite hard about them.

Some people say that if you can't measure something then it's not a benefit. But that narrow approach can be dangerous and lead to you missing out an important part of the project justification.

The following sections cover the three types of benefit that your project can bring to your organisation.

Direct savings

Some benefits result in a cash saving. You can see the money sitting in an account somewhere at the end of the project or soon after. One example is swapping a machine that has a high maintenance cost with a new one that has a low maintenance cost. When the new machine is installed, the leftover money remains in the maintenance budget. That money is measurable, visible, and real, and you can draw it out and hold it in your hand – if the finance director allows you to. Talking of finance directors, this sort of benefit is of great interest to them.

Quantifiable benefits

Quantifiable benefits are those where you can't draw out the money and hold it in your hand, but where the benefit is nevertheless measurable (ideally in monetary terms). The most obvious example is savings in staff time. For example, your organisation may be very concerned that your sales staff are having to spend too much time doing admin work and that this is reducing the time they have available to actually do the selling. Consequently a project is run to streamline the administration of the whole ordering system and one result is that it saves each salesperson an hour of admin work each day. That is a quantifiable benefit. You don't want to make any of the salespeople redundant; you're just pleased that they can spend more time selling, which is what you hired them to do. No direct saving is made, because the salary bill stays the same. But you can quantify the saving in hours, and you can also go on to state it in money terms by multiplying out the hours saved by the hourly pay rate of the sales staff. If you like, this is almost a measure of efficiency.

Non-quantifiable benefits

So now to the tricky one. Is something a benefit if you can't put a value on it? Well, yes. But here you need to be especially careful not to fool yourself. Claiming lots of wonderful benefits is easy if you can't measure them and no one can prove you wrong.

Suppose you work in a large organisation with a really old and dark reception area that's really off-putting to the many visitors to your HQ. The visitors get a poor impression of your company even before they talk to your receptionist, and a worse one still as they sit in a chair and look around while waiting for someone to come and meet them. This image may be very significant. If you run a project to refurbish the reception area to make it bright, pleasant, and welcoming, you drastically affect a visitor's first impression. How important is that impression and, if you do accept that it's important, how does the positive impression benefit the business?

This is an area where it's easy to bounce off at a superficial level and measure the wrong thing. For example, you may do a survey of customer impressions before and after. 'Good morning, can I ask you what you think of our dull and dark reception area; please give a number on a scale of 1 to 10. Minus 5? Okay. Now, after the refurbishment, what do you think? You score it a 10? Great.' The measurement shows that the new-look reception area positively impresses customers.

Your survey results may be good, albeit subjective, measurements, but they don't measure the business benefit. How does that customer impression translate into lost business or increased business? That's just about impossible to measure. Does that mean that you should leave the reception area cold, dark, and boring? No. You know that improving the area is worthwhile, but coming up with any meaningful measure of the business benefit is somewhere between hard and impossible. In such cases, instead of trying, you're usually better classifying the benefit as important but non-quantifiable.

Hybrid justifications

Just because a project is a compliance one or an enabling one doesn't mean that you don't get any business benefits at all. Some may well exist. Or you may say that as you have to do this project anyway you can adjust it a bit, perhaps by extending the scope, so that it does offer some business benefit. Although the benefits resulting from this adjustment may not cover all the project cost, it may offset at least part of the cost. In this case the Business Case may remain focused on a compliance element, which is the main justification, but then you go on to list what benefits the project delivers alongside that compliance.

Keeping It Current: A 'Living Document'

A UK Government report, the McCartney Report, made a really valuable point about project Business Cases.

> *The business case needs to be seen as a living document that will run for the lifetime of the project, not just as a mechanism to obtain funding. It is only by using the case as a tool for monitoring progress that it is possible to make sure the intended benefits of the project or programme are realised.*
>
> The McCartney Report
> – Successful IT: Modernising Government in Action

For many people, the Business Case is indeed something that you do at the beginning of a project in order to secure the funds and then forget about. The McCartney report stressed the importance of keeping the Business Case up to date – using the really neat term 'a living document' – because the projection of benefits dropping or increasing may change the view of the project. Simply put, if the project claims to save £2.5 million a year and costs just £1 million to run, everyone may agree immediately to running it on the grounds that it's justified on cost savings.

But suppose you find part way through the project that circumstances have changed and the project now costs £1.5 million and saves only £150,000 a year. If the main interest was savings, then almost certainly the correct decision is to stop the project. The up-to-date 'living' Business Case provides this essential ongoing management information.

The initial and usually very sketchy Business Case can be prepared even before PRINCE2 starts and in that case it comes into the method as part of the Project Mandate. The mandate is the 'trigger' that starts off Start Up. Often the organisation has some idea of why it wants to run a project and what the likely main benefits are. It may be wildly optimistic, but it's a start. If the Business Case isn't provided in the mandate, or it's included but not in enough detail even for the sketchy or *Outline Business Case* then you work on it during Start Up. Please turn to Chapter 4 for much more on Start Up.

The manual identifies four steps which cover the development of the Business Case, then keeping it up to date. These are:

1. **Develop:** Getting the information together in the first place.

2. **Verify:** Checking at intervals to ensure that the Business Case is still valid and the project is still justified.

3. **Maintain:** Keeping the Business Case up to date with the latest information, such as project costs and benefits projections.

4. **Confirm:** Checking that the benefits have been forthcoming or are likely to be.

Getting Help When It Gets Complicated

People often think that getting help is admitting weakness. Within reasonable limits, I consider asking for help as a sign of strength and professionalism. So when you develop a Business Case, don't hesitate to get help if things start to get complicated and you really need that help. Your organisation's finance people may be a good first port of call and you can think of them as part of the team. But you may need to call in bigger guns still if the Business Case is on a large scale, such as in some government projects that require large amounts of public funds.

One police force was developing a Business Case for building a new headquarters, complete with radio transmitters and a control room. The project required private-sector funding as a partnership project. The work to develop the Business Case was so substantial that the force decided to make it a project in its own right: The force created a project to develop a Business Case for the HQ project. The justification for the Business Case project?

I hope you got there before me – it was an enabling project. The project didn't deliver any business benefit itself, but put the information in place that secured the funding to allow the HQ project to proceed, and in turn that delivered substantial business benefit.

Principle 1 – Continued business justification.

A quick overview of Business Case development

Project Mandate

✔ The Mandate may include an Outline Business Case (a sketchy one) that the organisation previously worked on (perhaps in a feasibility study, for example).

Start Up

✔ The Outline Business Case is produced if it wasn't included in the Mandate, or checked and amended if it was.

First Project Board decision – end of Start Up

✔ At the end of Start Up the board must decide whether the project idea looks worthwhile and whether to authorise the Initiation Stage. The information in the Outline Business Case on ballpark costs, time, and benefits informs this decision.

Project Initiation

✔ In the first stage of the project, the planning or Initiation Stage, the Business Case is worked into full detail, with investment appraisal if required.

Second Project Board decision – end of Initiation Stage

✔ The full business case forms part of the Project Initiation Document (PID) which the Project Manager gives to the Project Board at the end of the Initiation Stage. The board must now decide if they want to accept the PID, including the Business Case within it, and commit to running the whole project. Please see Chapter 5 for more on the PID.

During stages

✔ During stages the Project Manager checks the Business Case to make sure that everything remains on track to deliver the expected levels of benefit. If some new information comes in, or something happens that affects the benefit levels, the Project Manager may need to warn the board immediately. This is part of the exception management control, which is covered in detail in Chapter 17 on the Progress theme.

At the end of each stage and third Project Board decision

Towards the end of each management stage the Project Manager works with the Executive, Senior User(s) and any others with an interest and updates the Business Case. This work involves making sure that the whole project is still viable as well as checking individual benefit projections. Then the Project Board decides whether or not to authorise the next stage. This End Stage work repeats for every stage in the project.

Dealing with Organisational Finance

Nearly every organisation is obsessed with controlling money. Finance people want to know exactly what everything will cost down to the last penny and they want to know that as soon as someone even breathes the word 'project'. Actually, this is more than illogical and not aligned with sensible business practice. How can you possibly say how much a project will cost, with absolute precision and to ten decimal places, when you're not even completely clear on what the project is yet?

PRINCE2 is much more sensible than that. When the idea is rough, so are the costings. As you do more work to plan the project out in Initiation, so you work through the costings in more detail and more accurately. What's the point of putting together an extremely detailed Business Case with detailed costings based on guesswork and ignorance? And worse, you and I know that once someone puts forward detailed stuff, changing it is very hard. Somehow the budget becomes set in concrete no matter how much anyone says that the costings are estimates and subject to change after the more detailed planning work.

Going with the organisational trend to provide detailed costings up front goes against the logic of PRINCE2. Instead of Start Up happening really quickly to sketch the project out, it becomes much more involved and everything begins to slow down. That's because when you try to work out detailed costings this early, you're doing Initiation-level work at Start Up. Do all you can to avoid getting bogged down in too much detail early on. Work hard to try to change any standard organisational approach that requires compiling detailed financial information in advance of the Initiation Stage of the project.

You normally run Start Up very rapidly in days or even hours, so make every effort to keep things that way. Don't try to do full project planning and get drawn into the detailed costings and calculations, which in turn require detailed plans to provide source data.

Many organisations have well-established formats for how you must present financial cases to decision makers, such as committees. In one sense those formats aren't a problem, but in another sense they can be because of overheads. Consider if you can combine the project needs (as represented by PRINCE2) with the organisational needs (as represented in the finance submission format). You may, for example, alter the content and layout of the Business Case so that you present the organisational items first, and the PRINCE2 elements that don't appear in the organisational format second – or even as an appendix. In this way you can have one document that covers both requirements and save on overheads.

As with the timings, though, if you think that the PRINCE2 content is well suited to the project and is better than the organisational format, then you may suggest change (shock, horror) to bring the organisational standard into line with the method.

Writing a Business Case

The method sets down some clear headings for what the Business Case includes in a PRINCE2 project. As always, you may want to adjust these headings to meet particular organisational or project needs.

The Business Case

Executive summary

Reasons

Business options

Expected benefits

Expected dis-benefits

Timescale

Costs

Investment appraisal

Major risks

Executive summary

The executive summary is both a summary and a commentary that explains the balance of the Business Case. For example, you may conclude that although the measurable benefits are limited, the non-quantifiable benefits are extremely important and that you can justify the project largely on these.

The executive summary is useful to inform those reading the Business Case of key points and the overall balance of the case. But the presence of an 'executive summary' is also dangerous in that it can give an impression to Project Board members that they just need to skim read this section and not bother with the others. That is not so and board members must not only read the whole Business Case, they have a fundamental responsibility to ensure that it's enough to justify the project.

Reasons

The reasons section says why you're running the project (or planning to). This is where you may say that the project is compliance justified, for example. You can also include some background; for example, the project may be the fourth in a series of five projects to upgrade production line machinery as set down in the corporate five-year plan.

Business options

The options give some further background information to set the project in context. Several things may have been possible to satisfy a business need, but here you explain why this one was selected for the project.

Beware of people and guidance – including the PRINCE2 manual – that say that 'doing nothing' is always an option. Sometimes doing nothing simply isn't an option, other than a very silly one. You have to do something. An example of this is an office move project where the lease on the current building is going to expire and you can't renew it, so you have to move. Saying that one option is to do nothing and wait to be killed by falling brickwork as the machinery moves in to demolish the building is nonsense and a waste of effort in a Business Case.

Expected benefits

Here you list the benefits you expect from the project together with the anticipated level of benefit. And you say how you plan to measure each benefit at the end of the project or, if you can't measure the benefit until some time after that, at a *Benefits Review* after the project. But remember that you may have some non-quantifiable benefits and by definition you can't measure these in a meaningful way.

Although the Project Manager probably does a lot of the work in writing the Business Case, and the Executive 'owns' it and must make sure that the project is value for money, benefits are the domain of the Senior User(s) on the Project Board. In PRINCE2 it's the Senior User role that must determine the likely benefit of the project, and then is responsible for delivering those benefits using the outputs of the project.

When setting down the benefits, it can be very helpful if you include an assessment of how reliable the benefits estimates are. The project may offer savings of £3 million and the Senior User and Project Manager are very sure of that; 99 per cent sure. Or it may offer savings of £5 million but you're only 50 per cent confident that this estimate is correct because, by their nature, these particular savings are hard to predict.

Expected dis-benefits

Dis-benefits are a negative outcome of the project. An example might be that a project that results in making processes more efficient means that some staff will be made redundant. That's a bad outcome for those staff in particular, but perhaps also for those remaining where well-established teams are broken up and there's likely to be a negative impact on morale, which may result in even more staff loss and also a drop in performance.

Don't confuse a dis-benefit with a statement of what will happen if the project doesn't go ahead. The dis-benefit is a disadvantage of running the project, in at least one person's eyes – not a statement of the negative consequences if you don't run the project.

Timescale

Timescale is second of two key factors that form the primary concern of many corporate managers. The first factor is cost, but if the cost doesn't sound too bad, their next question is almost always, 'When can we have it?' The timescale is likely to be a ballpark estimate in Start Up and gets more and more precise as you discover exactly what the project involves. As better and more precise information becomes available through the project, you update the 'timescale' section of the Business Case.

Costs

Like the timescale, the costs are a ballpark figure at Start Up that becomes more precise after you do project planning in the Initiation Stage, and then even more exact as you do more work in project stages and update the Business Case in the light of better and better information. With most projects, the time when you know exactly how much the project costs is when it has just finished, but sometimes not even then.

Investment appraisal

This section of the Business Case locks back into earlier sections of 'Expected benefits' and 'Costs', using techniques such as discounted cash flow (DCF), which show the benefits, costs, and future benefits at today's values. Check out the sidebar 'A bit more about discounted cash flow' for more on DCF.

Investment appraisal is about money – costs and benefits that you can quantify in financial terms. This may be only part of the story, because of non-quantifiable benefits and things such as the demand on scarce staff resources, which an appraisal just showing hourly rates doesn't adequately reflect. Although investment appraisal techniques are valuable, they're limited.

PRINCE2 doesn't cover investment appraisal techniques, but you can find plenty of information on the Internet or in techniques publications like Inspirandum's *Project Techniques Toolbox*.

Major risks

The risks section summarises all the risks in the project. Arguably, you may find it better to focus this section on summarising risks that may affect the Business Case, because from Start Up onwards every time you update the Business Case and present it to help with decision making you also update the Risk Register. But if the Business Case is to be circulated outside the project (perhaps to corporate managers) and without other project documentation such as the Risk Register then this section can be particularly helpful.

A bit more about discounted cash flow

For investment appraisal many people use techniques such as discounted cash flow (DCF, or 'net present value' – NPV – if you're into spreadsheets), return on investment (ROI), and internal rate of return (IRR), which is based on DCF. Have a search on the Internet to find out more about these if you need to or, better still for full detail, invest in a copy of *Understanding Business Accounting For Dummies* by Colin Barrow and John A. Tracy.

The concept of DCF can be a bit strange if you haven't come across it before, but actually the technique is very straightforward. Put simply, future money is not as valuable as today's money. For example, if (and please note the 'if') I offer to give you £5,000, would you like it today or in five years' time? You'd say 'today', partly because you're afraid that I may have changed my mind in five minutes' time let alone five years', but also because you know that the buying power of the £5,000 will be much less in five years' time. Even if you don't want to spend the cash straight away, you can put it in the bank and at least get some interest. DCF 'discounts' the value of future money and expresses it at today's values.

A £1 million benefit in five years' time may be worth only £800,000 at today's values. This is significant, because you incur costs on the project now, but often only get the benefits in the future. The further the benefit is into the future, the lower and lower its value, so the discount factor in the calculation increases year by year.

If I tell you that I'm going to spend £1 million on a project today and there aren't any savings for five years, but then I get a one-off benefit of £1.1 million, you may be tempted to think that the project pays for itself, though only just. Actually, as you've now seen, it doesn't even do that; it runs at a loss because of the lower value of future money.

If you have a pension plan, you're not too near pension age, and you can stand a shock, have a look at a personal finance software package. You can enter how much you have in your pension fund and what you pay in each month, and it then tells you how much money you'll have in the fund at your chosen retirement age. Wow! The sum looks fantastic and you dream of a life of ease in your old age as a multimillionaire as you see the huge total and the amount of money you'll receive each month in your retirement. Then you notice a click box at the bottom of the screen that says 'Would you like to see this at today's values?'. You click – oh, what a very different story. At this point people usually decide to increase their pension payments.

Setting down best case and worst case

Sometimes you just don't know exactly what the benefits may be because they depend on so many factors. In this situation you can put forward a best case, a worst case, and a most likely case. This is known as 'three point estimating'. Some prefer to use the average (the mean) rather than the most likely value (the mode) as the middle figure.

Being sensitive

One other approach PRINCE2 mentions is Sensitivity Analysis. Sensitivity Analysis refers to 'what if' scenarios and you may find it worth doing this for some of your projects. An example is with currency exchange rates. If project costs are being incurred in one currency and benefits realised in another, then exchange rates will affect the payback. You can perform 'what if' calculations to see how sensitive the costs and benefits are to exchange rate fluctuations and the point at which rate changes would start to impact on the project enough to make it non-viable.

Checking If a Benefit Really Is a Benefit

You have to be able to measure benefits, unless you've already identified them as non-quantifiable. At Benefit Reviews, you check the benefits to ensure that the project delivered what you expected, or more, or less. If the benefits are significantly more or less than target you also need to ask why.

A lot of misunderstanding surrounds identifying benefits and a quick look on the Internet reveals some quite strange Business Cases. I use a simple question to help check whether a benefit really is a benefit. If you can answer that question, the benefit is probably a good one; if you can't, it probably isn't. The question is simply: So what?

The new computer system will have an integrated database. So what? Well, it just will and that's good, isn't it, because all the best systems these days have integrated databases? This doesn't sound like a business benefit, at least not yet, because you have no proper answer to the question 'So what?'. This is actually a real example from a 'techie' Business Case. Business Cases written by technical specialists can sometimes focus on technical features rather than business benefits. These 'techie' Business Cases can be rather amusing sometimes, but I move on quickly in case you're a techie (not to be confused with Trekkie but, surprisingly often, people are both).

In saying that the integrated database is not a benefit, I slipped in the words 'at least not yet'. It could be that this is a benefit after all, but the author of the Business Case hasn't gone deep enough. If you tell me that because the database is integrated you input data only once, not five times into five separate systems, I may start to get interested. If you go on from that and say it saves 300 administrator hours per month at a particular hourly rate, then I may be even more impressed and say that you have indeed identified a benefit. The icing on the cake is when you then set down exactly how you can measure that benefit to demonstrate the saving at the end of the project. Now I'm positively drooling, particularly if I happen to be a corporate manager concerned about departmental efficiency and overheads.

Being Sure That You Can Deliver

If you're taking the Senior User role on the Project Board, when you claim that there'll be a particular benefit you need to be sure that you really can deliver it. If you can't be sure of delivery, then include very clear warnings to say *why* you may not be able to – in other words, spell out the risks.

One organisation moved its headquarters out of a city. Part of the Business Case was that the old HQ was in a prime location and would raise more money than the new, out-of-town HQ would cost. Tempting indeed, and common indeed. However, nobody wanted to buy the old HQ building, which was in a shopping area and not a business area. The building remained empty for over three years before the organisation finally found a buyer. In the meantime, the organisation incurred all the costs of the new HQ and the move.

Not claiming benefits that don't exist

Just because you can measure something doesn't mean that it's a benefit. You need to be really sure that you can deliver that benefit at the end of the project and, with the exception of 'non-quantifiables', can provide a meaningful and relevant measure.

A department was running a project that would considerably reduce the paper storage requirements for their business area. Part of their allocated space was a very large basement room in a large and prestigious building. The project team realised that the department would no longer need the room, and the team went to the accommodation department and found the value per square metre of the building per year. They measured the room and multiplied the area by the value per square metre and claimed the resulting sum on a discounted cash flow as a recurring annual saving. Because the room was large and the building prestigious, the saving was huge. But the project team failed to realise that if this large basement room was currently full of paper, but was then going to lie empty, there was no actual saving at all. It would only be a saving if the room could be used for something else that otherwise would have incurred expense. But the team had not identified any such use because other departments didn't want any extra space in the basement.

Being prudent

Management accountants have a principle of being prudent or conservative. They aim to slightly understate, not overstate, because that's safer. This holds very true for project Business Cases and for two important reasons.

First, if you overstate the benefits at the start, organisational managers or the Project Board may approve the project when they really shouldn't. Those authorising it make a judgement on faulty information. The knock-on effect may be that by authorising this project another project gets delayed, and that other project really should have gone ahead because it would have given more benefits more rapidly.

The second reason to be prudent relates to the perception of failure. If you claim massive benefits which then don't materialise, organisational managers consider the project to be a failure. If you promise less but actually deliver a bit more, then everyone sees the project as a success.

Avoiding benefits contamination

A further problem with benefits realisation is the isolation of benefits. The best way to describe this is to use a real-life example.

To be a member of a particular internationally respected professional organisation you need to pass exams, join, and then maintain that membership from year to year. The membership fees pay for the running of the organisation. Fairly standard stuff then.

Now, the organisation has competitors in this professional field and it wants a growing membership so that it can resource more things and stay healthy. So it decides to run a project to increase membership. The big question is: How can you tell whether the project is successful?

Say the membership goes up by 5 per cent over the period of the project. But perhaps the competitive organisations' membership also increases by 5 per cent over the same period and those organisations don't run any projects at all; it's just natural growth in the particular professional area. Or perhaps competitors' memberships go up by 10 per cent without them doing anything, so it seems that the recruitment project is working against the organisation and is putting people off joining rather than attracting them.

Now suppose that the competitors' memberships don't increase at all, but instead go down by 1 per cent, whereas our organisation's membership grows by 5 per cent. Is the project a success? Well, possibly, but perhaps people are joining for other reasons. Perhaps the organisation was involved in a court case where someone showed that she acted correctly and was supported by the professional organisation and so won the legal case. Other professionals saw the reports and many decided that they'd been meaning to join one of the organisations, and now this one has caught their eye because it helped so much in the court case. They're joining because of the newspaper headlines and not because of the project at all.

Contamination of benefits can be a tough area to deal with. You need to select benefits measures that isolate benefits from non-project factors and prove that they relate directly to the project. Depending on the benefit, isolating it may be relatively easy or may require significant thought and effort.

Taking the example of the professional organisation, the project staff have to think how to show that the membership growth is due to the project and not to other factors. A common and extremely simple method is to ask new members why they're joining. If the selected option is one of those that relate to the project, then the link is proven. Well, actually a small problem still remains, but that's enough to give you the idea.

Actually Measuring Benefits Delivery

The Business Case itself includes information on the benefits and how they'll be measured. But you also need a plan to show when benefits will come on stream, when they can be measured – which could be a while after they've come on stream – and who is to do the measuring. If you think that you're going to need some sort of Benefits Review Plan, then you'll be delighted to know that PRINCE2 has exactly that.

Measuring during the project, at the end of the project and after the project

PRINCE2 now recognises (at last!) that benefits can sometimes come on-stream during the project. It is not uncommon in business projects, for example, for project deliverables to be taken into operational use right through the project, not just in one 'big bang' at the end. If things are starting to be used during the project, then clearly benefits may start to be seen during the project as well.

You can often measure some benefits at the end of the project when major deliverables are taken into operational use. But for others, there'll be a gap between delivery and benefits measurement.

Seeing the gap between delivery and benefits

When you think about benefits and measurement, you need to think carefully about the nature of the project, the deliverables and the benefits themselves. Some benefits materialise very quickly in a way that can be accurately measured and reported. Some take a while to settle down so that you can give a realistic picture of the level of benefit actually achieved.

An example of quick measurement is with the replacement of an old, obsolete machine on the production line with a new one. The old one is expensive in terms of weekly maintenance but the new one has a long maintenance cycle and not only goes longer between maintenance checks, but the work is less expensive. As soon as the new machine is installed, you'll get the maintenance savings because the weekly checks can be stopped.

Immediate savings on a production line machine is very different to implementing a new and quite complicated business procedure. Although the new business procedure is more streamlined than the old way of doing things, it will nevertheless take staff a while to get familiar with it. You can't measure time savings the moment that the new procedure is launched because staff are still learning about it and are going slower than usual. It's only when they've got used to it and are working at a more normal speed that you can take a meaningful measure of the time savings.

That potential gap exists, whether you're measuring benefits during the project or after it. It's quite common, for example, to have a review some six months after the end of a project when the dust has settled, things have stabilised and benefits measurement can consequently be more accurate.

Understanding the responsibilities

Quite a few people, potentially, can be involved with measuring benefits, but the responsibility for specifying them in the first place and actually delivering the business benefit lies with the Senior User(s) on the Project Board. It's the Executive who has the primary responsibility for making sure that the Business Case is sound and that the project is worthwhile, but it's the Senior User(s) place to specify the benefits that they can deliver if the project goes ahead. Then everyone watches with interest to see the Senior User come up with the goods after the project has delivered! If you're a Senior User you may like to flip back to the section earlier in this chapter on 'Being prudent' and read it again – slowly!

You may well involve other people in measuring benefits though, even people outside the project. For example, finance staff often have a valuable role in helping measure financial savings.

Benefits Review Plan

Scope: What benefits are to be measured.

Accountability: Who is accountable for the benefits (usually the Senior User).

How and when benefits will be measured.

Resources needed for benefits reviews.

Baseline measures: If you say there'll be a 10 per cent saving, what is the existing cost?

How the whole project's product will be reviewed: This is measuring the success of the project as a whole as opposed to the individual measurement of benefits.

As you can see from the panel, the Benefits Review Plan content is obvious enough but, as always, adjust it if you need to.

For Benefits Reviews to be done during the project and at the end of it, don't forget to put the activities and resource on your Project and Stage Plans. For any review(s) after the project, don't forget to pass the actions back into the organisation at the end of the project as *follow-on action recommendations*.

Chapter 12

Deciding Roles and Responsibilities

In This Chapter

▶ Seeing how PRINCE2 really helps projects with clear roles and responsibilities

▶ Getting to grips with the PRINCE2 ideas behind project organisation

▶ Meeting the PRINCE2 Project Management Team

▶ Coming to terms with the Project Board, change and assurance roles

▶ Being clear on the Project Manager and Team Manager roles

▶ Understanding Project Support

*W*hat the method calls the *Project Management Team Structure* records the detail of the roles and responsibilities in a PRINCE2 project. You're probably well aware that many projects get into difficulties because people aren't clear about what they should do and what other people are doing. This leads to confusion, mistakes, and stuff falling through the gaps. Having clear roles and responsibilities is essential for good project control and PRINCE2 provides that clarity. Actually, it does that rather well.

The even better news is that the method approaches project organisation in a really flexible and practical way. A common misunderstanding when someone gets hold of the manual is for them to look at the organisation diagram and say, 'Okay, so we need ten or more people – and that's just for the PRINCE2 stuff.' In fact, you can adapt the project team structure remarkably simply and quickly for very large projects, very small projects, and absolutely anything in between. Quickly, that is, if you know how, and this chapter shows you how. But all that flexibility hinges on that one important word – roles.

Getting the Right People Involved

Before getting into the detail of organisation, you must be clear on one vital fact. You can have all the methods and approaches you like, but if you involve the wrong people then your project is likely to be in trouble. Equally, involve good people and, even if your approach is not that great, you may well end up with a successful project. Methods such as PRINCE2 are really impressive when you use them well, but the people are more important still.

Dick Parris, my manager for some years in a training and consultancy company and who taught me a vast amount, has a favourite expression: 'Projects are about people'. He's absolutely right. Having the right people is vital for success. But filling the right number of seats isn't enough. Organisations often wrongly build a team from whoever happens to have spare capacity, instead of choosing people with the right skills and experience who work well together.

Philipp Straehl, a highly experienced and successful project manager of large projects, said, 'Have you got the best people, or the best people available? Big difference'.

PRINCE2 doesn't cover the people factors, but that doesn't mean you can ignore them. So, WARNING in big red letters. Get the wrong people and you're heading for trouble, no matter what methodology or approach you use.

Understanding PRINCE2 Management

You need to get to grips with some key elements before drilling down into the detail of individual areas of responsibility. So here they are.

Having roles, not jobs

PRINCE2 describes responsibilities as *roles*. That isn't very dramatic, you may think; everyone calls them roles. True, but this is significant for two reasons in the method. The first is to do with people doing more than one thing and the second is to do with status – or actually a lack of status.

Taking on multiple roles and sharing roles

First, a role is not the same as a job because

- ✔ One person can have more than one role (with a few limitations)
- ✔ A role can be filled by more than one person (mostly)

A simple example where one person can have more than one role is with a smaller project. You may manage the project as Project Manager but also do some of the specialist work of the project – so you're also a team member. You manage your own work and possibly the work of others too. If you've been wondering why you get paid such a lot, that's probably the reason.

Though I deal mostly with business projects these days, I started out in IT as a systems analyst and designer. When I was made a Project Manager, I was still very involved in the design of the systems. So I had dual roles in my job as a team member who helped to build the system, but also as a Project Manager who managed the work of the whole project.

An example of where more than one person can share a role is in the Project Board – the group of managers with oversight of a PRINCE2 project. One of the roles on the Project Board is Senior User. This is a manager who represents the people who actually use what the project delivers. The Senior User is on the board primarily to make sure that the project delivers the right things – that they're suitable and usable – and to specify and then deliver the business benefits that result from running the project. Take a project that affects two departments. You may want to have two Senior Users, one from Department A and one from Department B, each to make sure that the deliverables work for their staff. The Senior User role is therefore split across two people; two project 'jobs' but sharing one role.

Keeping status out of the equation

The second important aspect of the word 'role' is that in PRINCE2 this isn't about status. Someone very senior in the organisation may have the role of a team member doing some of the work of the project, say checking out the legal policy. Someone much more junior may be the Project Manager. This doesn't matter, provided that the senior people don't get awkward about it. If you have to explain this to senior people who don't like the idea then you can describe the project management as 'co-ordinating' their work. If you speak slowly when you explain this to them, even the most senior people are usually able to grasp the point that someone has to co-ordinate things, even if they don't like the idea of someone 'managing' them.

The 2009 edition of the PRINCE2 manual has some strange references to roles and it talks of 'combining roles' which badly confuses the concept of roles and reduces clarity. You don't combine roles at all; it's just that one person's job on the project may cover more than one role. So just ignore those bits of the manual and go with what you've read in this chapter and you'll find things much clearer when you come to design the project organisation.

Sticking to small Project Boards

In PRINCE2, Project Boards need to be lean and mean. The minimum number of people on a board is one person, covering all three roles, but the maximum is really no more than about six. The PRINCE2 manual has now retreated in the face of the enemy – those determined to get themselves onto Project Boards! The manual no longer gives the guideline of six as an upper limit and instead just talks about keeping boards as small as possible. But 'as small as possible', in some people's eyes, is a committee of 25 – or more! If you're under pressure to have more than about six on the board, have a look at Chapter 10, which is about setting up and running successful Project Boards and has some ideas for ways to keep the number down.

If you have a few minutes spare and want some cheap entertainment, do a search for Project Initiation Documents (PIDs) on the Internet and look at the ratio of the number of people on the Project Board to the people actually doing the project work. One I saw had 12 on the board and just 2 on the team doing all the work. To use the old Wild West management joke, 'Too many chiefs and not enough Indians.'

Seeing the project from three viewpoints

The next aspect of management is powerful. PRINCE2 recognises three key viewpoints in the project: business, user, and supplier.

All three viewpoints are important and you must listen to all three carefully. The business and user interests are from the 'customer' side of the project, and the supplier viewpoint is – great surprise – from the supplier side, the people doing the project work. You can trace many project problems back to a lack of involvement of one of these viewpoints.

The business viewpoint

The business viewpoint is primarily 'value for money'. The project costs a lot and takes significant staff resources. Is it worth it? What will the project deliver and is this worth the cost and the effort involved? This view distils down to the Business Case, which Chapter 11 covers in detail. Although all three of the viewpoints are important, the business viewpoint is the most important of all.

The user viewpoint

The user viewpoint is mostly about the usability of whatever the project is producing, and also for specifying and then delivering the business benefits that will result from the project. The user viewpoint addresses the questions 'Will it work for our people?' and 'Is it fit for purpose?' Far too many projects deliver things that aren't what people really want. This can occur for a number of reasons, but a major one is not consulting the users enough. In PRINCE2, one of the users' own managers is on the Project Board.

The supplier viewpoint

The supplier viewpoint is again concerned about delivery, but in relation to whether the project is workable and the outcome sensible. This viewpoint represents those who work on the project to build the deliverables – in other words, the project teams. Problems crop up where the project does not cover this viewpoint or does not bring it in early enough. If you've ever been responsible for work on a project, you may have found yourself saying to managers in a business area: 'Why didn't you call us in earlier? You've set this up in a really difficult way and there are several ways of doing it that are much easier and better.'

Applying the viewpoints to roles

The three viewpoints are represented very clearly in the Project Board roles (see 'Viewing the Project Board as central', later in this chapter), and also in the 'audit' areas of Project Assurance.

Project Assurance. This is the Project Board audit function that checks that the project is run properly. PRINCE2 has three sub-types of Project Assurance: business assurance, user assurance, and supplier assurance.

Recognising a customer/supplier environment

The viewpoints are grouped in two broader categories, as you may have spotted earlier in the chapter. The business and user interests are from the customer side of the project, and the supplier is from the supplier side. The method recognises this _customer/supplier environment_ and manages the potential conflict of interest between the two. If you have an internal supplier for the project, such as your own IT department building the new computer system, then any conflict of interest is small; well, we live in hope anyway.

In recognising this split, PRINCE2 demonstrates that the project is actually the responsibility of the customer; it's not the supplier's project. In the world of IT, computer departments have been trying to get the message across for years that the systems don't belong to the IT department but to the business areas. The IT department is just the supplier that builds and then maintains the system on behalf of the real owner, which is the business area.

Viewing the Project Board as central

The Project Board is the group of senior managers who together own the project. Their place in a PRINCE2 project is extremely important. However, organisations that use the method often misunderstand and completely under-estimate the responsibilities of the board. Chapter 10 covers the effective working of the Project Board and explains the key points where it's involved in the project. You may understand the function of the Project Board better if you think of it as the Project Manager's boss.

The Project Board is a group of senior managers, but the word 'senior' is relative. On a very small project, for example, the board members may be quite junior in terms of organisational management. Again, the word 'role' is significant: As well as putting junior people in 'senior' positions, the reverse is true and senior people may hold 'junior' positions in the project. Project roles can radically alter the normal management hierarchy and reporting lines.

A police force ran a project to change its reporting structure. Police forces, by nature, are very 'command and control' oriented and someone's rank is rather important. On this project, the Project Manager was an inspector, just two hops up from the bottom of the pile (constable – sergeant – inspector). One of the team members doing important policy work on the project was the Deputy Chief Constable (DCC), just one step down from the very top. So in this project, the DCC was accountable to an inspector and the normal reporting lines were turned upside down. But, in fact, the DCC wasn't accountable to an inspector at all; a team member was accountable to a Project Manager. PRINCE2 is about roles, not status.

Keeping the Project Organisation stable

The project organisation must be stable, as far as possible within the limitation of roles. When appointing Project Board members and the Project Manager in particular, you need people who can see the project right through to the end. If you get changes – particularly on the board – during the project, you run the risk of moving goalposts. A new board member taking over part way through the project is likely to say, 'But I don't think that the project should be about this at all. What I think is . . .'

A couple of exceptions to this stability are Team Managers, where comings and goings are normal because different work is done on the project, and the Project Board role that represents the supplier viewpoint (see 'The Senior Supplier(s)', later in this chapter, for more detail).

Structuring the Organisation of PRINCE2

You document the PRINCE2 roles and how they fit together in the Project Management Team Structure, which you then keep up to date throughout the project.

There are four levels of authority in the organisation structure but the first is actually outside the project. Levels 2 to 4 cover the project itself:

1 **Corporate or Programme Management:** Who the board report to.

2 **Project Board:** Directing. The board has oversight of the project.

3 **Project Manager:** Managing. Takes day-to-day responsibility.

4 **Team Manager:** Delivering. A Team Manager runs a project team.

The roles of Project Board, Project Manager, and Team Manager together with audit (assurance), any change authority and project support (project administration) make up the *PRINCE2 Project Management Team,* see Figure 12-1. The 'Project Management Team' is more than just a label and actually represents a very important PRINCE2 concept.

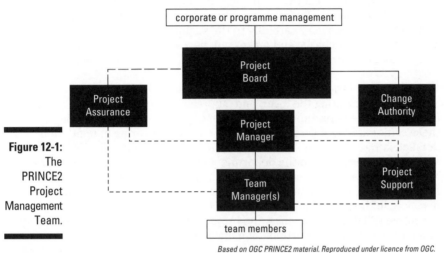

Figure 12-1:
The
PRINCE2
Project
Management
Team.

Based on OGC PRINCE2 material. Reproduced under licence from OGC.

Principle 3 – Defined roles and responsibilities.

The PRINCE2 Project Management Team

The word 'team' emphasises that the whole group works together to manage the project. Of course you have specialisms within the team, and levels of decision making. But the point remains that everyone on the team is on the same side. If a junior Team Manager has a problem, then potentially everyone has a problem and the whole Project Management Team, right up to Project Board level, may ultimately need to get involved to help solve it.

This PRINCE2 approach of managers working together as a team attacks a common problem in projects. Often, Project Board members somehow think that the project doesn't have much to do with them. Instead, they delegate the work to the Project Manager and then stay back at a safe distance until the end, when they come back to cut the red ribbon and take the credit if the project works well – or fire the Project Manager if not.

Examining the Project Board

Organisations using PRINCE2 often misunderstand the board responsibilities. To illustrate this area of management, consider a department in an organisation. If you think of the project as a temporary department, then you get the idea. One role, the Executive (representing the 'business' viewpoint), is like the department head. Obviously, you have only one head of department and although she listens very carefully to the senior managers in her department, she's ultimately in charge and makes any necessary decisions if disagreement arises. And, of course, she also takes responsibility for those decisions.

You can think of the two other roles on the board, the Senior User and Senior Supplier (representing the 'user' and 'supplier' viewpoints), as the senior managers in the department. The head of department values the views of these senior staff and listens very closely to them, bearing in mind their detailed knowledge within their specific areas of responsibility. Normally, this management team in the department agrees on the way to take things forward and reaches decisions by consensus. But in the event of disagreement and when push comes to shove, the head of department makes the decision. In the project and in the Project Board, that's exactly what the Executive will do. In that sense, the project management of the project is no different to ordinary departmental management in an organisation.

It follows that if the Project Manager is getting conflicting instructions from different board members, she should do what the Executive says.

The Project Board, not the Project Manager, owns the project and is responsible for it.

You can think of the Project Manager as a lower-level manager in the department. The senior staff must have great confidence in that manager; if not, why appoint her to the post? Although the Project Manager doesn't have ultimate responsibility for the project, she may still have huge amounts of authority and/or responsibility. (Turn to 'Getting to Know the Project Manager', later in this chapter, for more on this role.)

Understanding the three Project Board roles

The three roles on the Project Board represent the three key interests of business, user, and supplier.

- **Executive:** The 'senior' businessperson, who represents the organisation.

- **Senior User:** A manager who represents those who eventually use whatever the project delivers and who specifies and delivers benefits.

- **Senior Supplier:** A manager who represents the teams that do most of the work on the project.

As well as having oversight, the board is also responsible for providing resources for the project, both the finance and the people. The Executive usually secures the funding, the Senior User provides users to take part in the project, and the Senior Supplier authorises the team hours.

If insufficient resources are available then don't run the project. Imagine you're sitting in an airport departure lounge waiting to board your flight across the Atlantic Ocean. How would you like to overhear a Project Board member – sorry, I mean airline manager – say to the captain of the aircraft: 'Well, we haven't been able to give you quite as much fuel as we'd have liked – a bit less than half, actually – but take off anyway and give it your best shot.' If that's more than slightly reckless for an airline, how reckless is it for Project Board members to try to run a project when they already know that they have insufficient resources to do the job?

The Executive

The Executive represents the business viewpoint. She's senior within the organisation, relative to the project, and is responsible for making sure that the project is worth doing. The Executive 'owns' the Business Case (please see Chapter 11) and this sums up her interests well. Other board members remain concerned about the value for money of the project, but the Executive particularly focuses on this and takes overall responsibility for it. She analyses the costs of the project (in staff hours as well as capital investment) and the benefits the Senior User is claiming for the project.

The Executive also examines risk: if the benefits are low and the cost is high, the project may still be worth running because the benefits still outweigh the costs. However, if the risks are enormously high, then that may well tip the balance and stop the project running. Equally, a project with fairly low returns, but of negligible risk, may be worth doing.

You can only ever have one Executive – this is one of the two roles in PRINCE2 that can't be shared. To understand the reason for this, think of the project as a temporary department again. You only ever have one head of department, no matter how large or small that department is. Having two heads of department leads to confusion: Nobody has the full picture and nobody has the final authority in the event of disagreement. The same occurs with a project. In a PRINCE2 project, one person is ultimately in charge and that person is the Executive. The manager who is the Executive can also have another role, such as Senior User, but you can't have two Executives on a single project.

Major responsibilities of the Executive

You can find the full detail in the PRINCE2 manual, but here are the main elements of the Executive's role:

✔ Is ultimately responsible for the project.

✔ Appoints the Project Manager (unless the organisation did this).

✔ Appoints other Project Board roles (unless the organisation did this).

✔ Owns the Business Case and checks regularly that the project remains viable.

✔ Normally obtains funding for the project.

✔ Chairs all meetings of the Project Board.

✔ Communicates with organisational management and reports on project progress and any problems that need upward referral.

✔ Carries out Business Assurance, or appoints someone else and then receives the reports.

✔ Is available to the Project Manager to give advice when needed (ad hoc direction).

The Project Board isn't a voting democracy. The Executive works very closely with the other Project Board members and normally they make decisions by consensus and without difficulty. But if disagreement occurs, the Executive makes the decision. Managers in a department can't outvote a head of department, and neither can other Project Board members outvote an Executive.

As well as owning the Business Case, the Executive also has other important responsibilities. A major one is chairing all meetings of the Project Board. This responsibility underlines the point that the business viewpoint is the most important of the three, and that the Executive is ultimately responsible. The Executive is normally the main channel of communication between the project and corporate management and is therefore the person who'll usually report progress on the project and advise on things such as the levels of benefits expected.

Very importantly, the Executive is also responsible for business assurance, which means checking that the project runs well from a business perspective. The Executive can do this personally, or delegate business assurance to someone else, who does it on her behalf. See 'Looking at Project Assurance', later in this chapter, for more on business assurance.

In more formal projects, written and signed job descriptions may be necessary to back up the roles. But for many projects, naming the roles and the people without going into detail is enough, because the manual itself lists the responsibilities for each role. Good use of PRINCE2 can reduce project paperwork.

The Senior User (s)

The Senior User is a manager from the user side of the project. The users are those who use what the project delivers – the new headquarters building, the new computer system, or the new business procedure. The Senior User must make sure that the project delivers suitable or *fit-for-purpose* results. The Senior User role also sets down the benefits of running the project, and then must deliver those benefits. You can have more than one person in the Senior User role.

In a major and prestigious international hotel chain, the headquarters ran a project to upgrade tables and chairs in conference rooms in a European country. HQ sent each hotel enough new chairs and desks for their seating numbers. Unfortunately, some hotels had only small and medium-sized rooms with little free space and the new furniture was physically bigger than the perfectly acceptable existing furniture. The new tables and chairs immediately reduced the capacity of the conference accommodation in those hotels, and with it the profitability of their conference business. Nobody had consulted the hotel managers (the users) on the impact of the upgrade.

The Senior User doesn't spend endless hours talking to designers of the project deliverables: Remember that the Project Board doesn't do the work of the project. Instead, the Senior User makes sure that the right people in their business area have been talked to, and allocates user resources to make such time available.

Like the Executive, the Senior User role also has responsibility for Project Assurance. The Senior User is responsible for user assurance, which makes sure that the project runs properly from a user viewpoint. (See 'Looking at Project Assurance', later in this chapter, for more on user assurance.)

Major responsibilities of the Senior User

Here are the main responsibilities of the Senior User, but for the full detail see the PRINCE2 manual. The Senior User:

✔ Makes sure that the project delivers products that are fit-for-purpose.

✔ Specifies and then delivers business benefits that will result from the project.

✔ Provides user staff resource – for example, to help specify requirements and perform user testing.

✔ Carries out user assurance, or appoints someone else to do it and receives the reports.

✔ Liaises between the user area and the project, acting as a 'project champion'.

✔ Works to prioritise user requirements, including change requests.

✔ Is available to the Project Manager to give advice when needed (ad hoc direction).

The Senior Supplier (s)

The Senior Supplier is a manager from the supplier side of the project: the teams doing the bulk of the work. The person taking this role must have authority to commit resources to the project and to check that things are being done properly from that supplier perspective.

Choosing the Senior Supplier can sometimes be difficult, but taking the resource issue and turning it around usually pinpoints a suitable person. Just ask yourself, 'Who will be authorising the team hours for this project?' That takes you to the right area, and then you can select someone at the right level and with the right authority.

The Senior Supplier is a very important role on the board for a logical reason. The board can't make meaningful decisions about resources or timing without the Senior Supplier saying that the resources are available. Plans made without supplier input are just wishful thinking. This is also true with suppliers who are from inside the customer organisation. Many a manager has gone to an IT department and said, 'We need this work done this month,' only to be told that the IT people are already fully committed on other work for the next six months.

Things can get more complicated in a project with a lot of suppliers – perhaps several internal areas of interest and many outside companies working on the project too. Like the Senior User role, you can have more than one Senior Supplier. You may have one Senior Supplier from the customer organisation who has authority to authorise internal staff resources to the project, and one from the external supplier company who has authority to commit that company's staff hours. Not only is that split sensible, but you frequently find it's necessary, because an organisation is unlikely to want to give an outside company authority over its staff or vice versa.

Major responsibilities of the Senior Supplier

These are the main responsibilities of the Senior Supplier role on the Project Board:

✔ Making sure that the project delivers what was specified.

✔ Checking that the project deliverables achieve the user's objectives.

✔ Making sure that the project meets necessary industry and technical standards.

✔ Providing staff resources for the team work.

✔ Deciding how to do supplier assurance on the project, and either doing the assurance or delegating it.

✔ Giving informal advice to the Project Manager when asked.

If you have a lot of supplier interests in the project, an alternative is to identify a *lead supplier*, which is the company doing most of the work. That company can provide the Senior Supplier, who liaises with the other suppliers. The Senior Supplier may need to get agreements (possibly signed) to things like team resources in advance, and then commit to stages on behalf of all the suppliers.

Looking at Project Assurance

PRINCE2 has three types of project audit or *Project Assurance* within the project that reflect the three key interests of the Project Board:

- ✔ Business assurance
- ✔ User assurance
- ✔ Supplier assurance

To understand Project Assurance think about financial audit and then apply that to the project. In a financial audit, you check that the accounts are accurate and done to the correct standard. This same check applies with the project. Is the project being run properly? Are calculations that the stage is on track actually correct? Are the benefit projections sensible? Are risks being managed properly? Are the teams consulting the right users to make sure that the project delivers the right thing?

Although the Project Management Team structure shows assurance as separate to the Project Board, assurance is actually the responsibility of the Project Board. But board members can delegate the activity of checking to others in two situations: If the project is quite big and the Project Board members simply don't have the time to do all the checking; or if board members don't have the skills to do the checking.

Knowing that Project Assurance isn't optional

The bottom line is that you must do Project Assurance: It's not optional or negotiable. But unfortunately, Project Assurance is probably the most neglected part of applying PRINCE2: it's seldom implemented properly, and often not at all.

The only choice you have with Project Assurance is how and to what degree you do it. Thinking that you should carefully manage and audit a department because it spends £2 million a year, but you don't need to check a project that runs for a year and spends £2 million, is nonsensical.

A PRINCE2 overview was being given to a group of about 50 people and a senior manager was present in the audience. When the presenter got to the bit about Project Assurance, the manager got to his feet and said in a loud voice, 'I don't need Project Assurance on *my* projects. I trust *my* staff,' and sat down again. The presenter was a little taken aback. But I know exactly what I'd have said in reply: 'Fine. I guess that you don't have financial audit in your organisation either and for the same reason. You trust your staff!' Nobody questions the need for financial audit, and project audit is equally valid.

Deciding how to do Project Assurance

You can set up Project Assurance in four basic ways:

✔ Board members do their own assurance. The Executive does the business assurance, the Senior User does the user assurance, and the Senior Supplier does the supplier assurance.

✔ The board appoints three people (or three teams) to do the assurance work. One team does business assurance and reports back to the Executive, another team does user assurance and reports back to the Senior User, and the last team does supplier assurance and reports back to the . . . you guessed it. You're really getting the hang of PRINCE2!

✔ The board appoints one person to do all three types of Project Assurance and report back.

✔ The board splits the assurance between board members and dedicated assurance staff. For example, the Executive and Senior User may do their own checking, but someone else does supplier assurance and reports back to the Senior Supplier.

However you do Project Assurance, the Project Board must understand that although they can delegate the activity of assurance to other people, they remain fully accountable for the satisfactory running of the project.

The relationship between financial audit and the finance director is exactly the same. If the financial auditors find problems, you don't blame the auditors. The responsibility for the organisation's accounts rests firmly with the finance director. In the same way, the responsibility for the project running properly stays with the Project Board and they can't delegate that – however much they may want to – either to dedicated Project Assurance staff or the Project Manager.

Working with, and not against, the Project Manager

Some financial auditors are bad auditors. They think that they're only doing their job well if they cause trouble and find big problems. If these auditors can't find any big problems, they take some small ones and blow them up out of all proportion. You don't want that mindset in your Project Assurance staff. Project Assurance and the Project Manager are both on the PRINCE2 Project Management Team and so on the same side. The team should normally work very co-operatively together because they share one objective: to get the project right.

Major responsibilities of Project Assurance

Business assurance checks that:

✔ Project progress data is accurate.

✔ Financial records are accurate and meet any organisational standards.

✔ Benefit projections are realistic and correctly calculated.

✔ Benefit calculations show that the stage remains within benefits tolerances.

✔ Risk management actions are actually being taken, not just talked about.

✔ The evaluation of project Issues (problems, changes, and so on) by the Project Manager included checks for impact on the Business Case (business assurance also assists with that evaluation).

User assurance checks that:

✔ The right user staff have been consulted about their requirements for the project.

✔ User staff resources set down in the plans are in line with what was committed.

✔ The right user staff tested project deliverables.

✔ The evaluation of project Issues included checks for impact on the users and the usability of products (user assurance also assists with that evaluation).

Supplier assurance checks that:

✔ The correct technical standards (industry standards, codes of practice, and so on) have been identified and that products are built to those standards.

✔ Supplier staff named in plans to do particular work are suitably qualified.

✔ The correct staff build products as set down in the plans (not trainees substituted by an over-committed supplier company – watch big consultancy companies on this one!).

✔ Project and Stage Plans are realistic in order to build products to the appropriate standard.

✔ The right Team Managers and specialists have been consulted to help draw up the plans.

✔ Suitably qualified staff have been allocated in the resource plans to test and check (including, in some cases, being qualified by being ignorant!).

✔ The correct staff have tested products, as set down on the plans.

✔ All tests have been performed and none left out (the Quality Register helps here, because it lists all the quality actions you carry out in a stage and sign-offs for each).

✔ Supplier staff resources set down on the Project and Stage Plans are in line with what was committed.

✔ The evaluation of project Issues included checks for impact on the suppliers, notably impact on staff resources and product integrity (supplier assurance also assists with that evaluation).

Imagine you do a difficult bit of work and ask an experienced colleague to have a look at it to see whether it looks okay to her. Your colleague picks up a couple of points and you talk them through and clear them up. Then she says, 'Well, that all looks fine to me.' Your reaction is to feel very pleased and much more relaxed, because someone you trust checked out your work and gave it the thumbs up. Well, that's exactly how Project Assurance works. It's an independent but on-side check – an experienced pair of eyes.

Project Assurance staff must be careful to come into the project in a non-threatening way and Project Managers must be open, not defensive.

Blowing the whistle

Although Project Assurance aims to be helpful and co-operative, the staff do perform an independent check and are accountable to the Project Board. If the Project Manager hides bad news from the board, then Project Assurance reports that. Project Assurance is like a safety valve on the project that ensures the board get correct information.

Understanding Organisational Assurance

Before leaving the topic of assurance, one more needs a mention. PRINCE2 now calls this *Quality Assurance*. The name is actually rather misleading as it's not primarily about the quality of products, which is the normal context of this term, but rather of the whole project. It functions the same way as Project Assurance, except that it's not done by the Project Board or people that the board members appoint. Instead it's done from outside the project and is accountable to corporate or programme management. Being independent of the project is quite powerful because it allows checks to be made on the Project Board itself.

If the board members are fairly secure and mature, and not all – no, let's not climb up on that soapbox! If the board members see the true value of this independent check, they can actually ask for a Quality Assurance check of their project. Taken the right way, such a check is a real confidence boost that things are okay because people who don't have an axe to grind and who aren't closely involved have taken a look at the project and checked it out.

Don't give an organisational Project Office responsibility for carrying out Quality Assurance on the organisation's projects, much as some of them will push hard to get – or keep – such work. The Project Office is there to support projects, not check up on them. It makes for a confused and uneasy relationship if someone who is supposed to be helping you as your assistant, also has a role to check up on you and report over your head if you're doing something wrong. It also undermines the assurance. To make a financial analogy, how can you provide independent audit if you helped write the accounts in the first place?

Changing Things – Board Authority

It's normal and usually very sensible to give the Project Manager some authority, time and budget to authorise changes. If the Project Board only authorises what's on the plans, then even small changes must be referred back to the board because the Project Manager has no authority to do anything about them. So the first question the board faces on change is how much authority it wants to delegate to the Project Manager. Anything more than that then has to be escalated. However, a second decision now has to be made. When the Project Manager does escalate something beyond her authority, should it be to the board or someone else?

The Project Board has an option to set up a *Change Authority* with an intermediate level of authority between the Project Manager and the Project Board. If the Project Manager wants to escalate a change request, she'd then go to the Change Authority and only if it exceeded that delegated authority would it go to the full Project Board for a decision.

You can find more on change and the options for a Change Authority in Chapter 16. The chapter includes a dire warning of the potential for bureaucracy to sneak in here, with the consequent slowing up of the project. So, you have an incentive to read the chapter – unless you like bureaucracy.

Getting to Know the Project Manager

The Project Manager is responsible for running the project on a day-to-day basis on behalf of the Project Board. You can only ever have one Project Manager in a PRINCE2 project. This may sound a little strange if you're used to having more than one – for example, a Business Project Manager and a Technical Project Manager – but the rule is there for logical reasons.

Major responsibilities of the Project Manager

Here's an overview of the main responsibilities of the Project Manager:

✔ Planning the project and successive stages (but involving others as necessary).

✔ Giving out work assignments – Work Packages – to Team Managers.

✔ Monitoring progress and making adjustments to the running of stages as necessary.

✔ Warning the board if he projects that the stage or project will stray beyond set limits (time and so on).

✔ Examining and dealing with any questions, ideas, or problems (project Issues) that are sent in.

✔ Receiving completed work from Team Managers.

✔ Reporting on progress to the Project Board.

✔ Referring to the Project Board any matters that need board involvement or decision making.

A useful analogy for a Project Manager is the captain of a ship. I live in Weymouth on the south coast of the UK, where a high-speed car ferry operates out of Weymouth Harbour to the Channel Islands and St Malo in France. This small ferry has one captain. Now, compare that ferry to a huge passenger vessel like the *Queen Mary*. Surely, a ship the size of the *Queen Mary* must have lots of captains on a voyage, probably working shifts and with seven or eight on duty at a time? Absolutely not! No matter how big or small the ship, it only ever has one captain. One person knows what's going on and has the 'big picture'. So no matter how big or small the project, you only ever have one Project Manager for the same management reasons.

People who think a PRINCE2 project can have two Project Managers misunderstand PRINCE2 roles. The project may involve specialised areas of work, such as the business area, but Team Managers of the respective teams head these areas up, not multiple Project Managers. The Project Manager is exactly that – the manager of the whole project and not just one bit of it.

You may think that if the board owns the project, the Project Manager has very limited authority and responsibility. But that's not correct. Going back to the analogy of the *Queen Mary* passenger liner, does the captain have no authority and no responsibility? Clearly he does. But on that size of vessel the captain doesn't own the ship, and doesn't choose the voyage either. In PRINCE2, the Project Board owns the ship and chooses the voyage (the project and the scope); the Project Manager runs the project on a day-to-day basis and perhaps has very substantial authority to do so.

Although the Project Manager attends all the meetings of the Project Board, she isn't a member of the board and she can't take a role on the board. For example, the Senior User can't also be the Project Manager, because this undermines the Project Assurance function. To repeat the financial audit analogy, you don't help write the accounts and then audit them. The Project Manager can't be accountable to herself.

Considering Team Manager(s)

The teams are those people doing the work of the project and in PRINCE2 each team has a Team Manager. The Team Manager is the only role in the main organisational structure that's optional. On a very small, one-team project, the Project Manager may also manage the team. Most projects have more than one team, however, and some have many.

Teams can come from inside the customer organisation and from outside suppliers. Either way, they're project teams and are under the control of the Project Manager. In other words, although some teams may be from outside the customer organisation, they're nevertheless inside the project. This is quite an important point in PRINCE2 project and stage planning; Chapter 14 tells you more about planning and 'internal' and 'external' deliverables.

Team Manager. This person is in charge of a project team, and you may have many teams and therefore many Team Managers in a project. Where a project involves outside suppliers, they may well appoint their own Project Manager to control their part of the work. That's fine and the supplier can call that person a Project Manager – or the ruler of Zabazabadoo – if it wants. But in PRINCE2, and in this project, that person is a Team Manager.

Major responsibilities of a Team Manager

Here's a snapshot of the main responsibilities of the Team Manager role:

✔ Assisting the Project Manager in the development of Stage Plans for a stage that involves the Team Manager.

✔ Any necessary detailed planning of teamwork (Team Plans).

✔ Monitoring progress on Work Packages and reporting to the Project Manager.

✔ Checking that quality levels are being met, including that all tests are done.

✔ Warning the Project Manager if she projects that the work will stray beyond set limits (time and so on).

✔ Referring any problems or issues to the Project Manager where her involvement is necessary.

Knowing How Project Support Helps

Project Support is mostly an administration service for Project and Team Managers. Think of a good personal assistant (PA) and translate that into a project environment, and then you get the idea. Project Support is a person or people who are excellent administrators, but who also understand projects and PRINCE2.

Some argue that Project Support is also an optional role, but don't listen – there'll always be some administration work, even if the person who is the Project Manager does it herself. Often, this admin work falls to the Project Manager by default, and nobody really thinks about it. But if you accept that Project Support is a mandatory role, then adding it to the load of the person who is also the Project Manager is a conscious decision, albeit fully justified for a particular project.

In most cases, the Project Manager spending a large chunk of her time doing administrative work doesn't make sense. Getting someone else to do the administration – often at lower cost, faster, and better – is much more practical, and this frees up the Project Manager to concentrate on running the project, or perhaps more than one. But flexibility is always the order of the day in PRINCE2, so exceptions include the following scenarios:

- ✔ The project is geographically distant from where administrators are based and communications are problematic (not just physically, but in terms of the potential for misunderstanding too)

- ✔ The admin load is light and having the Project Manager do it is simpler and more convenient

- ✔ The Project Manager can be full-time on the project and can concentrate on it, rather than part-time and having to do non-project work as well

- ✔ The organisation has money to burn and insists on doing administration as expensively and inefficiently as possible

Many organisations seem to be very committed to the last of these scenarios. Interestingly, though, most of those organisations don't apply the same principle to their top organisational managers, who all have PAs or secretaries.

Setting up a Project Office

In larger organisations centralising the support function with a Project Office can be very effective. Project Offices can be excellent, or extremely bad – much depends on how organisations set them up.

Major responsibilities of Project Support

Project support can help with the following:

✔ Assisting with project and stage planning.

✔ Updating plans with *actuals* (staff hours and spending).

✔ Preparing for meetings (circulating invitations, booking rooms, and so on).

✔ Taking meeting notes (at Project Board meetings, quality reviews, and so on) and circulating them.

✔ Helping prepare reports, then distributing them.

✔ Setting up and maintaining the project filing.

✔ Operating version control procedures.

✔ Advising on the use of administrative approaches and computer tools.

If you set up an office with good staff who understand their role (support) and take professional pride in that, the Project Office can be stunningly good. It can actually take on a greater role than just administrative support and offer advice to Project and Team Managers in areas such as planning and risk management. In that way, Project Offices can act like an internal project consultancy unit.

Where Project Offices tend to go wrong is where the staff involved aren't content to support and want to control the projects. Then the office gets involved in monitoring and even enforcing standards. This confuses the role of support with assurance and is bad news indeed. In some cases, Project Offices have taken over so completely that they even bypass Project Managers and Project Boards and report on project progress – with beautifully standardised reports – directly to corporate management. This causes all sorts of problems, and if you translate this situation back to organisational management you can immediately see why: Imagine some small unit in a department telling more senior managers how to do their jobs and then reporting direct to the management board, bypassing not only those managers but also the department's own top managers and head of department. This locks back to the warning earlier in the chapter on not allowing Project Offices to get involved with Quality Assurance; the external auditing of projects.

If the Project Office sees itself as a service that's out on the edge and the project as the important thing in the centre, then it normally works well. If the office sees itself at the centre (and a surprising number of them do) and requires projects to fit in with its requirements, then things usually go from bad to worse. That 'worse' is then usually accompanied with a lot of paper – forms, forms, and more forms.

Chapter 13

Managing Project Quality

● ●

In This Chapter

▶ Understanding the importance of quality

▶ Creating the Quality Management Strategy

▶ Looking at quality at stage and team levels

▶ Checking and controlling quality

▶ Using the Quality Review technique

● ●

*M*anaging projects is about delivering on time and within budget – that's what you often hear. But that just isn't true. Whatever's the point of delivering a load of unusable garbage on time and within budget? Project management is about delivering on time, within budget . . . and to quality standards. Quality is a vital third dimension.

The PRINCE2 project management method is actually rather good at managing quality. Unfortunately, the chapter in the official manual is a bit obsessed with definitions and processes, so it doesn't explain too well how quality works. See whether you think this chapter makes a better job of it.

Given the obvious importance of quality in projects, its frequent neglect is a bit strange. But the problem is that people always think they'll get away with it. For this reason, quality is often the first casualty and an easy target if a project comes under pressure.

Given the strong focus in many organisations on only time and cost, you may need a bit of determination to push for good quality management. But in some projects quality is the most important element. In fact, even in projects where quality seems to have a low profile, it is often more important than you think. If a project delivers on time and to budget but the deliverables don't work properly, people are still complaining about it two or three years later and long after the problems have been fixed. In contrast, if a project delivers a couple of months late but everything works perfectly, two years later everyone has usually forgotten it was late.

The project to build a new air traffic control system for the south of the UK came under severe criticism for being late and over budget. But if you're in a passenger aircraft approaching London Heathrow – the busiest airport in the world – and you have to choose, would you rather they got the air traffic control system completed on time and within budget, or that they'd got it right? In some cases quality is overwhelmingly the most important factor.

Product Planning with Quality Built In

In Chapter 14 you can read about the powerful approach that PRINCE2 uses for planning that's 'product-led'. This is a very logical approach, where you define what you're going to produce – the deliverables or *products* – before you try to list the activities and resources you need to build them. But apart from being powerful in its own right, the product-led approach to planning also opens the door to very precise control over quality and this is the key point you need to take on board to understand quality management in the PRINCE2 method. You can't specify quality for an activity very easily, but you can specify measurable quality criteria for a product. In PRINCE2 projects you list these quality criteria on the Product Descriptions, which you use to define every product.

Product Description. You write a Product Description for every product identified at project level, and then again when the products are broken down into more detail in every stage. The Product Description defines what the product is but also sets down the exact standards that products must meet (quality criteria); how you measure them (quality methods); boundaries for quality, such as upper and lower limits of machine performance (quality tolerance); and who performs the quality checks (quality check skills needed and also responsibilities for the actual checking). The set of Product Descriptions also includes a Project Product Description for the whole project; usually the final deliverable. Chapter 14 has much more detail on products, Product Descriptions and the Project Product Description.

Just because this section is short, don't underestimate the huge precision that PRINCE2 brings to quality by adopting the product focus in its approach to planning and control – it's an extremely powerful aspect of the method.

Taking Quality Seriously, Very Seriously

Having established that quality is very important, you must take it very seriously in your projects. Organisations can easily play games and give the appearance of delivering quality when actually they're not. Compliance with international quality standards is an example of this mindset. How many organisations start with 'We want the quality certification label, now what's the minimum we have to do to get it?' rather than 'We care about quality so let's get the certification as evidence of that'? How many senior managers sign every page of quality manuals without actually reading the pages? You mustn't allow such games in a project – you have to get quality right.

Delivering appropriate quality

PRINCE2 is extraordinarily practical regarding quality and doesn't suggest that every project needs 'top quality'. Instead, the method focuses on *appropriate* quality. Not every project is safety-critical, where human life hangs in the balance – like the air traffic control example earlier in the chapter. If your project is 'quick and dirty' then PRINCE2 helps you deliver at that level. Equally, if your project really is safety-critical, then it helps you deliver at that level too.

Overstating the quality level you require often leads to two problems. First, you pay for high quality when you just don't need it. That affects the Business Case because of the costs, and it also affects the time you require, because the extra work lengthens the project. In turn, that also means that bringing the business benefits on stream takes longer, which again affects the Business Case. The second problem is that, where you set the quality level much too high, a common reaction when the pressure's on is to abandon quality completely: 'Well, never mind, we'll do the next project properly.'

Quality costs money, so don't overstate the level you require. But don't understate it either, because poor quality can turn out to be even more expensive in the long run. Have you ever bought something cheaply only to regret it later when it doesn't do what you want? And do you end up buying the more expensive but better-quality item you should have bought in the first place? Of course not, but you probably know people who do.

The Quality Management Strategy sets down, amongst other things, just what level of quality you need to achieve in the project. That strategy forms part of the Project Initiation Document (PID). The strategy is in the PID because the level of quality, as well as the way you achieve it, varies from project to project. If quality was always the same for every project, you wouldn't need to put a strategy in the PID. (For more on the PID, please see Chapter 5.)

Sticking to quality

Abandoning quality is a common problem in the IT community. When discussing quality on one site someone asked me, 'Haven't you ever heard of live testing?' This is where you go live with some vital computer system, and then you see whether it works or not. Rather amusing, but not so for another computer company whose senior sales staff commit to short deadlines in order to win business, but those deadlines don't allow enough time for testing. This company installs systems on customer sites that almost always fail and the supplier has to do the 'bug fixing' in full view of customer staff. This lack of attention to quality is seriously damaging the company's reputation and if the company doesn't get things under control soon it may lose its leading position in the marketplace, because its competitors have a more quality-led approach.

I'm not saying that after you decide a level of quality you can't reduce it. If the project comes under pressure, you can indeed lower the quality to save time or money. But that's a conscious decision involving the Project Board; you don't reduce quality just because a team left some of the tests out.

Specifying Criteria for Project Acceptance

Although there's power down at the 'rivet-counting' level with the products, PRINCE2 also works at the higher level to help you set down quality for the whole project and especially for any final deliverable. It does this at two levels, both of which are written into the Project Product Description.

Customer quality expectations

The *Customer quality expectations* are, as the name suggests, what the customer side of the project is looking for. These expectations tend to be a bit on the vague side. 'We need it to go fast' or, 'It needs to be durable'. In writing the Quality Management Strategy – more of that in the next section – these expectations are translated into something more measurable, the Acceptance Criteria.

Acceptance criteria

Acceptance criteria are for the whole project and must be measurable. They can be new as the Quality Management Strategy is written, or some may be refinements of the customer quality expectations. The idea is that the project will be accepted if the criteria are met. The criteria can include timings, such as the delivery date of the project.

IKEA, the Swedish furniture manufacturer, has display cases in its showrooms showing products being tested. One display I saw in a UK store was a machine opening and closing a drawer. An electronic display showed how many times the drawer had been opened and closed and you could see it clocking up with each movement. That gives a measurable definition to a customer quality expectation of 'durable'. IKEA design their drawers so that they still function without problem after a stated number of movements, which is a mind boggling number.

Writing a Quality Management Strategy

The Project Management Strategy sets down the level of quality you're going for in the project, what control mechanisms you use, and who's responsible for making sure that you actually deliver the correct level of quality. 'Strategy' is an important word here. The strategy doesn't contain the fine detail of exactly what tests you do and when because it's much too early for that: You create the Quality Management Strategy in Initiation (the first stage of the project, which is for planning only) and before you even produce the Project Plan. You cover the tactical planning of exactly what and who and when in your more detailed planning of each stage.

When thinking through the Quality Management Strategy you need to watch out for any constraints. These can come primarily from two directions and may override anything that the user actually wants (the Customer Quality Expectations). The first constraint is the Project Approach that you produce in Start Up (for more on Start Up, please see Chapter 4). The Project Approach may include things such as safety measures and other standards with which the project must comply, and so you must take them into account in the Quality Management Strategy. The second direction is any organisational standards, and in turn these may be influenced by other quality standards such as the International Standards Organisation 'ISO' series.

The Quality Management Strategy

Introduction: The purpose and objectives of the strategy (though this is normally self-evident), the scope and who is responsible for the strategy (normally the Project Manager).

Quality management procedure: How quality is to be achieved in the project and noting the interface with any organisational or programme-level procedures.

Quality planning: Specifying when detailed quality planning will be done; notably in stage planning but some may be left to team-level planning.

Quality control: The approach to testing. This may include industry standard tests for particular products (such as some electrical testing), how quality activity will be recorded (such as the use of Error Sheets) and what data is to be recorded so that a check can be made across the whole project for how quality is being achieved.

Quality assurance: How the quality and the running of the project will be checked from outside the project so that it's independent.

Tools and techniques: Here you list any tools needed, which may include specialised equipment, as well as particular techniques to be employed.

Records: What records will be used for quality management overall, as distinct from those just needed in quality control, which came under a previous heading. It also sets down where records will be stored, how and by whom.

Reporting: Setting down the reporting requirements for quality. For example, this may include what quality information is to be included in the End Stage reporting so that the Project Board can be satisfied that the project is meeting its quality targets.

Timing of quality management activities: Most quality activities are event driven (you test a product when it's been completed) so this section may be overkill in your project. However there may be things that you do need to specify if you're in a higher-quality project environment, such as how often quality audits will be carried out.

Roles and responsibilities: Who is responsible for quality management activities. This may include people not only from outside the project but also outside the organisation, such as building safety inspectors.

Quality Assurance and Quality Control. Where you see the word 'assurance' in PRINCE2, think 'audit' and you have the right concept. Quality Assurance is an independent check of the whole project. An example is if your organisation has a quality department with staff who check up on quality throughout the organisation, including its projects. Quality control is the actual testing or checking of something.

Here are a few suggestions of things you need to think about when working through some of the sections of the strategy.

Introduction

Although the PRINCE2 manual suggests that the next heading in the strategy, the Quality management procedure sets down variance with the organisational or programme quality management standards, it can make more sense if you mention it in the context of scope as well; covered in this section. The project strategy may have limited scope because for the most part, the project will follow the organisation's standard approach.

Tools and techniques

If you need to specify industry standard techniques, you don't need to copy them all into the strategy. It's quite okay to just reference other standards.

Records

As with other strategies, the manual suggests that you set down here composition and format information for registers, this time for the Quality Register, but that's not usually needed as it's self-evident what the composition and format is; just look at it! The content of the Quality Register is covered later in this chapter as is a bit more on other quality records you may need.

Timing of quality management activities

Timing here, for things like quality audits, can be 'random' but then you need to make quite sure that 'random' doesn't turn out to be 'never'. To avoid a problem, you can specify a minimum number of audits or a maximum time period between audits.

Roles and responsibilities

Don't get tied up in knots here, the manual explanation isn't particularly clear. Logically this section can only refer to responsibilities at a high level, though reading the manual you might wrongly conclude that it refers to all quality management activity including product testing. If you think about this, you can't yet specify responsibilities for quality management activities at a product level because you haven't even come up with the Project Plan yet, let alone the Stage Plans where the testing needs become clear.

Instead, this section must be high level but points out particular resource needs that'll be useful to know when you come to do the project planning. For example, you may identify that you'll need to have an external safety inspection of the building works that you already know are to be included in the project. You may then need to put on your plans that the building inspection needs to be booked in Stage 3 in order for the inspection itself to be carried out in Stage 5.

Planning Stage- (and Team-) Level Quality

In contrast to the strategic nature of the Quality Management Strategy, planning at stage and team level is tactical. You work on this mostly during stage planning, so you repeat this work right through the project, stage by stage. The quality activities are built into the Stage Plan although, regrettably, the 2009 edition of the PRINCE2 manual has withdrawn a heading of 'Quality Plan' where a note could be put to say how quality is being tackled in that particular stage. It's regrettable because that heading helped keep a focus on quality throughout the project and prompt some specific thinking about it when doing the stage planning. You should still do the thinking though!

This tactical level of planning sets down exactly what testing you need, and who does it, how, and when. Clearly, you can't specify these details in the Quality Management Strategy, because at that time you don't know the details of the stage products, the requirements for testing them, or the exact availability of the staff resources to do the testing.

You can take quality planning right down to team-level plans. This is unusual though, and I've never yet seen it used even on big projects. The Stage Plan will usually be enough, but the team level is there if you need it.

Controlling and Auditing Quality

Quality control is the testing that you do to check that a product meets the required quality criteria set down in its Product Description. Quality control applies to management products such as the Project Plan and Risk Register just as much as to specialist products – the things that the teams build.

The type of quality control or test depends very much on the nature of the product being checked. If the product is a document, you may well use the Quality Review technique (see 'Checking Products with Quality Review', later in this chapter), or you can use informal quality review where a colleague checks the document over. If it's a product like a bridge, you can get someone (else) to drive over it in a tank.

If quality checking is at all dangerous, always delegate it. Remember you're an important PRINCE2 expert and you need to live in safety and comfort to check documents, think important thoughts and do other vague but essential project stuff back at headquarters. Send an expendable team member to do the dangerous things. If you're a team member reading this and have just received a dangerous assignment, obviously your manager bought a copy of this book before you did.

Controlling quality

The PRINCE2 method always did have a bit of a problem with language that isn't exactly friendly if you're a business user of the method, not a project professional. Sadly, the 2009 edition of PRINCE2 has introduced even more for you to get your head around.

Quality control involves the actual testing of products, but also the documentation and, if required, any further actions needed to get a product formally approved. For the testing though, the method has now introduced two categories of test, one with two sub-categories – value for money then.

In-process and appraisal

The two higher-level categories are 'in-process' methods and 'appraisal' methods. In-process is the easiest to understand from the name and simply means testing that is done while a product is being built. For example, when building parts for a machine, the technician measures with callipers at intervals to make sure that the part is cut to the right size. Appraisal refers to checks after the product is finished to make sure it's okay.

Appraisal in turn splits down into two sub-categories of 'testing' and 'quality inspection'. You can think of these simply as objective and subjective testing. Testing is objective; it's a matter of fact and often of measurement. So, is the paper A4? Is the cover of the report blue? Quality inspection is subjective; it's a matter of judgment and even of opinion. So, is the report understandable? Is the teenager's bedroom tidy?

Auditing and the Quality Register

You can manage quality very effectively by setting up an audit trail for quality testing and checking the quality controls. Of course, the following conversation never, ever happens in your organisation's projects, but you may overhear people on the train from *another* organisation talking like this:

> **Project person 1:** 'Oh, by the way, I never saw the test results of the reverse separation flange ignition to make sure it was firing up okay.'

> **Project person 2:** 'Oh rats! I meant to remind the team to do that test, but then I forgot all about it and they must have too. And now they've built the flange ignition into the main transverse combustion housing, which is due to be shipped out tomorrow so we can't get at it – not without taking it all to bits again anyway, and we're up against the deadline as it is.'

Project person 1: 'Well, it was a pretty important test. How long would it take you to take it out, test it, and then rebuild the housing?'

Project person 2: 'Three weeks minimum.'

Together: 'It's going to have to stay where it is and let's hope it works.'

In a PRINCE2 project you simply can't forget a test. The Quality Register is a clever but simple mechanism that ensures you don't. As part of planning each stage you write Product Descriptions for every product you will build in the stage, each of which includes a section that specifies how you test the product. After these descriptions are complete you can copy all the tests from these *Quality Method* sections into the Quality Register. Then, when you do activity and resource planning for the stage, you can add in the test dates and details of the people to do the testing.

As the stage progresses and the tests are done, each one is signed off in the Quality Register and the Error Sheet is usually filed there too, even if it's a *nil return*, where no errors were found by the testers. If some corrective work is needed to a product then a re-test, that work is now listed in the Quality Register as well, and signed off when it is done.

Now, here's a clever bit because lots of people now check that register. While the work is being done to build and test the product, the Project Manager, Team Manager, and Assurance staff check the log regularly to see that the tests are being done. When the products in the work assignment are all complete, the Team Manager checks the register one more time to be sure that all the tests were done for those products. When he hands the completed products back to the Project Manager – you've guessed it – at End Stage a further check is done to assure the Project Board that the quality was delivered. Each of these checks takes mere moments. So, for a particular product, the three tests were done and signed off, and error sheets signed and filed. Thirty seconds, maximum, but highly effective to spot if a test got missed out.

The Quality Register is a very effective audit trail: It's quick and simple to set up, incredibly easy to maintain, and takes mere moments to check. This is a method at its best – fast, effective, and light years away from the dull, dry, and wrong impression that methods are about filling some forms in and having to mindlessly follow a lot of boring steps.

Now for a clever bonus in PRINCE2. Three registers are set up during the first stage of the project where the planning is done (the Initiation Stage). But of these, the Quality Register is set up first and immediately, right at the start of the stage. That means it's available for use to audit the testing of the management products being developed in the Initiation Stage for the Project Initiation Document and for the next Stage Plan. Now that's neat.

The Quality Register

Quality identifier: A unique reference, and most people just use a number series.

Product identifier(s): The unique identifier of the product that the quality activity will be done on. Please see Chapter 14 and product planning for more on this.

Product title(s): Again, please see Chapter 14 for more on products.

Method: What tests are to be done, taken from the Product Description again covered in Chapter 14 (as noted at the start of this chapter, quality is powerfully locked in with products).

Roles and responsibilities: Who is responsible for carrying out the quality activity, such as a test. It may be an individual or a group of people.

Dates: The planned and actual dates of the quality activity, and for any subsequent sign-off and approval.

Result: The outcome of the quality activity. For example, something may fail test and in turn this may lead to more quality activities to check the product after it has been corrected.

Quality records: Cross references to any other quality documentation, such as test logs.

Making sure of assurance

You have to check that someone actually does the tests you require. You can do this simply by using the Quality Register, but you may want something more than that. I made unkind comments earlier in this chapter about people signing things off when they haven't even read them, much less checked them. Quality Assurance and Project Assurance (the audit functions) may have to be a bit more probing then than just merely checking that tests have been signed off in the Quality Register.

Where Project Board members aren't doing their own assurance, they should talk very specifically to their Project Assurance staff about exactly what will be checked and how. Ultimately the Project Board is responsible for the project and for delivering the required quality and they must be assured that it has all been checked. (See Chapter 12 for more on assurance.)

Checking Products with Quality Review

PRINCE2 doesn't have much in the way of project techniques and it expects you to find and use suitable ones. But it does cover Quality Review, which is a useful technique, provided you do it well. If you don't do it well it quickly becomes a sham and a waste of time.

A Quality Review is a meeting you use primarily to check products that are documents. People involved with the product 'walk it through' (hence the common alternative name of 'quality walkthrough') section by section to see whether anyone found any errors and, if so, how severe they are.

Roles in the quality review

Four roles are used in the review technique. People are appointed to these roles for each Quality Review as part of stage planning, when you establish the need for the review and plan the resourcing of the stage.

- ✔ **Chair:** Someone with skills in running a meeting who checks that the product is ready for review, and then runs the meeting.
- ✔ **Presenter(s):** The person or people who can talk knowledgeably about the product under review and send it round in good time before the meeting. It's often the person or people who actually produced the product.
- ✔ **Reviewer(s):** A person or people who can say whether the product is right or not.
- ✔ **Administrator:** Someone who helps arrange the meeting and then notes down any errors found and details of any corrective work needed.

These roles have absolutely nothing to do with the Project Board, so be careful not to confuse them. Project Board members don't do any of the work of the project. If someone on the Project Board is qualified to take part in a review, then that's a completely separate role to his Project Board work.

Finding, not correcting, errors

Quality Review is about finding and noting errors, not correcting them during the meeting. Where Reviewers find errors before the review meeting itself, they can send details to the Administrator, who puts them on the agenda for discussion on how severe they are.

Don't allow error correction in Quality Review meetings. Doing a quick fix is almost certain to miss out some of the implications and lead to more problems. The Quality Review meeting takes place just to find any errors, but the Project Team fixes them.

Staying 'ego-less'

Quality Reviews are not about ego. If the producer(s) of the product are also acting as Presenters in the review, they mustn't be defensive and the Reviewer(s) mustn't attack. The focus is simply on finding any errors so that they can be put right. If Reviewers go on the attack, then the Presenters are likely to defend. But the review isn't about attacking people or defending reputations. It's simply about checking to see if a product is right or not.

Be particularly careful of young and junior team members who are involved in a review. They tend to be far too proud of their work, having worked extremely hard on it, and they can feel hugely disappointed and very protective of their product if anyone finds an error. They can then sometimes try to rush a review meeting on to the end before anyone finds another problem with their precious work.

When working as a full-time Project Manager in IT, I used to devote a fair bit of energy to getting the right concept of Quality Reviews into the heads of junior team members, albeit kindly I hope. I used to explain 'We don't make our reputation out of error-free Quality Reviews. We make our reputation out of delivering computer systems that work. If someone finds an error in one of our documents, they've just helped us deliver a system that works.'

Signing off – the three options

At the end of a review meeting the members must agree what the outcome is. It may be one of three logical alternatives:

- ✔ **The product is fine and the team has done a great job:** The product can be signed off at the end of the meeting and the review result put in the Quality Register.

- ✔ **Errors were found that must be corrected, but they're not serious:** The errors are noted on an Error Sheet and the required action listed in the Quality Register, and the meeting closes. When the errors have been corrected the product is taken back only to those who found the errors in the first place. If they're happy, they sign off that entry on the Error Sheet. When all errors are signed off, the product is signed off.

- ✔ **One or more errors have been found that are more serious and require some effort to change:** Because this affects the whole product, the review meeting decides that individuals can't sign off the errors (as in the case of less serious errors), but rather that everyone needs to see the product again to make sure that it's now correct. The product must be put through Quality Review again after the corrective work.

Recording Quality

If you're going to check that quality has been delivered, then clearly you need something to physically check. This is where the records come in. As always, be careful with records because you don't want a paper mountain or the electronic equivalent. But you need some form of record. This section is last in the chapter because most of the possible documents covered here have already been mentioned in earlier sections.

PRINCE2 quality records

PRINCE2 expects that quality requirements are recorded at a strategic level, product level and then an audit trail that quality activities were carried out. The Quality Management Strategy is the strategic document, then Product Descriptions for quality criteria for individual deliverables, then the Quality Register to list quality activities together with confirmation that those activities were carried out. These are all explained earlier in this chapter.

Generic quality records

These records aren't specified by PRINCE2, but you'll probably need something in this area. Here are a couple of examples.

Test logs

You can't put huge lists of very detailed tests into the Quality Register. Instead you're likely to have dedicated test documents such as test scripts, and then log the results of the tests. The test log is a common document for doing that and provides a checklist to ensure that every test is done, and an audit trail for others to see that the test was done and what the result was.

Error sheets

Already mentioned earlier in the chapter, Error Sheets are great. Someone has asked what is worse than biting into an apple and finding a worm. The answer is, biting into an apple and finding half a worm – guess where the other half is! What is worse than finding an error? Finding it twice. You hit a problem and then realise that it was spotted earlier but somehow it got forgotten and slipped through without being corrected. The Error Sheet makes sure that all errors are listed, albeit simply, and that they have now been put right. You can use it in informal review – peer-level checking – as well as formal review. It's also helpful to retain 'nil returns' so that you have a record that the check was done and a confirmation that in this test no errors were found.

Correspondence and meeting records

If there's discussion on the quality of a product, this may need to be recorded. It may be simply a copy of emails, memos and letters but it could include minutes of meetings held to discuss and decide on quality issues.

Chapter 14

Planning the Project, Stages and Work Packages

. . . .

In This Chapter

▶ Understanding why you need to plan

▶ Fitting in with organisational formats and requirements

▶ Achieving huge planning power with the product-based approach

▶ Fitting activity planning in with the products

▶ Planning resources

▶ Looking at levels of plan – project, stage, and team (Work Package)

▶ Knowing who does the planning and who checks it

. . . .

*W*elcome to planning – probably the most exciting chapter in the book! This chapter covers an amazingly powerful approach to planning in projects, but one that the PRINCE2 community widely misunderstands and completely undervalues. Many people leave out this approach because they can't really see what product planning is all about. And many PRINCE2 trainers don't really understand product planning either.

Without planning you have no effective control, and many projects go wrong right at the start because people try to cut back on planning or leave it out altogether in order to save time. But unless you know where you're supposed to be in the project, you aren't able to detect whether you're off track. But the plans are also important to help you find problems and find them early, so that you can solve problems on the plan, not in the project.

Part of a resistance to planning is experience of over-planning in projects where managers have seen piles of documents and diagrams that are never referred to again once they have been approved. But the answer to the problem of over-planning – or under-planning for that matter – is not to go to the opposite extreme. The answer is the correct level of planning, in line with the control needs of the project.

Some people think that they can speed things up by leaving out planning. This doesn't work. However, the popular 'never mind all this planning – get on with the real work' approach forms the core of another project method in widespread use – JFDI or 'just *flipping* DO IT'. Sadly, the failure to plan and so avoid the obvious problems has led to many JFDI project disasters.

Thinking about the Planning

The answer to the problem of under-planning or over-planning is some careful thinking to getting the level of detail right. Over-planning hurts the project: The plan takes longer than necessary to draw up during Initiation, and then that plan has to be maintained right through the project, wasting further time. Under-planning in its turn means that important things go unnoticed and obvious conflicts, such as double-booking project staff, don't get seen with the result that problems hit the project later on when it's much harder to deal with them.

So your evaluation of what degree of planning and control you need in any particular project is an important one. But you base that decision on the nature of the project and the environment you run it in, so you can't look up any easy calculations in a book. Instead, the decision is a matter of judgement and the Project Manager and Project Board must work it out between them.

For example, if you run a project that's pretty similar to six previous ones that all ran successfully, then your planning may be relatively light because you know exactly what you're dealing with. If you work with very experienced staff, you may need to give them less detailed information on building project deliverables than if they're very inexperienced. Again, a project that is time-critical needs much more careful planning than one where the timing isn't so vital. The list goes on and you can add your own factors for your own project environment.

Considering organisational requirements

Before doing the planning, you need to check whether there are any organisational constraints on how you do the planning and how you present the plans. If you're a consultant this is especially important, because you need to make sure that you work in line with your client's corporate standards.

Thinking about money

You also need to think about types of budget when drawing up plans. A PRINCE2 Project Manager has three areas of budget to control. The first pot of money is for the planned work and is always available to the Project Manager. But the other two (the change and risk budgets) are conditional and can only be used under specific circumstances.

Budgeting for project, stage, and team plans

After the project is planned out you can cost it and have an idea of the total budget. For the more detailed Stage Plans, a stage budget can be calculated and approved for that stage, and you do the same at the Team Plan level for a Work Package. It can be cyclical though. If the project plan shows the project to be too expensive, then the plans more easily allow adjustments to things such as scope and resource to get the cost down to what is affordable.

Budgeting for change

But what about finance for elements that aren't planned for? Allocating a change budget avoids the Project Manager running back to the board for every change in a stage, no matter how small. The change budget allows the Project Manager to carry out changes up to a certain level without having to refer back to the board each time. This can be made more refined still if you decide to make use of an intermediate level of authority between the Project Manager and the Project Board; a *Change Authority*. You can find more information on change control in Chapter 16 that covers the Change theme.

Change budgets are conditional. If nobody wants any changes, the Project Manager doesn't have authority to use that money. The Project Manager can't use the budget to make up for any overspending on planned work.

Budgeting for risk

The overall risk budget is normally calculated when the Project Board agrees the risk control actions, but the general operation of the risk budget is decided early on in Initiation when the Risk Management Strategy is prepared. For example, if a risk-related spend is above a certain threshold, the board members may decide that they want to be consulted before the money is committed, even if the Project Manager has identified and costed the risk as part of the risk analysis and planning.

Like the change budget, the risk budget is conditional. If a risk doesn't happen, then the Project Manager has no access to the part of the risk budget set against that risk. She can't use those funds for any other purpose, such as to offset over-runs on planned work or to pay for a change. In case you think that over-running on planned work is a risk and so is a neat way of tapping into the risk money, think again! Over-running is an impact, not a risk and Chapter 15 has more detail on this point if you need convincing.

Planning with Products

Now to the actual planning itself. Although PRINCE2 does expect the use of planning techniques that you're probably familiar with – such as the Gantt chart with its horizontal bars representing the tasks or activities of the project, and possibly activity networks – the method doesn't expect you to start there. Instead PRINCE2 expects that you'll be using some techniques up front that require a totally different approach when thinking about the project; techniques associated with 'product-based' or 'product-led' planning.

Products and outcomes. Project deliverables in PRINCE2 are known as products. But although the deliverables are usually physical products, occasionally a deliverable may be a soft product or 'outcome'. This may be something like a changed customer perception of the company. You can't hold or kick a changed perception.

Looking at the planning problem

The traditional approach to planning that starts off with the familiar Gantt chart has a problem, which the following example illustrates. To draw a Gantt chart, you start off by listing the activities or tasks down the left side of the Gantt. Here's a task you can put on the list for one of your projects: 'Build the wall'.

First of all, do you agree that 'Build the wall' is an activity or a task? You do? Good, because it is. That's step one. Step two is to draw a bar onto the Gantt chart to show how long this activity should take. So how long does it take to build a brick wall?

You may immediately start thinking of questions: 'How long is it? Is it one or two bricks deep? How high is the wall, because we may need scaffolding?' However step two isn't to start an argument but rather to draw a bar on a Gantt chart; so please answer my question on how long it takes to build the wall.

Focusing first on what you must produce

If those sorts of questions did cross your mind, then great, because you already think in the 'product-led' way. First you define 'wall'. When you are as clear as you can be about what you're building, then you can much more easily come up with the activities you need to do to build that deliverable and more accurately predict how long the work will take. In other words, the focus first of all is on what you produce – the *products* – and not the activities that build the products.

Products. Like a number of other approaches that use this 'deliverables' focus, the PRINCE2 name for 'deliverables' is *products* – what the project produces.

If you're heavily into activity planning, you may argue that you already think about what you're going to produce in order to come up with meaningful activities and timescales. If so, great. You're already convinced of the value of the product-led approach and will feel at ease that it's expected in PRINCE2. But you may find that this approach has considerably more power than you think, and not least for progress control.

So, thinking 'product' before 'activity' is actually rather logical. How can you come up with meaningful activities and sensible estimates to build a wall unless you know what 'wall' actually is in this case? In fact, many projects go wrong right at the beginning because people do indeed list activities and estimate durations (as instructed by books and computer scheduling software) before knowing what the project requires. In turn, that is often because project planners push for this information to get the plan done.

Product-based planning. With this approach you identify and plan the deliverables or products first, then turn your attention to the activities you need to build those products. This is different to the more traditional activity-driven approach, which starts with identifying activities and drawing up activity networks and Gantt charts. You need activity planning and that's a vital element, but the approach 'front ends' that work with powerful product planning, hence it is a product-led or product-based approach to planning.

Thinking 'product' is not particularly natural, whereas thinking 'activity' is. When you understand products, the approach is pretty easy. Some people understand the concept immediately, whereas others struggle for a bit, and then get it. And often it's the people with the most planning experience that find the idea tricky at first. Don't worry; so did I, and then it clicked.

Identifying products in the project

The first step in product-based planning is to think what the products are. You can simply make a list (although see 'Giving the product list some structure', later in this chapter, for a technique that can help). In a Project Plan, you look for between 15 and 30 products to cover the whole of the project at a fairly consistent level of detail.

So what exactly is a product?

Put simply, a product is something that one of the project teams builds or produces. As an example, imagine that I carry out a review of a business area and look at what work it does. The business process is outdated and in need of overhaul and simplification – for example, many of the forms the business uses have sections that just aren't relevant and people leave them blank. The review is to identify the problems and make improvements, and then launch a revised procedure with new form designs as needed.

So, what are the products? Remember that products are something that the team builds, so they're things you can hold in your hand or, if they're too big for that, things that you can kick. In this example the products are small:

- Existing desk instructions (staff instructions on current procedures)
- Diagram of the present procedures
- New procedure definition
- New form designs
- New form supplies
- New desk instructions
- New business procedure – the new procedure up and running

Identifying 'external products'

When I look at the list, I now realise that the supplies of the new forms don't come from within the project but rather from a local print shop, which is, quite obviously, not one of my project teams. I supply the shop with the designs and it prints the forms and glues them to a card back to make pads. The shop's work is not part of my project: The printer's staff activities to do the work aren't on my Gantt chart, and the shop doesn't send me progress reports or time sheets. The forms are important to launch the new business procedure, but they come from outside the project boundary.

I also realise with a sudden flash of insight that the product 'existing desk instructions' must already exist. So although this is an important document in the project, the project team doesn't have to create it. The 'existing desk instructions' product is therefore external as well – it comes over the project boundary from outside.

Using the Product Flow Diagram

The next step in product planning is to identify the sequence in which those products will be created, using a Product Flow Diagram (see Figure 14-1).

The symbols in the diagram are simple: a rectangle for an 'internal' or team product, an ellipse for an 'external' product, and an arrow to show the dependencies or sequence. This diagram is really powerful and well worth the effort of drawing it.

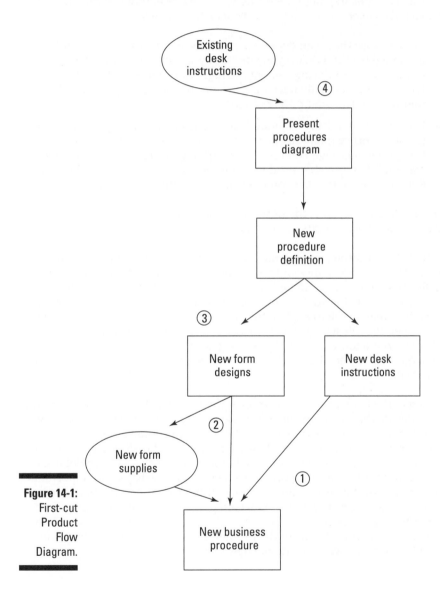

Figure 14-1:
First-cut
Product
Flow
Diagram.

Performing the 'bottom-up' checks

The next step in product planning is to do the *bottom-up* checks. As the name suggests, you start at the bottom of the diagram and work back up to the top. This is a vital step but interestingly successive editions of the PRINCE2 manual have never mentioned it. You check the following:

- ✔ Are you sure that each dependency arrow leading to the product being examined is correct? Are you sure that you can't develop the lower product without having each of the higher products in place? If you find you don't actually need one or more of the higher products, then remove the dependency lines to them.

- ✔ For the product being examined, do you need any other product to be produced other than the ones with arrows leading to it? In other words, is anything missing? You may find a missing product or two, and you may find that a related product is on the diagram somewhere but without an arrow to the one you're examining at the moment.

Going back to Figure 14-1, the bottom-up checks reveal four issues, which are at the numbered points on that diagram.

Starting at the bottom, the dependencies to the new forms and the new desk instructions seem fine, but when I ask whether I need anything else, I realise that I must have trained staff. The new business procedure isn't ready to go unless the staff are clear on how to use it. In turn, I realise that I need a training outline to explain the changes and show staff the new forms. I don't need the full supply of new forms, though. The designs are enough and I can print a few copies of those designs as part of the training outline and hand them round. So, I add in two missing products: training outline and trained staff.

Looking at the left side of the diagram at the bottom, I find a couple of issues. First, I decide that the dependency arrow is redundant between 'New form designs' and 'New business procedure'. 'New form supplies' serves that dependency. But when I look at 'New form supplies', I realise that the shop needs an order from the team to specify the quantities and billing details. So, I identify another missing product – a small one perhaps, but important. Continuing with the bottom-up check, I identify two other missing products. One is the existing form designs on which to base the new ones, and at the top of the diagram I decide that there are bound to be some interview notes and these will record details of the problems and requirements which will be needed to come up with a workable new procedure.

A revised diagram (Figure 14-2) shows the newly found products and adjusted dependencies. By the way, don't worry if the diagram gets a bit messy and you need to re-draw it a few times. This is quite common, especially when you don't know the project very well and lots of new information comes to light. Whiteboards are great for diagrams like this.

If you don't have an electronic whiteboard, take a digital photograph of your diagram at every version. Writing 'Please don't rub this off' at the bottom of the whiteboard isn't enough. That's what the cleaners come to last, just after they've destroyed your work, starting at the top of the board. Years ago I was doing consultancy work with a major bank who had hired a hotel conference room for a couple of days . . . no, sorry, the memory is still too painful! But ever since I've always carried a camera with me.

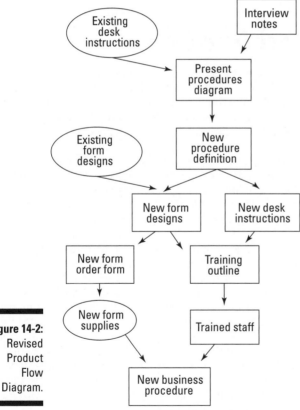

Figure 14-2:
Revised
Product
Flow
Diagram.

Specialist Products and Management Products. The method refers to two categories of product: specialist and management. The specialist products are basically the ones that the teams build (although a few specialist products may be external and come into the project from outside). The management products are the things being used for project management, including products such as the Risk Register, the Business Case, and the Project Initiation Document. You use the management products to manage the production of the specialist products. In the diagrams, you normally model the specialist products only.

Products for quality and for progress milestones

Using a product-based approach to planning also opens the door to very specific quality control and also superb progress monitoring. Chapters 13 and 17 respectively give more detail.

Writing Product Descriptions

I worked for the UK government for some years, but I'm nearly better now; I just get the occasional nightmare. One thing that has stuck with me is a loathing of forms. However, I really like the Product Definition or, as PRINCE2 calls it, the Product Description. Every product on the Product Flow Diagram has one and the description really spells out what that product is.

Some people think that writing Product Descriptions is just doing some form filling. This is both wrong and rather dangerous. Coming up with the Product Descriptions is primarily a thinking exercise that helps you understand the product and you put the results of that thinking on the form. If you resort to form filling, you focus on the paperwork, not on understanding the products.

I ran a planning workshop for nine people on an important industrial project. One Product Description form took the ten of us four hours to complete: that's 40 staff hours to fill in one form. Did the group think that this technique was bureaucratic and wasteful by the end of that four hours? No, they were delighted. The product was absolutely critical in this high-risk, year-long project and nobody properly understood the product when we started. After four hours, which we mostly spent discussing and thinking, everyone understood the product and all were agreed on the description. For such an important product on a business-critical project, everyone thought the time was very well spent. In the same workshop, two people went off to produce a Product Description for a different product and came back ten minutes later with it finished. That product was much more straightforward.

The Product Description poses some really useful questions that help pin down exactly what the product is.

Product Description

Identifier

Title

Purpose

Composition

Derivation

Format and presentation

Development skills required

Quality criteria

Quality tolerance

Quality method

Quality skills required

Quality responsibilities

Identifier

Usually numeric, this can cross reference to symbols on the product diagrams.

Title

Easy enough, but the title needs a bit of thought. Remember three things about product titles:

- ✔ Make sure that you pick a nice short title that you can use easily on the diagrams. Whatever you do, don't resort to using numbers on product diagrams, which then means that you can't read the diagrams without looking up a list all the time.

- ✔ Make the title descriptive, so you can easily understand what the product is.

- ✔ Use the language of the business area. If you change all the business area terminology to different terminology, the business staff can't understand the diagrams and so can't spot any mistakes.

Purpose

The purpose is simply asking why you want to build this product in this project. Often, that question is a no-brainer to the point that you wonder why the heading exists. But just sometimes you stop and realise that although you may normally do something on this project you don't actually need to this time. If you don't know why you need a product, find out or don't build it.

Composition

Composition is the first of the more awkward headings. A better name would be 'description', because that's what the composition mostly is. In this section you describe the product, but that may well include sub-products that comprise this one.

Don't confuse the Product Description with a specification, which is a separate document in its own right. Where you do have a more detailed specification, that becomes the product, and you then write a Product Description that explains exactly what the specification covers and how it will be presented.

Derivation

Derivation is a rather strange heading, but an easier way to think of it is as 'dependencies'. What must be in place before you can build this product? Normally, you need to build other products immediately before this one (the products that the arrows come from on the Product Flow Diagram). However, it may just be that the product is 'external' and comes from a source outside the project, and if so you note it here.

Don't worry if the 'internals' and 'externals' aren't quite clear for the products at first. You may intend to have a team build something (internal product), but then decide for speed to buy it in from outside the project (external product). So you simply change the symbol on the diagram and note the detail on the Product Description.

You may think that this section is rather unnecessary, but surprisingly it often catches any products you miss from the Product Flow bottom-up checks (see the earlier section 'Performing the 'bottom-up' checks'). The dependency may also be on something other than a product, such as a confirmation from the finance director that the funds are in place so that you can proceed with the work of building this product.

Format and presentation

Many products don't have requirements for format and presentation, so don't hesitate to leave the section blank if need be. But reports, for example, may need to comply with a house style. Equally, in projects involving computer systems, data often has a required format, sometimes a very strict one.

Development skills required

This section is obviously useful for resource planning. In the early part of product planning though, and particularly before the product is clear, you may not be quite sure of skills yet, so you can leave the section blank until you know the detail.

Quality criteria

Set down what quality criteria the product must satisfy for it to be complete and then approved. You need to be able to measure quality criteria or you can't determine whether the product meets them. Having said that, defining quality isn't always so easy – Chapter 13 offers more detail.

Quality tolerance

Quality tolerance is a rather strange area added for the first time in the last edition of the PRINCE2 manual. A tolerance, by definition, has a plus and minus boundary to the stated measure. Many project products just aren't like that, but one example is the speed of a new machine for the production line that's being procured in the project. Producing a unit with the machine mustn't take more than three seconds, but shouldn't be faster than two seconds because this is unnecessarily expensive as well as disruptive to the rest of the production line. Most products in business projects don't have a tolerance, so again just leave this section blank if it's not relevant to the product.

Quality method

The quality method section specifies how you measure whether the product meets its criteria. How you do this depends on the nature of the product. Sometimes, you can measure with a ruler – the report must be on A4 paper, for example. Other times, the measure is a judgement – the managers agree that they can understand the report.

Quality skills required

You need to think carefully about skills for the quality checks. Introducing the word 'skills' into the heading is actually a bit dangerous though, because you may want to choose someone precisely because of her lack of skill. For example, if you have an instruction manual for a new computer system, the last person you want to check that manual is a team member who helped write the system and who already knows exactly how it works. Instead, you need someone who's never seen the system before – you sit her down in front of a screen and keyboard with the manual and you say, 'Please enter a new customer record.' But for some technical products you may indeed want a highly skilled and professionally qualified person to conduct the tests.

Quality responsibilities

This refers to who is to produce, check and approve the product. The second two of these three can be the same person.

Defining the project

Now that you've looked at the product description as it applies to all products, or deliverables, in the project, it's necessary to go back a bit to a product description that you do first of all, and which is slightly different. This is the product description for the final deliverable of the whole project; the *Project Product Description*.

Project Product Description

Title

Purpose

Composition

Derivation

Development skills required

Customer quality expectations

Acceptance criteria

Project-level quality tolerances

Acceptance method

Acceptance responsibilities

The Project Product Description is produced during Start Up but can be amended during Initiation when the PID is written and things are being thought through in greater depth. You'll see from the headings that some of the normal Product Description headings are omitted because they're just not relevant when thinking about the project as a whole. Other headings have been adjusted slightly because this is the 'whole project' product. So, acceptance criteria are the criteria that the whole project must satisfy in order to be accepted.

Giving the product list some structure

For the Product Flow Diagram earlier in Figure 14-1, I started with a simple list of products. But my thoughts were a bit random in making the list. If you know the project area well, then you can use another diagram that allows you to think systematically through all the areas of the project to determine what products are in those areas or under those categories.

The *Product Breakdown Structure* or PBS is a simple hierarchy diagram with categories and sub-categories of products, and the products themselves are at the bottom level. This bottom level forms the list of products, from which you can then go on to develop a Product Flow Diagram.

Returning to the new business procedure project, used as an example earlier in the chapter, the PBS may look something like Figure 14-3.

On this diagram you can see the product list at the lowest level. The products are shaded to make them easy to see. The higher-level boxes are the category boxes that give the structure some . . . well, structure. To show that these are just categories or 'groupings', you have an option to make them a different shape. The very top box on the PBS represents the whole project and is the same box as the final box on the Product Flow Diagram. This is the Project Product, subject to the Project Product Description mentioned earlier in the chapter. When the final product on the Product Flow Diagram is complete, that's the whole project done.

Structuring the structure

No rules exist for determining the categories in the structure of a PBS. You use the categories and structure that help you to think the project through systematically. Another project planner may break the project down differently and that's fine, but you both come up with the same bottom line, albeit in a different order.

If we both build a house, you may have main categories of brickwork, woodwork, and electrics. I may have grouped my products by anticipated resources: the things I plan to build personally, the things that supplier A will do for me, and the things that supplier B will do for me. We both end up with light switches on the bottom line somewhere. I have them under a sub-category of 'fittings' under the resources block, which covers the work I intend to do myself. You have them under a sub-category of 'lighting products' under the 'electrics' main block. But we both have light fittings on our diagrams and in both cases we take that product forward to the Product Flow Diagram.

In very large projects, you can have PBS blocks to reflect the groups of products making up the different contracts to be let.

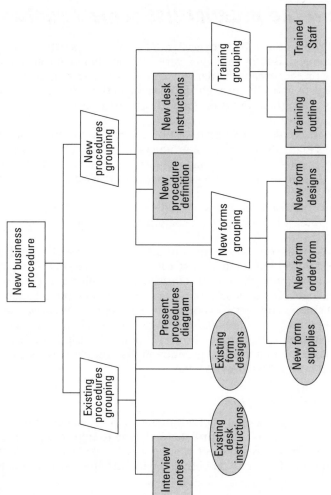

Figure 14-3:
The Product
Breakdown
Structure.

In terms of the depth of the structure, you want this to be fairly evenly balanced; in other words, going to about the same level of detail throughout. You want 15 to 30 products across the plan and about the same level of detail of product. On the house project, for example, having 'roof' as a bottom-level product in one part of the diagram and 'top screw of left side of bottom hinge on kitchen door' in another would make for a bad PBS.

Planning when you don't know the project area

If you don't know the project area well, the PBS diagram often can't help you because you don't know what that structure is in order to be able to think systematically through it. A feature of the PBS is that it works from the top down. If you don't know what the top level is, then you have a problem. In that case, simply leave out the PBS and go straight to Product Flow. But if you do have some knowledge of the area, the PBS can be a real help, both in making sure that you think the product right through and in speeding you up – sometimes quite dramatically.

In one project I was giving consultancy help to a client for Start Up and Project Initiation. I didn't understand this new business project as I was new to the project, and neither did the client, which was partly why I was asked to provide consultancy. A PBS wasn't going to help because nobody knew what the top-level categories of this project were. Nor was the scope clear. I suggested using a Product Flow Diagram first and, unusually, we did this in Start Up rather than Initiation. Because the Product Flow Diagram is a network diagram, we could start anywhere. I was working alongside the Project Manager and together we drew the bits we knew about and went and talked to a lot of people, and over three or four days the whole Product Flow came together, which also neatly defined the scope for the Project Brief. We never did draw a PBS for that project.

Getting to the Product Flow Diagram from the PBS

Moving on to a Product Flow Diagram is very easy if you keep in mind that the bottom level, or 'leaves of the upside-down tree', form the list of products. You use exactly the same boxes on the Product Flow Diagram, only this time you put them in the sequence in which you plan to produce them, and the final product on the flow is the same as the top box on the PBS.

Making one exception to the rule – integration products

Just occasionally you may have a product that's made up of other products. For example, for the product 'engine', the lower-level products may include 'radiator', 'big end', 'butterfly spring', and 'battery'. You can see immediately that 'engine' is not a category. If you take the big end, the butterfly spring, and the other bits and pile them up on the floor, you don't have an engine. An engine is a product in its own right, not a category or grouping, so here you have an option of modelling a higher-level rectangle on the PBS, and the lower-level rectangles underneath it are the components that go to make up the engine. A product that is made up of other products like this is known as an *Integration Product.* In this case, you take the higher-level Integration Product box forward to the Product Flow Diagram as well, and so break the 'bottom level only' rule. In other words, all rectangles and ellipses form the list of products and you take all of them forward to the Product Flow Diagram.

Moving On to Activity Planning

Activity planning is quick to explain, but takes some time to do. You look at each product and decide what activities you need to build it. Here, you consult different people such as suppliers, team specialists, and Team Managers. But it is much easier for them in PRINCE2 because you have the Product Descriptions that say both what the product is, and how it will be tested.

You can easily be too simplistic about activity planning and say that if you identify the products, you already have the activities – so for the product 'machine', the activity is simply 'build the machine'. In turn, that leads people to draw the wrong conclusion that product planning is basically the same as activity planning. But it is often more complicated than one activity for each product anyway. Even if the machine is a very simple one, you may still have two activities of 'build it' and 'test it', each using very different resources.

For the specialist products you can write the activities against each box on the Product Flow Diagram, or you can just list them down the left side of a Gantt chart. Although the computerised scheduling or 'project management' software doesn't usually cover product planning, it allows you to specify milestones as headings and then group tasks under them as follows:

New form designs

> Identify usable content from old forms

> Design new forms

> Check new design with business users

New forms order form

> Establish quantities with business area

> Complete and send the order form

You have two things to remember here. First, don't forget the management products such as Stage Plans. The diagrams show the specialist products so you can work systematically through those, but allow for the management products too. Second, don't forget that external products may have a time duration. If you send a 'windows specification' (internal product) to a window manufacturer who then sends you the 'windows' (external product) for your team to produce the 'installed windows' (internal product), don't imagine that the manufacturer can produce the windows in zero time.

Estimating – the Easy Bit

Yes, the heading is meant to be a joke. Estimating is one of the hardest bits of project planning but PRINCE2 only mentions it in passing by listing a few techniques. Project techniques toolbox publications, such as the Inspirandum *Project Techniques Toolbox*, explain some techniques. But don't go looking for magic formulas that give you perfect estimates every time because you're doomed to disappointment; they don't exist and estimating is a tricky business.

Estimating can be sub-divided into two basic approaches: *top-down* estimating, which you do across the whole project, and the more detailed *bottom-up* approach, when you have the detailed activities in stage planning and can estimate them and add them together to get a total.

Some techniques rely on you knowing how long things have taken before; what's *normal* in your organisation. If your project staff have lots of support work to do alongside their project work, don't expect them to be as productive as staff who can concentrate just on project work. This variation in the working environment is one reason why you can't have an easy estimating formula.

Imagine that I ask you to paint a wall for me, and I tell you the size of the wall and that I've already prepared it for painting. What's the most valuable bit of information you need to answer the question of how long the painting takes you? That information is how long it took you last time you painted a wall. Now, perhaps this wall is only half the size of the one you did before, but you can take that into account when calculating the time you need.

Most organisations are really bad at storing historic information. If it exists at all, the information is in the depths of old Project Plans where finding it is really difficult, even if you can remember which projects involved this sort of work anyway.

The construction industry is much more mature than most when it comes to estimating costs. In the UK, *The Architects' and Builders' Price Book* holds statistics on how much the various bits of building work cost, and Spon publishes this every year. So, for each element of building you can just look up the detail and find out materials costs and labour costs for the stated unit, such as per square metre. This is how builders can give you a reply so quickly when you ask for an estimate for a job on your home. They just look up the different elements, multiply them by the number of units, and then tell you the total. Even that doesn't help with getting accurate time estimates though, as most people who've had building work done in the UK can tell you . . . between heart-wrenching sobs and with their head in their hands.

Scheduling and Resourcing

The work of scheduling and resourcing is very integrated with estimating and you move backwards and forwards between these jobs.

You estimate the amount of time you need to do an activity, but then the estimate depends on what resources are available. And making a decision isn't as simple as dividing the work hours by the number of people either. If you have a 500-hour job and one person available, how long does the job take? Perhaps 500 working hours. If you have a 500-hour job and five staff, how long does it take? Well, certainly not 100 hours. It may be considerably more because of arguments about it (with five people you can probably reckon on at least six opinions) and the fact that Joe makes the tea while Mary produces the team news sheet. What if you have two people? Again, the work may not take 250 hours because they work so well together that synergy sets in, so they may do the job in just 200 hours. Then, what about the level of experience? In most cases, trainees work more slowly than very experienced staff and make more mistakes, which adds time while the errors are corrected. So, estimating, resourcing, and scheduling are very much bound together.

You can use different techniques for scheduling, but most project planners use activity networks and Gantt charts. Actually, most people just use Gantt charts because they don't really understand activity networks. But you can use a timeline if you prefer.

Activity networking and precedence networks

This book focuses on PRINCE2 and can't go into the detail of precedence networks and Gantt charts, but do consult *Project Management For Dummies* by Stanley E. Portney (Wiley) for more information. Having said that, this section covers the basic concepts to help you draw up a simple network and Gantt chart if you're not already familiar with the techniques.

Activities have dependencies, just like products. You can't test the new machine until you build it. Although Gantt charts are really great (see the next section 'Activities with Gantt charts'), they don't show dependencies very well. Most computer tools display arrows on the Gantt chart to try to show dependencies, but the arrows just make the chart really confusing. The first thing I do when loading a new version of any scheduling software is to find the option where you turn the arrows off. A different diagram is much more powerful and suited to the job – the activity network. There are two basic sorts of activity network but the most used one is the *precedence network*. The precedence network is much more straightforward than the alternative and all the popular software tools use it.

The good news is that constructing a precedence network is dead easy, contrary to the common perception. Figure 14-4 shows some activities from the example of the new business procedure project set down in the precedence network. The diagram simply shows in what order you can do the activities. You can see that you can do some activities at the same time, and the dependencies show that as well.

The precedence network can show timings and this is where the power of the technique starts to emerge. Products don't have a time as such, but rather the activities to build that product take time. In putting the times onto the network, you can work out the total time the project requires. Figure 14-4 shows only part of the project, but it illustrates how the technique works.

You can see that the pathway through the bottom of the diagram is longer than the pathway across the top; six days and one day respectively. You don't have to be too much of a mathematician to calculate that the part of the project covered by the diagram takes 17 days in total, leaving a bit of spare time across the top path; in fact, five days of spare time.

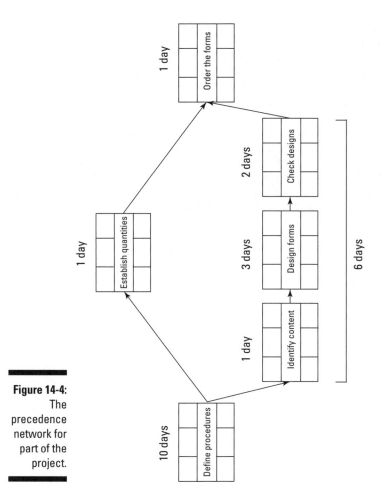

Figure 14-4:
The precedence network for part of the project.

In the top set of boxes, you can put the estimated duration in the middle, then the earliest start data (ESD) in the left box, and the earliest finish date (EFD) in the right one. This example uses day numbers (day 1, day 2 and so on) but if you use computer software it works with calendar dates. The earliest finish date is simply the earliest start date for the activity, plus the duration.

You can now see those figures entered on the top line of each box (Figure 14-5). The earliest start of an activity is the same as the earliest finish of the previous one because it follows it immediately. Where two lines feed in, as in the box on the extreme right, you use the highest figure as the ESD, which in this case is 16 from 'Check designs'.

Now, using the bottom set of figures, the return journey from right to left, you can calculate the amount of free time, or *float*, on each activity. The first step is to copy down the ESD from the top right box to the bottom right box on the very last activity. In this case, that figure is 17. That figure becomes the latest finish date (LFD) by which you must complete the activity. Now, to fill in the bottom left box, you need to determine the very latest time that activity can start without going beyond the LFD. In this activity example, the latest finish is the end of day 17 and the activity is one day long. Therefore, if you start it any later than day 16 then the activity is going to be late finishing. You calculate LFD minus duration to give the latest start date (LSD).

You copy back the LSD of the activity you've just calculated to become the LFD of all preceding activities directly connected by an arrow. In Figure 14-5, you see that there are two activities that come directly before the final activity 'Order the forms' and both of these carry 16 as their LFDs. Where an activity has more than one line feeding back into it, as into the first activity on the example, you take the lowest of the LSDs feeding in. In this case that's 10.

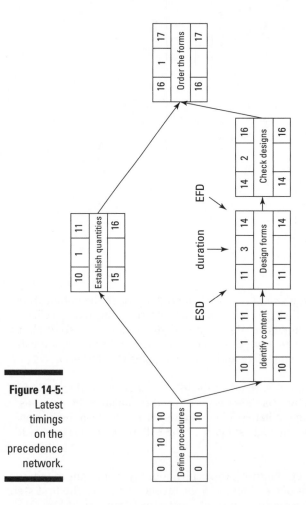

Figure 14-5:
Latest
timings
on the
precedence
network.

You calculate the amount of float on each activity by comparing the end pair of figures in each activity box, the EFD (top right), and the LFD (bottom right). You put the amount of float in the bottom middle box.

Now you can show the longest path by following the line of zero floats (see Figure 14-6). This longest path determines the length of the project and is known as the *critical path*. If any activity along this line gets delayed, it lengthens the longest path and the project end date slips. When you look at the top line of the diagram, you can now see that the float for 'Establish quantities' shows five days: The lower path is five days longer than the top one and so the lower path determines the length of the project.

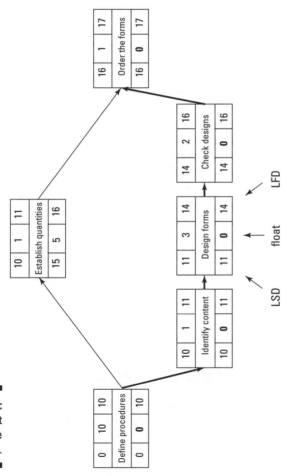

Figure 14-6:
Zero float and the critical path.

Activities with Gantt charts

The Gantt chart is probably more familiar territory (Figure 14-7). After you get the precedence network together, constructing a Gantt chart is very easy. If you draw the Gantt chart by hand (unlikely), the bar for each activity is fixed from just three of the figures from the same activity on the precedence network – top left, top right, bottom right; or, to use the professional expression, earliest start date (ESD), earliest finish date (EFD), and latest finish date (LFD). Remember, if you work with day or week numbers rather than calendar dates, the figures refer to 'end of day' or 'end of week'. Figure 14-7 shows part of the Gantt chart built from the Precedence Network data.

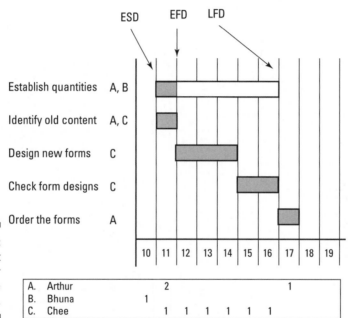

Figure 14-7: The Gantt chart for part of the project.

Activities and resource levelling

The last bit of activity planning checks for resource conflict. The Gantt chart in Figure 14-7 shows a resource conflict, because Arthur is scheduled to work full-time on two activities at once. The grid along the bottom showing the resources shows this. You need to resolve the problem and 'smooth' or 'level' the resources to get the required resources down below the level of available resources. Smoothing or levelling involves three basic steps:

1. If an activity is not on the Critical Path, delay its start until a time when the person is available. You can slide activities along within the person's free time or float.

2. If you still have a problem, see if you can get more resources, if that helps. The Project Board may be able to give you more people with the same skill set. This lifts the level of available resources and so may resolve the problem.

3. If you do steps 1 and 2 but you still have a problem, then the project end date moves. In the example in Figure 14-7, Arthur has to do one activity and then the other one a week later, which takes the duration out to 18 days for this part of the project.

Resource levelling can be hard work, and all the more so where you need to level resources between projects as well as within your own. But don't give up. A plan with resource conflicts just doesn't work and you hit the problems in the project only, rather than in the planning.

Checking Risk

You should be checking for new project risk – risks that come from within the project itself rather than from the outside – right through the planning work. However, if while checking project risk you notice an external or business risk, you deal with that as well.

Project risk may include things like multiple points in the project where you need advice on legal matters, and that advice may take time to arrive and so delay the project. After the resource planning you may notice that nearly all the project staff are available for part of their working week only, because they're working on other projects at the same time. That situation is likely to slow the staff down because they have to stop and start all the time. Plus, if one of the other projects comes under pressure and has a higher organisational priority, staff's time on your project may get cut even further.

As with all risk analysis, you record risks that'll be formally managed in the Risk Register, and you build actions into the plan. You're very likely to update the plan then, and any contingency time you require alters the timing of the project activities and perhaps the overall timescale of the project.

For much more on risk analysis and management, including the use of the Risk Register in PRINCE2, please see Chapter 15.

Some questions to check for project risk

Here are a few questions to ask when you're considering project risk:

- **Estimates:** Are estimates likely to be wrong because you have no previous experience of the type of work involved?

- **Staff:** Are you using a lot of trainees on the project who may be slower and make more errors?

- **Suppliers:** Are suppliers already over-stretched with other work and likely to cause delays?

- **Supplier history:** Are you locked into using a supplier who's let you down before?

- **Timing:** Do you have a fixed end date that allows little room for delay?

- **Finance:** Is the money for the project readily available or are funding problems likely to cause delay (for example, hold-ups with external government funding)?

- **Experience:** Is the project a completely new experience where unforeseen work is likely to occur, despite the Product Flow Diagram checks?

- **Project environment:** Is the project running in a highly changeable business environment where significant change requirements may cause setbacks?

- **Inter-project:** Do inter-project dependencies exist with products, staff, or both where a delay in another project may affect this one?

- **Multi-agency:** Is the project running in a public area where a lot of bodies need to authorise things, which builds in great potential for delay and extended debate over trivial things?

Explaining the Plan

The last thing to do with the plan, at whichever level of detail you're working, is add textual explanation and also any other elements you require that the products and the activities don't cover. The most important of these other elements is a finance plan.

Adding explanations for those who read the plan

Sometimes the Project Plan can look a bit strange unless you know why it's been set up like that. The text of the plan explains anything unusual. In the case of the Project Plan, a number of people are likely to need to look at it, but notably this includes Project Board members, who must sign off the plan and need to understand why it's been set up the way it has.

Sometimes a gap can occur in the activities. This can look very odd, but valid explanations for it include:

- ✔ **Risk contingency (time):** A fallback action allowing for delay where this is likely.

- ✔ **Waiting for an external supply:** You ordered something and the gap allows time for a supplier who's completely outside the project to build the item.

- ✔ **Waiting for staff to come from another project:** You know that the designers aren't available until week 32.

You may need to comment on other things as well though, such as your level of confidence in the estimates that underpin the activity plans. If experienced people helped with the estimating of a fairly standard project, then you may be, say, 90 per cent confident that the estimates are correct and that the project will run closely to the plan. However, if this is a novel project and nobody has much relevant experience, you may be only 20 per cent confident that the estimates are correct. This second case gives early warning to the board and any others that the project may fluctuate significantly either side of the estimates.

Financial planning

Strangely, PRINCE2 says virtually nothing about financial planning within the project. As financial planning is an important part of project planning and control (the territory of PRINCE2), this remains a big gap in the method.

You need to draw up a budget for the project and then monitor project spending and compare it with that budget. As with all planning in PRINCE2, your financial planning goes into more detail at stage and team levels. You can have a high-level project budget, and then a more detailed stage budget, and beyond that team budgets for each unit of work. You do most monitoring at stage budget level, but you must also maintain the project budget. For example, information may come to light in stage 4 that affects the level of spending in stage 6 and consequently the costs of the whole project.

Most people use a spreadsheet for the budget. This allows you to show the costed elements of the plan, the actual costs you have so far, and the variance between planned and actual costs incurred. A spreadsheet also allows 'what if' projections on costs.

If early-stage activities are more expensive than you expected, part of the project control is to investigate why. If you now think that you underestimated the project across the board, you can do a 'what if' projection on the spreadsheet to increase costs of all activities and so help evaluate the impact on the whole project.

Planning at Three Levels

The approach to planning covered in this chapter applies to all the levels of planning in the project. You plan at three levels, and use the same techniques for all three, as shown in Figure 14-8.

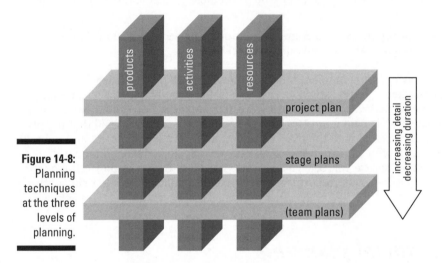

Figure 14-8:
Planning
techniques
at the three
levels of
planning.

The Project Plan

You develop the Project Plan in the Initation Stage and it forms part of the Project Initiation Document or PID (for more on Initiation and the PID, please see Chapter 5). The Project Plan covers the period from the end of the Initiation Stage to the planned end of the project, and shows all the delivery stages of the project. You maintain the Project Plan throughout the project and update it at least at every stage end. In reality, updating is usually continuous, at least for activities, because in computer scheduling tools the Project Plan and then successive Stage Plans are all within a single file.

The Project Manager is responsible for producing the Project Plan, but she discusses it carefully with other people – including Project Board members, team specialists, and key suppliers – to get it accurate.

The Project Plan also involves *Project Assurance*, the audit function of the project to check that it's correct. For example, Project Assurance can check whether you mistakenly planned any activities over public holiday periods, and whether the total amount of user resources stays within the limits set down by the Senior User(s) on the Project Board.

The Stage Plan

A Stage Plan covers just one management stage and you draw it up just before that management stage begins. After Project Initiation, you keep the Project Plan up to date from the latest information in the Stage Plans.

The Project Manager is responsible for Stage Plans, but takes advice from others, particularly from Team Managers.

Team Plans

Team Plans are optional. In smaller projects especially, the Stage Plans often incorporate sufficient detail to control the team work assignments, or *Work Packages*, as PRINCE2 calls them. Where the Stage Plan doesn't have sufficient detail (notably where a Work Package is particularly complex), the Team Manager may decide that she needs a more detailed plan to control that work and so develops a Team Plan for that Work Package.

Where a project is particularly supplier intensive, the Project Manager may ask the Team Managers to produce a Team Plan for each of the Work Packages they're involved with, and then work with the Team Managers to create a Stage Plan from the Team Plans, as shown in Figure 14-9.

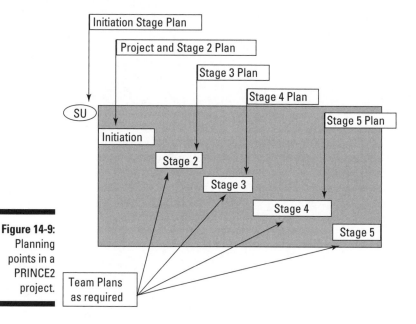

Figure 14-9: Planning points in a PRINCE2 project.

Chapter 15

Managing Project Risk

. . . .

In This Chapter

▶ Defining risk

▶ Deciding how to handle risk in the project

▶ Identifying individual risks

▶ Assessing the risks and thinking about how to handle them

▶ Planning and implementing your risk actions

▶ Using the Risk Register and Daily Log

. . . .

Many projects neglect risk management, and that's a common cause of project failure. This is a sad state of affairs, because risk management isn't difficult to do, it's often not that time-consuming, and it's actually rather interesting.

At its very simplest, risk management is just asking 'What can go wrong with this project?' and then doing some simple management stuff to prevent that happening or at least to control it. Some argue that risk management is all negative and unnecessary. They say you're just looking for trouble and wasting time looking at things that mostly never happen. In fact, as you'll probably agree immediately as a wise user of PRINCE2, risk management is very positive. You do it to protect the project and to prevent or control things that otherwise may cause problems to the point of complete project failure. Actually PRINCE2 also covers 'good' risk and the work to try and increase the chances of something advantageous happening in the project.

In this chapter is good news and bad news. One bit of good news to mention at the outset is that overall PRINCE2 is quite good with its risk management. The method has limits in what it covers though, and you may well want to go further if you're involved in a high-risk project. But more good news is that it's easy to add in additional risk techniques and controls. The bad news is that the 2009 edition of PRINCE2 has made the area of risk management more complicated – so really you should have learned PRINCE2 earlier and bought the previous edition of this book! This complexity is because the method has abandoned some of its project-oriented roots in favour of alignment with another UK government approach that covers all organisational risk, not just project risk. But in this chapter I give you useful information including, in a couple of places, harking back to the 'good old days'.

Starting with the Basics: What Is Risk?

A dictionary definition of risk is 'the adverse consequences of future events'. In other words, risk is future trouble. That's what risk management in projects is mostly about: seeing what trouble may come and taking action now to control it and in some cases even prevent it. However, although that trouble-focused view used to be the PRINCE2 definition, the method now defines risk as 'an uncertain event or set of events that, should it occur, will have an effect on the achievement of objectives'. This reflects the UK government's risk-management method M_o_R® (Management of Risk). Although this definition is a bit of a mouthful, it reflects the point that a risk can be a positive thing – the risk of something good happening as well as the risk of something bad happening.

An example that the chief examiner of the M_o_R® method has used to explain this is the stock market. If you buy shares you take a risk, but the shares may go up in value as well as down. The risk is positive as well as negative. That's a neat example.

You still need to remember the dictionary definition, though, because although a particular risk may indeed have a positive outcome, the emphasis in projects is still primarily on what can go wrong and how you can contain that.

Risk management has been around for a long time and a lot of modern thinking on risk is based on an explosive time for the development of risk management in the early 1600s – no, that's not a typo. Like many other risk approaches, PRINCE2 uses two elements of risk measurement suggested in a paper produced in a monastery outside Paris back at that time: impact and probability. Don't you feel good knowing that you work with something that's so bang up to date? If you want to know a bit more about the development of risk thinking, a fascinating and very readable book is *Against the Gods: The Remarkable Story of Risk* by Peter L. Bernstein and published by John Wiley.

Deciding your strategy for handling risk

Before getting in too deep with the handling of individual risks, you need to think through your overall approach, or strategy, for handling risk in the project. That strategy is going to vary from project to project, so your approach on a small, low-impact, low-risk project is going to be rather different from that on a huge, high-risk and business-critical project.

The Risk Management Strategy

Introduction	Scales
Risk management procedure	Proximity
Tools and Techniques	Risk categories
Records	Risk response categories
Reporting	Early warning indicators
Timing of risk management activities	Risk tolerance
Roles and responsibilities	Risk budget

To record your risk approach on this particular project, PRINCE2 includes the *Risk Management Strategy* which you develop in the Initiation or planning stage of the project and which then gets put into the Project Initiation Document. As with quite a few of the PRINCE2 management products, it can look a bit daunting at first sight, but as always, adjust it to keep it as simple as possible in line with the control needs of your project.

Understanding the sections of the strategy

Introduction

The purpose, objectives, scope and responsibilities for risk management in the project. Apart from responsibilities, the areas here are often fairly self-evident and you may find you need to put little in this part. But the section will be more important if your project is part of a programme of projects because you'll almost certainly need to spell out the scope clearly to show what project risk management covers and what will be addressed by risk management activity at the higher, programme management, level. The same applies if you work in a place where a formal risk management approach has been adopted across the whole organisation.

Don't ever struggle to 'pad out' a section of the Risk Management Strategy, or any other PRINCE2 management product for that matter, to make it look a respectable size. If there's little to say, then say little.

Risk management procedure

Any procedures you use for managing risk in the project are recorded in this section, such as how people should report new risks. The areas to cover relate to the risk management procedure diagram that comes later in this chapter. Where the project is using existing organisational standards you can just reference them; you needn't write out or copy in information that's recorded in other places, provided that those places are readily accessible.

Tools and techniques

There may be particular techniques that you intend to use in the different parts of risk management, such as the Ishikawa diagram – explained later in this chapter – to help identify risks. But tools may include computerised risk management tools or risk analysis questionnaires.

Records

This sets down how risks will be recorded. You normally use the Risk Register for risks to be formally managed, and the Daily Log for those to be informally managed. The manual also suggests that you define the Risk Register in this section, showing what headings are to be included. Personally I think this is a bit over-the-top in most cases as it's rather clear from the Risk Register itself what headings are included! In a very formal and high-risk environment, there may be some discussion on this and the strategy may need to be agreed before the Risk Register is set up, and in that case it may be fair enough to spell out the contents in this Records section. But you can get the wrong idea that PRINCE2 is huge if you just read the manual as you're likely to draw the natural but incorrect conclusion that this detail is the norm.

Reporting

The Communication Management Strategy overlaps a bit here. For more on the Comms Strategy, have a look at Chapter 5. Arguably it's better to have all the reporting set down in one place, that is, the Comms Strategy rather than split the reports across the different strategies. However risk reporting does need to be specified somewhere. You need to think through and get agreement on risk reporting requirements.

Part of your risk reporting might be the regular circulation of the p-i grid (probability–impact) described later in this chapter. The grid can be really helpful because it provides a visual representation of where risks are, and it can also be used to show changes since the last reporting point. You can read how you do this later in the chapter.

Timing of risk management activities

This is a sensible section, but the manual is rather limited in its explanation of the heading. It talks about risk management activity at an End Stage Assessment (the Project Board's review of the project at the end of each management stage). Now while the board must check over the risk position at an ESA, the members are hardly likely to be getting up to that much risk management activity in just one part of a 40-minute meeting! What is much more significant on timing is how often risk will be reviewed *during* stages. For example, in a higher-risk project, it may be that the Project Manager should go through a formal review of all risk every two weeks and do that together with the risk specialist who's been appointed to the project. This sort of work is included in the activity 'Review the Stage Status' in the process 'Controlling a Stage' which is covered in Chapter 7.

Roles and responsibilities

This refers to who is to do the various bits of risk management. The previous comment on timing gives an example. Risk will be regularly reviewed by the Project Manager and the appointed risk management specialist on this high-risk project.

You can get a dangerous side-effect when you state who's responsible for a particular risk – the same danger exists in organisational risk management. The problem is that when you set down who's responsible, everyone else thinks that they're not responsible. You can put a 'catch all' in the roles section to say everyone has a responsibility to report risk, but you almost certainly need to vocalise this in any project staff briefing as well.

Following on from the last Tip, if some junior team member does report a risk, be careful how you react. If the warning is silly, but actually the team member did it in good faith – for example, he didn't realise it had already been discussed and discounted – nevertheless thank him for being vigilant. If you jump on someone for being stupid, what will he do when he spots a new and major risk in a few weeks' time that nobody else has seen? Report it perhaps? No way – he'll put his head down and keep quiet. And probably not to get his own back either but rather to be quite sure he doesn't get shown up again.

Scales

Have a look at the section on the p-i grid later in this chapter for more on this. But for now, just take on board that different projects have different scales for things like impact. A £10,000-risk impact is usually going to be very much less significant on a project with a £2 million budget than one with an £11,000 budget.

Proximity

Proximity is how soon a risk can happen. You can read more about this in the 'assessing' section later in the chapter.

Risk categories

Categories can be useful to indicate who should have responsibility for different risks and who else may need to be informed of them. Have a look at the suggested set later in this chapter.

Risk response categories

The nine suggested PRINCE2 response categories again are listed in a panel later in this chapter, but the good news is that you'll find an alternative and shorter set provided too. Under this heading in the strategy, you put down what categories you're going to use in the project. As always, be careful to take note of any organisational standards.

Early warning indicators

I'd like to be able to offer you a clear explanation here, but I can't. There is a rather enigmatic explanation in the PRINCE2 manual that talks about tracking to determine if pre-defined levels have been reached. The problem is rooted in the fact that early warning indicators are normally related to individual specific risks, not to all risk. Therefore it makes more sense to put most of the information on early warning indicators against particular risks in the Risk Register rather than in the strategy. There are instances where you may want to have a project-wide indicator and one is to spot the cumulative build-up of risk in the project. For example, if all 100 risks were rated 'low' probability but they all moved up to 'medium' probability then looking at just one of those risks may not set off alarm bells. But the fact that all 100 have been upgraded raises a concern because the cumulative risk of the project has increased significantly.

Risk tolerance

A tolerance is a statement of authority limits, plus and minus. It fits particularly well with probability and impact and the p-i grid covered later in the chapter. If a particular threat becomes more dangerous and enters the high score zone on the grid, the fact must be reported immediately. Or, on the minus side, if it's found to be less dangerous and drops out of that zone, the fact must also be reported immediately. But some types of risk may need to be reported straight away if they start to materialise and there's no flexibility at all. You set down these factors in this Risk Tolerance section.

Risk budget

Decisions need to be made on whether to have a separate budget, and if so how it's to be handled. The next section of this chapter examines the options.

Managing the Risk Budget

You can adopt one of two basic stances on the risk budget:

1. Don't have one. Just roll any risk-related budget into the project and stage budgets.

2. Have a risk budget where risk-related funds are kept separate from the main budget for the planned work.

Where the Project Manager is very experienced and has a lot of delegated authority for the project, it may be appropriate to just let him manage the risk with its associated costs, just as he manages the rest of the work. Indeed, a Project Board may want this to be the case and not be involved with the detail of authorising specific risk amounts. They just authorise a total and the Project Manager gets on with bringing the project in within this total.

Usually though, separate risk budgeting is advantageous so everyone can see what money is set aside for risk and the amounts against specific risks can be pre-authorised by the Project Board. If the risk happens, the Project Manager already has the authority to spend the funds to deal with it and the board knows what it has signed up to.

If another project is delayed it creates the risk that staff won't be released in time for our project. A fallback is that if this happens, we hire in some additional staff, and this response is costed and approved. If, later in the project, it's found that the other project is indeed delayed and staff won't be released, then the risk has been realised and the Project Manager can hire in some extra help using the risk funds. There's no need to go back to the Project Board because the board has already agreed this action and has already approved the funds.

Just in passing, and because I can't resist it, critics of PRINCE2 say the method is procedure-bound and causes delay to projects with documentation and over-management. But you can see from this example of the risk budget how the Project Manager can react extremely quickly to a risk happening. He doesn't then need to involve the Project Board with some risk-spending-approval procedure, and that's simply because the actions were set down in the Risk Register together with any financial provision, and approved in one go.

Using a Risk Cycle

Enough of the high-level planning then, and on to specific risks. The PRINCE2 method now has a 'procedure' for risk management and has abandoned the use of a risk cycle to think through the handling of each particular risk. I think that's a step backwards because the risk cycle in the previous edition was a particularly good one because it's simple – so simple in fact that after you get used to it, you can keep the cycle in your head. As promised at the beginning of the chapter, this book is including a couple of older things that you may find helpful on projects, so we have kept in that cycle; just ignore this section for the moment if you're about to take the PRINCE2 exams.

In line with many other approaches, the cycle divides neatly into two halves – risk analysis and risk management (see Figure 15-1). The point of this is that after analysing the risk you may well decide that no management is necessary, so you don't move to the second half of the cycle. That point is lost in the new procedure, which covers the handling of all risk in one go, and the procedure also loses the advantage that the cycle shows identification of a particular risk as out of the main loop because you only do this once.

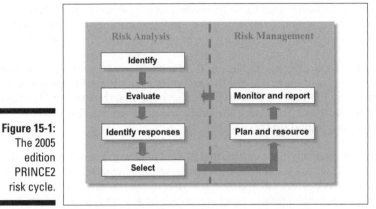

Based on OGC PRINCE2 material. Reproduced under licence from OGC.

Figure 15-1:
The 2005 edition PRINCE2 risk cycle.

Managing Risk with the Risk Procedure

PRINCE2 now models risk management with a procedure. The risk procedure seen in Figure 15-2 has four elements and because these go round in a circle they don't function as a cycle but rather they handle all risk in the project en bloc.

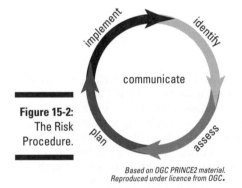

Figure 15-2:
The Risk Procedure.

Based on OGC PRINCE2 material.
Reproduced under licence from OGC.

The next five major sections in this chapter are to look at each of the five parts of the risk procedure – the four arrows and the 'communicate' function in the middle – so the model gives you a roadmap for most of the rest of the chapter.

Although the PRINCE2 manual doesn't provide too much in the way of techniques you can find lots to help with risk management and especially with risk identification and assessment. For details look around the Internet for publications that are 'project techniques toolboxes'. You'll find several including one from Inspirandum that's designed to fit particularly well with PRINCE2 and another from John Wiley. Having said that, as this chapter continues in its 'helpful mode', and follows the model round, you'll find a few useful techniques that you can apply easily.

Identifying Risk

First, you identify what the risks are. Lots of techniques can help with this and most are simple, such as using a risk checklist.

Risk categories and the Risk Checklist

You can find lists of risk categories in different risk publications, on the Internet and in risk software tools. There is one example in the next panel which is based on – yes, the previous edition of PRINCE2! Some use a simpler list such as the PESTLE acronym – political, economic, sociological, technological, legal, and environmental. Categories are useful because they help you break the risks up a bit so you can think them through in a more structured way, and also because it may help determine who should be responsible for managing them or even providing funds for management.

You can use risk categories (with common risks listed under each of them) as a Risk Checklist, which is the first of the risk techniques.

Commercial Risk Checklists can be very helpful, but a tailored list of headings and risks that are more precisely relevant to your own organisation is more valuable still. At the beginning of each project, after doing other risk identification activity, you can use your Risk Checklist as a safety net to see whether you missed anything. Risk specialists suggest that you don't use the checklist first, as you're likely to miss new risks.

A set of risk categories

- ✔ Strategic
- ✔ Commercial
- ✔ Economic
- ✔ Financial
- ✔ Market
- ✔ Legal and regulatory
- ✔ Organisational/management

- ✔ Human factors
- ✔ Political
- ✔ Environmental
- ✔ Technical
- ✔ Operational
- ✔ Infrastructure

If you have a Project Office that provides administrative support (have a look at Chapter 12 for more on the Project Office), then that's a good place to keep an organisational Risk Checklist. But other project staff mustn't disown the checklist. If they see a new risk that may affect other projects, staff must ask the Project Office to add it to the list so that all projects consider it during planning. Equally, if someone finds that a particular risk just can't happen in the organisation any more, then he needs to ask the Project Office to remove that risk from the list. That way, the Risk Checklist is always up to date, relevant, and extremely useful, and only a small overhead is required to maintain it.

Identifying causes, events and effects

For each risk it's helpful to break it into three parts. Different approaches use different names for this but PRINCE2 uses:

- ✔ Cause
- ✔ Event (the risk itself)
- ✔ Effect

Although you can simply list these for each risk, another option is to use a diagram. Inspirandum's 'Project Techniques Toolbox' suggests a notation with a triangle for a cause or trigger, a rectangle for the risk event and a circle for the effect, as shown in Figure 15-3. Diagrams like this can be particularly helpful because you can readily see the interaction between the different elements. For example, a particular cause may trigger more than one risk. You can also show chain reactions in risks where the effect of one risk is actually a cause of another, and the effect of that sets off yet another risk. It gets really interesting when you start to consider not only the effect of each risk if it happens on its own, but also combined effects if more than one risk happens at the same time. If you're working in a project with any significant amount of risk you need to move towards this sort of detail in your risk analysis.

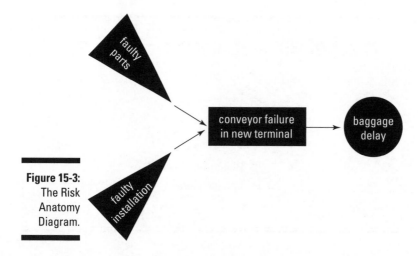

Figure 15-3:
The Risk
Anatomy
Diagram.

Opportunities and threats. Picking up on the point that risk can be good or bad, PRINCE2 makes a further distinction on risk causes. The risk of something good happening is triggered by an 'opportunity' while the risk of something bad happening is a 'threat'.

Differentiating between risks and impacts

People often confuse risks and impacts. In someone's Risk Register you may see:

> *Risk 3 – The project will overspend.*
>
> *Risk 4 – The project will be late.*

These are not risks but impacts. The risks are what may cause the project to go over budget and what may cause it to be late.

Understanding this opens the way to using a very helpful risk analysis technique, which is worth mentioning in passing because it can be so helpful in a systematic review of risk, and because it fits so well with using risk categories. It's the Ishikawa or fishbone diagram (see Figure 15-4), which is sometimes known as a 'cause and effect diagram'. The impact is the effect and you can systematically look at the causes, the risks that may give that impact.

You can use the chosen risk categories, as set down in the project's Risk Management Strategy, as the primary fish bones and enter the individual risks as the secondary bones. This is simply a hierarchical diagram, but it's really helpful because it takes you systematically through every area of risk and so gives structure to this part of your risk analysis. The technique makes you think about every area and so helps find risks that you may not otherwise realise are there.

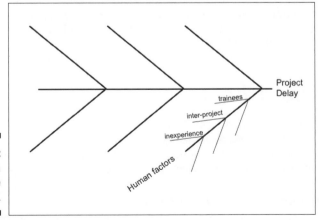

Figure 15-4:
An Ishikawa fishbone diagram.

Figure 15-4 shows a partly completed fishbone diagram for the impact of delay in a project. It considers the human factors:

- ✔ **Trainees:** The project must use a lot of trainees who are slower and are likely to make mistakes.

- ✔ **Inter-project:** Some of the teams come from other projects, so if those projects get delayed then those teams may arrive late.

- ✔ **Inexperience:** Team members have very limited experience in this technical area, and the budget doesn't allow for getting help from outside.

You can use two other techniques for identifying risk instead of, or as well as, Risk Checklists and Ishikawa diagrams and just two are:

- ✔ **Interviewing:** Talk to the Executive and other board members, team specialists, Team Managers, external suppliers, and Project Managers who've managed similar projects.

- ✔ **Examine the Product Flow Diagram:** For each product box, ask whether anything may go wrong with its development. See which external products may affect the project badly if they're delayed or if the supply doesn't materialise. If you think a particular risk may always affect the project badly, don't forget – for some of the externals at least – that you may have alternative sources of supply. Turn to Chapter 14 for more on this planning technique.

You may like to run a risk workshop. You can get key people from the project together and spend some time listing on a flipchart what the risks are and how you can deal with them. This is quite good fun as well as being fast and highly effective. It also has the powerful advantage that key players on the project are already well aware of risk because they went to the workshop and joined in the discussion. Often, the memory of the workshop is more powerful than just reading about risks in the Risk Register later on. You can use quite a few of the risk techniques, such as the Ishikawa Diagram, very successfully in a workshop setting.

Assessing risk

The next step in the risk procedure is to put some measures on the risks you've now identified. The two common measures are impact and probability – back to the monastery outside Paris mentioned at the beginning of the chapter – but you also need to consider proximity, which is how soon the risk may happen.

Calculating impact on a scale of one to . . .

Impact can be tricky and you need to define your scale carefully. You may do this just for a particular project, or you may have a standard scale in your organisation. Either way, it's set down in the Risk Management Strategy. What PRINCE2 can't offer is a standard scale that all organisations can use.

If you work for a multinational organisation with an annual turnover of £23 billion (like one of my clients) then, on a scale of 1 to 5, what's the impact of a loss of £1 million, assuming you're not insured for it? If you work in a company with just two people and an annual turnover of £250,000, what's the scale of impact of a loss of £1 million?

Areas of risk impact

Here are a few areas to think about when considering the impact of a risk:

- ✔ **Time:** This includes delays to the final project delivery, but also to parts within the project. For example, do you have other deadlines, such as taking products into operational use at different points in the project, not just at the end?

- ✔ **Cost:** Consider the total amount but also the timing. For example, if a risk may cause delay, then some costs that you expected the project to incur in this financial year may instead fall in the next one.

- ✔ **Physical resources:** You may face impacts on availability of specialised equipment or accommodation, for example. If something gets delayed on your project, you may need some specialised equipment for the next activity in November rather than October as you originally planned. But another project has already booked that equipment for November.

- ✔ **Staff resource:** As with physical resources, timing can have a big impact. But although machines don't have feelings (unless you count Marvin in *The Hitchhiker's Guide to the Galaxy*), people do, so additional risk impacts such as low morale and demotivation may become significant.

- ✔ **Other projects:** Where other projects depend on this one, perhaps to receive one or more of the products or because a team moves to another project after working on a part of this one, certain risks may lead to significant impacts for them. That may affect your choice of management actions and justify more expense to speed up this project so that it doesn't affect other ones.

- ✔ **Business benefit levels:** A risk can affect projections of the project's benefits. For example, if a competitor runs its project faster and so beats you to market with a new product, that may mean you have to reduce your sales projections.

- ✔ **Business benefit timing:** The level of benefit may be the same (£1 million saving per month), but it may now start three months after the end of the project rather than the two months you previously expected.

- ✔ **Quality:** A risk may affect quality, which is an example of interactions between risk impact areas. Pressure on time because of a risk happening and a fixed project end date may mean that you can't do some of the planned tests, with the risk that the project may deliver reduced quality.

- ✔ **Reputation:** Often forgotten, this is another interaction between impact areas. A quality impact can lead to an impact on reputation if you give a faulty product to a customer.

- ✔ **Scope:** A risk can affect scope in two ways. It can be interactive: for example, if you face a timing problem you no longer have time to do everything and you have to reduce the scope of the project to deliver by the fixed deadline. But a further impact in complex projects may be that something just isn't technically possible after all, which obviously affects the scope.

Most people involved with the management of projects are obsessed with time and cost. One impact you can easily overlook is reputation damage. Sometimes the knock-on effect of this is huge, and just one element going wrong somewhere can kill even a large multinational. Carefully think through impacts and don't just stick with those that relate to time and cost.

Strangely, reputation damage works the other way round to financial impact in terms of large and small organisations. If a multinational company or government department has a major project problem, it's picked up in the press and featured in newspapers with international circulation. If a small company has a major project problem, the press are rarely interested and it can go unreported and therefore not have any significant impact on reputation. So, if you work for a large organisation or one with a high public profile, watch out.

Where a project goes into an unknown area and you don't know whether doing something is even theoretically possible, you can think about including a 'proof of concept' product early on in the project to prove it is possible. You can even make this a 'bottleneck' product in the Product Flow Diagram – consult Chapter 14 on planning for more on this powerful technique.

Assessing probability

Impact can be a tough thing to work out, but it's easy compared to probability. Probability has been described as 'the Achilles' heel of risk management'. The difficulty in working out probability revolves around a lack of information.

You can sometimes calculate probability on the basis of previous cases that are relevant to the current project. Examples of this occur in medicine, in insurance, and in oil exploration at sea.

In the North Sea, the weather can get very bad, which stops companies carrying out survey work. When a survey is needed on part of the sea bed around an oil field, a ship with a mini-submarine goes out to do it using a variety of techniques including sophisticated ultrasound. But bad weather may mean that the ship can't launch the mini-submarine and the crew has to wait on station until the weather calms before carrying out the survey. This waiting can sometimes last as long as two weeks. To help plan, companies draw on historic weather stats. The North Sea has been divided up into a grid and weather statistics are kept for every cell in that grid, so a company can determine the probability of bad weather in that part of the North Sea in any given week of the year. This helps quantify the risk of adverse weather causing delay.

In many cases though, there's no algorithm you can use for working out the probability and precious little in the way of repeated earlier experience. So the probability rating is based on your best guess – sorry, estimate.

Determining proximity

Proximity is simply how soon the risk can happen. In the strategy you set down what categories you have for specifying it. That can be helpful to see what risks can happen at any time, in a current stage, in the project and beyond the project (the categories suggested in the PRINCE2 manual) but you need to be aware of two other dimensions in the risk proximity:

- **Fixed:** Fixed proximity is always a set time away. This includes the 'now' proximity. An example is a staff member going off sick: He may walk up to the Project Manager in five minutes' time and say that he feels really ill and needs to go home. But fixed proximity can also be a set time into the future. Today, the proximity of the risk is four weeks. But in two weeks' time the proximity is still four weeks. That may sound odd until you consider a simple example – a team member resigning and leaving the organisation. If the period of notice in his contract is four weeks, then if he resigns today he actually leaves the team in four weeks' time. But if he resigns in two weeks' time, he still works his period of notice and leaves four weeks after that.

- **Date-specific:** Some proximities are fixed to calendar dates. If you face a risk that the project isn't able to recruit enough bricklayers in October when you're due to start the brickwork, then the proximity gets shorter and shorter as you get nearer to October.

Using a probability-impact (p-i) grid

For the two measures of impact and probability you can use measures of very high, high, medium, low, and very low, or a numeric scale of 1–5 or 1–10. You can then plot the risks on a grid as shown in Figure 15-5. This technique is very useful because you see the big picture of where risks are. For example, have you got a lot of low-impact but high-probability risks?

The diagram is called a p-i grid here because that's what most people call it. In the PRINCE2 manual, though, it is known as a *Summary Risk Profile,* with the p-i grid then being the same matrix, but with values set for each cell to give each one a severity factor, after deciding an exact scale up each axis.

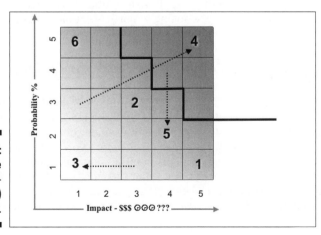

Figure 15-5:
The Probability-impact (p-i) grid.

Some people like to use a simpler grid with just three measures on each axis of high, medium, and low, but risk experts recommend never using a scale of less than five, otherwise you just don't think hard enough. But equally in most projects you're best not going above ten – or you may find yourself in deep mental anguish when you try to decide whether a risk is a level 647 or a level 648 on your 1–1,000 probability scale.

Where you decide to use numbers for risk and probability measures, you can then multiply them together to give an overall assessment of severity. One that has low probability and low impact, like Risk 3 in Figure 15-5, has a severity of 1 (1x1). One with very high probability and very high impact is more worrying, like Risk 4, which has a severity factor of 25. Although the higher the number, the greater your concern and the more attention you need to give to the risk in risk management, you also need to be careful about some of the lower numbers. Don't play number games here because they don't work. Risk 6 on the profile has very low impact, but its probability is so high that you need to do as much work on Plan B as you do on Plan A.

The profile is also great for showing movement since the last reporting point. The dotted arrow lines show which risks have moved since the last report. In addition, the profile shows risk tolerance. The top right of the profile is the high-severity area. The Project Board may define a zone at the top right like that shown on Figure 15-5 but it doesn't have to be exactly that shape. The board want to be told immediately if any risk goes into or comes out of that zone. You must report that to them the same day and not wait for the next regular progress or Highlight Report. In the case of Figure 15-5, new information shows that Risk 5 now has a much lower probability than you previously thought. You must tell the board straight away that this highly dangerous risk is now much less likely. This helps board members sleep better at night instead of waking up with a nightmare about a risk that's now only rather mild.

One of the drawbacks of the grid is that it can get rather busy. Imagine a project with 100 risks or more. In that situation, a solution is to split the risks up and have several grids, each specialising in particular risk categories.

Making the 'before or after' decision

Looking at the 2009 edition of the PRINCE2 manual, it's good to recognise quite a few bits of advice built into the last edition of _PRINCE2 For Dummies_! Perhaps we should charge a fee! With the assessment of impact and probability you need to think about the measures before you take risk control actions and after. There are advantages in ultimately recording both and the PRINCE2 _Risk Register_ now covers that point too (more on the Risk Register towards the end of the chapter). But at first you may circulate a copy of the p-i grid showing the 'before' or _inherent_ values. Then, when action has been decided, you can change this to show the position 'after' risk management actions are taken into account, the *residual* risk. For ongoing reference during the project you need to show the new, 'after', assessment of impact and probability after the effect of risk management actions, otherwise your assessment doesn't reflect the present state of the risk that you're managing.

Even when you arrive at the 'after' position it's still helpful to record the 'before' ratings in the Risk Register as well. Otherwise managers looking at the probability and impact measures may think a risk is insignificant being 'very low – very low' and not worth managing. But the true picture may be that without those management actions the risk will revert to its 'before' measures of 'very high – very high'.

If you don't have many risks, you can get really clever, assessing both before and after, and linking the two points on the p-i grid. If you see that in a future edition of the PRINCE2 manual please remember, you saw it here first.

Planning how to deal with a risk

Consider all the possible actions that you can take to control a particular risk. You have to think broadly here: Don't limit your response to throwing money at the problem. Sometimes you can come up with an imaginative solution that requires brain power rather than money.

Do remember the word 'suitable' when you consider risk actions. Although silly ideas have their place because they can sometimes trigger sensible ones, you don't want the risk analysis sessions, particularly those involving any young and junior team members, to descend into farce. All this analysis costs the project money in terms of staff time, so although identifying risks and then actions can be fun, don't allow it to waste time. The world being hit by a giant toxic meteor shouldn't usually be in the Risk Register of a project to enhance the payroll system.

Categorising the responses

Different risk approaches use different categories for the types of response. PRINCE2 has got a bit enthusiastic about this which, unfortunately, reinforces an impression that it's complicated. It uses ten response types; six for downside risk – threats – and four for the upside risk – opportunites – as again it prioritises alignment with the UK government risk method. The 'share' response appears in both sets though.

If you're looking for a simpler set of risk responses, you may like to consider the American PMI (Project Management Institute) ones. For downside risk it uses avoid, transfer and mitigate, and for upside risk it uses exploit, share and enhance.

Responses to threats – the downside risk

✔ **Avoid:** Can you stop the risk happening? If a plastic component may melt if the new machines overheat, replace it with a steel component that heat doesn't affect.

✔ **Share:** Is it possible to reduce your own exposure to the consequences, such as by sharing the financial impact with another organisation?

✔ **Reduce:** This response reduces the probability of something happening, or reduces the impact if it does happen. If you're likely to face a delay travelling on the roads, go by train. You may still run into a delay, but that's less likely by rail than by car (theoretically!).

✔ **Accept:** This is a strange 'action' because you do nothing. But you do record a decision not to act on a risk. Perhaps, for example, the cost of any action is disproportionate to the impact of the risk.

✔ **Fallback:** With this response, you allow for the risk happening. This may involve:

• Contingency time in the plan.

• Contingency budget (money pre-authorised by the Project Board to use if a particular risk happens).

• Contingent actions (alternatives so that if something happens that means Plan A can't work, you move to Plan B).

✔ **Transfer:** Can you pass on the risk to someone else? An example is subcontracting for a fixed fee, so that if things prove more complicated than expected, the subcontractor has to find the additional staff resources to deal with it. Insurance is another example of risk transference.

You can use risk management actions in combination. With home insurance, for example, two actions are in force. If you have an insurance policy it probably says that you must close the door and lock it when you go out. This prevents someone just walking in. But your locks are only prevention to a certain level and you're not required to recruit your own personal round-the-clock security force. Just lock the door, and after that the insurance company accepts the transfer of the risk, albeit for a generous fee (have you seen the smart headquarters buildings of all the insurance companies?).

Just in case you're studying this book at a time when you have a PRINCE2 exam coming up and need to memorise this stuff, drowning is a downside risk so to keep safe your response needs to be AS RAFT (an acronym that spells out the threat responses). If the risk is a good one then to take advantage you need to be as wise as a SEER. Check out the nearby sidebar 'Responses for opportunities – the upside risks' for more on this acronym.

Deciding which of the possible actions to take and which not to is a human judgement. Given that many of the actions require money, or staff time that represents money, this decision belongs to the board and especially the Executive, who owns the Business Case and is responsible for value for money.

Responses for opportunities – the upside risks

✔ **Share:** How kind. You'll share the advantage with others.

✔ **Enhance:** Can you make it even better when it happens?

✔ **Exploit:** Can you increase the probability of it happening?

✔ **Reject:** Although it would be good, you'll turn it down. Perhaps because it would be too expensive or you don't have time to make use of it.

Selecting the responses to act on

The PRINCE2 manual suggests that you base the decision on a balance between the cost of taking that particular action and the probability and impact (severity) of the risk. That's absolutely right, but it leaves out the time factor. Occasionally, the time impact on the project rather than the cost is significant in a potential action. For example, if a project proves more complicated than I thought, I may find that I don't have enough skilled staff available. This situation is highly likely and the resulting impact is also very high. I can identify an action of training up more specialists, but that action may not be as suitable as hiring in skilled staff. This isn't for cost reasons – training may actually be cheaper – but because of the time needed to carry out sufficient training. Arguably, more dimensions exist, but you get the picture.

Implementing the Risk Responses

Risk management isn't always necessary, though it usually is. If you simply 'accept' a risk then by definition no management action takes place. But you still need monitoring in some cases, because if circumstances change, acceptance may no longer be a sensible response.

You need to build the risk actions into the Project Plans and also Stage Plans as appropriate, to show the necessary activities and resources. Clearly, this may have implications for the overall cost of the project and the time you require to do it, but the Project Board are well aware of those implications because they're involved in deciding the risk actions. You also need to be clear on who is in control of a risk and who is to take action if it occurs.

Risk owner and risk actionee. The person who's best placed to monitor the risk and control any action is the 'risk owner'. The person who takes any action is the 'risk actionee'. It's possible that for a particular risk, the person who owns it may also be the actionee.

As with the rest of project management, it's important that if risk actions are at all dangerous, you appoint someone other than you to be the actionee. Because of your advanced skills, you need to survive to run another project.

Actually taking the planned action

Implementing is the final section of the external part of the risk procedure model and may sound a bit obvious. But two important points emerge about this. The first is that you must make sure that the risk actions are indeed taken. Projects have come to grief because although risks were spotted and countermeasures planned, they were never actually carried out.

The second important point exposes another downside of the PRINCE2 risk procedure; it doesn't mention monitoring. But risk factors change. For this reason you must have monitoring in place and you must not neglect this when thinking about implementation. Risk factors can change in two areas: the project and the business environment outside the project. That outside area splits into two as well; outside the project but still in the organisation, or in the wider world beyond the organisation. All these factors can change the status of the risk and so necessitate a re-evaluation of the risk and the measures being taken to control it. If you use the risk cycle illustrated earlier in this chapter you'll get the idea as the monitoring brings the risk cycle back round into the analysis half, returning it to evaluation.

Communicating Information About Risk

The final part of the risk procedure in PRINCE2 is the bit in the middle of the procedure model, 'communicate'. This is going on all the time. In communication you need to keep others up to date with the risk position in the project as well as to get input into the risk management process. For these communications you may find the information you stored in the Communications Management Strategy helpful – see Chapter 5 – and in particular the two final sections where you listed stakeholders and others who need to be informed.

Communicating risk information needs to be carried out in the most appropriate way; 'appropriate' communication is what the Communication Management Strategy is all about. In some cases, risk information can be included in the standard reports used for reporting progress and for reporting project status at set points, notably at the end of project stages.

Be careful that risk reporting doesn't have to go through too many layers. For the Inspirandum project risk workshop, we've come up with the expression 'one-bounce risk reporting'. In other words, someone at the coal face shouldn't have to go through more than one other person before reaching whoever is responsible for the risk, otherwise it's likely that the message gets diluted as it goes up the chain. We use the example of 'A major crisis' becomes 'A serious concern' becomes 'Something of a problem' becomes 'A bit of a snag' becomes 'Are you free for lunch? I know a nice little place . . .'.

Registering a Risk . . . or Not

You must regularly review the Risk Register and keep things like status up to date. At a minimum, you do this at each stage end, where the PRINCE2 process builds in this action. But you may need to review the risk assessment during the stages as well, particularly if your project is high risk. Equally, you also need to check the risk impact of any problems or other issues. Chapter 6 looks at stage boundaries and Chapter 7 covers running the stages.

In PRINCE2, you document all risks by making a record for each one in the Risk Register. You open this in Start Up with entries for just the main risks and a bit of detail on each one. In the Initiation Stage (the first project stage that covers the full planning of the project) you fill in the Risk Register with all the risks you identify, giving full details for each one. Flip to Chapter 4 for more on Start Up and have a look at Chapter 5 for more on Initiation.

The Risk Register

Risk Identifier

Risk author

Date registered

Risk category

Risk description

Probability, impact and expected value

Proximity

Risk response categories

Risk response

Risk status

Risk owner

Risk actionee

Making a Risk Register entry

You complete a Risk Register entry for every risk that's been identified and where the risk is to be formally managed. In Start Up the information may be quite sketchy, and at that time is noted in the Daily Log, but is filled out when you do the risk analysis during the Initiation Stage. After that you keep the register up to date throughout the project, changing the information on the risk as necessary (such as a change of status requiring you to modify the control actions).

Safely Leaving Out Risk Management

Some people ask whether you can ever safely leave out risk management, such as in small projects. No, you can't. Although a project being very large may be a risk factor in its own right, other than that, risk isn't related to project size. A very large project may be quite low risk whereas a very small one could carry very high risk.

A London finance house ran a very small project that took two staff just 6 weeks to complete – 12 staff weeks of work. However, the project carried enormous commercial risk. If it went wrong, it would have a potentially unrecoverable impact on the reputation of that finance house, including all its share-dealing services, which were worth billions. It was a tiny project but with huge risk, so significant risk management action was fully justified.

Someone has said that the right question isn't, 'Should we do risk management?' but, 'How much risk management should we do?'

Interestingly, small projects are higher risk in some respects than larger ones. If you have a project team of 100 and one person goes off sick, what's the impact? Just 1 per cent, although that person may feel he's much more important than that. But if you have a project with just two staff and one goes off sick? That's 50 per cent of staff resource.

In a low-risk project you may not do very much risk management, and adjusting the degree to which you use PRINCE2 activities allows for this. But don't ignore the method where it calls for risk-management work. Instead, always look for risks and so protect the project from the obvious things that may cause trouble later.

Chapter 16

Controlling Change and Versions

· ·

In This Chapter

▶ Controlling change and stopping scope creep in its tracks

▶ Getting to grips with the different types of project Issue

▶ Dealing with Issues and changes

▶ Tracking change with version control – configuration management

· ·

*I*f someone wants a change to a building, a computer system, a business procedure – anything at all in fact – they nearly always start with 'just': 'We just want one extra power socket by the door'; 'We just need an extra report from the system'; 'We just need . . .'.

One major project killer is *scope creep* – uncontrolled change where people add very small things to a project, one thing at a time, small item by small item: a 10-minute job here, a 20-minute job there, just a 5-minute job after that. And the project is a year long and costs £20 million, so surely you can accommodate a five-minute job? But the small changes build up, and of course you aren't given any extra time, staff resources, or budget for them. Eventually, the cumulative effect is so great that it kills the project because the changes now represent substantial extra work.

In PRINCE2 scope creep can't happen – well, almost. After you set up and agree the project, all changes come under change control. The response to the request may well be to say 'yes', but then the Project Board gives the time, budget, and staff hours to do the extra work. The project isn't supposed to somehow absorb all this unplanned work with no impact.

What may seem a bit strange is that the handling of all project Issues comes under change control in PRINCE2. This is odd, because an Issue can be about anything at all; it doesn't have to be a change. But either way, this is where Issues come in the method. This chapter covers controlling change, Issues and two special types of Issue, which are Requests for Change and Off-Specifications, usually referred to as RFCs and Off-Specs. The chapter also covers controlling versions of things or, to use the up-market name, configuration management.

Allowing Change, but Not Scope Creep

People often assume that change control is all about *preventing* change but that simply isn't true in PRINCE2. If someone has a good idea that may help run the project faster, better and cheaper, you may well want to implement it. The emphasis is on *controlling* change and that includes accommodating and resourcing it.

Taking control

Scope creep or incremental change can be very damaging and is often high up on lists of causes of project failure. Many projects barely have time to achieve what they plan to do. Imagining that they can take on a whole heap of extra work and still stay within the original bounds of scope, quality, budget, and time is illogical and entirely unrealistic.

I was talking to a group of managers in a multinational company, including a senior manager with a great deal of project experience, Paul Beaton. We were discussing the need for contingency time in Project Plans and I used the analogy of going to the airport. In the UK, getting to London Heathrow can be a huge problem and delays are very common. Nobody in their right mind allows only the minimum travel time in order to get to the airport at the last possible moment for check-in, with no contingency allowance for travel delay. If you need contingency just for a flight, I said, how much more do you need it for a project? Paul added to that thinking: You're rushing to the airport with barely enough time to catch the flight when you get a call telling you to divert and pick up a package from Gatwick airport, some 40 miles away, before going back to catch the flight at Heathrow. That's exactly what scope creep is. You only had just enough time to get to the airport in the first place, but now you have an extra 80 miles on a congested London motorway and a pick-up to do as well. And you still expect to make the flight?

Avoiding a change freeze

Apart from killing the project, uncontrolled change or scope creep can have another really bad effect on the project – a change freeze. Scope creep happens until someone realises that the project is getting overwhelmed and is in danger of not delivering anything at all. So the Project Manager makes an announcement that after the end of this week the project won't accept any more changes – none at all: there's a change freeze. Oh, great. Up to now all sorts of minor and unnecessary changes were accepted without question, but after the end of this week all changes will be turned down, no matter how beneficial or how important.

Most projects happen in a dynamic business environment and unfortunately that environment doesn't have the good manners to stay still while the project runs. If the project implements a change freeze, it inevitably gets more and more out of step with the business environment.

The answer is not scope creep and then a change freeze – the answer is change control. That means that you can accept a change even very late into the project if you can justify and resource it, but you turn down a change that you can't justify, even in the early days of the project.

Defining a Project Issue

In the PRINCE2 method, change control covers all Issues in the project.

Issue, Issue Report and Issue Register. A project Issue is a communication from anyone in the project (or if you prefer, anyone at all with an interest in the project – see the next tip) direct to the Project Manager. An Issue can be sent at any time during the project and it can be about anything – it doesn't have to relate to change. As soon as the Issue is received it's logged in the Issue Register so it can be tracked or, if the Project Manager decides that the matter can be handled informally, into the Daily Log. If it goes into the Issue Register, the Project Manager first records the full detail of the Issue on an Issue Report.

The PRINCE2 manual says that anyone with an interest in the project can send in an Issue. You may want to think about that. I've worked in organisations with a few control freaks who want to try to influence everything, whether in their area or not. If project Issues are wide open, people like that are likely to bombard the Project Manager with lots of Issues in an attempt to swing the project the way they want it to go. An alternative is to restrict Issues to people inside the project. If a person outside wants something, then he can talk to the Senior User on the Project Board. If he convinces the Senior User, then the Senior User can put in the Issue.

Categorising Issues

PRINCE2 has three sub-types of Issue, but you process them in exactly the same way in terms of recording them, tracking their progress, and noting how you resolve them.

General Issue or 'Problem/concern'

The 2009 edition of the PRINCE2 manual has gone back to giving this first sub-type of Issue the name of 'Problem/concern'. That name is a bit misleading because just about everyone thinks of 'a concern' as being something bad. If someone says something is a 'cause for concern' you aren't expecting good news. But as the manual itself points out in the text, an Issue can be about anything at all and it doesn't have to be bad stuff. Issues can also be good ideas or questions – anything at all, in fact.

Request for Change (RFC)

An RFC is a special type of Project Issue where someone wants a change to a product that has already been 'baselined'.

Baselined. This means a product has been quality checked and signed off. This is a configuration management term.

An RFC can be submitted for a specialist product (something that a team built) or a management product (something like the Project Initiation Document that you use to help manage the project).

After a product has been baselined, any change always goes through the change control procedure. Not to do this means that quality is abandoned. There's no point in quality control staff carefully checking a product against set criteria and signing it off as compliant if a junior team member can walk in five minutes later and completely change it. After something is quality checked and signed off, nobody must touch it except under change control. Even if someone has a really good idea for an improvement and it may not take long to do, this may not be the right time to do it – such as the night before an important demonstration in front of customers.

Off-Specification (Off-Spec)

You declare something Off-Specification if it fails to meet its quality criteria during testing and you can't easily correct the problem. You can sometimes submit the Off-Spec even before the test, because the team can see that the product is never going to meet its quality criteria.

Normally, if something isn't up to standard and it fails the test you just take it away and work on it until it does meet the standard and passes the test. But doing that may not always be so easy. Perhaps, for example, some components are now obsolete. Or maybe the correction would take so long that it would threaten the project as a whole.

An Off-Spec is usually for a product that's below its quality criteria – it's substandard. But occasionally an Off-Spec can be because a product *exceeds* its specification. That can also cause a problem.

A company wanted a new software package written to transmit data to handheld computers used by their field staff. The company agreed the requirement with the supplier and said what handheld computers it was using. However, the supplier gave the company an adapted version of their very latest software package to give really good value and give additional functionality – in excess of the specification agreed. It worked fine in testing with the supplier's handhelds. However it failed at the customer site because the customer company's handheld computers were older and didn't support the technical requirements of the new system. The new software was Off-Specification because it was too good. In the end the supplier company bought new handheld computers for the customer, at the supplier's expense, because the original specification was clear and it was cheaper to buy new kit for the customer than to start all over and re-configure the software package. Lesson One in 'How to wipe out your profits'.

Conceding a concession

When you find that a product is Off-Spec, you may be better off just accepting it as it is. Bearing in mind that Off-Specs usually relate to things that are below standard, this may sound a bit odd. But if the project can live with the item being below standard and time is short, accepting it (which PRINCE2 calls making a *concession*) may be better than losing the whole project because you can't correct it in time.

The PRINCE2 manual says that only the Project Board can make a concession, and for the vast majority of projects that's fine. However, in technically complex projects you may want to think about delegating decision making on concessions to the Team Manager or even team specialist level. In such projects the board are often only able to ask, 'What does the Chief Engineer say?', and rubber stamp that evaluation. The board members are often unable to validate the technical evaluation in either direction.

You can combine a concession with a *Follow-On Action* to create, effectively, a temporary concession. If something is substandard but you don't have time to correct it without missing the fixed project delivery date, you can make a concession and accept the product, but only temporarily. You require the supplier to provide a new product that's up to standard and come back some time after the project to install it. You pass a Follow-On Action to a manager in the organisation, who takes responsibility for it after the project closes down and makes quite sure that the supplier provides the improved product. Chapter 9 has more on Follow-On Action Recommendations.

Handling an Issue

The flow of control for an Issue goes through five simple steps and the next sections in this chapter work through the sequence.

Step 1 – capturing the Issue

When the issue is received the Project Manager has a decision to make. Should this Issue be handled formally and tracked, or can it be handled informally? If the answer is that the Project Manager can handle it informally then she makes a note of it in the Daily Log. If the Issue needs formal handling, then she records the full detail on an *Issue Report* and then records the tracking information (who sent it in, current status and so on) in the *Issue Register*.

As with all of the PRINCE2 logs and registers, think of the Issue Register as a control document and then you can see how it's used. The Issue Register provides an overview of all of the current Issues showing when each was received, what action is being taken on it and whether or not it's been resolved. Well, actually a bit more than that as the panel shows. The Issue Report records the full detail of a single Issue.

Where you have project staff such as Team Managers who are very familiar with PRINCE2, you have the option of asking them to submit any Issues in Issue Report format, completing the sections that they can. Nothing is lost if the Project Manager decides to handle the Issue informally as much the same information is needed whether the matter is handled formally or informally.

Issue Report

Issue identifier: A unique reference, often just a number.

Issue type: RFC, Off-Spec or Problem/Concern (or use 'General' for the third category if you want to avoid the negative impression of problem/concern).

Date raised:

Raised by: Nearly always the name of the person, but it could be a team.

Issue Report author: Usually the Project Manager, but it can be a Team Manager or team member.

Issue description: The details of the Issue, including the cause of any problem and also including the impact. Details of the impact may be filled in later after investigation.

Impact analysis: Details of the impact of the Issue after investigation. This could be in terms of the need to change products or impacts in one or more of the six PRINCE2 control areas of cost, time, quality, scope, risk and benefits.

Recommendation: What the Project Manager recommends as a resolution of the Issue and why.

Priority: This could be high, medium, or low, or using a scale that was decided during Initiation and recorded in the Configuration Management Strategy. For example, a change may be prioritised as 'essential' through to 'nice to have if possible'.

Severity: Again this will use a scale decided in Initiation and recorded in the Configuration Management Strategy. In turn the severity can indicate who is authorised to make a decision on the Issue.

Decision: The outcome, such as to reject a Request for Change or to make a concession on an Off-Specification.

Approved by: Information on who made the decision. It could be the Project Manager, the Project Board or, if you have one, the Change Authority (see later in this chapter).

Decision date:

Closure date: In the case of an Issue where no action is taken the closure date will be the same as the decision date, but where action was needed, then it will be some time afterwards.

The Issue Report then, covers the full information on a single Issue, including all the action taken on it. A summary of the control information is duplicated in the Issue Register, but slightly modified, as set down in the next panel.

Don't confuse the Issue Register with the Risk Register. People commonly mix these two up, and some even try to combine them. Remember that the information in these two registers is very different, and the way you handle them is very different as well. Some people argue that a risk is an Issue that hasn't happened yet and an Issue is a risk that has. Not true, because an Issue can be about anything, such as a question or a good idea; it doesn't have to be risk-related at all.

Issue Register

This register is a control document that gives an overview of all Issues. For the most part the register repeats key control information taken from the individual Issue Reports.

Issue identifier

Issue type

Date raised

Raised by

Issue Report author

Issue description (This would not normally be in the same amount of detail as that held on the Issue Report.)

Priority

Severity

Status (This is an item of information not included on the Issue Report, though arguably it should be.)

Closure date

As part of capturing the Issue the Project Manager allocates the severity and priority ratings. However, the appropriate rating may not be clear until after the next step of examining the Issue. In that case you can set a provisional rating and modify it when things are clearer. For example, a team member may have reported a severe problem, but after investigation it's found that this young and inexperienced team member got a bit over-excited and, although there is indeed a problem, it's been very much exaggerated.

Step 2 – examining the Issue

If the Issue is significant, other people as well as the Project Manager, may need to help analyse it. You may need to involve Team Managers, team specialists, and external supplier companies. The PRINCE2 manual also suggests that you involve Project Assurance to help assess matters like impact on the Business Case, but that may detract from their impartial position as the project audit function that's independent of the Project Manager. How can assurance staff check whether an Issue was handled correctly if they themselves helped decide what to do?

Impact areas to consider

In considering the impact of an issue, include these areas:

- ✔ Business benefits and project justification

- ✔ Cost

- ✔ Delivery time for the whole project

- ✔ Time impacts for the present stage and knock-on effects to future stages

- ✔ Impacts on a programme or interfacing projects

- ✔ Quality

- ✔ Risk

- ✔ Staffing levels and staff availability

When planning the project and especially the stages, think what the level of Project Issue-related work is likely to be – in terms of the likely number and the likely complexity. You need to include resources and time in your plans for the impact analysis, which in some projects can be substantial.

Step 3 – proposing action

Deciding what to do about an Issue potentially involves three levels of decision-making authority: the Project Manager, a Change Authority and the Project Board. If something requires action that is beyond the Project Manager's delegated authority, it needs to be 'proposed' to whoever is authorised to approve that action. You can find an explanation of the three levels of responsibility later in the chapter in the section 'Understanding Authority Levels'.

Step 4 – deciding action

If the Issue is being handled informally, the Project Manager just notes her decided action in the Daily Log. If it's being formally handled that detail goes in the Issue Register and on the relevant Issue Report. If the Issue has been escalated to a Change Authority or to the Project Board then the decision is taken at that level.

It's tempting to just think of decisions as 'yes' or 'no' but you have some other possibilities, so do stay flexible. First, the board or Change Authority may hold off a decision because they want more information. In that case the Project Manager goes away and finds it and then brings the matter back a second time for a decision. The decision itself provides a range of possible outcomes. Taking a requested change as an example the response could be:

- ✔ Yes, we'll do it.

- ✔ No, we won't do it.

- ✔ Perhaps we'll do it later in the stage. If it's early in the stage and the change isn't high priority, the Project Manager can put the request on hold. If some change budget is left at the end of the stage, the change will be done then. If the budget is exhausted at the end of the stage then this particular change won't be done. It would be bad management of a change budget to agree all sorts of trivial changes at the front end of a stage and then find that there's no money or time for more significant changes later.

- ✔ Perhaps we'll do it in a later stage. Because of a fixed deadline, there may be no capacity to carry out this change in the current stage, but it's a good idea and the work can be added to at a later stage in the project.

- ✔ Perhaps, but not in this project. It may be that the proposed change is a great idea, but there just isn't time or budget to carry it out in this project, which is up against a fixed deadline. It may then be recommended back to the organisation as a *Follow-on Action*. If organisational managers agree it's a good idea, they can get the work done in another way; perhaps by including it in a future project.

Step 5 – implementing any work

If the decision is to go ahead, then the Project Manager puts the work in hand. That may involve some re-planning. When the work is complete, the Issue is closed down in the Issue Register, on any Issue Report or in the Daily Log.

Going into exception deliberately

An exception occurs when something goes significantly off plan. If you have to run the stage differently from this point because of a problem, you can't go on using the existing Stage Plan because that won't reflect how you will intend to complete the stage. So you draw up an Exception Plan that replaces the rest of the current Stage Plan. You can find more about this in Chapter 17.

You can use exactly the same mechanism to resource a significant change. For example, if a team member comes up with a great idea that may save a huge amount of money, but requires additional work to implement, then the board may agree it in principle and ask for an Exception Plan. The Project Manager produces a new plan showing all the work to accommodate the change and presents this to the Project Board for approval.

If you're changing a product – deliverable –, don't forget that you also need to change its Product Description. Chapter 14 on planning explains the nature and use of Product Descriptions.

Understanding Authority Levels

Deciding how to handle Issues, including change requests, is a matter for the Project Board as 'the boss'. Board members must decide how much authority they're willing to delegate to the Project Manager and at what point they require the Project Manager to come back to them for a decision. One obvious threshold is budget. They may be happy for the Project Manager to authorise something costing £1 but not so happy at the idea of the Project Manager quietly committing the project to an extra £5 million.

But authorising changes isn't just about money. Even though the Project Manager has a change budget, she may not be able to make decisions that affect the operation of the whole organisation, for example, no matter how cheap and fast this is. Even the Project Board probably have to get other authority for changes of that kind. Please see Chapter 5 for more about where levels of authority and the control mechanisms are set up and recorded.

Setting up a change budget

Giving the Project Manager a change budget makes sense. This can be set up and authorised stage by stage, or for the whole project. Having a change budget to accommodate unforeseen changes avoids the Project Manager constantly calling in the Project Board to approve every single change, no matter how small. If the board doesn't authorise a budget and only authorises the Stage Plan, then every change has to be escalated because, by definition, a change isn't on the plan and so the work isn't authorised.

For a finer degree of control, a change budget can specify individual change amounts and a cumulative amount. For example, the Project Manager may have a change budget of £60,000, but no one change can cost more than £10,000. If she needs to make a change that costs £15,000, or costs £10 but takes the total change for the stage over the £60,000 limit, then the Project Manager has to take the change to the Project Board.

Paying for Off-Specs and RFCs

The cost of an Off-Spec often, though not always, falls to a supplier because the supplier hasn't delivered to the customer's specification. Often, the cost of an RFC falls to the customer, because it's a change from what the customer originally agreed.

If a decision is within the Project Manager's authority but she wants to talk to one or more board members in any case, she can always do that using the facility in PRINCE2 for getting *ad hoc direction* – in other words, 'running it past the boss'. One time you may need to do this is in the case of priorities for RFCs. Imagine that the Project Manager has 20 RFCs from different junior members of staff in the business area. Guess what priority every single person put on their RFC? Yes – number one, top priority. So in this situation the Project Manager may go to the Senior User, explain that she has time to do only five of the RFCs, and ask the Senior User to reassess the priorities and tell her which RFCs are really useful.

Setting up a Change Authority

If the Project Board doesn't want to be involved in all changes that are beyond the authority it's willing to give to the Project Manager, then it has the option of setting up a Change Authority between the board and the Project Manager and with an intermediate level of authority. If cold fear has now gripped you and visions of long forms and endless committees are rushing before your eyes, you have good reason; but more of the downside in a moment.

A Change Authority can actually be quite a good thing – sometimes. In fast-moving projects but where the Project Board is very senior or geographically spread out, the delay in getting change approval from the Project Board can be problematical. If the board has set up a Change Authority that can react very quickly to change requests, perhaps even the same day, that can be very practical. The Change Authority can make a rapid decision and clear its lines with the Project Board later as necessary.

Okay, on to the nightmares and the downside. Some organisations set up the Change Authority in a very bad way. If a Change Authority is used it should not slow things down, and preferably should speed things up.

One large company has centralised the Change Authority: it's a committee that meets once a month. Any project that wants any change, no matter how small, has to write a paper and put it to the Change Authority. The committee reviews all of the changes and decides which to allow and which not to. That means that any change in a project can take up to a month to get to a decision point. Where changes can involve knock-on effects to other projects and operational areas such a mechanism may be justified as part of a change management procedure. But to apply it to *all* change?

In a fast-moving project, the Project Board could decide that the Executive will be the Change Authority for urgent changes. Changes beyond the Project Manager's authority go to the whole board, but where an urgent reply is needed, the Executive will give a same-day decision and sort things out later with the other board members.

Controlling Versions – Configuration Management

PRINCE2 uses some really unfortunate language. Unfortunate, that is, if you happen to be a business user of the method rather than a career project specialist. 'Configuration management' is one of the worst terms if the objective is to make the method readily understandable. *Configuration management (CM)* is basically version control; you may know it as 'versioning'. Actually, CM is slightly more than that, but not much more, and certainly not enough to worry about.

You can't escape CM in any project, and won't want to after you've read this section. To give a simple example of why you need it, say I have two different documents, one called 'Revised Project Plan' and the other 'Project Plan – Revised'. Now, which one do I use? Clearly, the document needs something like a version number on the bottom or perhaps a date, so that I can see which one is more recent. But actually neither of the documents may be the latest version and there's another one, more recent still, that I don't know about. A central record would tell me that both of the ones I have are now superseded. That's a simple example but it shows the need for configuration management and also how CM can help avoid problems and confusion. The rest of this chapter covers how, who, and also what you may and may not want to control.

Deciding How Much CM to Do

How much CM do you need in your particular project? You can choose one of two opinions:

- ✔ You only configuration manage what you may change. If you're not going to change something after you deliver it, you don't need version control. For example, do you want to roll back the foundations of the building to an earlier version? Unlikely, to say the least.

- ✔ You configuration manage just about everything. Even if the product isn't likely to change after you complete it, you still want to know how far through it is in its development. So, you're not going to change the foundations, but are they finished and signed off? This is status accounting, which can be useful not only for checking progress during stages but also as a double check at the end of a stage to make sure that you've done everything.

The Baseline Management Products

Benefits Review Plan

Business Case

Communication Management Strategy

Configuration Management Strategy (see later in this chapter)

Plan (Project, Stage and Team)

Product Description

Project Brief

Project Product Description

Quality Management Strategy

Risk Management Strategy

Work Package

Status Account. This is a report in PRINCE2 and is a snapshot of a set of products at a particular point in time to know what *state* they are in.

The trouble with CM is that you can tend to focus just on the specialist products – the specifications, new business procedures, brick walls, and computer programs that the teams are busy building. But you have to think about management products as well – such as the plans that you use to manage the project. These change and you need to know which is the latest one. Some of the PRINCE2 management products are classified as *Baseline Management Products* and it's expected that you'll configuration manage these.

Writing the Configuration Management Strategy

How are you going to do CM on this particular project is decided in Initiation and set down in the Configuration Management Strategy along with the other change management decisions. In that strategy you set down your objectives for change and CM and details such as what procedures you have and who runs them. The PRINCE2 manual defines the CM Strategy, but as always, don't let that put you off if it looks too detailed, because you can always adapt the headings if you want to hold slightly different information.

Configuration Management Strategy

Introduction: An explanation of the purpose of configuration management, the scope of it in this project and who is responsible for the strategy.

Configuration management procedure: How CM is to be carried out, including procedures such as 'booking in' and 'booking out' and the identification system to be used (usually numbers). This section can refer to corporate or programme standards but in that case should also note any variance from them.

Issue and change control procedure: How Issues will be managed and the procedure for change control. Often you will use the PRINCE2 approach as it is and so have little or nothing to say in this section.

Tools and techniques: CM computer tools are available, or your organisation may have an established database standard for maintaining CM information. If you're using something like that, this is where you explain that so everyone is clear.

Records: According to the manual, this defines the composition of the Issue Register and Configuration Item Records (for CI Records, see later in this chapter). But that's not awfully intelligent since everyone uses templates for such things in their projects so it's self-evident what the content is. The manual authors seem to have been very focused on consistency between the strategies and having the same headings in each, whether relevant or not. That isn't particularly helpful where PRINCE2 is already charged with being heavy on documentation. But, as noted before this panel, leave out what you don't need.

Reporting: The composition of the Issue Report and Status Account. See the critical comments under the last heading in relation to the content of documents! The manual also says to set down the timing of the documents. As both are event driven, this is even more strange. The authors must have been having a really bad day when they did this bit.

Timing of CM and Issue and change control activities: This is explained in the manual as relating to the formal activities. Again it is nonsensical in the case of most of change and CM because it's all formal in the sense that it's being tracked in the change documentation and not in the Daily Log. However the one bit you may want to specify here is the frequency of checks on things like the CM records to make sure that they're accurate.

Roles and Responsibilities: Who will be responsible for the different procedures. This may be Project Support dealing with things like booking in and booking out, and issuing reference numbers. But if the CM is to be done by a corporate or programme service (such as a Programme and Project Office) this is where you would say so. In the context of change, you also need to record authority levels and budgets in this section, including that for any Change Authority (see earlier in this chapter).

Scales for priority and severity: The scales give an indication of who should take decisions on Issues, especially those relating to change. You may have an organisational scale that you can adopt, and if so just reference it in this section.

Keeping CM Information on Products

You need to hold information on each item being managed. In PRINCE2 this information is held on something called a Configuration Item (CI) Record. The CI Record content contains very relevant information. Some of it may be excessive for your project but, as always, reduce the headings where you can to keep the record as simple as possible. Don't hold information you don't need.

Configuration Item Record

Project identifier: Really useful where products are being passed to other projects and received in from them.

Item identifier: Usually a number.

Current version: Again usually a number, but it could be an alpha-numeric format.

Item title: Preferably short and descriptive, following the advice given in the planning chapter, Chapter 14, so the titles fit into the diagram boxes without a problem.

Date of last status change: For example, a product-passed test.

Owner: Who will take ownership of the product when it's handed over. Because the owner of the product may not be a technical specialist, you may want to hold additional information in the CI Record to cover that – please see the 'Additional CI Information' section after this panel.

Location: If the product is complete, this section says where it is. That may be in a particular drive on a network or in a project library if it's hardcopy, or a compound if it's something big and physical like a pre-fabricated part of a building. Or it could be back out with a team who are modifying it as a result of a requested change.

Copy holders (where relevant): For some products, like the Project Plan, if you make a significant change you need to circulate fresh copies to people. This section holds the list of who.

Item type: This simply says what the item is. It could be a single product, or it could be a set of products that are being tracked as a group (sometimes known as a baseline, using a second meaning of that word, or release).

Item attributes: Here you can hold information on what the item is, such as an engineering drawing, a plan, a programme or a report. In the case of a product bought in from outside the project, it's also helpful to record the make and model number. Have you ever tried to match things like door handles some time after you bought the original set and have long since thrown away all the packaging?

Stage: The stage in which the product will be, or was, produced.

Users: Who will use the product. This can be useful to find who to consult when constructing or changing it.

Status: The current state of the product such as 'draft' or 'delivered'. PRINCE2 suggests that you list the status types you'll use in the Configuration Management Strategy. That may sound like overkill, but it can be helpful where people may otherwise make up their own and then you can't find stuff in searches of a project database. This is because one person has set the status to 'in development' while someone building a different product has labelled theirs 'in progress' and a third decided on 'under construction'.

Product state: This is broadly similar to the previous heading, but refers to planning where a single product may be modelled once even though it goes through different states. The planning chapter earlier in this book (Chapter 14) doesn't advise this approach and I strongly recommend that you follow the way of doing things set down in that chapter. Merging states into a single entity serves to seriously undermine the great power of product planning in effective progress control.

Variant: Where a product might be varied from another, such as documents also made available in a large print format for those with sight problems.

Producer: The person or team who built the product or who procured it from outside the project.

Date allocated: The date on which a Work Package was issued to authorise the start of work on building or procuring the product.

Source: If the product was procured from outside the project. In the case of an external supplier, this can be useful, combined with the make and model information suggested under the heading of 'Item attributes' if you need to buy further items of the same type in the future.

Relationship with other items: The PRINCE2 manual suggests that this should record links of things that need to be changed if this one is changed, and other things which, if changed, would affect this item. A specific context is 'parent and child' relationships. If a particular item is used as a sub-component of a range of other products, then if you want to change it you need to be able to check that it's going to fit with all of the bigger products that use it. Similarly, you need to know what sub-components go to make up this particular larger product.

Cross-references: Finally, on this very long list, a reference of related project documentation. Predictably that's going to be the item's Product Description (see Chapter 14 for more on planning, including Product Descriptions) but also things like risks, Issues-related correspondence and other technical records.

If you use a CM computer tool you may have little or no choice about how you identify products, as the tool may have an inbuilt coding system. You may also have organisational standards that dictate how you identify products, particularly if the organisation is experienced in this area and has to control a large number of products in their working life, such as with IT products and computer departments.

Additional CI Information

Please sit down before reading this section: the author of *PRINCE2 for Dummies* is about to break with his usual practice and suggest *adding* things to a PRINCE2 product instead of taking things out! You may like to include the following items in the CI Record as and when you need them. The first two are from the previous edition of the PRINCE2 manual but they've been mysteriously dropped in the 2009 edition, and the third goes back even further. They're mentioned here, because the information can be valuable

Lifecycle steps for the product

To help with status accounting, you may like to record the lifecycle steps so that you can compare this with the current status to know where the product is in its development. To give a simple example, the lifecycle steps of a report might be 'draft', 'final' and 'approved'.

Knowledgeable person

The previous meaning of the term 'owner' related to recording the name of a person or team that understands a particular product, such as a technical specialist. Often this would be the person who built or installed it in the first place, but remember that CM goes on into the working life of products and so perhaps for many years. The person who built the product may have long since moved on, but you still need to know who to consult if you're thinking of changing the product.

Security requirements

This heading was dropped some two editions of the PRINCE2 manual ago, but it's actually rather useful. I suspect it was taken out because PRINCE2 was seen as being something for business, not just for government users, so readers were unlikely to be dealing with classified information. However, remarkably often this information is needed, even outside of government. Commercial information often needs to be handled with care, such as customer records. In a medical environment, confidentiality of patient information is clearly vital. If your project is dealing with information and any of it is confidential, you may like to think of adding this heading in to your CI Record to indicate what security is needed to look after it.

Construction location

You may also want to add even more elements to your record such as a location code for where the team builds a product, as distinct from the 'location' heading, which says where the product is at the moment, and even a country code with international projects. Such information can be very useful in problem solving and problem avoidance too, such as when things go wrong with measurements and you can see immediately that some products were built in a country using imperial measurements while other interfacing ones were built in a country using metric.

Copenhagen Airport in Denmark owns Tyne Tees Airport in the UK. Some of its projects involve work in both countries and its project staff need to be able to identify what products teams are building and where. In circumstances like this a country code can be very useful.

Change history

Usually, recording information on change history is also useful. The record then not only shows that something has been changed, but also why. If the change looks a bit odd, knowing why the change was made in the first place may prevent someone being tempted to reverse it.

Seeing that CM Is a Different Control

CM is inherently different from the rest of PRINCE2 controls (with the possible exception of part of risk management) because CM carries on when the project, and PRINCE2, stops. You need CM in the working life of products.

If you want a new oil filter for a car, you go into a motor spares shop and look at the reference card for the make, model, and year of the car. The card tells you what version of oil filter you need from the wide range on the shelf below. That's CM, but in the working life of the product. The project to design the car may have finished a number of years before.

At the end of the project, you need to pass information on versions and possibly the procedures back into the organisation as a Follow-on Action Recommendation.

Follow-on Action Recommendation. This is something the project recommends that the organisation does after the end of the project. In the case of CM, that action is ongoing control of the versions.

How CM helps prevent confusion

The information held as part of CM isn't complicated, but it's useful and can prevent time-consuming or even damaging problems in a project. Here are a few examples of problems together with the elements of CM information that can be effective in helping to prevent them:

✔ **Lost product:** The location information, and also information on who's currently working on the product.

✔ **Argument over who has the latest version:** The version number on the product identifier.

✔ **Not knowing whether you updated something or not:** The version number and also any change history information.

✔ **Not knowing whether a change may have an impact on something else:** The 'relationships with other products' information, but also the additional 'knowledgeable person' information if you're holding it.

✔ **Not knowing what other things a sub-component is used in:** The 'relationships' parent–child information.

✔ **Not knowing where to get a replacement for a broken part:** Supplier information, together with make and part number in 'Item attributes'.

Chapter 17

Monitoring Progress and Setting Up Effective Controls

In This Chapter

▶ Looking at time-driven and event-driven controls

▶ Managing by exception and saving senior staff time – big time

▶ Understanding tolerances and exceptions

▶ Checking progress and keeping control of projects

C ontrols in PRINCE2 are simple but extremely effective. If you use controls well they save time and make progress on the project extraordinarily clear. In fact, one progress control – which is a natural progression from the product planning covered in Chapter 14 – is one of the clearest available and involves no extra work if you do your planning well.

The main control during the project stages revolves around a management approach called *Exception Management*. This idea comes from accounting and works very effectively in a project. The key principle in Exception Management is that if everything goes to plan, actually you don't have too much to talk about. Only when something happens that's significantly different to what you expected do you need to sit up and take notice. And yes, this chapter deals with what 'significantly' means too.

Controls in PRINCE2 break down into two groups: event-driven controls and time-driven ones. Most controls are event driven, which means that they're triggered when something happens rather than when a certain period of time elapses. There are three time-driven controls; two progress reports at two different levels and an optional team meeting.

Controlling at Different Levels

As well as working with two basic types of control, event-driven and time-driven, the PRINCE2 controls also work at and between specific levels of management within the project. Some controls work at more than one level.

Breaking down the levels of control

Here's a breakdown of the management levels that are also mentioned elsewhere in the book because they affect things like communications as well:

✔ **Corporate or programme management:** The individual or group who commission the project.

Then, within the project itself:

✔ **The Project Board:** The managers who are responsible for the project.

✔ **The Project Manager:** One person who has day-to-day responsibility for the project and who's accountable to the Project Board.

✔ **Team Manager(s):** Each project team has a Team Manager who's responsible for the work given to that team (this role may not be needed though – see Chapter 12 to find why).

The project-level roles form part of the Project Management Team and you can read more about them in Chapter 12.

Reporting: Time-Driven Controls

The two time-driven reports in the method are both progress reports – the *Highlight Report* and the *Checkpoint Report*.

Highlight reporting

A Highlight Report is a regular progress report that the Project Manager gives to the Project Board members. The content of the report is largely predictable – schedule, budget, delivery, and information on any major problems. The Project Board specifies the frequency and exact content of the report and this is recorded in the Communication Management Plan, which is part of the Project Initiation Document or PID (there's more about this in Chapter 5).

Although the Highlight Report is intended for the Project Board, it may have a circulation beyond that. For example, where a project is part of a programme, you normally copy the Highlight Report to the Programme Director – or Senior Responsible Owner – and Programme Manager.

Checkpoint reporting

The second time-driven progress report is from a Team Manager to a Project Manager that explains how work on a Work Package is going.

Work Package. An instruction from a Project Manager to a Team Manager to build one or more products or deliverables. The Work Package includes things such as reporting requirements and problem notification, including Work Package exception. For more on Work Packages please see Chapter 14.

Team Managers give these *Checkpoint Reports* at the frequency and with the contents set down in the Work Package instructions, and this builds in great flexibility. You can vary the frequency of Checkpoint Reports between Work Packages. So one Team Manager may produce a Checkpoint Report every two days, while another doing work at the same time produces one every two weeks. As with the Highlight Report, the idea is to keep things simple and, as with any PRINCE2 report, you may decide that it can be verbal.

A Team Manager normally produces a Checkpoint Report after a regular team meeting. Although there's no requirement to hold team meetings, or to match Checkpoint reporting to team-meeting frequency if you do have them most people do. That meeting is actually the third time-driven control.

Using the Event-Driven Controls

The event-driven controls happen when the associated trigger event happens. The most important of these event-driven controls are the project stages.

Controlling the project with stages

You can't say the word 'control' in PRINCE2 without immediately thinking 'stages'. The stages (you may know them as *phases*) are the big controls in the method. A stage is a block of project work that the Project Board is willing to authorise to be done in one go.

Stages aren't a uniform length in PRINCE2. You never, for example, say that a year-long project divides into six stages of two months each. Well, you can, but I may then call you in to cut your buttons off, crumple your hat, rip up any PRINCE2 certificate you hold, and point a sword towards you. Dangerous stuff, so don't even think about it.

No, the stages are different lengths because they relate to the nature of the work, not to the turn of a page in a calendar. To determine the length of a stage, you consider things like the amount of risk in that part of the project and major decisions about the project. The stages are event driven, so when you reach the point you defined, the stage ends. If the work is slightly delayed, then the stage takes slightly longer and the Project Board meeting at the end of the stage is slightly later. If the stage finishes early, then the Project Board . . . ah, you're getting the idea of event-driven controls rather well.

Thinking 'management' stages not 'technical'

You must appreciate that in PRINCE2 the stages are management stages and not technical stages. The management stages are the units of work that the Project Board is willing to authorise and a particular management stage may contain several technical stages. You may align some of the management stage boundaries to technical stage boundaries, almost certainly not all of them or you're just running with the technical stages and missing out on the power of the management stage concept.

The stages in PRINCE2 give the Project Board superb control and means that it doesn't have to authorise all the money and staff resources for the project at the beginning. The Project Plan sets down the spend of money and the use of staff and then the board authorises these in a controlled way – one stage at a time.

Deciding how many stages to have

Some people ask whether you can have a standard number of stages for a particular type or size of project. The answer is emphatically 'no'. You just can't define a calculation or algorithm because there are too many variables.

The bottom line is that the Project Board decides the number of stages and these factors are set out in Chapter 10 which covers the Project Board work. If you're a Project Board member, do have a look at that chapter, because in PRINCE2 your work on the project is much more important than you may at first realise.

Counting the cost of stages

You need to be careful when thinking about the number of stages and where the stage boundaries are. The more stages, the more control you have, but the higher the cost. The fewer stages, the lower the cost but also the lower the degree of control. The Project Board must strike this balance. The board meet at the end of each stage and meetings can be expensive when you cost out everyone's time. And don't forget that the greater the number of stages, the greater the number of Stage Plans too, and they can take a lot of effort.

Approving stages – with a pen

No stage can start in PRINCE2 unless the Project Board gives its authority to do so. This makes the stage a powerful control, because you make a clear and recorded decision to carry on into the next stage. The project doesn't just roll on because nobody said to stop.

Although the method doesn't specify how the board give that authority, the pen is hard to beat. It's a wonderful instrument for getting commitment. Wherever possible, board members should physically sign these authorities. You know yourself that a world of difference exists between telling someone 'It looks all right to me' and then actually signing your name to confirm your approval. That signed authorisation doesn't have to be difficult – I'm not suggesting some handwritten parchment with a red ribbon round it. It can simply be a signature panel on the front of a Stage Plan.

Principle 4 – Manage by stages.

Making decisions at four key points

The stage boundaries form key decision points for the Project Board. Even before the first stage the board must decide whether the initial work of Start Up (see Chapter 4) shows the project to be viable and at least worth planning in more detail. If it does, the project starts to run the planning or Initiation Stage (see Chapter 5) and produces the Project Initiation Document or PID. The board must now decide whether the project should carry on or whether, after all, it's not worth conducting and must stop. Then the board meet at the end of each stage for an *End Stage Assessment* to decide whether everything is okay and whether or not to authorise the next block of work, the next management stage. At the end of the last stage, the board check that everything is complete and authorise project closure.

End Stage Assessment (ESA). The Project Board meeting at the end of a stage in which board members review the stage just completed, check that the project is viable, and then either authorise the next management stage or stop the project.

Ordering Project Closure at Any Time

The Project Board can decide not to authorise a stage and stop the project instead. But it has another, more immediate control. PRINCE2 incorporates a mechanism where the board can order immediate closure of the project without waiting until stage end. In response to an event at any point in the project, the board can call in the Project Manager and instruct that the project goes into its close-down process. This could be in response to a serious problem that has taken the project out of control, or perhaps because of some new information that shows the project just isn't needed any more.

A project was being run in an insurance company to upgrade and simplify some of its business procedures. But the project was suddenly stopped part way through. The insurance company had been taken over very suddenly by another company. There was no point in continuing the project to review the existing procedures because the new parent company had instructed that all business operations must now follow the existing parent company standards.

Managing 'By Exception'

Financial and retail management uses *Exception Management* as a control. This is a simple device that PRINCE2 brings into the project environment. Basically, the Exception Management approach says that if everything goes as expected, you may want a report that confirms you're on track but no decision has to be made.

A project stage contains a lot of plans – product plans, activity plans, resource plans, and financial plans. The Product Checklist provides excellent progress monitoring and gives you a lot of milestones for tracking delivery of project products very closely (see 'Monitoring Progress and Controlling Projects', later in this chapter). If everything runs pretty close to those plans, and demonstrably so, the argument is that little or nothing needs to be discussed.

In PRINCE2, the monthly progress meeting is gone – it's history. The Project Board doesn't meet until the end of the stage unless something goes 'significantly' off track, which means finishing outside the *tolerances* (limits) that the board itself specified. Cutting out the monthly progress meeting saves large amounts of senior staff time. Instead PRINCE2 has the Highlight Report, which is both informative and quick to prepare.

If you're a Project Board member and worry that you may not be getting wholly accurate information on the Highlight Reports, remember that Project Assurance, the audit function in the project, checks the information. If the information you receive is wrong, assurance staff tell you immediately. Please see Chapter 12 for more on Project Assurance.

Principle 5 – Manage by exception.

Specifying the Limits: Tolerances

Very few projects, stages, or even Work Packages run exactly to plan. Suppose I'm a Project Manager in a $500,000, 10-week stage in a multimillion, 15-month project, and you're a member of the Project Board. In Week 2 my latest projections from team estimates and other information are that the stage won't cost $500,000 after all; it's going to cost $500,002 – $2 more. Should I call you in with the rest of the board to discuss the $2 projected overspend? I don't think so, although when I posed this question once somebody answered, 'It depends on whether there's a free lunch', which I thought was an extremely good answer.

But wait, I miscalculated. I'm afraid that this stage is going to cost £8 million – a £7.5 million overspend on a £500,000 stage. Should I call you in now? The same person answered, 'It depends on whether there's a free lunch,' which I thought was an even better answer. But I think that most people would be slightly concerned at this degree of overspend and if you're on the Project Board you'd want the Project Manager to call you in – and fast.

This leaves one question: At what point do I call you in? Is it £3, £500, or £7 million? What's the point between £2, where you don't want me to call you in, and £7.5 million, where you do?

The limits, both upper and lower, are the *tolerances*. If something comes in at significantly lower cost than expected, you want to know that as well. Perhaps you need to inform others in the organisation and certainly this affects the Business Case, because the project now has even better justification.

You can do the same with time. If the Project Manager projects that the stage will take ten weeks and one hour, rather than the ten weeks initially agreed, do you want him to call you in? If the project is 42 weeks over and the Project Manager now estimates that it will take a year rather than 10 weeks, do you want him to call you in? A tolerance is specified on this too with plus and minus limits, which you can set down as a percentage or a number of days, say 10 weeks, plus or minus 10 per cent, or you may say plus or minus three days. The lower limit can be as important as the upper one, because if the project comes in a lot earlier than expected, taking advantage of this may have all sorts of business implications.

Setting unequal tolerances

The plus and minus amounts specified for a tolerance don't have to be the same, and they don't have to be the same across all types of tolerance. For example, you may decide on plus or minus 10 per cent on time, and plus 5 per cent and minus 15 per cent on cost. Actually those figures are often used because underspends are generally less sensitive than overspends, but not always, so you need to think about the sensitivity in the context of the business environment in which you work.

For time and cost, you can show the tolerances graphically. Figure 17-1 shows the expected expenditure and time, with upper and lower limits. Those limits form a box at the top right of the graph, the *tolerance box*.

The box represents the Project Manager's delegated authority to manage the stage. All the time that the projections end in the box, the Project Manager can keep going, though he regularly reports progress with a Highlight Report. Exception Management gives the Project Manager some space to get on with his job without undue interference and without unnecessary meetings.

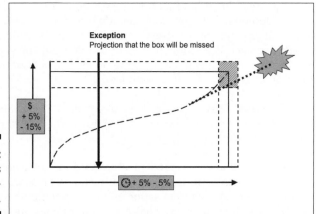

Figure 17-1: Tolerances and the tolerance box.

In his '100 Rules for NASA Project Managers', Jerry Madden says:

> *Rule #3: Management principles are still the same. It is just that the tools have changed. You still find the right people to do the work and get out of the way so they can do it.*

The tolerances allow the Project Board to get out of the Project Manager's way, but within limits that board members themselves set.

A lot of misunderstandings occur among those people using PRINCE2 who don't have the intelligence and foresight to buy a copy of *PRINCE2 For Dummies*. These people quite often say that if a stage is high-risk, you apply zero tolerance. Zero tolerance may be fine as a concept in managing crime, but it simply doesn't work in projects – not unless you provide sleeping accommodation for the Project Board, because they end up in permanent session. Bringing in a Project Board for a penny's projected overspend, then a penny's projected underspend, just isn't workable. Even if the board approve the new cost, they then have to start reviewing the project's timing because now the stage is five minutes over the planned ten weeks because you didn't include that meeting in the plan. Use a tight tolerance maybe, but not zero.

Guarding against wishful thinking – tolerance lines

You may have encountered a problem if you manage staff who have budget allocations. The staff give their spending profiles to you at the beginning of the financial year with fairly modest spending plans. You approve the budget, and then after three months you get their first spending report. Your staff spent rather more than planned, but they reduced the estimates for the rest of the financial year and it all meets the original total. Then, after another three months, another overspend occurs, but the staff reduce the remaining six-month forecast and maintain the annual limit. Same story after another three months, except they now say they won't spend anything at all in the last quarter. Then comes the report for the last quarter, which shows spending higher than the previous three periods all added together.

This problem stems from wishful thinking. 'Yes, things are a bit overspent, but we're bound to save some money later.' 'Yes, we're a bit behind, but the team's bound to get faster as the stage goes on.' Really? Perhaps, but if you're a Project Board member you may just want to check that.

Using the graphical approach again, you have an option to include *tolerance lines* all the way up the S curve (see Figure 17-2). If the Project Manager forecasts that the stage will go outside this 'tolerance corridor', as someone has aptly named it, the Project Manager calls the board in, even if the projection is that the angle may ease off later and the stage will finish inside the tolerance box.

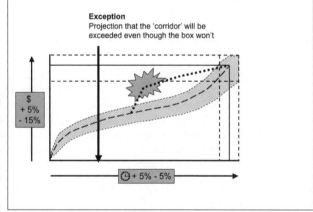

Figure 17-2: The tolerance lines and tolerance corridor.

If the board aren't concerned about deviations during the stage as long as the Project Manager projects that the stage will finish inside the box, then they can just specify the box limits and not the lines.

You may want to think about whether to bring the tolerance corridor into force a little while into the stage and not from the beginning. In the first part of the stage the corridor is very narrow and can send the stage into Exception much too easily. In that first part, you may be better off not having lines at all and using the box only, or specifying a set tolerance amount and time for that first period, not a variable one depending on the distance along the S curve. If you play around with a spreadsheet you can see that an overspend of, say, £1,000 causes a minor blip towards the end of a stage, but the same amount sends the stage well into exception at the beginning.

Outlining the six types of tolerance

You can specify tolerances in some or all of the six PRINCE2 control areas. Time and cost are the most common areas.

- ✔ **Time:** Few projects run exactly to time, so having a margin is sensible, to avoid calling the board in for minor variations in the predicted end point.

- ✔ **Cost:** As for time, there's no point in calling the board in over minor variations. Doing so may cost more in senior staff time than the amount the variation involves.

- ✔ **Scope:** In some projects carrying out some changes in scope without reference to the board may be acceptable. A common example is in Rapid Applications Development (RAD) projects to build computer systems within a set time limit. The team is empowered to 'de-scope' products to fit the specified 'time box'.

- ✔ **Risk:** If a risk dramatically increases in severity, or new information shows that a really severe risk has gone and now can't damage the project, then the board want to know immediately. Chapter 15 has more on risk management and how to show risk tolerance against impact and probability.

- ✔ **Business benefits:** If the projection of benefits changes to go outside a given range, then the board want to know at once. If new information shows that the project will now give considerably more benefits than previously estimated, the board want to know so that they can boast to – sorry, inform – corporate management. But if new information shows that benefits may be significantly less than predicted, the board may want to consider closing the project down immediately.

- ✔ **Quality:** Upper and lower limits may apply on quality variations, for example on the number of errors found.

Quality tolerance can sound a bit odd in the context of errors. If you find more than a certain number of errors then you have a clear quality problem that the board need to discuss. But strangely, not finding enough errors can be serious too, and may be enough to bring a board in very quickly.

Safety-critical computer developments have a norm for errors. If you find significantly fewer errors, they result from two possible causes and the board will want to know which applies. The first is that the team has written the software to a particularly high standard and fewer errors are present than expected. But the other reason is that the testing is inadequate. The errors are there, but the tests aren't finding them. That means errors can go through into a safety-critical system, which is, obviously, extremely serious. One way of checking is to do more stringent testing of some sample areas to see whether this confirms that no more errors are present, or whether many more come to light and so show up weaknesses in the original testing regime.

Tolerances and project finances

A stage includes three areas of funding and you need to understand financial tolerances in this context.

✔ **Stage budget:** This is the budget for what you plan to do. This spend is subject to tolerance, because few stages run to plan to the penny.

✔ **Change budget:** This is for things that, by definition, aren't on the plan. But the money is conditional: If nobody asks for any changes, then you don't have access to this fund. Tolerance doesn't apply to change budgets.

✔ **Risk budget:** This is money set aside as part of risk management. If a risk occurs then the money is pre-authorised to deal with it. Again, the money is not subject to tolerance and is conditional because if the risk doesn't happen, you don't get access to the money.

The Project Manager would be abusing any of the funds if he used them outside their designated purpose. Project Assurance, the audit function, checks to make sure that the money is used correctly.

Reporting Projections Outside of Tolerance: Exception

If you project that you're going to break any tolerance limit, you must report it immediately. The stage is 'in Exception' and this reflects the name of this approach – *Exception Management*.

In Exception. When the projection is that something will finish outside the tolerance limits specified. If you can manage the situation with your own delegated authority so that things now stay in tolerance – it alters the projections – then you're not in Exception. You're in Exception as soon as you establish that you can't complete that part of the project within the limits. Exception isn't when you finally go outside the tolerance corridor or miss the box. If you project in week 2 that you can't complete a stage within the upper limit of week 10, you're in Exception in week 2, not in week 10.

Giving an Exception Report

A stage exception is reported using an *Exception Report*. PRINCE2 is just so complicated sometimes, isn't it? You 'give' an Exception Report, though, so that doesn't necessarily mean write it. You can make a phone call to each Project Board member, for example. The Communication Management Plan in the PID sets down what needs to be in the report and how to give it.

The Exception Report

This report is used to pass on information about an exception that may affect the current stage or even the whole project.

Date: This heading isn't actually listed in the PRINCE2 manual, but is clearly advisable on a written Exception Report.

Exception title: A description of the type of exception, such as a risk exception. The PRINCE2 manual suggests that this should be an overview of the exception, but that is surely a little lengthy for a title! Such detail would be better placed under the next heading.

Cause of the exception: The description of what's gone wrong and why.

Consequences of the deviation: The impact within the project and beyond it if the problem is not dealt with. Of course there may still be impacts if the problem is dealt with, but that's covered by the next heading.

Options: The alternatives for action and the impacts of each. For example, re-working a product to deal with a quality exception may have significant impacts on time and cost.

Recommendation: Of the options put forward, which does the Project Manager recommend and, importantly for the Project Board's understanding, why?

Deciding what to do

When the Project Manager recommends an action for a stage-level exception it's just that, a recommendation; the Project Board actually decide the action. This is the first part of the Exception Management procedure. The board members take very careful note of what the Project Manager thinks and they may then follow his recommendation, but they may not.

The Project Board may decide on an action that doesn't have any impact on Stage or Project Plans. For example, the board may decide to close the project. Or perhaps the cost of a piece of equipment goes up a lot and takes the stage into cost Exception. The board may simply authorise the additional funds and the Project Manager just needs to note this on the budget. You don't have to do any re-planning because the timing of the stage, the staffing, and the activities and products are the same. This board give their decision to the Project Manager and that ends the first part of the procedure.

Revising the plans

If you have to run the stage very differently to recover from an exception, clearly the original Stage Plan isn't much use. You need to re-plan to show the changed products, activities, schedule, and resources. But re-planning what you've already done so far in this stage is pointless.

Revising the plan forces an extra stage boundary. Because you don't want to re-plan what you've already done, you close that work down as if this was the end of a stage. You even produce an End Stage Report for it. You re-plan the remaining work in the stage as if it were a new stage and that plan is an *Exception Plan*. There's more on this in Chapter 6, and on the detail of planning in Chapter 14. Whereas the Exception Plan is normally exactly the same as a Stage Plan, it's usually a bit faster to prepare, and this is for two reasons. First, it doesn't cover the whole of the stage, only the bit that's left. Second, it is very unlikely that everything will have changed and some parts of the existing Stage Plan are almost certain to be usable.

Exception Plan. A replacement plan for a stage that covers the period from the point of the exception until the end of the stage. It may also need to include an updated Project Plan if, for example, this stage now takes longer to complete, that timing change knocks on to the timing of the other stages and the project end date.

The Project Board must see and approve any plan at stage level. You then need to hold an End Stage meeting to check things out and either approve the plan or stop the project. This behaves exactly like a planned End Stage, but because you didn't originally intend it – you're reacting to the exception – the meeting has a different name; an *Exception Assessment.*

Exception Assessment. A meeting of the Project Board that works just like an End Stage Assessment except you didn't originally plan it. You hold it to consider an Exception Plan.

Using Tolerance at Different Levels

The discussion on Exception Management so far in this chapter relates mostly to the stage level. But one of the strengths of Exception Management is that you can use it for control between all the management levels in the project:

- ✔ **Project Tolerance:** Corporate management or the Programme Director can give the Project Board tolerances for the whole project.

- ✔ **Stage Tolerance:** The Project Board give the Project Manager stage tolerances for each stage.

- ✔ **Work Package Tolerance:** The Project Manager can put tolerances on Team Managers for individual work assignments or *Work Packages.*

Tolerances can run right down the levels of the project, but they can also trigger exceptions running right up to the top. An exception on a Work

Package can send a whole stage into Exception, which in turn could trigger a Project Exception and require the Executive to report to corporate or programme management.

In its handling of Work Package exceptions PRINCE2 yo-yos from one edition of the manual to the next, so I guess you can feel even freer than usual to make your own mind up. The present position is that a Team Manager won't use an Exception Report to notify an exception, rather, he'll usually submit an Issue. However, the exact mechanism to be used is set down on the Work Package itself so there always was flexibility.

Monitoring Progress and Controlling Projects

The PRINCE2 method incorporates different ways of controlling work during a project and checking progress.

Controlling teams with Work Packages

In PRINCE2 the Project Manager controls the flow of work by authorising Work Packages. A Team Manager can't start work until he receives the package. While the team works on the products, the Team Manager reports progress from time to time using a Checkpoint Report. Chapter 7 explains the Work Package control. The concept of the Work Package is used by many project management approaches, not just PRINCE2, but as already hinted in this chapter, the idea is a great one because it allows fine-tuning of controls. Different controls such as reporting frequency and exception handling can be applied to different Work Packages, though you may well define some default settings, which you then use for most of them.

Measuring progress with the Product Checklist

PRINCE2 has a very powerful progress-measuring mechanism, the Product Checklist. You develop it as part of product planning (you can find out more about this in Chapter 14) and the checklist is simply a list of products or deliverables together with their target delivery dates and, later, their actual delivery dates. These form highly effective milestones within a stage because the products are unambiguous in terms of delivery. Either a product is delivered, which means quality checked and signed off, or it isn't delivered. You can't have a halfway house of 'nearly delivered'.

Product planning typically identifies 15 to 30 products in each stage, which gives 15 to 30 milestones where you know exactly where that stage is with no debate at all.

Avoiding 'percentage complete'

Most project approaches, including computer scheduling tools, use the 'percentage complete' measure on activities to determine progress. However, percentage complete is unreliable and activities can stay 'nearly finished – 90 per cent' for a remarkably long time.

Beware of strange views on product planning. If you stick to the approach set down in this book you'll be fine. Some people argue that different 'states' of a product don't matter: They're the same product and you should model them as one thing. Not only is that illogical (try convincing a child that a muddy potato is exactly the same thing as a packet of nice crispy fries in their favourite fast-food outlet) but it also undermines quality (the quality criteria are different), activity planning, resource planning (the resources are often different for arriving at the different points in development), but now it also undermines progress monitoring and use of the Product Checklist.

You can extend the Product Checklist slightly by putting in other dates such as the expected and actual dates for testing. That can be really useful as an early warning of delay, but the key information is the delivery information.

Controlling quality

The PRINCE2 method includes some highly effective ways of controlling the quality in the project. This exploits the power of product-based planning. For the detail on these, please see Chapter 13 for quality and Chapter 14 for product planning, including setting quality criteria for the individual products.

Looking for Financial Controls

If you're looking for an effective way of controlling project finance in PRINCE2, then you're going to be terribly disappointed. Other than the S curve and cost tolerance (see 'Guarding against wishful thinking – tolerance lines', earlier in this chapter), the method doesn't offer anything. This is a major omission in PRINCE2, which targets project planning and control, of which financial control is clearly an important element. You need to look outside PRINCE2 for help on financial control.

As a start on financial planning, you can make a spreadsheet with budgeted costs, actual costs, and the variance. That's easy to construct. Then you can also look for information on the Earned Value Analysis technique, because that fits PRINCE2 well and again is fairly simple to use.

Part IV
The Part of Tens

The 5th Wave   By Rich Tennant

'Hey, Phillip! We haven't finished appointing our Project Management Team yet!'

In this part . . .

Every *For Dummies* book has a Part of Tens, a handful of concise chapters that really pack a punch.

These chapters are all helpful pointers towards making PRINCE2 work at the best possible capacity for you. I hope you find them helpful.

Chapter 18

Ten Ways to Make PRINCE2 Work Well

In This Chapter

▶ Staying flexible in how you use the method

▶ Building PRINCE2 into the organisation so that it becomes normal

▶ Maintaining the audit function to make sure that the project runs well

A lot of people get tied up in knots with PRINCE2 and think that the method is only for very big projects because of all the overheads. Sometimes they've been given the impression by others that PRINCE2 is all about documentation – form filling. That's so far from the truth. PRINCE2 is a powerful and dynamic method, but you need to use it intelligently, like any tool. Here are ten tips to help you on the way to PRINCE2 success.

Staying Flexible – Using PRINCE2 Differently

How you use PRINCE2 can be as different as your projects are from each other. Even when you repeat a project, you may want to use the method differently. Yes, yes – I know that some people say that you can't repeat a project, but I disagree. Saying slight differences may exist is just splitting hairs.

One company involved in deep-sea surveys sends remotely operated vehicles (mini-submarines on a control cable) down to survey the sea bed, to move an oil rig or build an undersea pipeline. The company sets up and runs each survey as a project. One survey is pretty much like another, except that the sub surveys a different part of the sea bed. In a different organisation, a review of accounting procedures for compliance with the Sarbanes-Oxley Act regarding financial disclosure may involve several projects examining different parts of the business, but the projects are all pretty similar.

Back to the point, then – even on similar projects you may use PRINCE2 differently. For two similar projects, one with a very experienced Project Manager and one with an inexperienced one, the two Project Boards may decide on very different management stages. The board with the inexperienced Project Manager want more stages and more points at which they check the state of the project. They may also require more rigorous audit (Project Assurance), and more detailed progress reports (Highlight Reports). Those variations are just three of the things that may be different just because of one factor – the experience of the Project Manager.

At the start of each project you must ask, 'How are we going to use PRINCE2 this time?' Keep things flexible. You have to fit PRINCE2 to the project or you end up with problems and almost certainly with unnecessarily high overheads.

A danger point for many organisations is about 12 to 15 months after they start using PRINCE2 across their projects, when they begin to 'stiffen up'. Instead of maintaining the in-built flexibility of the method, organisations start to say, 'This is how we do it here.' Even worse is when a poor Project Office (see Chapter 12 for more on the Project Office) starts to impose standards so that it can get nicely uniform reports from nicely uniform information about nicely uniform projects. Unfortunately (well, for the report formatters anyway), projects are different – the important thing is running the project well, not slavish adherence to an inappropriate but 'Project Office -friendly' standard.

One very large multinational company used PRINCE2 very well and went past the 12 to 15 month period with no apparent 'stiffening' problems. I was really impressed, but then a few months later one of its Project Managers told me that he wanted to keep one of the PRINCE2 registers on a spreadsheet. He wanted to be able to use the powerful spreadsheet functions to sort entries in different ways; for example, into items still unresolved, items from a particular area of the project, and items that were high priority. I thought this was a really sensible idea, but the Project Manager told me he wasn't allowed to do it. Project Support had told him that the company standard was to use a word-processor table and not a spreadsheet and that he must comply. Project Support staff had gone off track with documentation standards and were now applying an unnecessary limitation even though it worked against good project management.

Keeping the Documentation Down

PRINCE2 users often complain that the method is paper-hungry and involves lots of unnecessary documentation. That's actually not true. If a document is unnecessary, why is it being produced? Why isn't the project's audit function – Project Assurance (please see Chapter 12 for more information) – jumping up and down and questioning why valuable project time is being taken up in writing this document that isn't needed, and then creating more unnecessary work for others who now have to read it?

You must make sure that you need every document that you produce in your project and that the content included is all necessary too. And even if the content is right, you need to ensure that the way you communicate it is appropriate. For example, do you really need to write that information down? Can you use a phone call instead?

Use the Communication Management Strategy in the Project Initiation Document (PID) to think through and record exactly what you require and the most effective and efficient way of communicating the information. Please see Chapter 5 for more on the strategies and PID.

Making PRINCE2 a Standard

So simple? Well yes, almost. PRINCE2 needs to become 'the way we do things around here' – part of the organisational culture, not an optional add-on. As with anything else, people gain familiarity and best practice becomes ingrained. 'Lessons learned' from one project feed forward into future projects.

Be careful that you don't fall into the trap of the *standard approach* where people think you use PRINCE2 exactly the same way on every project. Instead, the familiarity and experience can lead to ever-improving and ever more intelligent use of the method.

Insisting on PRINCE2

Insisting that PRINCE2 is used? You may be thinking, 'Hmmm. Easier said than done in my organisation.' You need to get senior corporate management on board to make sure that you use PRINCE2 for all your projects. Now you're probably thinking, 'You *really* don't know my organisation.' I agree that getting top management support can be tricky – but not tricky with accounting. I expect that your organisation's finance staff prepared the accounts properly and professionally last year and are preparing them equally properly and professionally this year. And I don't anticipate any arguments about whether the finance staff will prepare the accounts properly next year either. Managing accounts professionally and well is routine and indeed necessary.

In the same way, the organisation needs to be as determined and as professional with managing its projects every single time. This needs top management support to work well – but not unknowing, mindless support. Senior managers need to see the logic of PRINCE2 and appreciate the business impact of failure where projects aren't run well. That business impact applies whether the organisation is public or private.

Training People in PRINCE2

I'm not trying to sell training here – organisations can do some training in-house. But whichever way you choose, all the people involved in the project need to understand the method they work with. And don't forget the Project Board, the senior management group with oversight of the project (Chapter 12 covers the detail). Board members can't fulfil their function of making sure that the project runs properly if they don't understand the method, any more than senior managers of a department can check whether the department functions well if they don't have any idea what their staff do.

The project board is actually a big failure point for PRINCE2. A lot of project problems can be traced back to the board not doing its job properly. The project is like a department or even a whole organisation. If you have problems in the board room, you usually have problems in the company. As far as you can control or influence your organisation's use of PRINCE2, try to make sure that you don't have problems of ignorance in your project 'board room'. Make sure that your people know what they're doing.

Implementing Project Assurance

Some people think that you do financial audit as a matter of routine but that project audit (Project Assurance) is somehow optional and unnecessary. But this is a strange and rather contradictory approach, especially given that some projects are incredibly important.

Project Assurance is essential, but it's also really helpful. It's essential because you must check that things are correct; it's helpful because Project Assurance supports the Project Manager. Project Assurance is like having a colleague check something over for you – a colleague who's sensible, co-operative, and constructive, not nit-picking and awkward.

Project Assurance is a valuable PRINCE2 safeguard and is an essential part of the way the method works. Don't leave it out. Instead, implement Project Assurance properly and everyone's happy, including those being audited.

Actually Doing the Benefit Reviews

The Business Case for the project sets down how you will measure the benefits and the Benefits Review Plan describes who does this and when. The project and the organisation need to make sure that the reviews happen partly by Project Board Members and senior organisational managers making sure that they get the results. For more on the Business Case and Benefits Review Plan, please see Chapter 11. For more on the Project Board's Project Assurance responsibilities and the external organisational check of Quality Assurance please see Chapter 12.

You need to be particularly careful about any benefits reviews that are planned for after the end of the project. At the end of the project, the PRINCE2 Project Management Team is disbanded, so you need to be sure that the responsibility for post-project benefit reviews is passed to someone in the organisation who'll make quite sure that they happen and that the results are reported.

Maintaining Product Planning

Product-based – or product-led – planning is a very powerful approach that PRINCE2 assumes you'll be using. Many users misunderstand product planning and so leave it out, thereby missing out on an extremely valuable planning approach that feeds forward into progress and quality control. At this point, depending on when you read this, you may be thinking any of the following:

- ✓ If you read Chapter 14 in this book, which deals with planning, you may be thinking, 'Oh no, he's raving on about the benefits of product planning again!'

- ✓ If you haven't read Chapter 14 but have already used PRINCE2, you may be thinking, 'Oh yes, product-based planning; I never did get the point of all that.'

- ✓ And if you're completely new to PRINCE2, you may be thinking: 'Whatever's product planning? Surely we don't need more planning techniques in projects?'

Whichever applies to you, do get to grips with this planning approach and then use it – it really does help. Product planning is a bit awkward at first because it isn't a natural way of thinking, but is actually very logical, so persevere. In the end it becomes easy. Product planning is a great step forward that pays its way time and again and can really help you, so don't leave it out.

Using the Product Checklist

The Product Checklist is a superb progress-monitoring tool and is much more effective than the normal 'percentage complete' progress check based on activities. This is because the checklist is factual and unambiguous. The Product Checklist emerges naturally from product planning, as Chapter 14 explains. The products you deliver in each stage act as milestones – the Product Checklist simply shows whether a product is complete (which means quality checked and signed off) or not. With 15 to 30 products in each stage, there are 15 to 30 points where the Project Manager and Project Board know exactly where the project is, with no debate at all. That's more than useful.

Keeping the Plans Up To Date

The PRINCE2 method has three levels of planning – but the thing about plans is that you need to keep them up to date. Too many people in projects draw up a plan to get the funding at the beginning, and then put the plan in a drawer and forget all about planning until the start of the next project. But a plan is only useful if it's up to date. This takes effort, but is vital for control.

The ongoing planning work involves making forward projections so that you can see any problems coming and take action in good time. For example, imagine that you're driving a car and you see a brick wall in the distance. You have time to steer to avoid the wall. But if you only look up and see the wall filling the whole windscreen at the last minute, no matter how violently you steer, you crash. Project Assurance should check at intervals to ensure that plans are up to date as well.

Plans are essential for effective control. No up-to-date plans – nothing to measure against – means no effective control.

Chapter 19

Ten Tips for a Good Business Case

*T*he Business Case is the most important element of a PRINCE2 project. It's the justification – the reason you do the project. You don't run projects for fun, though they may *be* fun. You run projects to deliver a business benefit or meet a business imperative. Although some projects have complicated Business Cases and developing them involves huge amounts of work, most are much simpler. Here are ten pointers to help you produce a good Business Case, and then keep it up to date.

Measuring Benefits – Wherever You Can

Wherever possible, you need to be able to measure business benefits so that you can show that they were achieved. Sometimes measuring is hard and it takes a lot of thinking to work out how to do it, but as far as possible have measures, even if it is only for part of the benefit. Beware of 'non-quantifiable' benefits because, although sometimes real and valid, they're by definition not measurable and you can easily fool yourself that the project is delivering more than it really is; more of that later in these tips.

Benefits can come on stream at different points, not just after the project. Particularly where things are being taken into operational use during the project, benefits may start to be seen during the project as well. Think carefully about this because even if only some benefits can be measured during the project, it gives everyone an indication of whether the project is headed for success or, for example, that the benefits projections were wildly optimistic. Chapter 11 gives you more on planning benefits reviews during the project, at the end of the project and after the project where benefits won't be clearly visible until sometime after the project has closed down. Chapter 11 also has full details on the Business Case itself.

Be careful also to isolate benefits correctly, so that you can genuinely attribute them to the project. It's easy to make the mistake of bouncing off too quickly and coming up with benefits measures that aren't precise enough and which get contaminated by other factors. For example, an increase in sales of 20 per cent may sound like a good benefit. But if sales do go up by 20 per cent, how can you be sure that this is just down to the project? Perhaps sales have risen for other reasons that aren't connected with the project at all. Perhaps the market has grown by 25 per cent and the project actually worked to reduce sales!

When working the Business Case into full detail in Project Initiation state clearly against each benefit how you plan to measure it. Then, in the Benefits Review Plan, you set down when the checks will be made and who is to make them. Chapter 11 has more on avoiding benefits contamination.

If the project is claiming a percentage change as a benefit – such as increasing the speed of fulfilling orders by 10 per cent or reducing the time needed for particular business processes by 5 per cent – don't forget to take baseline measures at the start of the project if you don't know the current stats. That way you can show the change after the new procedures are up and running.

Understanding that Some Projects Don't Have Benefits

Just occasionally you have a good reason to run a project that has no business benefits in the normal way in which that term is understood, or for which realising benefits is secondary to the main purpose. Here are three instances of when this may happen:

> ✔ **Compliance projects:** Sometimes you have to run a project, whether it has benefits or not. The justification is 'we've been told to'. Perhaps you received an instruction from headquarters that all divisions have to do this, or perhaps it's a legal requirement. The justification for the project is 'compliance'. The project may have some benefits as well, but you run it even if it hasn't got any benefits at all because you have to.

> A senior officer in a UK police force was very worried about the Business Case for one of his projects, because he couldn't see any benefits and didn't know what to write. When asked why the project was being planned, he replied that the Home Secretary (the government minister responsible for UK police forces) had written to all chief constables in

all UK police forces asking (which means telling) them to run a project to implement a particular change. The justification or Business Case was therefore very simple: Why are we running this project in the police force? Because we have no choice; the Home Office told us to.

✔ **Enabling projects:** Sometimes a project may not deliver any benefit, or any significant benefit, but you still run it because it allows one or more other projects to run that do deliver benefits. The justification for the project is therefore 'enabling'. That's a perfectly valid reason.

✔ **Non-quantifiable benefits:** Benefits are normally measurable, but an exception exists. Some genuine benefits of a project simply cannot be measured, or at least can't be measured meaningfully. They can be very powerful though, so need to be included in the Business Case. An example is with quality and company image. Perhaps you have a project to boost the customer's perception of your company. You can measure that a bit, but how the improved perception then affects order levels is much harder to measure. But if perception problems are losing business, not to address your company image may end up with the loss of the whole company. Similarly, quality can be hard to measure sometimes.

In such cases clearly state that the primary justification is, for example, compliance and although there may be some benefits also, these are secondary and the project is needed whether the benefits are delivered or not. You can use the Executive Summary section of the Business Case to spell that out.

Reviewing the Business Case Regularly

The Business Case is a vital and 'living' document in PRINCE2. Keep it up to date throughout the project. Don't just use the Business Case as a mechanism to get funding at the start, and then file it away and forget it. If the Business Case deteriorates you may need to stop the project – quickly. You can't make decisions on the ongoing viability of the project, such as at the End Stage, unless you have current information to hand.

As a minimum, update the Business Case just before the end of each stage, so that you have it ready for the Project Board to check at the End Stage Assessment, their end of stage meeting. Chapter 6 covers the End Stage update of the Business Case.

Being Prudent (1)

Being prudent or conservative is a principle of accounting, and it holds true in project Business Cases too. Be careful not to be over-optimistic with benefits projections when you're doing Start Up and Initiation so that you don't start a project that really shouldn't be started. That won't help the business, and may stop another project which actually would have been more beneficial.

Being Prudent (2)

Another reason to be prudent about benefits is so you don't undermine the success of a project. If you promise unrealistically high benefits and then fail to deliver them, the project can end on a sour note and the organisation may well see the project as a failure. But if you're prudent and keep your estimates of benefits conservative, then when the project delivers, or even slightly exceeds, the promised benefits, the organisation sees the project (and you) as a success.

Owning the Business Case

The Executive must own the Business Case and not delegate this to the Project Manager. The Executive represents the business viewpoint for the project and delivering value for money. The Senior User(s) specify what benefits they can deliver from the project, and must then deliver them, so they have an important input into the Business Case as well. In line with the role of the Project Board as a whole, the Senior User(s) and Executive must realise that they're responsible for the project overall, including the Business Case, even though the Project Manager may do a lot of the spade work for them.

Aligning the Business Case with Corporate Requirements

Many organisations have internal procedures for applying for funding, and have documents that you must prepare in a set way. Don't make work for yourself by producing a Business Case according to the PRINCE2 list of contents, and then having to do the work all over again to re-format it and adjust the information to meet your organisation's needs for finance submissions.

Instead, work out a format that serves both purposes in one hit. If the PRINCE2 Business Case includes elements that are useful to the project but aren't necessary for the corporate application, put these elements in a separate section and don't submit that section as part of the corporate procedure.

Change PRINCE2 where you need so that it fits your organisation.

Standing Firm on the Figures

Many organisations ask for huge financial detail as soon as anyone even murmurs something about a potential project. Try not to get sucked into this and end up doing a full Business Case in Start Up. Start Up is supposed to go fast and the Business Case at that point is just a ball-park outline. Please see Chapter 4 for full detail on Start Up, including the _Outline Business Case_.

If you give in to organisational pressure to produce detailed costings at that early point, you end up doing Initiation in Start Up and it all takes far too long. Instead, try to explain the PRINCE2 approach to your finance people and get them to see that you're not ignoring the detailed financial work, but that you're doing it as part of the planning when all the necessary detail from the Project Plan is to hand.

Updating the Business Case During Stages

PRINCE2 focuses on updating the Business Case at the end of each stage. But don't simply do that and forget all about the Business Case _during_ each stage.

In the regular review of the stage to check progress you need to check the benefit projections from time to time as well. If new information comes to light as part of the stage work that affects the benefit levels, it may have a knock-on effect on the viability of the whole project and you may need to warn the Project Board.

The Project Board may require a warning on benefits projection and set a tolerance level for benefits. So if the projections go outside the band they've specified, the Project Manager must warn the board immediately that the stage is in 'benefits exception'. You can find more information in Chapter 17 on tolerances and exception handling.

Thinking 'Business Case' in Issue Handling

When dealing with a project Issue (something anyone brings to the Project Manager's attention, such as a problem), don't forget to look at any implications for the Business Case or benefits projections. For example, if the project is to put on a sports event and the problem is that you can't obtain clothing in the right colour, this may affect sponsorship if it's the main sponsor's corporate colour. Please see Chapter 16 for more on Change Control and how to handle Project Issues.

The PRINCE2 method suggests that you consult Business Assurance to help check out this side of the Issue impact analysis, but everyone involved needs to have the Business Case continually in mind, not least the Project Manager.

Chapter 20

Ten Things for Successful Project Assurance

In This Chapter

▶ Making sure that you actually do assurance

▶ Avoiding the list tickers and nit-pickers

▶ Making assurance helpful and co-operative

*P*roject Assurance is the audit function in a PRINCE2 project. Project Board members can do it themselves, or they can delegate the audit checks to other people, who then report back to the board members. You can read much more about Project Assurance in Chapter 12.

Project Assurance is a hugely neglected part of PRINCE2 (except where users of the method read *PRINCE2 For Dummies* and realise how important this audit function is). But Project Assurance really is a vital part, just as financial audit is a vital part of financial management. Here are ten tips for making Project Assurance work well.

Making Sure You Do It

Okay, telling you to ensure that you do Project Assurance may sound a bit basic, but actually I'm making a very important point. Project Assurance is probably the most neglected part of PRINCE2. Few organisations question the need for financial audit, but a great number don't think they need to bother too much about 'project audit', even for large and expensive projects.

In many cases organisations neglect Project Assurance because they had unpleasant experiences of bad financial auditors (oh, all right then, lots of unpleasant experiences of lots of bad financial auditors) and they think that PRINCE2 auditing will be just as annoying. Financial audit can be very productive, but it often becomes an ordeal because of auditors who have a poor approach and even worse interpersonal skills. But this problem is bad news in financial audit, let alone within the management team of a PRINCE2 project.

The correct approach to Project Assurance is a co-operative one, which is rather like a colleague checking work for you. You really appreciate your colleague's input and are grateful for any problems that she finds because then you can put them right.

The velvet glove contains a steel fist though, because Project Assurance is independent of the Project Manager and has a direct reporting line back to the Project Board to feed back what it finds. So if assurance staff find that the Project Manager is giving the Project Board incorrect or misleading information, they report it – and rightly so. But that's an unlikely situation in the vast majority of projects.

The responsibility for making sure that Project Assurance is actually carried out lies firmly with the Project Board, and board members must not neglect this.

Being Flexible about Assurance

Project Assurance reflects the three PRINCE2 viewpoints of business, user, and supplier – see Chapter 12 for more on the viewpoints and how they fit with project roles. But delegation of assurance isn't all or nothing. For example, the Senior Supplier may delegate supplier assurance to a specialist, while the Executive and Senior Supplier on the Project Board decide to do their own business and user assurance respectively.

Think carefully about the best approach for assurance in each particular project. Don't get stuck in a rut with people saying, 'This is how we always do assurance on our projects.'

Selecting Experienced People

For effective Project Assurance you need to choose people who

- Understand projects
- Understand PRINCE2 *properly* – as a flexible and adaptable method, not as some bureaucratic beast that they found out about on some inadequate training course run by people who don't understand it properly either, or from misunderstanding the PRINCE2 manual
- Know the common problem areas and where things can go wrong
- Know what to look for – the tell-tale signs of problems

Don't use inexperienced people who can only say, 'Well, it all looks fine to me, but actually this is the first time I've ever seen one of these.' Or worse still, 'Well, the PRINCE2 manual says . . .'

If you're really stuck for people inside your organisation, you can hire in experienced people from outside. But then make sure that those external consultants do what you want, and only what you want, and don't set up assurance as some small industry. And make quite sure that the people you use understand PRINCE2 properly too (back to avoiding bureaucracy) or they can push you down the road of too much paperwork and an inflexible implementation of PRINCE2.

Avoiding List Tickers

Those doing assurance need to check things thoroughly, not bounce off at a superficial level. For example, assurance staff must make sure that the right people quality-checked a product to the right standard. They don't just check to see whether a control document has merely been signed.

The focus needs to be clearly on making sure that things have been done as planned for the project, not just getting some boxes ticked off on a check sheet. Beware: Those who don't understand the method and think it's all about documentation can turn this powerful project method into a list ticker's paradise – and at the cost of very high project overheads.

Steering Clear of Nit-Pickers

Project Assurance is co-operative and helpful – and not about looking for trouble and causing project delays by making small problems seem unduly important. The project has enough to do without getting sidetracked on unimportant trivia picked up by nit-pickers.

Working Co-operatively

Do brief your Project and Team Managers to work co-operatively with assurance staff. And explain that Project Assurance is like having something checked over by an experienced colleague – something to be welcomed as part of the Project Management Team.

Separating Assurance and Support

Don't give Project Support staff the responsibility for assurance. Project Assurance must be independent, whereas Project Support gets involved in the actual work. If you're not quite convinced, just think of finance. You don't have people helping write the accounts and then the same people checking them. That undermines the audit because these people aren't impartial. Those doing Project Support are there to help Project Managers, not to check up on them, and combining the two areas makes for a very unhappy as well as completely ineffective relationship.

Being Careful When Using Other Project Managers

Some organisations get Project Managers to do Project Assurance on each other's projects. Doing this can work, but be careful because it can go badly wrong: 'She made my life terrible on my last project. Right, now I can get my own back on her project!'

Getting Project Board Ownership

If dedicated Project Assurance staff do the assurance work, make sure that the Project Board members fully understand that they're still responsible for the correct running of the project. Project Assurance staff do the work on the board's behalf, but they aren't ultimately responsible for assurance. To go back to the financial audit example, a finance director remains responsible for the quality of organisational accounting, even though other people do financial auditing and report back to the director.

Following on from this, also make sure that dedicated assurance staff communicate well with respective Project Board members, both to determine what the assurance staff must check and then to talk through what they find and what they need to follow up.

Where you do delegate Project Assurance, remember that assurance staff aren't Project Board members. Don't expect them to attend Project Board meetings. Instead, have Project Board members pick up and deal with any assurance issues well in advance of any Project Board meeting.

Being Clear on What You're Assuring

To get assurance right, you need to think through each project very carefully to decide what you need to audit and what you don't. Remember that Project Assurance takes time and also takes project staff (such as the Project Manager and Team Managers) off their work for a while. The Project Board members, who either do the checking or ask others to do it on their behalf, need to strike a balance here.

Do this thinking and decision making in the main project planning stage, the Initiation Stage, after the Project Plan itself is in place and you have some detail to work with.

Part V
Appendices

The 5th Wave   By Rich Tennant

NUCLEAR
POWER TOOL
RESEARC

'I think that formally decommissions the project,
don't you?'

In this part . . .

Love PRINCE2? Think it's the best thing since Torvill and Dean? Appendix A gives you a quick peek into PRINCE2 qualifications, if you're thinking about taking your skills to the next level.

Appendix B is a helpful glossary of PRINCE2 terms to refresh your memory when you need a prompt.

Appendix A

Looking into PRINCE2 Qualifications

●●●

*T*he PRINCE2 qualifications are at two levels: Foundation Certificate and Practitioner Certificate. The Foundation Certificate concerns basic knowledge of the method and how it fits together, and Practitioner Certificate indicates that the holder is able to apply PRINCE2 to a project. Of the two, the Practitioner Certificate has more value and is increasingly recognised worldwide. The Foundation Certificate is of very limited value, because it doesn't show any proficiency in using PRINCE2 and in fact the Foundation syllabus doesn't cover all of the method. You need to pass the Foundation Exam before going on to take the Practitioner but if you do them on a training course you can do them both during the same training event.

Choosing PRINCE2 Training

Although the Practitioner Certificate is an indication of practical knowledge of PRINCE2, it is only that. Unfortunately, many qualified practitioners know little about using the method effectively, often because their training was focused on how to pass the exam rather than use the method well on projects. Many practitioners learn about PRINCE2 structure and documentation and return to their organisations to set up a very bureaucratic, form-filling application of PRINCE2 and have no real idea about adapting the method to suit different project needs.

If you want to go on a training course to back up the information that you gained from this book, select your training company with great care. Choose one that covers the practical and flexible use of the method on projects, with tutors who have good experience of using PRINCE2 on projects rather than just general project management experience. That way you get a thorough knowledge of the method and also the confidence that you can go back and use PRINCE2 on your projects, use it well and make the method really pay for itself. That's very different from theory and 'exam cram'.

Accreditation is a minimum standard, not a uniform standard, and a common misconception is that all accredited PRINCE2 training courses and training companies are the same. In fact, course objectives, standards, and the practical experience of trainers in actually using PRINCE2 vary significantly.

Looking at Sample Papers

Sample papers are available from training organisations but not past papers. Unlike many exams that run once or twice a year, the PRINCE2 exams run about once a week. Writing 50 or more complete papers each year would be a huge effort, so the questions in the pool are re-used. The PRINCE2 exam boards don't release the past papers because the past papers are also the future papers!

The Foundation Exam

The Foundation exam lasts one hour and comprises 75 multiple-choice questions. Of the 75, five will be new questions being checked out by the exam board. They don't count, but you won't know which five they are. The pass mark is 35; so 50 per cent of the 70 live questions. The exam is *closed book*, which means you can't have help or refer to the PRINCE2 manual. Wrong answers aren't penalised; they just don't score a mark. A good strategy if you don't know the answer to a particular question is to guess. With four options, you have a 25 per cent chance of hitting the right answer.

The exam doesn't have trick questions as such, but the wording of some questions can be rather tricky, so read each question very carefully.

A typical Foundation question looks like this:

What is the name of the PRINCE2 product that may be used by a team member to inform the Project Manager of a problem?

A. Risk Identification Form

B. Issue

C. Checkpoint

D. Problem Report

In case you're wondering, the correct answer is at the end of this Appendix.

The Practitioner Exam

The Practitioner exam lasts for two and a half hours and is also in multiple-choice format. However, the multiple-choice question styles vary – such as *matching questions* where you match items in one column against answers in another – and aren't just the classic multiple choice like the Foundation exam.

The exam contains nine areas of questions, each on a different part of PRINCE2, so a paper doesn't test all the method. Each area is worth 12 marks, so the paper has a total of 108 marks. In this exam, the pass mark varies to even out slight differences in the standards of the different papers. It will usually be between about 50 and 55 per cent, so you have to score 60 or more to be safe. This mark is across the whole paper; in other words, you don't have to pass each of the nine sections and good marks in one area can compensate for weaker marks in another. Most of the questions are based on a project scenario that the paper provides with the questions. The scenario outlines a project and may have supplementary information that you need to use with specific questions. Some of the questions may be about the nature and structure of PRINCE2 itself, not the application to a particular project, such as the reasoning behind the PRINCE2 roles and responsibilities.

The Practitioner exam is *open book*, so you can take your PRINCE2 manual into the exam room. However, that means only your manual. You can't take in any added sheets or sticky notes, though you can use tabs as a fast index to help find sections quickly.

Table A-1 shows a sample question in the 'matching' style of multiple-choice questions.

Column A lists a number of items of information. For each one, please select the PRINCE2 management product in Column B that would contain that information. An item in column B may be used for more than one answer or not at all. No marks are deducted for wrong answers.

Table A-1	Sample question
Column A	*Column B*
1. Proximity	A. Business Case
2. Method	B. Exception Report
3. Investment appraisal	C. Issue Report
4. Timescale	D. Risk Register
5. Decision	E. Quality Register
6. Expected dis-benefits	F. Highlight Report
7. Options	
8. Impact analysis	

You can find the correct answers at the end of this Appendix.

Staying Up to Date

The Practitioner qualification is valid for up to five years and you must take a top-up exam between three and five years after your last exam. However, the good news is that this top-up exam isn't a full-sized Practitioner exam, but just one hour long and one-third the size of the initial Practitioner exam – three sections instead of nine.

Getting Qualified and Locating Exams

You can only gain the PRINCE2 qualifications by taking the exams – unlike the membership requirements for some of the professional project organisations there is no 'project experience' route to PRINCE2 Practitioner. APM Group Ltd currently administers these exams on behalf of the Office of Government Commerce, the UK government body that owns the PRINCE2 method.

Accredited training providers for PRINCE2, such as Inspirandum Ltd (www.inspirandum.com), can run exams for their clients in open (public) courses as well as for 'in-company' events. But you can also take exams arranged directly by APM Group Ltd. APM Group has a number of offices in different countries and you can find out more by visiting its Web site at www.apmgroup.co.uk. APMG are always very helpful so do contact them if you need any assistance with booking into one of their open exams.

Getting Help with the Exams

Exam guides are available including one from TSO called 'Passing the PRINCE2 Examinations 2009' and a more substantial one that includes strategy advice as well as revision and practice questions called 'Passing Foundation and Practitioner' that is available directly from Inspirandum (www.inspirandum.com).

Answers to the Sample Questions

- ✔ Foundation: B – Issue
- ✔ Practitioner: 1D, 2E, 3A, 4A, 5C, 6A, 7B, 8C

On the Practitioner answers, you may notice that A was the correct answer for a number of questions while F was not the correct answer to any of them. This follows the information in the question that an answer in column B may be used more than once or not at all.

Appendix B

Glossary of the Main PRINCE2 Terms

• •

Acceptance Criteria. Set down in the Project Product Description, these are measurable factors used to decide whether or not to accept the project. This sounds strict, and sometimes it is, to the point of being the base of a legal contract. But in many cases you don't refuse the project because it doesn't meet some criteria, but you must certainly discuss these criteria. Please see Chapter 14 for more on the whole area of product planning and the Project Product Description.

Activity. Something you do on the project which is recorded in the activity plans. But activities are also the name given to the list of suggested things you do in each of the seven PRINCE2 Processes.

Activity Plans. These plans show what activities you need to build the products. PRINCE2 doesn't specify what techniques you use for activity planning, but most people use activity networks and Gantt charts. You do activity planning at all three levels of planning detail in PRINCE2 – project, stage, and team plans.

Administrator. A role in a Quality Review. This person helps set up the review meeting and then keeps notes of any errors found in the product under review.

Approval. This is an acceptance of a product (deliverable) that may in turn authorise action. For example, when the Project Board approves a Stage Plan, it is giving the Project Manager permission to start work on the next Management Stage on the basis of that plan. Specialist products must be approved too, often by those who are testing the products and signing them off as correct, but sometimes it needs authority beyond that for formal approval.

Assurance. Basically an audit function. For the auditing done inside the project, please see Project Assurance. For the auditing done by the organisation – outside the project – please see Quality Assurance.

Baseline. This term is used in two senses, both to do with Configuration Management or version control. First, any project product that has been quality checked and signed off is said to be 'baselined'. This is significant, because after this point any change to the product is done under change control. Some of the PRINCE2 management products, such as the Business Case, are defined as 'baseline management products' because if you change them then you need to keep track of that. The other use of the term identifies a set of products of known versions that you then handle together. They form a baseline, or if you're in a computer development environment you may call them a 'release'.

Benefit. A good result of doing the project, such as a cost saving or faster delivery to customers. PRINCE2 says that benefits must be measurable, but most people recognise than non-quantifiable benefits are not only real but can be extremely important too. Please see Chapter 11 for more on this.

Benefits Review Plan. Sometimes benefits can come on-stream in the project, not just at the end of the project or after it. The Benefits Review Plan sets down when benefits should be measured, who should do it and when.

Business Case. This document is the justification for the project and incorporates the business benefits that the project brings. The Business Case may be provided on the Project Mandate, but if not, is first developed in Start Up. After this it is kept up to date throughout the project – making it a 'living document'. The Project Board refer to it at all key decision points to ensure that the project is still viable and worth continuing with.

Change Authority. A group or person with the authority to approve changes, at an intermediate level of authority between the Project Board and the Project Manager. One use of it is to speed things up in a fast-moving project where getting a change decision from the Project Board takes too long. Beware of bureaucracy though. Please see Chapter 16 for more detail.

Change Budget. An amount of money given to a Project Manager to fund changes without having to go back to the Project Board or Change Authority. This can be controlled by setting an overall amount, or an overall amount plus a cap on the cost of any individual change.

Change Control. This set of procedures makes sure that things cannot be changed without proper consideration. With change control, a change may be refused or agreed, but if agreed, then care is taken to make sure that the time and resources are given to implement the change – unlike scope creep, where the project is supposed to absorb the change somehow. How change control is done in the project is set down in the Configuration Management Strategy. See Chapter 16 for more detail on managing project change.

Checkpoint (Checkpoint Meeting). A progress measuring point for a team working on a Work Package, this often takes the form of a Checkpoint Meeting, where the Team Manager gets together with the team to discuss progress and any problems, and to look at the work in the next period. As a result of the meeting, the Team Manager usually gives a progress report (the Checkpoint Report) to the Project Manager.

Checkpoint Report. A progress report from a Team Manager to the Project Manager that gives information on how work is progressing on a Work Package. Each individual Work Package specifies the frequency and exact content of this report, allowing the Project Manager to vary it from one Work Package to another.

Communication Management Strategy. A plan developed in the Initiation Stage and which then forms part of the Project Initiation Document (PID). The strategy outlines project communications and so helps thinking communications through to make sure that they're both complete and sensible. Over-communication is as much of a problem, or even more, than under-communication, so this thinking is important. The strategy lists the information that moves around (such as progress information), who produces it, who receives it, and when and how it will be communicated. A particular communication may be verbal, such as a phone call.

Concession. This means accepting a product that's off-specification. Normally, if a product is found to be off-spec when it's tested, it's re-worked until it passes the test and meets its specified quality criteria. But if for some reason achieving this is difficult or even impossible, or it causes other problems such as unacceptable delay to the project, then the best thing may be to make a concession and accept the product as it is. That's not good, but better than the impact of correction. The PRINCE2 manual says that only the Project Board can authorise a concession, but for some very technical projects that's debatable, as Chapter 16 discusses.

Configuration Management (CM). This is basically version control or versioning. CM covers the control of management products that are likely to go through more than one version and also most specialist products. It includes holding information about products and why changes occurred (change history), as well as version information. The way that Configuration Management will be done in the project is decided in the Initiation Stage and recorded in the project's Configuration Management Strategy that goes on to form part of the Project Initiation Document (PID).

Configuration Management Strategy (CM Strategy). The Project Manager produces this strategy, often with the advice of Project Support and specifically any person within Project Support who specialises in configuration management. The Configuration Management Strategy sets down the procedures for managing change in the project, including the version control procedures. The CM Strategy forms part of the Project Initiation Document (PID) and is maintained throughout the project.

Contingency. PRINCE2 no longer uses this term and instead refers to *fall back.* There is more on this in Chapter 15 on risk.

Daily Log. This log, set up in Start Up, is effectively the Project Manager's diary but Team Managers can use Daily Logs as well. It can save on documentation because its simple notes help avoid more formal and lengthy communications. If the Project Manager decides that an Issue or risk does not need to be formally managed, the details can be recorded in the Daily Log rather than in one of the registers. The Daily Log is also a 'catch-all' for any information that other PRINCE2 management products don't cover.

Deliverable. See Product.

Dis-benefit. A disadvantage of running the project, such as disruption to business operations while building work is carried out. Unlike a risk that might happen, a dis-benefit concerns an effect that will happen.

Embedding. Adjusting PRINCE2 to fit the needs of the organisation for all of its projects. Adjustments within that to meet the needs of individual projects is called *tailoring.*

End Project Report. The Project Manager produces this report at the end of the project and presents it to the Project Board. It's the Project Manager's assessment of how well the project went and to what extent it met the objectives set down in the Project Initiation Document.

End Stage Assessment (ESA). At the planned end of a management stage the Project Board attend this meeting to review the completed stage, check that the project is still viable against its Business Case, check that the risk is still acceptable, and then give approval for the next stage on the basis of its Stage Plan. The board always have an option to close the project instead of authorising the next stage.

End Stage Report. The Project Manager produces this report at the end of each management stage. The report focuses on how the stage ran, and covers things like the final cost, final time, delivery of quality, and any problems that are likely to flow through to the next management stage. Like other reports, the End Stage Report doesn't necessarily have to be written. The Project Manager can present it to the Project Board verbally, and the details can then be noted in the record of the meeting.

Event driven. This is one of two categories of control, the other being *time driven*. An event-driven control is one that is fixed to a particular event, so if that event is delayed or doesn't happen the control will be late or won't kick in. An example is an End Stage Assessment (ESA) which is fixed to the end of a stage. If the stage finishes early, the ESA will also be early.

Exception. This is the state when a Work Package, stage, or project is projected to finish outside the tolerances set for it. PRINCE2 works on an Exception Management principle: All the time the work goes to plan there's relatively little to communicate between control points apart from progress confirmation. But if it's projected that the project is going significantly off the plan ('significantly' meaning outside the specified tolerances) then the fact must be reported immediately. At stage or project level, this is usually done using an Exception Report. This control mechanism isn't only sensible and practical; at stage level it can save considerable Project Board time. Chapter 17 has a full explanation.

Exception Assessment. This is when the Project Board meet to consider an Exception Plan. This meeting is very like an ordinary End Stage Assessment, but is a forced stage boundary where you have to completely re-plan the remainder of a stage because of an exception or the need to accommodate a major change.

Exception Management. See Exception.

Exception Plan. This is a plan used after an exception. When corrective work, or additional work required to accommodate a major change, substantially changes things, then the existing plan won't be usable any more. If this happens to a stage, it triggers a stage boundary. The work done so far in the stage is closed down and reported with an End Stage Report; there's no point in re-planning what's already completed. An Exception Plan is used to re-plan the remainder of the stage from this point until the end of the stage. The Exception Plan may have a knock-on effect on other plans, notably the Project Plan, and if so, then that revised plan is also included in the Exception Plan.

Exception Report. The Project Manager uses this report to inform the Project Board that a stage is now projected to finish outside a specified limit (tolerance). The report could be verbal, such as a phone call.

Executive. This is a role on the Project Board and the person who takes this role represents the business viewpoint, which means primarily thinking about value for money. This role may not be shared, so a project can only ever have one Executive. Also, the Executive must be a person, so a committee can't act as the Executive. Although the whole of the Project Board own the project and are responsible for it, ultimately it's the Executive's project.

The Executive always chairs board meetings and is the ultimate owner of the project. Some still refer to this role as Project Executive to avoid confusion with other executive roles in the management of the organisation.

Follow-On Action Recommendations. At the end of the project, the Project Board may recommend that the organisation does some things after the project has shut down. The recommendations can include good ideas generated during the project but where there was not enough time or resources to implement them, and suggestions for changing project management standards as a result of experience gained during the project.

Highlight Report. The Project Manager gives this regular progress report to the Project Board. The contents and the frequency of the Highlight Report are set down in the Communication Management Strategy. The report may also go to other interested parties, notably to programme management if the project is part of a programme.

Initiation Stage (Initiation). This is the first stage of any PRINCE2 project and is devoted solely to project planning. The main deliverable of this stage is a package of plans called the Project Initiation Document. At the end of the Initiation Stage, the Project Board decides whether or not to commit to the whole project with the intention of running it through to the end.

Issue. This is a direct communication from anyone in the project from the Executive through to the most junior team member, straight to the Project Manager – the PRINCE2 manual suggests it can be from anyone with an interest in the project. A project Issue can be about anything to do with the project and it can be submitted at any time. So, quite flexible then. There are three sub-types of Issue which are Problem/concern, Request for Change and Off-Specification. Issues that are to be tracked formally are recorded on an Issue Report and then in the Issue Register. Issues to be informally controlled are recorded in the Daily Log.

Issue Register. A control document set up during Project Initiation in order to track all Project Issues that are to be formally managed. The Issue Register records information such as who submitted each Issue and its current status.

Issue Report. A record made by the Project Manager when an Issue is received.

Lessons Log. As the name suggests, this log records lessons learned from this project that may help improve the management of future projects but it also notes lessons from previous projects (and other sources) which may be of help in this project. The Lessons Log is closed and turned into a Lessons Report at the end of the project.

Lessons Report. This is produced from the Lessons Log at the end of the project. But more frequent reporting is possible if significant lessons need to be passed back into the organisation before the end of the project, such as end stage. The report is stored somewhere accessible (such as a Project Office) so that Project Managers can easily check it for advice for future projects. The Lessons Report is a very positive document, not a post-mortem report that focuses on bad news and whose fault the problems were. The report records problems and how they can be avoided in the future, but also contains information on what worked really well in the project that may benefit future ones.

Logs. These are informal records and there are two; the Daily Log and the Lessons Log. Things that need more formal control are recorded in registers.

Management products. These are the products that you use to manage the project. The Project Initiation Document, Risk Log, and Business Case are examples of management products. See also Product.

Management stage. Project stages in PRINCE2 are management stages and not technical stages. A management stage is a block of work that the Project Board authorise the Project Manager to do before coming back to them for approval to do the next management stage. You may have several technical stages within a single PRINCE2 management stage. The stage boundaries form powerful control points for the Project Board and are the single most important control in the method. The Project Manager can't start work on the next stage until the board has given permission by authorising the Stage Plan.

Milestone. This is a progress measuring point. *PRINCE2 For Dummies* strongly recommends, contrary to the PRINCE2 manual, that all stage-level products should be used as milestones. Chapter 14 explains why.

Off-Specification (Off-Spec). This is a sub-type of Issue used when a product fails to meet the quality criteria on its Product Description and can't easily be corrected. An Off-Spec can also be used in advance of a test if a team can see that a product isn't going to meet its required quality criteria. The resolution may be to accept the product in this state as a concession, or authorise a more substantial re-working of the product, which may then involve altering the plans to accommodate the extra time and resources needed. Chapter 16 covers Project Issues, Off-Specs, and concessions.

Outcome. The use of the project's deliverables or 'output' (see next item) to bring about a change. So, the project may deliver new tools, and the outcome is that production work can be done faster and capacity is thereby increased. In turn, this outcome may lead to the benefits of increased sales through lowered prices and so to increased profitability of the manufacturing plant.

Output. The products or deliverables generated in the project.

Phase. Some non-PRINCE2 project management approaches and planning tools use this term to mean a section of the project. The PRINCE2 equivalent is *management stage*.

Presenter. One of the roles in a Quality Review, this is the person or people who understand the product that the review meeting checks.

Principle. One of the seven things that the method suggests you should be doing in order to claim that your project is being run under PRINCE2. Principles include things such as defined roles and responsibilities and using the exception management principle. You will find more on them in Chapter 2.

Process. Part of PRINCE2 which indicates *when* things should be done in a project. Each process has a number of suggested activities. There are seven processes and these are covered in Section II of this book.

Product or Project Product. Things that are being *produced* in the project – the deliverables. The two categories of product in PRINCE2 are management products and specialist products. The management products are things like the Risk Register and Project Initiation Document that are being used to manage the project. The specialist products are mostly what the team build, although a few may be obtained from outside the project. For specialist products, PRINCE2 incorporates a very powerful product-led, or product-based, planning approach. Chapter 14 has full details.

Product Breakdown Structure (PBS). This is one of the diagrams used in product-led planning. The PBS is a hierarchical diagram and is useful when thinking through what products you need to build. You group products in categories, which helps you think through the whole project systematically. Chapter 14 contains information about this diagram and how to use it.

Product Checklist. This is a simple but very powerful progress monitoring tool. The checklist provides unambiguous milestones during each stage and records what products will be produced in the stage together with their target and actual delivery dates. The Product Checklist can also be used at team level to monitor progress on building the products in a Work Package.

Product Description. A form that defines a particular product and sets down related information, such as how that product will be tested. The description is part of the product-led planning approach explained in Chapter 14. Take great care when writing Product Descriptions because this is largely a thinking exercise; it's not a form-filling one.

Product Flow Diagram. This diagram shows the sequence in which you produce the deliverables or products. It's extraordinarily powerful and is a part of the product-led planning approach that Chapter 14 explains.

Product-led planning (Product-Based Planning). A powerful 'front end' to the more traditional activity planning approach. Product-led planning sets out to understand the nature of what the project is to produce (products) before trying to establish what needs to be done to produce them, what resources are needed, and how long the project may take. It also opens the way to particularly effective progress monitoring and quality management. Chapter 14 describes product-led planning and the associated techniques.

Product Plans. PRINCE2 uses product planning alongside activity plans and resource planning, but the products are planned first – a product-led planning approach. Product plans are used at all three levels of detail of planning in the method: Project Plans, Stage Plans, and Team Plans. Please see Chapter 12 for the full detail.

Product Status Account. A report giving the current status of a set of products, such as all of the products being developed in the current stage. Status settings may show things such as 'under construction', 'ready for test', and 'delivered'.

Programme. This is the name given to a group of projects that you need to manage together in order to co-ordinate them. For example, perhaps all the projects need to finish at the same time or they have significant inter-dependencies. PRINCE2 does not cover programme management, but being part of a programme affects the way you set up a PRINCE2 project. For example, the Project Plan may have to fit in with the programme plan.

Project and Programme Office (PPO). When the project is part of a programme, you may centralise the administrative support at project level and programme level in a PPO that serves both levels.

Project Approach. You develop this management product in Start Up and then maintain it throughout the project. The Project Approach sets down things that affect how you plan and run the project and things that constrain the project outcome, such as legal requirements, the type of staff you use on a project (perhaps solely contractors or solely customer staff), and security requirements.

Project Assurance. This role performs an audit function in the project. The Project Board members may do their own assurance or they may appoint one or more other people to do it on their behalf and report back. Project Assurance isn't optional and must be independent of the Project Manager.

Project Board. This comprises a group of senior managers (relative to the project) who own the project and are responsible for it. The board incorporates three roles: Executive, Senior User, and Senior Supplier. You can have fewer than three people on the board if a board member fulfils more than one role, or you can have more than three if people share roles but boards of more than six tend to give problems. The board isn't a voting democracy and other board members can't outvote the head, the Executive.

Project Brief. The Project Brief is like a sketch of the project idea. It's a short document produced in Start Up and so before the project begins. The Project Board use the information in the brief to decide whether starting the project and doing the full project planning in an Initiation Stage is worthwhile.

Project Executive. Please see Executive.

Project Initiation Document (PID). You produce this key PRINCE2 document during Initiation and it defines the project and exactly how you manage it. Although the PID is a single document you can think of it as like a folder containing many other plans and documents such as the Business Case, Project Plan, Risk Log, Project Organization, and Project Quality Plan.

Project Issue. Please see Issue.

Project Management Strategy. A document that sets down the level of quality required in the project, how it will be delivered, and who's responsible for making sure that the project delivers quality. The strategy forms part of the Project Initiation Document and is maintained throughout the life of the project.

Project Management Team. This comprises all the management roles in PRINCE2 with the addition (rather strangely) of Project Support, which actually doesn't do any management. The roles are the Project Board roles of Executive, Senior User, and Senior Supplier, and then Project Assurance, Change Authority, Project Manager, Team Manager, and Project Support. The concept of the Project Management Team underpins the important point that the team are 'in this together'. For example, the Project Board can't just delegate the whole project to the Project Manager and walk away.

Project Management Team Structure. The document showing the Project Management Team for the project, often in the form of an organisation chart.

Project Manager. This manager runs the project on a day-to-day basis on behalf of the Project Board and is accountable to the board. The board decide the amount of responsibility and authority the Project Manager has. In turn, the Project Manager may have one or more Team Managers reporting to her.

Project Mandate. Programme or corporate management produces this document, which contains high-level information about the project idea. The mandate is the trigger that starts PRINCE2 off and names the project's Executive, at least, but often the Project Manager as well.

Project Office. An office that centralises Project Support for all the organisation's projects in order to give enhanced expertise and also economy of scale. A very large project may be big enough to justify its own office. When the organisation runs one or more programmes, an option is to combine the support at both levels in a Project and Programme Office.

Project Plan. This is the high-level plan of the whole project from the end of the Initiation Stage to the end of the project i.e. the delivery stages. It contains product plans, activity plans, and resource plans, together with textual explanation and financial planning.

Project Support. This is primarily administrative support to the Project Manager and Team Managers. However, Project Support can also function in an advisory capacity. Project Support may be provided in a number of different ways, from a centralised Project Office to a personal assistant given to each Project Manager to provide admin support. On smaller projects especially, the person who is the Project Manager may also do her own administration and so have a second role of Project Support.

Project Support Office (PSO). The name formerly given by PRINCE2 to the Project Office. PRINCE2 has now aligned with other project approaches.

Quality Assurance. A check or audit from outside the project to ensure that it is being run properly and that information about it is correct. Quality assurance is independent of the project, including independent from the Project Board. This is unlike Project Assurance which is the responsibility of the Project Board and is only independent of the Project Manager.

Quality Control. The testing or checking of something to check if it meets its quality criteria as specified on its Product Description and any further standards that the Product Description refers to.

Quality Register. This lists the quality activities, including tests and checks, to be done in each stage (entered when the Stage Plan is built) and then the results of those activities. It forms a simple but very powerful audit trail to ensure that no planned test is missed out. If a test hasn't been done then the Quality Register makes that obvious because the entry isn't signed off. The register is checked frequently.

Quality Review (Quality Walkthrough). A technique in the form of a meeting held to check a product. This technique is used mostly to check paper-based products such as reports and specifications.

Registers. Control documents used by the Project Manager for things that are to be formally managed. The logs are for things to be informally managed. There are three registers in PRINCE2; Risk, Issue and Quality.

Request for Change (RFC). A sub-type of project Issue, an RFC is used when a change is wanted to a product that has already been baselined (signed off). After a product has been quality checked and baselined, any change to it must be controlled or quality is completely undermined.

Resource plans. These set down who performs activities to build products and when, but you can use them to schedule physical resources (such as equipment) as well as human resources. PRINCE2 doesn't cover this area and expects users of the method to look up information in other project management sources. However, *PRINCE2 For Dummies* gives you a bit of information in Chapter 14. Computer tools for activity planning usually include facilities for resource planning, but they're generally rather limiting. Project Managers of projects of any size use the software for activity planning, but then often turn to a spreadsheet to do resource planning.

Reviewer. One of the roles in a Quality Review, this person checks whether the product is correct and meets its specified quality criteria.

Risk Actionee. Someone who is appointed to take action on a particular risk. This may or may not be the same person who is that risk's Owner.

Risk Management. The work involved in identifying, analysing, and managing risks in the project. Each identified risk is entered into the Risk Log. Risk management is important in PRINCE2 and is built into the method. Chapter 15 gives full information.

Risk Owner. A person appointed to monitor and control a particular risk. This may be outside of the project. For example, some risks may be 'owned' by programme management or corporate risk management even though it is recorded in the project because it has particular implications for the project.

Risk Register. This register, opened in Initiation, records all the risks in the project that are to be formally managed, along with key information on each one, such as the probability of something happening, the impact if it does, and what actions are being taken to limit the possibility. The register is kept up to date throughout the project and reviewed systematically at the end of each management stage so that the Project Board can see the very latest position on risk when deciding whether or not to authorise the next stage in the project.

Role. This is an important term in the context of the Project Organisation Structure and is a key to flexible use of the method. With two exceptions (Executive and Project Manager) more than one person can share a role. Equally, one person, again with some limitations, can have more than one role. This gives considerable flexibility when applying the method, including using it on small projects that involve very few people.

Senior Supplier. This role on the Project Board represents the supplier viewpoint of the project. One or more managers who provide the teams that build the project's products fill this role. They're on the board to be sure that the project delivers something realistic and workable and to authorise the team resources. One or more people from outside the customer organisation may fill this role where external suppliers provide one or more teams on the project. For more information please see Chapter 12.

Senior User. This Project Board role represents the user viewpoint. One or more managers fill the role and represent those who use what the project delivers. They ensure that the project deliverables are suitable and fit for purpose, they provide user resources (such as to help specify requirements) and they also specify the business benefits that will result from running the project and are then responsible for delivering those benefits. For more information on this role, go to Chapter 12.

Specialist Product. The specialist products are the deliverables of the project that are not management products (such as the Risk Register). PRINCE2 classifies these in two ways: the internal or team products that project teams produce, and external products that come over the project boundary from outside the project.

Sponsor. This isn't a PRINCE2 term or concept. The PRINCE2 equivalent is somewhere between the project Executive and Senior User on the Project Board. Chapter 12 tells you more about these roles.

Stage. See Management stage.

Stage boundary. At a stage boundary one management stage finishes and another one starts. The Project Board decides the stage boundaries during Initiation, because these are the board's control points. An additional stage boundary can occur if a stage goes significantly off its plan, goes into exception, and then requires an Exception Plan. That exception planning triggers a stage boundary that you didn't originally plan; this new stage boundary is reactive and part of the handling of the exception. The board meeting at an originally planned stage boundary is an End Stage Assessment. The board meeting on a reactive stage boundary is an Exception Assessment.

Stage Plan. A plan produced by the Project Manager for a single management stage. Stage Plans are always created at the end of the previous stage except for the Initiation Stage Plan, which is created at the end of Start Up.

Stakeholders. These are individuals or corporate bodies with an interest in the project and its outcome.

Start Up (Starting Up a Project). This part of PRINCE2 happens before the project starts. During Start Up, you produce a Project Brief that provides the information that the Project Board need in order to decide whether going forward to full planning work is worthwhile.

Tailoring. The name given to fitting the PRINCE2 method to a particular project. How this is being done in a project will be recorded in a dedicated section of the Project Initiation Document (PID).

Team Manager. This manager is responsible for a project team, which may be from within the customer organisation or from an external supplier but which is nevertheless under project control. This is the only role in the Project Management Team that's optional. In a very small project with just one team, the Project Manager may also manage the team.

Theme. The name given in PRINCE2 for advice on *how* things are done in the project as opposed to the processes which indicate *when* things should be done. There are seven themes which are covered in Part III of this book.

Time Driven. One of two categories of control, of which the other is event driven. Time-driven controls are at a set frequency. An example is with progress reporting from the Project Manager to the Project Board which is at set intervals, such as every four weeks, right through the project.

Tolerance. PRINCE2 uses this term to mean the limits above and below a specified amount. Project work doesn't often go exactly to plan to the precise minute and precise penny. So having some flexibility makes sense, or else the Project Board would be called in every five minutes to hear reports of something not going to plan. But the board don't expect to be told about major problems only late in the day when it's too late to react. Tolerances can be set for cost and time which are the most common, but also for quality, benefits, scope and risk. If work may finish outside the tolerance band, the fact must be reported to the Project Board immediately. This is an exception and PRINCE2 makes use of Exception Management. Tolerance can be set at project, stage, and Work Package levels. Chapter 17 has more information on this and other controls.

Work Package. The Project Manager gives this instruction pack to the Team Manager. The Work Package asks the Team Manager to produce a product or perhaps more than one, and give instructions on how to do this. Those instructions include things such as how to report problems and how often to submit Checkpoint Reports to report progress. Each team works through a series of Work Packages in each stage.

Index

• Numerics •

"100 Rules for NASA Project Managers"
(Madden), 302

• A •

Acceptance Criteria
  customer quality expectations, 212
  defined, 337
  meeting, 133
  in Product Description, 54, 337
  for product quality, 213
  for projects, 212–213
acceptance level for risk, 155
acceptances, checking for, 133–134, 163
accountability loops, avoiding, 157
accredited training providers for PRINCE2,
    333, 336
activities
  adjusting degree of doing, 31
  altering sequence of, 31–32
  as checklists, 17, 30, 42
  Gantt charts for, 246
  gap in, 249
  leaving out when not needed, 30–31
  planning, 227, 239–240, 337
  precedence network for, 242–245
  resource levelling, 209–210
  shifting between processes, 32–33
  in Start Up, 41–42
ad hoc direction, 18, 93, 103, 146, 161, 286
adapting PRINCE2 for projects
  acid test for adjustments, 32
  altering sequence of activities, 31–32
  degree of doing activities, 31
  doing without a Project Plan, 33–34
  embedding, 340
  as key to success, 30
  leaving out activities, 30–31
  need for, 28, 132
  overview, 88
  parallel initiation to save time, 33

size of project, 13
  staying flexible, 313–314
administrative work, 206
Administrator for Quality Review, 337, 347
appraisal testing method, 217
approval, 127, 337
The Architects' and Builder's Price Book, 241
assumptions, 60, 89
assurance, defined, 337
authority levels
  Executive, 192
  overview, 192–193
  Project Board, 147, 192, 203
  Project Manager, 83–84, 151, 152–153,
    192, 203, 285
  setting up a Change Authority, 48, 286
  setting up a Change Budget, 225, 285–286
authority to proceed, 107, 161, 162. See
    also sign-offs

• B •

Barrow, Colin (*Understanding Business
    Accounting For Dummies*), 180
baseline, 64, 278, 288, 320, 338
Benefits Review Plan. See also business
    benefits
  in Closing a Project, 143, 164
  contents of, 186
  in Controlling a Stage, 120
  described, 91, 108, 170, 338
  in Directing a Project, 165
  in End Stage Assessment (ESA), 162
  implementing, 186
  in Initiating a Project, 91
  measuring early benefits, 163
  in premature project closure, 135
  preparing, 87
  after project closure, 136–137, 317
  when to measure benefits, 104
benefits-driven projects, 171–173, 319
bottom-up checks, 230–231
boundaries. See stage boundaries

budget. See also costs
  for change, 152, 225, 285–286, 305, 338
  controls, 310
  financial planning, 249
  for plans, 224–225
  for risk, 153, 225, 258–259, 305
  tolerances for, 305
  unrealistic, 10
bureaucracy, 14, 29, 203
business assurance, 149–150, 196
business benefits. See also Benefits
    Review Plan
  in Business Case, 178
  checking truth of, 181–182
  contamination, avoiding, 183–184
  defined, 338
  direct savings, 171–172
  early, 163
  ensuring delivery of, 182–184
  gap between delivery and benefits, 185
  measurability issues, 319–320
  measuring after project closure, 136–137,
    163, 184–186
  measuring during the project,
    104, 184–185
  non-existent, not claiming, 182
  non-quantifiable, 172–173, 319, 321
  projections for, reviewing, 105
  projects without, 170–173, 319, 320–321
  prudent approach to, 183, 322
  quantifiable, 172
  risk impact on, 265
  Sensitivity Analysis for, 181
  tolerances for, 304
Business Case. See also Outline Business
    Case
  aligning with corporate requirements,
    294, 322–323
  altering sequence of doing, 31
  best and worst case, 180–181
  building in Initiation Stage, 86–87
  business options section, 178
  in Controlling a Stage, 120
  costs, 179, 323
  defined, 91, 310, 338
  delivery of benefits, ensuring, 182–184
  development of, 175

deviations from, 138
  in Directing a Project, 165
  dis-benefits expected section, 178–179
  as driver of PRINCE2 projects, 169
  End Stage Assessment (ESA), 162
  End Stage Report information, 95
  End Stage review of, 106, 115, 138
  Executive owning, 170, 178, 185,
    293–294, 322
  Executive summary section, 105, 177
  expected benefits section, 178
  help with, 174–175
  in Initiating a Project, 91
  investment appraisal section, 179
  Issue implications for, 324
  justifying the project, 55, 169,
    170–173, 319
  in Managing Stage Boundaries, 108
  measurable benefits for, 181–182, 184–186
  organisational finance procedures, 176
  outlined in Start Up, 53–55, 86
  overview, 21, 169, 338
  project failure due to lack of, 10, 11
  in Project Mandate, 175
  Project Report review of, 138
  prudent approach to, 322
  reasons section, 177
  reviewing, 104–105, 293, 321
  risks section, 179
  sections of, 177–179
  Sensitivity Analysis, 181
  timescale section, 179
  updating at Stage End, 106, 115, 165, 295
  updating at Start Up, 153
  updating during stages, 173–174, 323
  writing, 53–55, 177–181
business options (Business Case), 178
business risks, 137
business viewpoint, 149–150, 190, 341

cash flow, discounted, 180
Change Authority
  defined, 49, 338
  project Issue escalated to, 283–284
  setting up, 48, 203, 286

Change Budget
  allocations for, 152
  defined, 338
  overview, 305
  setting up, 152, 225, 285–286
change control
  baseline, 64, 288, 320, 338
  change freeze, 276–277
  defined, 338
  need for, 275
  Off-Specs and RFCs costs, 285–286
  overview, 23, 338
  project failure due to lack of, 10, 11
  scope creep issues, 10, 275, 276–277
change history of product, 293
checklists. See also Product Checklist
  activities as, 17, 30, 42
  Risk Checklist, 261–262
  what you don't need to do, 17
Checkpoint Meeting, 128–129, 339
Checkpoint Reports
  in Controlling a Stage, 112, 120
  defined, 112, 125, 130, 339
  outline of contents, 111
  project completion check, 133
  for Work Package(s), 112, 125–129, 130
Closing a Project
  checking business benefits, 136–137
  checking the work environment, 135–136
  closing logs and registers, 142
  diagram, 132
  documentation for, 132
  End Project Report, 138–139, 143, 163
  follow-on actions, 137–138, 140, 143
  Lessons Report, 139, 140–142, 144
  making sure you're done, 133
  management products for, 143–144
  overview, 19–20, 131–132
  planned closure, 133–134
  premature closure, 134–135
  Project Board responsibilities, 162–164
  Project Closure Notification, 163
  recommending project closure, 142–144
  reviewing the project, 137–142
  sign-offs and acceptances, checking,
    133–134
  storing project records, 142–143

coding system for products, 291
commercial supplier environment, 36
Communication Management Plan, 305
Communication Management Strategy
  alternatives to paper documents, 80, 315
  communicating information about
    risk, 272
  communication needs, 81
  defined, 339
  external communication needs, 81
  in Initiating a Project, 9
  outline of contents, 82
  over-communication, 79, 80
  overview, 79, 82, 339
  reporting stage progress to the Project
    Board, 116–118
  updating, 85
  using verbal reports, 80–81
  writing, 79–80
communications
  explaining the plan, 248–249
  by Project Board, 148
  project failure due to lack of, 10
  risk management, 272–273
  verbal reports, 80–81
complexity, 154, 171, 253–254
compliance projects, 171, 320
computer files, storing, 142–143
computer rapid application development
    (RAD) projects, 124
computer system, 53, 56
concessions, 138, 279, 339
Configuration Item Record
  change history of product section, 293
  in Closing a Project, 143
  construction location of product, 292–293
  in Controlling a Stage, 120
  defined, 78, 91, 108, 130
  in Initiating a Project, 91
  knowledgeable person section, 292
  outline of contents, 290–291
  product coding system, 291
  product information in, 290–293
  Project Manager creating, 112
  security requirements, 292
  using, 290
Configuration Librarian, 42, 269, 311

Configuration Management
  baseline management products, 288
  confusion prevented by, 294
  deciding extent of, 287–288
  defined, 339
  follow-on actions, 164, 293
  keeping product information, 290–293
  language unfortunate for, 287
  overview, 23, 76–77
  project completion check, 133
  specialist versus management
     products, 288
  Status Account report, 288
  uniqueness of, 293
  Work Package requirements, 124
Configuration Management Strategy
  defined, 91, 339–340
  outline of contents, 289
  in Stage Boundary management, 108
  updating, 77
  writing, 77, 288–289
constraints
  Project Approach considerations, 56–57
  Project Definition, 60
  in Project Initiation Document (PID), 89
  in Quality Management Strategy, 213
  on scope, 60, 125
  in Work Package(s), 125
construction location of product, 292–293
contamination of benefits, 183–184
control, level of
  deciding on management stages, 153–155
  determining Highlight Reporting, 155–156
  evaluating, 70
  Project Assurance issues, 156
  Project Manager authority levels, 151,
     152–153, 192, 203, 285
  Quality Assurance issues, 156–157
  risk acceptance level, 155
Controlling a Stage
  capturing project Issues, 280–282
  correcting a stage, 119
  diagram, 110
  escalating project issues, 119–120, 283
  Exception Report, 116, 119–120
  Highlight Report, 117, 120
  monitoring and progress reporting,
     115–118

overview, 19, 109–111
  products used by, 120
  risks and issues, 113–115
  status check, 116
  Work Package, authorising and receiving,
     111–113
controls. See also Exception Management;
     tolerances
  areas of, 24–25
  budget, 310
  event-driven, 297–299, 341
  financial, 309–310
  levels of, 295–296
  management stages as, 82–83
  need for, 70
  ordering project closure, 299
  percentage complete measures, 309
  Product Checklists as, 308–309
  progress control, 23
  quality, 214, 216–219, 309, 347
  setting up, 82–85
  time driven, 296–297, 350
  Work Packages as, 308
Corporate or Programme Management, 192
corporate risk management, 137
correspondence and meeting records, 222
costs. See also budget
  Business Case section, 179, 323
  estimating, 240–241
  management stages, 153, 154
  Off-Specification (Off-Spec), 285–286
  organisational finance procedures, 176
  of overstating quality levels, 211
  Request for Change (RFC), 285–286
  risk budget, 258–259
  risk impact on, 265
  tolerances for, 300–301, 304, 305
  unreasonable, project failure due to, 10
critical path, 245
customer, 54, 172–173, 191, 212

• *D* •

Daily Log
  closed, 143
  creating, 50–51
  defined, 340
  entering a risk into, 72

outline of contents, 50
  in Start Up, 65
deliverables. See also management
    products
  defined, 226
  Product Description for, 54
  as products, 227, 266
Delivery Stage, 87, 97, 161
derivation/dependencies, 234
deviation from the plan, 118
diagrams. See also Product Flow Diagram
  Closing a Project, 132
  Controlling a Stage, 110
  Directing a Project, 17, 146
  Initiating a Project, 68
  integration, 26
  Ishikawa fishbone, 263–264
  Managing Product Delivery, 123
  Managing Stage Boundaries, 94
  precedence network, 243, 244
  process model, 17
  Product Breakdown Structure (PBS), 238
  Product Flow, 228–232
  Project Management Team, 193
  Risk Anatomy, 262
  risk procedure, 260
  Start Up (Starting Up a Project), 42
  themes, 20
  Work Package(s), 111
direct savings, 171–172
Directing a Project. See also Project Board;
    specific processes
  diagram, 17, 146
  giving ad hoc direction, 146
  management products of, 164–165
  overview, 18, 145–146
dis-benefits, 178–179, 340
discounted cash flow (DCF), 180
documentation. See also filing; *specific
    kinds*
  for Closing a Project, 132
  correspondence and meeting
    records, 222
  keeping simple, 80
  minimizing, 71, 314–315
  PRINCE2 not method of, 28
  quality management, 217, 221–222
  references in Project Brief, 63

• E •

earliest finish date (EFD), 243, 246
earliest start data (ESD), 243, 246
Earned Value Analysis technique, 310
EFD (earliest finish date), 243, 246
embedding, defined, 340
enabling projects, 170–171, 321
End Project Report
  for Closing a Project, 138–139, 143, 163
  creating, 90
  defined, 165, 340
  in Directing a Project, 165
  Lessons Report in, 140–141
  measuring early benefits, 163
  storing and filing, 140
  writing, 140
End Stage Assessment (ESA)
  defined, 97, 162, 340
  key information for, 95–96
  known as stage gate, 97
  overview, 107, 340
  Project Assurance appointment for, 96
  Project Board decision point, 162
  triggering, 96–97
End Stage Report
  defined, 105, 340
  described, 108
  in Directing a Project, 165
  key information for, 95–96
  outline of contents, 106
  preparing, 105–107
  Project Board sign-off for, 107
environment of a PRINCE2 project, 26,
    34–38, 248
error sheets, 218, 221, 222
errors, 220, 221
ESA (End Stage Assessment)
  defined, 97, 162, 340
  key information for, 95–96
  known as stage gate, 97
  overview, 107, 340
  Project Assurance appointment for, 96
  Project Board decision point, 162
  triggering, 96–97
ESD (earliest start data), 243, 246
estimating, 240–242, 247–248, 249
event-driven controls, 297–299, 341

Example icon, 4
Exception Assessment, 161, 307, 341
Exception Management
  as a control, 300
  deciding what to do, 306
  'in Exception' defined, 116, 305
  overview, 153, 341
  Project Manager authority levels, 153
  Project Manager reporting on, 152
  tolerances, 116, 152, 305–307
Exception Plan
  building, 100–101
  defined, 97, 165, 307, 341
  in Directing a Project, 165
  Project Board sign-off for, 107
  for project Issues, 284–285
  in Stage Boundary management, 108
Exception Report
  in Controlling a Stage, 116, 119–120
  defined, 341
  in Directing a Project, 165
  giving, 305–306
  outline of contents, 119, 306
  as Project Board decision point, 161
  by Project Manager, 119–120
  by Team Manager, 308
exceptions
  defined, 341
  End Stage triggered by, 96
  'in Exception' defined, 116, 305
  reporting, 108, 116, 305–307
exclusions in Project Definition, 60
Executive. See also Project Board
  appointing, 45–46
  authority level of, 192
  business assurance responsibilities,
    149–150, 196
  as Business Case owner, 170, 178, 185,
    293–294, 322
  as Change Authority for urgent
    changes, 286
  defined, 49, 149, 195, 341–342
  Executive summary section (Business
    Case), 105, 177
  Programme Manager role integrated with,
    dangers of, 37

  as Project Board head, 40, 46, 130,
    194, 195
  role and responsibilities, 47, 149–150,
    195–196
  single person needed for, 49, 195
external products, 228, 234, 240

• F •

failure of projects, 9–11, 52–53, 183
fallback, 249, 259, 270
feasibility study, 67
filing
  communication records, 82
  End Project Report, 140
  in Initiation Stage plan, 64
  project records, 142–143
finance procedures, organisational, 176
finances. See budget; costs
financial controls, 309–310
financial risks, 248
financial tolerances, 305
fishbone diagram, 263–264
fitting PRINCE2 to the project, 34–38
flexibility principle, 29, 30, 313–314
float, 243–244, 245
follow-on actions
  for Benefits Reviews after the project, 186
  for Closing a Project, 137–138, 140, 143
  after Closing a Project, 164
  concessions, 279
  Configuration Management, 164, 293
  defined, 342
  in End Project Report, 139, 140
  for Issues, 164
  risk management, 137, 164
  in Stage Boundary management, 108
Foundation Certificate, 333
Foundation exam for PRINCE2, 334

• G •

Gantt charts, 101, 155, 226, 246
government projects, 13–14
'The Green Book' (UK Treasury), 52

• H •

handovers, 134, 139
Highlight Report
  contents of, 155–157
  in Controlling a Stage, 117, 120
  defined, 342
  in Directing a Project, 165
  outline of contents, 117
  progress meetings replaced by, 153, 155, 157
  reporting to the Project Board, 116–118, 342
  writing, 116–118
hybrid justifications, 173

• I •

icons in margins of this book, 4
impact
  analysing for project Issues, 113
  areas of risk impact, 265
  of an issue, 283
  probability-impact (p-i) grid, 267–268
  risk versus, 263–264
in Exception, 116, 305
infrastructure projects, 170–171
Initiating a Project. See also Project Initiation Document (PID)
  Business Case, building, 86–87
  combining with Start Up, disadvantage of, 37–38
  Communication Management Strategy, preparing, 79–82
  Configuration Management Strategy, preparing, 76–78
  deciding on management stages, 153–155
  Delivery Stage, preparing, 87, 97
  diagram, 68
  feasibility study versus, 57
  management products of, 91
  overview, 18, 68–69
  Project Board responsibilities, 159–160
  project controls, setting up, 82–85
  Project Initiation Document (PID), creating, 88–90

Project Plan, creating, 85–86
quality management in, 73–76
Risk Management Strategy, preparing, 71–72
Stage Plan, creating, 85–86
Initiation Stage. See also Initiating a Project
  defined, 64, 342
  feasibility work, planning, 57
  as mandatory, 69
  need for, 69–70
  overview, 18
  parallel initiation to save time, 33
  planning, 97
Initiation Stage Plan
  creating, 63–64
  defined, 164
  described, 65
  preparing, 97
in-process testing method, 217
Inspirandum Ltd accreditation provider, 72, 240, 261, 262, 336
integration products, 239
Interfaces in Project Definition, 61
internal products, 234
inter-project dependencies, 35
investment appraisal, 179
Ishikawa fishbone diagram, 263–264
Issue Register
  in Closing a Project, 143
  in Controlling a Stage, 120
  defined, 342
  described, 108
  in Initiating a Project, 91
  outline of contents, 282
  recording Issues in, 277, 280
  Risk Register versus, 281
  setting up, 78
Issue Report, 113, 120, 280–281, 342
Issues
  analysing impacts, 281
  Business Case implications of, 324
  capturing, 280–282
  categories of, 277–279
  in Controlling a Stage, 113–115
  deciding on action to take, 283–284
  defined, 78, 113, 277, 342
  escalating, 119–120, 283

Issues *(continued)*
  examining, 113–115, 282–283
  Exception Plan for, 284–285
  follow-on actions, 164
  handling, 84, 113, 280–285
  in Highlight Report, 155
  involving Project Board in, 114–115,
    117, 283
  logging/recording, 277, 280
  Off-Specification (Off-Spec), 278–279, 343
  Project Manager dealing with, 113–115,
    156, 283–284
  Request for Change (RFC), 278, 285–286
  statistics on, 141

• J •

justification for projects, 105, 170–173, 319,
  320–321

• K •

Key Point icon, 4

• L •

latest finish date (LFD), 243–244, 246
latest start date (LSD), 244
legal issues, 56, 134, 135
Lessons Log
  closing down, 143
  in Controlling a Stage, 118
  creating, 51–52
  defined, 342
  outline of contents, 52
  in Stage Boundary, 108
  in Start Up, 51, 65
Lessons Report
  in Closing a Project, 140–142, 144
  in Controlling a Stage, 118
  defined, 343
  described, 108
  in Directing a Project, 165
  in End Project Report, 139, 140–141
  in premature project closure, 135
  storing, 142
  writing, 140
LFD (latest finish date), 243–244, 246

lifecycle steps for product, 292
List Tickers, 30–31, 327
location of product, 290
logs. See also Daily Log; Lessons Log
  closing down, 142
  defined, 343
  function of, 72
  overview, 72
  Risk Log, 72, 106
  test logs, 222
LSD (latest start date), 244

• M •

Madden, Jerry ("100 Rules for NASA
    Project Managers"), 302
management products
  baselined, 288
  for Closing a Project, 143–144
  Configuration Management for, 288
  for Controlling a Stage, 120
  defined, 232, 343
  for Directing a Project, 164–165
  for Initiating a Project, 91
  for Managing Product Delivery, 130
  for Managing Stage Boundaries, 107–108
  Request for Change (RFC) submitted
    for, 278
  specialist products versus, 288
  for Starting Up a Project, 65
management stages. See also Managing
    Stage Boundaries
  cost issues, 153, 154
  deciding on, 153–155
  defined, 343
  overview, 82–83
  parallel initiation to save time, 33
  planning in Start Up and Initiation, 97
  professional approach to, 38
  technical stages versus, 153
  time requirements, 154
  triggering an End Stage, 96–98
Managing Product Delivery
  diagram, 123
  management products of, 130
  overview, 19, 121–123
  receiving a Work Package, 127

Managing Stage Boundaries
  building an Exception Plan, 100–101
  diagram, 94
  management products of, 107–108
  overview, 19, 88, 94
  Planning a Stage, 98–100
  Project Board sign-off, 107
  Project Manager responsible for, 94
  start points, 94
  triggering an End Stage, 96–98
  updating a Project Plan, 101–102, 250, 318
  updating Risk Register, 102–104
Mandate. See Project Mandate
McCartney Report (UK Government
    report), 173
milestone, defined, 343
misunderstandings about PRINCE2, 13–14,
    27–28, 80
multi-agency risks, 248
multi-organisation environment, 37

• *N* •

Next Stage Plan, 165
nit-pickers, avoiding, 328
non-disclosure agreements, 36
non-quantifiable benefits, 172–173, 319, 321

• *O* •

objectives
  checking on the achievement of, 90
  in Project Definition, 60
  project failure due to lack of clarity,
    10, 11
  put into Project Initiation Document
    (PID), 88
  reviewed in End Project Report, 139
Office. See Project Office
Office of Government Commerce (PRINCE
    manual - *Managing Successful Projects
    with PRINCE2*), 1
Off-Specification (Off-Spec), 278–279,
    285–286, 343
"100 Rules for NASA Project Managers"
    (Madden), 302

opportunities and threats, 263, 271
optimism bias, 52–53
organisational finance procedures, 176
organisational handovers, 134
organisational standards, 164, 213
outcome, 88, 226, 343
Outline Business Case. See also Business
    Case
  approving, 55
  avoiding detailed costs in, 62, 323
  described, 61–62, 65
  development of, 175
  in Project Brief, 61–62
  in Start Up, 65
  writing, 53–55
output, defined, 343
outside suppliers, 75, 77

• *P* •

PBS (Product Breakdown Structure),
    237–239, 344
percentage change, 320
percentage complete measures,
    avoiding, 309
phase, defined, 344
PID (Project Initiation Document). See also
    Initiating a Project
  in Closing a Project, 144
  creating in Initiation Stage, 88–90
  defined, 64, 68, 91, 164, 346
  keeping simple, 89
  other names for, 68
  outline of contents, 70
  overview, 18, 67, 70–71
  parallel initiation to save time, 33
  Project Board commitment to whole
    project, 90–91
  Project Brief versus, 58
  Project Manager responsible for, 71
  quality level stated in, 211
  sections of, 88–89
  sign-offs, 92
  uses for, 90–91

planning. See also Initiating a Project;
    product-led planning
  activities, 227, 239–240, 337
  bottom-up checks for, 230–231
  budget for plans, 224–225
  checking project risk, 247–248
  creating a Project Initiation Document
    (PID), 88–90
  creating a Project Plan, 85–86
  estimating, 240–241
  evaluating planning needs, 70, 224
  explaining the plan, 248–249
  financial, 249
  finding problems during, 69
  for Initiation Stage, 63–64
  levels of, 250–251
  need for, 69–70, 223–224
  over-planning, 70, 223, 224
  overview, 18, 85–86
  Product Breakdown Structure (PBS) for,
    237–239, 344
  Product Flow Diagram for, 228–232
  product-based, 227, 232
  project failure due to lack of, 10, 11, 67
  risk management, 71–72
  sorting out problems during, 69
  Stage Plans, creating, 98–100
  traditional approach, problems with, 226
  updating Project Plans, 101–102, 250, 318
Portner, Stanley E. (*Project Management
    For Dummies*), 242
Post Project Benefits Review, 163
PPO (Project and Programme Office), 345
Practitioner Certificate, 333
Practitioner exam for PRINCE2, 334–335
precedence networks, 242–245
Presenter(s), 220, 221, 344
PRINCE manual - *Managing Successful
    Projects with PRINCE2* (Office of
    Government Commerce), 1
PRINCE Speak icon, 4
PRINCE2
  acronym explained, 8
  adapting to specific projects, 34–38
  flexibility of, 29, 30, 313–314
  history of, 16
  insisting on use of, 315–316
  integration diagram, 26
  language unfortunate for, 217, 287

  making part of organisational culture, 315
  misunderstandings about, 13–14,
    27–28, 80
  overview, 1, 8
  principles, 23–24, 344
  process model, 16–20
  professional approach to, 38
  as public domain project method, 12
  qualifications, 334–335
  reasons for using, 12–13
  shutting down, 136–137
  techniques, 23–24
  tool nature of, 28–29
  understanding, 127
Prince-iple icon, 4
principles, PRINCE2, 23–24, 344
probability, calculating for risk, 266
probability-impact (p-i) grid, 267–268
process model. See also *specific processes*
  activities within as checklist, 17
  getting things going, 17–18
  overview, 16–17
  process, defined, 344
  repeating as necessary, 18–19
  shutting down/closing a project, 19–20
Product Breakdown Structure (PBS),
    237–239, 344
Product Checklist
  as control, 308–309
  in Controlling a Stage, 118, 120
  defined, 344
  preparing, 98–99
  as progress-monitoring tool, 318
  project completion check, 133
  reporting on progress with, 118, 157
  used in Highlight Report, 118
  usefulness of, 118, 157, 318
product coding system, 291
Product Description
  acceptance criteria in, 54, 337
  creating, 53–55
  defined, 53, 65, 134, 210, 344
  derivation/dependencies, 234
  outline of contents, 54, 233, 236
  in Project Brief, 62, 65
  quality criteria, 235
  Quality Method section, 218
  quality tolerance, 235
  sections, 233–236

specification versus, 234
in Start Up, 65
title of project, 233
in Work Packages, 103
writing, 232–236
Product Flow Diagram
bottom-up checks using, 230–231
creating from Product Breakdown
Structure, 239
defined, 344
first-cut example, 229
for identifying risks, 264
photographing, 231
as planning tool, 228–232
revised example, 231
product plans, 345
Product Status Account, 345
product-based planning. See product-led
planning
product-led planning
defined, 22, 345
identifying products in, 227–228
importance of, 85, 317–318
overview, 23, 226–227
products. See also management products
baselined, 278, 288
categories of, 232
Closing a Project, 143–144
defined, 344
deliverables as, 226, 227
external, 228, 234, 240
handovers, 139
identifying, 227–228
integration products, 239
reviewed in End Project Report, 139
soft products or "outcome," 226, 343
specialist, 232, 240, 278, 288, 349
professional approach to PRINCE2, 38
Programme Manager, 37
Programme or Corporate Management, 192
programmes, 34–35, 345
progress controls, 23
progress, monitoring, 31, 308–309
Project and Programme Office (PPO), 345
Project Approach
as constraints on quality, 213
defined, 56, 345
documenting, 56–57

outlined in Project Initiation Document
(PID), 89
updating, 102
Project Assurance
appointing at End Stage, 96
audit function of, 38, 199
avoiding List Tickers, 30–31, 327
avoiding nit-pickers, 328
business assurance, 149–150, 196
clarity on what you're assuring, 329
co-operative approach to, 326, 328
defined, 49, 149, 191, 325, 345
delegation by Project Board, 156, 199,
219, 325
ensuring, 48
flexible approach to, 326
need for, 219, 316–317
not optional or negotiable, 48, 199–200,
325–326
other Project Managers for, 328
overview, 199
in Project Plan, 156, 250
Project Support separated from, 328
roles and responsibilities, 201–202
selecting experienced people for, 324, 327
Senior User responsibilities, 197
setting up, 200
user assurance, 150
working with Project Manager, 200–202
Project Board. See also Directing a Project;
specific roles
accountability loops, avoiding, 157
appointing, 40–43, 192
authority level of, 147, 192, 203
availability of, 148–149, 192
being professional, 38
as central to projects, 191–192
Change Authority of, 286
Closing a Project responsibilities, 162–164
closing down, 164
commitment to whole project, 90–91
communication needs from, 148
concessions made by, 279
consulting about Project Quality Plan, 61
decision points for, 158–164
defined, 18, 46, 145, 345–346
End Stage Assessment by, 95–96, 107, 162
Executive as head of, 40, 46, 130, 194, 195

Project Board *(continued)*
  Initiating a Project responsibilities,
    140–141
  involved in project Issues, 114–115, 117
  keeping small, 47, 148, 149, 189–190
  listening to Project Manager, 152
  as managers, not workers, 147
  ordering project closure, 219
  as owners of project, 47, 145, 147,
    194, 329
  pitfalls to avoid, 157
  PRINCE2 understood by, 127, 316
  Project Assurance delegation by,
    156, 199, 219, 325
  Project Manager communications,
    158, 181, 281
  as Project Manager's boss, 18, 145
  quality decision-making, 74
  recommending project closure, 142
  reporting stage progress to, 116–118
  risk consultation with, 103
  roles, 18, 49, 146–151, 156, 191–192,
    194–199
Project Brief
  checking project viability, 52–55
  defined, 58, 65, 164, 346
  exclusions in, 60
  keeping simple, 58
  level of detail in, 57–58
  outline of contents, 58
  Project Initiation Document versus, 58
  sections, 59–63
Project Charter. See Project Initiation
    Document (PID)
Project Closure Notification, 163
Project Definition
  defined, 59
  in Project Brief, 59–60
  in Project Initiation Document (PID), 88–89
Project Definition Report (PDR). See
    Project Initiation Document (PID)
Project Executive. See Executive
Project Initiation Document (PID). See also
    Initiating a Project
  in Closing a Project, 144
  creating in Initiation Stage, 88–90
  defined, 64, 68, 91, 164, 346

keeping simple, 89
  other names for, 68
  outline of contents, 70
  overview, 18, 67, 70–71
  parallel initiation to save time, 33
  Project Board commitment to whole
    project, 90–91
  Project Brief versus, 58
  Project Manager responsible for, 71
  quality level stated in, 211
  sections of, 88–89
  sign-offs, 92
  uses for, 90–91
project Issues
  analysing impacts, 281
  Business Case implications of, 324
  capturing, 280–282
  categories of, 277–279
  in Controlling a Stage, 113–115
  deciding on action to take, 283–284
  defined, 78, 113, 277, 342
  escalating, 119–120, 283
  examining, 113–115, 282–283
  Exception Plan for, 284–285
  follow-on actions, 164
  handling, 84, 113, 280–285
  in Highlight Report, 155
  involving Project Board in, 114–115,
    117, 283
  logging/recording, 277, 280
  Off-Specification (Off-Spec), 278–279, 343
  Project Manager dealing with, 113–115,
    156, 283–284
  Request for Change (RFC), 278, 285–286
  statistics on, 141
Project Management For Dummies
    (Portney), 242
Project Management Strategy, 347
Project Management Team. See also
    Project Board; Project Manager; Team
    Manager(s)
  choosing, 48–50
  defined, 48, 49, 150, 193, 346
  diagram, 193
  roles, 48, 150–152
  updating, 100

Project Management Team Structure,
63, 89, 108, 346
Project Manager. *See also* Controlling a
Stage
appointing, 46
authority level of, 83–84, 151, 152–153,
192, 203
Closing a Project responsibilities,
131, 162–163
Configuration Item Records created
by, 112
Controlling a Stage responsibilities,
109–113
creating the Business Case, 170
Daily Log set up by, 50
dealing with Issues, 113–115, 280
deciding on management stages, 154
defined, 49, 204, 346
End Project Report produced by,
90, 140, 340
Exception Report responsibilities,
119–120
experience of, 314
Highlight Report given by, 342
logs used by, 72
making Quality Register entries, 76
managing risk costs, 258–259
one person needed for, 203–204
over-extended, 46
PRINCE2 understood by, 127
Project Board as boss of, 18
Project Plan as responsibility of, 250
Risk Register set up by, 72
roles, 46, 151, 194–199, 200–205, 206
Stage End responsibilities, 93
Stage Plans as responsibility of, 251
as Team Manager, 123
Work Packages given to Team Manager,
111–113, 122
Project Mandate, 44–45, 153, 175, 346
Project Office
defined, 346
imposing standards, 314
Lessons Report filed with, 142
responsibilities of, 49, 203
Risk Checklist kept by, 262
setting up, 206–207

Project Organisation. *See also* Project
Management Team; roles
getting the right people involved, 187–188
keeping stable, 192
levels of authority, 192–193
putting in place, 18
PRoject Organisation, Management and
Planning Technique (PROMPT II), 16
Project Plan
in Closing a Project, 144
creating, 85–86
defined, 91, 347
doing without, 33–34
explaining, 248–249
in Initiating a Project, 91
overview, 250
Project Assurance in, 156, 250
Project Manager responsible for, 250
risk management in, 271
updating, 101–102, 250, 318
Project Product, 344. *See also* Product
Description; products
project risk, 137, 247–248
project stages. *See* management stages
Project Support. *See also* Project Office
defined, 49, 347
making Quality Register entries, 76
overview, 206
Risk Register set up by, 72
roles and responsibilities, 49, 206–207
separating from Project Assurance, 328
Project Techniques Toolbox, 240,
260–261, 262
project tolerance, 307
PROMPT II (PRoject Organisation,
Management and Planning
Technique), 16
proximity determination for risk, 257, 267

qualifications for PRINCE2
Foundation exam, 334
locating training and exams, 336
Practitioner exam, 334–335
sample papers, 334
staying up to date, 336

Quality Assurance
  defined, 214, 347
  ensuring, 219
  need for, 202, 219
  overview, 156–157
  Project Office and, 203
quality management
  appropriate quality, 211
  audit processes, 217–218
  baseline, 278
  compliance standards, 211
  controls, 214, 216–219, 309, 347
  cost issues, 211
  customer quality expectations, 212
  documentation, 217, 221–222
  importance of quality, 209–211, 212
  in Initiation Stage plan, 64
  overview, 21–22
  persisting in, 212
  planning stage, 216
  records, 215
  risk impact on, 265
  roles and responsibilities, 214, 215
  scope of, 215
  standards as constraints on, 213
  taking seriously, 210–211
  testing of products, 217
  time requirements, 214, 215
  tolerances for, 304
  tools and techniques, 215
Quality Management Strategy
  constraints, 213
  defined, 91, 213
  effectiveness of, 141
  in Initiating a Project, 91
  level of quality, appropriate, 72–75, 211
  organisational standards, 213
  outline of contents, 214
  outside suppliers and, 75
  overview, 73–74
  quality records, 221–222
  sections of, 214–215
  updating throughout the project, 76
  writing, 74–76, 213–215
Quality Register
  closing, 144
  in Controlling a Stage, 120

defined, 91, 347
as effective audit trail, 217, 218
error sheets for, 218, 221, 222
in Initiating a Project, 91
outline of contents, 219
preparing, 76
reviewed by Team Manager, 129
setting up, 218
Quality Review
  Administrator, 337, 347
  defined, 347
  for finding, not correcting, errors, 220
  overview, 219–220
  Presenter(s), 220, 221, 344
  Reviewer(s), 220–221, 348
  roles in, 220, 337
  sign-off options, 221
  staying ego-less, 220–221
  test logs for, 222
quality tolerance, 235, 304
quantifiable benefits, 172

• R •

RAD (computer rapid application
    development) projects, 124
registers. See also Issue Register; Quality
    Register; Risk Register
  closing down, 142
  defined, 348
  function of, 72
Remember icon, 4
reputation, impact of risk on, 265, 266
Request for Change (RFC), 278,
    285–286, 347
resources
  availability of, 69
  checking for conflicts, 246
  constraints, 56
  estimating integrated with, 241
  overload as common problem, 69
  precedence networks for, 242–245
  Project Board availability issues, 148–149
  resource levelling, 209–210
  resource plans, 348
  risk impact on, 265
Reviewer(s), 220–221, 348

RFC (Request for Change), 278, 285–286, 347
risk actionee, 271–272, 348
Risk Log, 72, 106
risk management
  acceptance level for risk, 155
  assessing risk, 264–268
  'before' and 'after'decision, 268–269
  budgeting for risk, 153, 225, 258–259, 305
  Business Case risks section, 179
  categories of risk, 257, 261–262
  communicating about risk, 272–273
  in Controlling a Stage, 113–115
  corporate risk, 137
  costs, 258–259
  defined, 254, 348
  follow-on actions, 137, 164
  identifying risk, 261–264
  impacts versus risks, 263–264
  in Initiation Stage plan, 64
  Ishikawa fishbone diagram for, 263–264
  leaving out, 274
  monitoring risk, 272
  need for, 22–23, 271, 274
  new project risk, 247–248
  opportunities and threats, 263
  overview, 260–261
  planning how to handle risk, 269–271
  probability assessment, 266, 267–268
  procedures, 255–256, 260–261
  Product Flow Diagram used in, 264
  project failure due to lack of, 10, 11
  project risk, 137, 247–248
  reporting section, 256
  responses to risk, 257–258, 269–272
  Risk Anatomy Diagram, 262
  Risk Checklist, 261–262
  risk cycle, 259–260
  risk, defined, 254
  roles and responsibilities, 195, 257
  statistics on risk, 141
  time requirements, 256–257
  tolerances for risk, 258, 304, 305
  workshop for, 264
Risk Management Strategy
  deciding on, 254–255
  in Initiating a Project, 91

outline of contents, 255
overview, 71–72
sections of, 255–258
risk owner, 271, 348
Risk Register
  described, 91, 256, 348
  Issue Register versus, 281
  making an entry, 72, 274
  non-disclosure agreements, 36
  opening, 72
  outline of contents, 273
  reviewing, 102–104, 115, 273
  updating, 102–104, 108, 165, 273
roles. See also *specific roles*
  appointing, 45–50
  avoiding neglect of, 157
  combining, 189
  Configuration Librarian, 42, 269, 311
  defined, 348
  jobs versus, 188–189
  Project Brief section, 63
  right people selected for, 187–188
  sharing, 189–190, 348
  status versus, 189, 192
  viewpoints applied to, 191

• **S** •

safety-critical products, 73–74, 211
scheduling
  activity networks for, 242
  critical path, 245
  estimating integrated with, 241–242
  Gantt charts for, 155
  precedence networks for, 242–245
scope
  creep, 10, 275, 276–277
  in Project Definition, 60
  project failure due to lack of clarity, 10
  in Project Initiation Document (PID), 88
  risk impact on, 265
  tolerances for, 304
security constraints, 56, 292
Senior Supplier(s)
  defined, 48, 49, 195, 349
  role and responsibilities, 48, 150, 198–199, 349

Senior User(s)
  benefits as domain of, 178, 185
  choosing, 47
  defined, 47, 49, 195, 349
  interest of, 148
  multiple, 150
  role and responsibilities, 47, 150, 197,
    322, 349
Sensitivity Analysis, 181
sign-offs
  authority to proceed, 107, 161, 162
  checking for, 133–134
  at End Stage Assessment (ESA), 107
  external, 134
  importance of, 92
  Project Initiation Document (PID), 92
  Quality Review, 221
  Stage Plans, 92, 107
  suppliers, 134
simple projects, adapting PRINCE2 for, 35
small versus large companies, 36, 274
soft products, 226
specialist products
  activity planning, 240
  defined, 232, 349
  management products versus, 288
  Request for Change (RFC) submitted
    for, 278
specification document, 234
Sponsor, 349
staff resource
  in premature project closure, 135
  risk impact on, 265
  risks, 248
  unrealistic, 10
Stage 2 Plan, 164
stage boundaries. See also Managing Stage
    Boundaries
  authority to proceed at, 107
  cost issues, 154
  defined, 349
  management products used, 107–108
stage budget, 225
stage gate. See End Stage Assessment
    (ESA)

Stage Plans. See also Exception Plan;
    planning
  building the products, 127–129
  Business Case, reviewing, 104–105
  in Controlling a Stage, 120
  creating, 85–86
  defined, 63, 349
  End Stage Report information, 95–96
  extract of, 126
  for Initiation Stage, 63–64, 65, 97
  for next stage, 65, 98–100, 108
  overview, 65, 251
  presenting with Project Initiation
    Document (PID), 91
  Product Checklist prepared for, 98–99
  Project Board sign-off for, 107
  Project Manager responsible for, 251
  revising, 306–307
  sign-offs, 92, 107
  in Start Up and Initiation, 97
  using without Project Plan, 33–34
stage tolerance, 307
stages. See management stages
stakeholders, 61, 82, 349
standard approach, PRINCE2 versus,
    27–28, 29
Start Up (Starting Up a Project)
  activities in, 41–42
  appointing project roles, 45–50
  Business Case outlined in, 53–55, 86
  checking project viability, 52–55
  choosing Project Management Team,
    48–50
  Daily Log created during, 50–51, 65
  deciding to start a project, or not, 65, 159
  defined, 350
  diagram, 42
  feasibility study versus, 67
  Initiating a Project combined with,
    disadvantage of, 37–38
  Initiation Stage preparation, 63–64, 97
  Lessons Log in, 51–52
  management products for, 65
  need for, 42–43
  overview, 18, 41–42
  Project Approach, defining, 56–57

Project Board responsibilities, 159
Project Brief, writing, 57–63
Project Mandate, 44–45
time requirements, 43–44
workshop, 44
Status Account report, 288
status versus roles, 189, 192
storing records. See filing
structure of PRINCE2
    principles, 23–24, 344
    process model overview, 16–20
    project techniques, 25
    putting it all together, 25–26
    six control variables, 24–25
    themes, 20–23, 350
sub-processes. See activities
Supplier Assurance, 150
supplier environment, 36, 191
supplier viewpoint, 150, 190–191
suppliers. See also Senior Supplier(s)
    checking project risk, 248
    Configuration Management concerns, 77
    outside, 75, 77
    Project Board representation of, 148
    quality management concerns, 75
    risks, 248
    sign-offs at project completion, 134

• *T* •

tailoring, defined, 350
Team Manager(s). See also Managing
        Product Delivery
    appointing, 49–50
    authority level of, 192
    concessions made by, 279
    defined, 205, 350
    giving Checkpoint Report to Project
        Manager, 112
    Project Manager as, 123
    Quality Register reviewed by, 129, 218
    roles, 49–50, 205
    submitting Issues, 280
    Work Packages received by, 111–113, 122,
        127, 130

Team Plans
    building the products, 127–129
    in Controlling a Stage, 112, 120
    as optional, 251
    overview, 251
    produced by Team Manager, 130
    use with Work Packages, 251
technical versus project stages, 153
technology, 56, 102
test logs, 222
testing of products, 217, 218
themes, 20–23, 350
time requirements
    for Business Case, 179
    estimating, 241
    float calculation, 243–244
    for management stages, 154
    misunderstandings about, 14, 29
    precedence network showing, 242–245
    quality management, 214, 215
    risk impact on, 265
    Risk Management Strategy, 256–257
    risks, 248
    for Start Up, 43–44
    tolerances for, 301, 304
time-driven controls, 296–297, 350
Tip icon, 4
tolerances
    budget, 305
    business benefits, 304
    defined, 61, 125, 301, 350
    Exception Management, 116, 152, 305–307
    financial, 300–301, 304, 305
    in Highlight Report, 155
    levels of, 307–308
    limits, 61, 301
    need for, 300–301
    in Product Descriptions, 235
    project, 307
    in Project Definition, 61
    Project Manager monitoring, 152
    quality, 235, 304
    reporting exceptions, 116, 305–307
    for risk, 258, 304, 305
    scope, 304
    setting, 301–302

tolerances *(continued)*
  stage, 307
  time, 301, 304
  tolerance box, 301, 302
  tolerance lines and corridor, 302–303
  unequal, 301–302
  Work Packages, 103, 125, 307–308
  zero tolerance, avoiding, 302
tool nature of PRINCE2, 28–29
Tracy, John A. (*Understanding Business Accounting For Dummies*), 180
training for PRINCE2, 316, 333–336
Treasury Green Book, 52

• U •

Understanding Business Accounting For Dummies (Barrow and Tracy), 180
User Assurance, 150
User(s). See also Senior User(s)
  in Project Definition, 61
  in Project Initiation Document (PID), 89
  user interests, 148
  user viewpoint, 150, 190

• V •

verbal reports, 80–81
version control. See Configuration Management
viability of project, checking, 52–55, 323
viewpoints, 149–150, 190–191, 341

• W •

Warning! icon, 4
Work Breakdown Structure, 36
Work Package(s)
  approval method, 127
  building the products, 127–129
  checking progress on, 112
  Checkpoint Reports for, 112, 125–129, 130
  in Controlling a Stage, 110–111, 120
  controls, 308
  defined, 120, 130, 134, 350
  diagram, 111
  giving out, 112
  need for acceptances noted in, 134
  outline of contents, 122
  received by Team Manager, 111–113, 122, 127, 130
  receiving completed products, 112–113
  reporting exceptions, 307–308
  returning completed products, 129–130
  sections, 123–127
  tolerance agreement, 125
  tolerances for, 103, 307–308
workshops, 44, 264

• Z •

zero float, 245
zero tolerance, avoiding, 302

FOR DUMMIES®

Making Everything Easier!™

UK editions

BUSINESS

978-0-470-51806-9

978-0-470-74381-2

978-0-470-71382-2

FINANCE

978-0-470-99280-7

978-0-470-71432-4

978-0-470-69515-9

HOBBIES

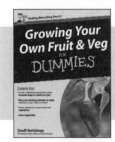

978-0-470-69960-7

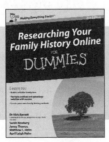

978-0-470-74535-9

978-0-470-75857-1

British Sign Language
For Dummies
978-0-470-69477-0

Business NLP For Dummies
978-0-470-69757-3

Competitive Strategy For Dummies
978-0-470-77930-9

Cricket For Dummies
978-0-470-03454-5

CVs For Dummies, 2nd Edition
978-0-470-74491-8

Digital Marketing For Dummies
978-0-470-05793-3

Divorce For Dummies, 2nd Edition
978-0-470-74128-3

eBay.co.uk Business All-in-One
For Dummies
978-0-470-72125-4

Emotional Freedom Technique For
Dummies
978-0-470-75876-2

English Grammar For Dummies
978-0-470-05752-0

Flirting For Dummies
978-0-470-74259-4

Golf For Dummies
978-0-470-01811-8

Green Living For Dummies
978-0-470-06038-4

Hypnotherapy For Dummies
978-0-470-01930-6

IBS For Dummies
978-0-470-51737-6

Lean Six Sigma For Dummies
978-0-470-75626-3

8041_p1

FOR DUMMIES®

A world of resources to help you grow

UK editions

SELF-HELP

978-0-470-01838-5

978-0-7645-7028-5

978-0-470-74193-1

Motivation For Dummies
978-0-470-76035-2

Overcoming Depression For Dummies
978-0-470-69430-5

Personal Development All-In-One For Dummies
978-0-470-51501-3

Positive Psychology For Dummies
978-0-470-72136-0

PRINCE2 For Dummies
978-0-470-51919-6

Psychometric Tests For Dummies
978-0-470-75366-8

Raising Happy Children For Dummies
978-0-470-05978-4

Sage 50 Accounts For Dummies
978-0-470-71558-1

Succeeding at Assessment Centres For Dummies
978-0-470-72101-8

Sudoku For Dummies
978-0-470-01892-7

Teaching English as a Foreign Language For Dummies
978-0-470-74576-2

Teaching Skills For Dummies
978-0-470-74084-2

Time Management For Dummies
978-0-470-77765-7

Understanding and Paying Less Property Tax For Dummies
978-0-470-75872-4

Work-Life Balance For Dummies
978-0-470-71380-8

STUDENTS

978-0-470-74047-7

978-0-470-74711-7

978-0-470-74290-7

HISTORY

978-0-470-99468-9

978-0-470-51015-5

978-0-470-98787-2

FOR DUMMIES®

The easy way to get more done and have more fun

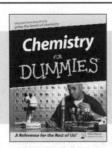

FOR DUMMIES®

Helping you expand your horizons and achieve your potential

COMPUTER BASICS

978-0-470-27759-1

978-0-470-13728-4

978-0-470-49743-2

DIGITAL PHOTOGRAPHY

978-0-470-25074-7

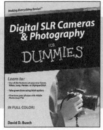

978-0-470-46606-3

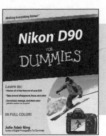

978-0-470-45772-6

MAC BASICS

978-0-470-27817-8

978-0-470-46661-2

978-0-470-43543-4

Access 2007 For Dummies
978-0-470-04612-8

Adobe Creative Suite 4 Design
Premium All-in-One Desk Reference
For Dummies
978-0-470-33186-6

AutoCAD 2010 For Dummies
978-0-470-43345-4

C++ For Dummies, 6th Edition
978-0-470-31726-6

Computers For Seniors For Dummies ,
2nd Edition
978-0-470-53483-0

Dreamweaver CS4 For Dummies
978-0-470-34502-3

Excel 2007 All-In-One Desk Reference
For Dummies
978-0-470-03738-6

Green IT For Dummies
978-0-470-38688-0

Networking All-in-One Desk Reference
For Dummies, 3rd Edition
978-0-470-17915-4

Office 2007 All-in-One Desk Reference
For Dummies
978-0-471-78279-7

Photoshop CS4 For Dummies
978-0-470-32725-8

Photoshop Elements 7 For Dummies
978-0-470-39700-8

Search Engine Optimization
For Dummies, 3rd Edition
978-0-470-26270-2

The Internet For Dummies,
11th Edition
978-0-470-12174-0

Visual Studio 2008 All-In-One Desk
Reference For Dummies
978-0-470-19108-8

Web Analytics For Dummies
978-0-470-09824-0

Windows Vista For Dummies
978-0-471-75421-3

**Available wherever books are sold. For more information or to order direct go to www.wiley.com
or call +44 (0) 1243 843291**